THE POLITICS OF
RELIGION AND
SOCIAL CHANGE

THE POLITICS OF RELIGION AND SOCIAL CHANGE

Religion
and the
Political Order
Volume II

**Edited by Anson Shupe
and Jeffrey K. Hadden**

A New Era Book

Paragon House
New York

First edition, 1988

Published in the United States by

Paragon House Publishers
90 Fifth Avenue
New York, NY 10011

Copyright © 1988 by Paragon House Publishers

A New Ecumenical Research Association Book

Manufactured in the United States of America

Library of Congress Cataloging-in-Publication Data

The Politics of religion and social change / edited by Anson Shupe,
   Jeffrey K. Hadden.—1st ed.
      p.   cm. — (Religion and the political order ; v. 2)
   Rev. versions of papers originally presented at a conference at Hilton
Head Island, S.C., in 1985.
   Includes bibliographies and index.
   ISBN 0–913757–76–4. ISBN 0–913757–77–2 (pbk.)
      1. Religion and politics—Congresses.   2. Religion and state—
Congresses.   3. Religion and sociology—Congresses.   I. Hadden,
Jeffrey K.   II. Shupe, Anson D.   III. Series.
   BL65.P7R433 1986 vol. 2
291.1'77 s—dc19
[322'.1]   87-24480
                                                                          CIP

Contents

Religion and Social Change: The Critical Connection

Anson Shupe and Jeffrey K. Hadden

EVEN CURSORY EXAMINATION of current events in most places in the world reveals that something is afoot in religion. Terrorism, political upheavals, challenges to regimes, societal transformation, and institution-building are everywhere and religious leaders seem to be right in the middle of the action. From the United States to Iran to Malaysia to Northern Ireland to Latin America, there is an indisputable link between social change and religion.

This apparent causal link between religion and social change does not mean that there is some single worldwide pattern. The sources of unrest that draw religion into the role of handmaiden of change are clearly not all the same. Different traditions influence the social order in different ways. Even within the same religious traditions there are competing interests and orthodoxies.

The prospect of finding parallel patterns among the seemingly diverse ways in which religion and the social order interface is a challenge of the first order for the social sciences.

The sociocultural contexts of various nations and regions simply are not easily comparable. For example, the conditions of India's religioethnic pluralism are quite different from the pluralism of the United States, even though both involve democratic societies. Still, the goal of science is the search for hidden likeness. The discovery of parallel patterns and processes where none were previously thought to exist would enrich our understanding of religion in the modern world.

Clearly religion plays a critical role in contemporary social change. But there is much we do not know regarding how religion functions in the modern world. All the spiritual ferment and its accompanying impact ought to be grist for the recantations of social scientists (and even some theologians) who once confidently predicted the demise, even extinction, of religion's influence in secular Western civilization.

There is growing evidence to indicate that such forecasts were premature (Hadden and Shupe 1986; Hammond 1984; Hadden 1987). As we rush toward the conclusion of the twentieth century, it is evident that the prophecies of the collapse of religion offered by virtually every nineteenth century social theorist and rehashed by most theorists of the current century were badly out of sync with empirical reality.

This is not to deny the dramatic secularizing forces in the world. But in the United States and around the world, the religious factor is alive and thriving. Religion has not disappeared even in those societies that have sought vigorously to suppress faith and organized religion.

The challenge to the social sciences is not to "fix" secularization theory. Rather, our challenge is to free ourselves from the grip of this theoretical orientation. Beyond its grasp is a world teeming with religious influence, waiting to be understood. This volume is a modest step toward charting new ways of understanding religion in the modern world.

The essays in this volume demonstrate that religious sentiments, beliefs, and organizations are at the heart of a large number of contemporary social transformations—violent and orderly, Oriental and Occidental, conservative and liberal.

Contrary to some scholarly and much media imagery, most of the contributors to this volume do not believe that the global religious ferment we are witnessing is merely a fundamentalist, anti-modernist rejection of science or industrialization. Despite popular stereotypes, many of the leaders as well as the rank-and-file participants of the significant religious movements of the twentieth century are not throwbacks to another age. Rather, they are very much men and women of their time.

On the surface, rhetoric from such disparate religious leaders as Iran's Ayatollah Khomeini and the New Christian Right's Reverend Jerry Falwell appears to have in common the goal of "restoring" pristine traditions of some earlier romanticized moral Golden Age. But this surface appearance should not be allowed to obscure the fact that, however else they may be different, both offer a search for new solutions to new challenges. While both may exhibit some qualities properly identified as reactionary, perhaps the more important quality is that both, to a large extent, are realists.

Religion's involvement in social change manifests a bewildering range of directions and degrees. There are unmistakably liberal (or progressive) movements that seek fuller extension of democratic and human liberties. The church-led civil rights movement in the United States and, now, the South African effort to dismantle apartheid are critical cases in point.

Alternately, religion can spearhead the consolidation of traditional ethnic identities with conservative religious values and thereby solidify intergroup conflict. The tensions between Sikhs and Hindus in India, and Protestants and Catholics in Northern Ireland, are prime examples of this process. Likewise, some movements with a religious thrust seek only to reform one or more institutions within particular societies. Others, like Khomeini's Iran-based Islamic Revolution, intend to spill over into other societies and create sweeping alterations.

This volume is the second in a series of three designed to explore selected issues involving the role of religion in the transformation of the political order. The first volume in this series, *Prophetic Religions and Politics* (Hadden and Shupe 1986), attempted to develop a broad comparative schema for conceptualizing how religion and politics interface. This second volume examines the role of religion in transforming the political order. World-transforming religious movements, particularly liberation theologies, are examined in more depth than was possible in the first volume. We examine also the reaction of minority religious groups to tensions within the dominant social order. Volume III will reassess the status of the concepts of secularization and of fundamentalism in the context of the dynamic processes these concepts represent.

Drafts of the papers for these three volumes were written for conferences convened in 1984 and 1985. The first was held on the island of Martinique, the second at Hilton Head Island, South Carolina. Both conferences had approximately two dozen participants representing several scholarly disciplines. Assembled around the table at each conference were experts on most of the world's major religions.

From a purely conceptual standpoint this diversity confronted us with a staggering and intimidating challenge to theory-building. The assumption that we could all familiarize ourselves in some depth with the interests and issues involving religion and the political order among different faiths in different regions of the world proved to be a far more ambitious undertaking than we had imagined. To paraphrase one of the participants who is a specialist in communications, W. Barnett Pearce, the more we learned, the less we were sure about. The more we heard and read, the less prepared we were to give precise definitions and generate broad propositions. We became more cautious about our generalizations, more willing to allow qualifications for concepts which had previously seemed unambiguous.

Yet we also became more impatient with those who have resisted generalizing, assuming, as a matter of principle, that the social order is too complex and diverse to permit any generalizations or comparative propositions. The tension between area specialists and comparative theorists is, of course, an old one in social science (though not too old—it would have seemed curious to Marx, Weber, Durkheim, and other Founding Fathers). Area specialists, who are frequently idiosyncratic and qualitative in their intellectual styles, immerse themselves in the details and nuances of a limited realm, be it a historical era, a single culture, or a polity. Masters of the unique and the individual, they are often preoccupied with the nominal-order, qualitative type that is the thing they study. They deny the possibility and value of its comparison with other "types" that, within a larger framework, become simply points or variables on a continuum.

Continua are the stuff of nomothetic, quantitative, comparative researchers. These investigators take individual cases and ascend to the necessary level of abstraction until the types become different values of a single dimension. Comparative scholars do not fear generalizations across many cases; indeed, they seek them.

It became obvious to us that anything less than a willingness to test the utility of concepts and theories in the comparative arena was a surrender to provincialism—not just to a parochial view of any single discipline, but also to the limits of cultures, geographies, even of epochs (including our own). Thus, despite the problems posed by so many viewpoints and orientations as well as substantive information, we determined that we needed more, not less, diverse regional studies and attempts at comparative synthesis if the religiopolitical nexus was to be better appreciated. For that reason also we envision each volume in Paragon House's *Religion and the Political Order* series as more than simply a new (and, hopefully, more insightful) contribution to the field of comparative social science and human understanding. Rather, each volume is in a real sense a further step in the maturation of thinking by the contributors whom we have specifically challenged to join in this larger analytic endeavor.

In some measure, the issue of specialist/comparativist has been rendered somewhat obsolete in recent years by a reconceptualization of social processes on a vastly different scale. This new formulation is no longer concerned with propositions and generalizations limited to nations, regimes, or even regions. It is a truly global view. It may eventually reconcile area specialists and comparative researchers. For comparative analysts, this global view offers the appeal that all nations and cultures are to provide the substantive meat for social change theories. For area specialists a reconceptualized sense of area is profered. That is, in the jargon of statisticians, an N of one emerges: the entire world is becoming a unified political-economic system.

Globalization and the Religious Factor

During the 1970s and 1980s a new perspective has emerged out of comparative, historical, and economic theories. It postulates the globalization of earth's societies into an integrated, evolving "world system" of economic-political relations (Wallerstein 1974a, 1974b, 1983). Roland Robertson (1984) defines this new conceptualization as a series of "processes by which the world becomes a single place, both with respect to recognition of a very high degree of interdependence between spheres and locales of social activity across the entire globe *and* to the growth of consciousness pertaining to the globe as such." As Robertson points out, this new theoretical viewpoint is heavily influenced by Marxist economic theory. Most importantly, it takes the "strong version" of the secularization hypothesis (a faith in the ultimate demise of organized religion as a significant social force) as a *fait accompli*.

At the same time there are certain "opposing trends" in globalization that its original theorists seem not to have anticipated. As Robertson notes, one of these is the expansion of nation-states' "spheres of operation under the guises of enhancing the quality of life" crossing over an institutional line into religious, or at least quasi-religious, realms. Governments become embroiled in disputes and value conflicts associated with what Talcott Parsons (1978) termed *telic matters*, i.e., those ultimate concerns of destiny and meaning which occur to all thoughtful human beings and which religions purport to resolve.

Robertson and Chirico (1985) argue that "The modern state 'invites' religious encroachment . . . because it is increasingly concerned with matters traditionally associated with the religious domain." Indeed, in their view, "The globalization process itself raises religious and quasi-religious questions."

As a result, any secularization that accompanies globalization, insofar as it involves culture conflict and challenges to the truth-claims of various traditional religions, is self-limiting. In other words, secularization turns in on itself and creates the very conditions for a resurgence of religious influence (though there are no guarantees that it will be a familiar or traditional brand of religion). At some point, globalization sets in motion the dynamic for a search for ultimate meaning, values, and resacralization.

There is another aspect of globalization that is frequently misunderstood, and that has important implications for religion's future in affecting social change—the electronic revolution in mass communications. Recent advances in commercial and state applications of this technology have led many observers to suggest that, as citizens of a planet now linked inextricably by transmitters, satellites and receiver dishes, cable television networks and relays, we have become a global community. Instantaneous communications capabilities now make instantaneous awareness of events half a world away a daily reality. Twenty years earlier media gurus Marshall McLuhan and Quentin Fiora (1968) prophetically stated, "Today, electronics and automation make [it] mandatory that everybody adjust to the vast global environment as if it were his little home town."

It is true that computers and satellites can speed information from one distant point to another at unprecedented speed. But, as media expert Ben Bagdikian (1971) asked over a decade ago, is faster necessarily better? Bagdikian reminded those enthralled by hi-tech communications that

> communications systems are amoral—they transmit lies, errors and paranoia with the same serene efficiency with which they transmit truth, accuracy, and reality. . . . There are real disadvantages to the swiftness and pervasiveness of modern communications.

Put another way, the two-dimensional and superficial portrayal of much electronic news, including a myriad of sociopolitical issues, is legend, well documented by social scientists. Sociologist Donald Luidens, a participant in the 1985 conference at Hilton Head, suggested that the media community may actually contribute to a rise in interfaith hostility rather than promote tolerance. This is because, Luidens argues, the mass media is very much akin to traditional society. It focuses on caricature and the particularistic. Its two-dimensional format encourages simplistic reductions of issues into black and white. It not only understands conflict better than cooperation, it perceives reality in these terms. Conflict, rather than harmony, is commercially marketable "news."

Luidens' perceptive observation about mass media's shaping of religion's probable influence on social change concluded:

> If we are moving towards an intersocietal or global village or global city, then it's going to be traditional in its framework. The question becomes, who is it that plays the media game most adeptly, or who can mobilize the traditional resources most effectively? I would suggest that it is those groups specifically who are good at reductionist, absolutist, simplified frameworks of reference and understanding. I think that's part of the attraction of things that we've been discussing, like the New Christian Right and Global Fundamentalism. As they streamline their messages, they package them for greater consumption— highly mediagenic in their framework.

By implication, we as planet Earth's inhabitants have become part of a global community in technological, electronic, communications, geopolitical, economic, or whatever terms. Yet intellectually and behaviorally we are light-years from such unity except as competitors and combatants. The superficiality of much of the media, and the rapid transmission of resultant images, probably exacerbates as much as defuses social class, interfaith, interethnic, and interest-based political conflicts. Passions and prejudices can now be carried as quickly and effectively as logic and reason.

Most "world-system" theorists seem to have ignored the fact that globalization involves more than the mere interface of economic and political units and systems. Globalization also entails national and regional identities. The mass media has rekindled and reinforced these identities, not broken them down. By inadvertently stimulating a return to religious questions and issues, the globalization process may well guarantee a substantial measure of prejudice, hostility, and conflict rather than the solidarity and harmony assumed by earlier commentators.

In sum, globalization enhances the likelihood that religion will be caught up in social turmoil. For this reason the comparative analyses assembled here and in Volume III take on enormous significance. Comparative analysis offers hope of comprehending the underlying source of religiously grounded conflict. And comparative scholars may contribute to anticipating and even defusing such strife.

Organization and Content of This Volume

The essays in this volume are contributions to understanding what may indeed be a process of globalization in the religion–social change nexus. On the grim side, the authors all recognize religious conflict and hatred as accepted facts of life in various world regions. More constructively, their separate analyses point to the roots of these problems. Implicit in the papers assembled is the hope that through understanding the destructive prospects of religiously guarded conflict can be reversed. Before definitive statements about the impact of the globalization process can be articulated, studies such as those presented here will have to be accumulated and integrated. Our effort is but a step toward this goal.

The essays have been arranged under four themes. Part I examines "The Politics of World-Transforming Religion." This is the style of religion that most readers associate with social change: charismatic, prophetic, aggressive, crusading. However, as the four essays demonstrate, world transformation does not always proceed in spectacular leaps. Sometimes it involves a fair amount of accommodation and stepwise progress.

Theodore E. Long ("A Theory of Prophetic Religion and Politics") takes up Max Weber's concept of prophecy and carries on where Weber failed to elaborate systematically on an important possible impact: politics. Long's intent is to develop a theory of how certain contingencies—social conditions and characteristics of a given prophetic religion—may account for prophetic religiopolitical linkages.

Long envisions politics as a dependent variable at three possible stages: interest-formation, activity, and consequences. Out of his formulation Long then deductively generates hypotheses as to the more likely roles prophecy might play in a globalizing world. Interestingly, one of these possible roles concerns the utilization of mass media as a prophetic group presses its truth-claims before the world.

Eileen Barker ("Kingdoms of Heaven on Earth: New Religious Movements and Political Orders") uses the broad wave of new religious movements appearing in the West since the 1960s as a base from which to generalize about how such groups analyze a problem-stricken world and how they seek to transform it. She points out that not all new religions seek to alter the world. Some abandon the quest and withdraw. Others simply accept the world as it is and concentrate on individual change. Still others affirm and may even glorify the existing social order.

Among the world-transforming groups there is a wide range of concerns about what needs transforming. Some take aim at capitalism, materialism, and sensate culture. Racism, on the other hand, is of major importance for groups like the Third World Rastafarians, as well as for members of the Unification Church.

Explanations of how the world went astray and what must be done to restore a desirable social order differ considerably. The problem may be original sin or ego, but Barker finds that in every case it will be an important ideological component of the future order to come.

Perhaps as important as the political impact on the outside world are the politics of internal change within these religious groups. In seeking to establish a more perfect world in microcosm (i.e., within the group's structure), members and leaders have to come to grips with a host of challenges and pressures that preoccupy much of their energies. Gradually these "kingdom builders," as Barker's analysis demonstrates, revise their expectations of the world and even revise the very transformative process they first envisioned.

The Church of Jesus Christ of Latter-Day Saints, the most successful of America's homegrown sects, is currently the fastest growing religious body in the world. If present trends continue the Mormon church is destined to become one of the world's major religions. Two essays examine important dimensions of the LDS church in America and abroad.

These two essays, by Armand L. Mauss and M. Gerald Bradford ("Mormon Assimilation and Politics: Toward a Theory of Mormon Church Involvement in National U.S. Politics") and Anson Shupe and John Heinerman ("State-Within-a-State Diplomacy: Mormon Missionary Efforts in Communist and Islamic Countries"), offer a contrast with the first two essays in this section.

At a conceptual level, Long deals with the prophet and the consequences of prophecy. Barker looks at cult-sect groups, most of whom are destined to minimal success and even oblivion. The latter two essays, however, examine a mature religious movement and one headed by an executive believed by his followers to possess prophetic powers (by virtue of Weber's class "charisma of the office"). The LDS president is considered "seer, revelator, and prophet," yet he simultaneously heads a large bureaucracy and oversees through its pyramidal structure many corporate decisions affecting billions of dollars and millions of members.

Mauss and Bradford investigate claims that Mormons have been involved conspicuously in American politics, particularly on the conservative side. At the state level the claim is valid. With seventy percent of Utah's population Mormon, the church's influence, both direct and subtle, is no mystery.

At the national level, Mauss and Bradford conclude "that involvements by the Mormon Church in national U.S. politics for the most part can be understood more by reference to whether or not the Church is in an assimilationist cycle vis-à-vis American society than by reference to doctrine or to polity." When the Mormon church has been confronted with persecution and repression, it has kept a low profile and "went with the flow" of mainstream politics and society. In times when the church is more confident of survival and, in fact, is in danger of being assimilated into mainstream American society, say Mauss and Bradford, "church leaders have shown much more inclination to stand against national trends, as in the issues of race relations, abortion, ERA," and so forth. Thus Mormon involvement in politics cannot be simply explained by a "denominationalization" thesis. The relationship is cyclical, depending on the Mormon Church's perception of where it stands with the outside non-Mormon cultural environment.

Shupe and Heinerman consider the LDS church's missionary activities abroad. Missionary efforts still are motivated by the evangelical, prophetic message of founder Joseph Smith. But the pace is definitely Fabian and the style, smooth public relations. In Communist and Islamic countries where religious freedom is sharply curtailed and/or given only lip service, Mormon missionaries can hardly do otherwise. Shupe and Heinerman chronicle how the LDS church managed to gain a foothold in the People's Republic of China and in the Soviet bloc nations as well as in Islamic cultures, using a low-key but persistent approach.

Unique to the strategy of the LDS in winning such access is its ability to act as a state-within-a-state. Mormons essentially conduct their negotiations with Communist officials apart from the U.S. Government's normal diplomatic channels. This approach sometimes meets rude indigenous reaction, as Mormon missionaries discovered in Somalia and Saudi Arabia (Moslem countries where proselytization by non-Moslems is illegal), but in the larger picture it has been proven quite effective.

Part II looks to another form of religion playing a significant role in transforming society: liberation theology—or, more correctly, varieties of liberation theology. As the papers in this volume well document, there is no monolithic phenomenon of liberation theology.

Thomas C. Bruneau ("The Role and Response of the Catholic Church in the Redemocratization of Brazil") analyzes the changing role of the Roman Catholic Church in Brazil, a country slowly "redemocratizing" after an era of strict military rule. During the dictatorial period political parties and freedom of expression were severely constrained. The Catholic Church was thrust into the position of being the sole institutional opponent to the regime, much as the Polish Catholic Church has become in that country. Not only has the church been in the forefront of leading the movement for a return to liberal democracy, it has also experienced popular participation through its Basic Christian Communities, which now number in the many tens of thousands.

With the "redemocratization" of Brazilian society, Bruneau argues, the church's prophetic oppositional role will change. It will become more pastoral and less inclined to join actively with political activists. But there are many questions remaining. For example, the Basic Christian Communities were the avenue of popular participation in discussions of public policy for many citizens. How will this grassroots political consciousness forum fare if the church pulls back from the political arena?

Michael Dodson ("Nicaragua: The Struggle for the Church") deals with another Third World nation affected by a variety of liberation theologies. The 1979 overthrow of Anastasia Somoza Debayle was the culmination of his own corruption and political bankruptcy. In Nicaragua, the Roman Catholic Church played a prominent role in delegitimizing the repressive regime and encouraging the development of, as Dodson notes, "an extraordinary effort of mass mobilization among the Nicaraguan people."

Since the revolution, however, the church has become divided over how to respond to the revolution and the Ortega regime. The various components of the Nicaraguan Catholic Church have been united only in their formal opposition to the brutal years of the Somoza dictatorship. Some church officials fear a materialist, humanist, irreligious thrust to the new regime's policies. But some in the church hierarchy, Dodson suggests, may be out of touch with the sentiments of grassroots Christians who helped bring about the revolution.

Dodson's essay presents a case in which an established *ecclesia* acts prophetically to help bring about revolution and then has to find its way through the uncertainties of postrevolutionary society.

William R. Garrett ("Liberation Theology and the Concept of Human Rights") issues a warning to those who uncritically embrace liberation theologies that promote Marxism. Western Christianity and Marxism, Garrett argues, hold distinct and irreconcilable understandings of human liberties. For Christians these rights are inalienable and God-given, beginning with freedom of conscience and religion and extending to "a whole panoply" that Americans now know as the Bill of Rights. For Marxist theory, there is totalitarian democracy, i.e., the idea that freedom must be obtained collectively, even at the expense of individuals.

Garrett is not optimistic that any alliance between Christian religionists and Marxist revolutionaries, however well-intended, will end as amicably as it may have begun. He considers naive the belief that the religionists will be able to militate the usual bloodshed and reprisals that accompany revolutions and civil strife in the name of the People.

A solid example of humanistic sociology, Garrett offers a philosophical critique that demonstrates how opposed are the traditions of Marxism and Western liberalism.

Bonganjalo Goba presents a different case of liberation theology in the making ("The Influence of Certain Political Movements in South Africa on the Church's Role in the Struggle for Liberation"). In South Africa the churches' part in the struggle against apartheid was slow to emerge but gradually has crystallized, along with secular movements, around the issue of Black

Consciousness. Under the leadership of young black men such as Steve Biko, the movement grew out of black college students' frustration with white-run student organizations and a sense that the time had come for black men and women to chart their own goals and destinies in ways radically different from the philosophy of apartheid.

Himself a part of the black awakening, Goba writes from a personal viewpoint. His candid account of how Black Theology evolved from Black Consciousness is remarkably free from anger or bitterness. Goba's essay represents a valuable look at the dynamics of how political grievances coalesced into what is now one of the most significant human rights struggles in world history.

Part III, "Religious Minorities and Integration," contains three essays dealing with the tinderbox of ethnic/religious conflict in Asia (particularly South Asia). Hostilities here can be traced back as far as a millennium. In Communist nations, the issue has been compounded by a new quasi-religion, Marxism, competing with the older faiths for political and cultural hegemony.

Jerry G. Pankhurst ("Muslims in Communist Nations") examines the politics of Muslim minorities in the Communist nations of Albania, Bulgaria, Yugoslavia, and the Soviet Union. Almost eleven percent of all Muslims live in Communist countries from Yugoslavia to China, with the Soviet Union comprising the fifth largest "Muslim power" in the world. Yet, as Pankhurst observes, "There is no overall structural unity of the Muslim population in any of these countries."

A fundamental tension exists between Muslims and the Communist states over institutional prerogatives, such as education of children. Although the situation differs by region and regime, religion, when tied to ethnic identity, retains more influence as an interest group. Muslim "ethnoterritories," in other words, gain for their citizens some degree of self-determination. They exist as the result of pragmatic recognition by Communist authorities that they help prevent further destabilization of their power. And, in some measure, at least, they appease opinion in Middle Eastern/Third World Muslim nations.

K. L. Seshagiri Rao ("The Roots of Hindu–Muslim Conflict in India: British Colonialism and Religious Revival") deals with the partitioning of India into Hindu and Muslim (Pakistan) nations. Muslims were the political rulers of the Indian subcontinent from the twelfth to the eighteenth centuries. During that time, superimposed Islamic culture made few inroads into the entrenched Hindu infrastructure, and the two religions mixed no better than oil and water. Thus, the anti-colonial revivalism that eventually displaced British rule had an inherently unstable basis.

British rule had only suppressed, not extinguished, centuries of old civil strife. Following independence, Gandhi sought unsuccessfully to establish a lasting peace and unity between the two religious traditions. Muslims, however, never felt confident that they would be treated fairly in a unified India and pressed for the partitioning. The conflict that erupted after independence, therefore, was merely a continuation of an interfaith struggle between a once-powerful, disliked, ruling Muslim minority and a newly reenfranchised Hindu majority.

Arvind Sharma ("The Sikh Crisis in India: A Question of Identity") also examines religious conflict on the Indian subcontinent. The Sikh religion, founded in the fifteenth century, blends elements of Islam and Hinduism, but is considered an independent tradition much as Christianity is from Judaism.

Identity is a critical problem for the Sikhs—not merely religious identity but also ethnic and political identities. For example, the Sikhs have had to share power with co-religionists in different factions and/or with non-Sikhs. The problem has recently grown more acute with increased factionalism, escalating violence and government reprisals, and the alienation of Sikhs from a democratic government. Sharma leaves the religiopolitical scenario up in the air—where it will remain, barring some new dialogue between the Hindu authorities and the radicalized Sikh minority.

Part IV, "Precarious Pluralism: The Case of Israel," presents three very different views of religious pluralism and strain in modern Israel. These essays help underscore how the diversity of faiths contribute to making Israel the beleaguered state that it is.

Donald Luidens ("Self-Preservation and the Embattled Church: The Case of the Greek Orthodox Patriarchate of Jerusalem") analyzes the delicacies of maintaining an interfaith homeostasis nominally headed by the Greek Orthodox Patriarchate. In reality, it is a precarious entity carefully negotiated and often renegotiated by a conference of various churchmen. The Patriarchate is engaged in a "hazardous balancing act" that includes not only the Greek Orthodox leadership versus competing faiths, but also its relations with its Arab members. In addition, the Patriarchate has to contend continually with secular forces to maintain its "most privileged" status in the Holy City. Luidens' essay provides a clear picture of how a traditional interfaith status quo is maintained under constant pressures to undermine it, including compromise, conflict, and the pettiness of bureaucratic legalism.

Roland Robertson ("Christian Zionism and Jewish Zionism: Points of Contact") demonstrates a considerable history behind Christians' eschatological hope for a Second Coming of Christ that includes the reestablishment of a sovereign Jewish state. Some readers will be surprised to learn that Christian Zionists actually antedate Jewish Zionists. Often quarreling over puzzling cryptic biblical prophecies, the Christian Zionists were stimulated by Charles Nelson Darby's nineteenth century Dispensationalism theology. Dispensationalism holds that human history can be divided into a series of successive stages, or dispensations, which culminate in Judgment Day.

Robertson demonstrates that the two social movements display a parallel

development, overlapping at times when their mutual interests have intersected. Since the 1970s a renewed interest by conservative Christians, particularly neo-Fundamentalists such as Jerry Falwell, has occurred. Though
the reasons for this revival are complex, they involve Israel's key geopolitical
role in the oil-rich Middle East, U.S. foreign policy objectives, a strong
American pro-Israel lobby, televangelism, and a lucrative "last days"/Arma-
geddon industry in American religion.

Finally, journalist Grace Halsell offers a critical view of Christian Zionism
much different from the perspective of Roland Robertson. Her thesis is that
many Americans have a naive, barely literate biblical understanding of modern
Israel, either geopolitically or in any other sense.

Evangelical Christians have romanticized the Middle Eastern situation in
terms of the *Book of Revelation,* the battle of Armageddon, and the Second
Coming of Jesus Christ. In so doing, many of the Christian tourists and
banquet-level supporters of Israel have totally disregarded the issues and rights
of other ethnic and religious groups in the region. These supporters are
preoccupied with Israel either in crude chauvinist terms (if Jews) or in the
mindset of Hal Lindsey's immensely popular *The Late Great Planet Earth.* In
any event, argues Halsell, the scene is set for more misunderstanding and
conflict, not less. If anything, she argues, fundamentalist Christians, with
their own premillennial convictions, will only exacerbate the tensions of the
situation, not ease them.

This second volume in Paragon House's *Religion and the Political Order*
series is a rich trove of current interdisciplinary and comparative social science
research that addresses one of the world's most significant and ongoing developments: the reentry of religion to center stage in affecting social change.
We invite you to use it as a resource in reconceptualizing and reinterpreting
current events as well as the broader frameworks within which they are seen
to occur.

References

Bagdikian, Ben H. 1971. *The Information Machines.* New York: Harper & Row.
Eppstein, John. 1974. *The Cult of Revolution in the Church.* Huntington, IN: Our
    Sunday Visitor, Inc.
Hadden, Jeffrey K. 1987. "Toward Desacralizing Secularization Theory." *Social Forces*
    65 (March 3), 587–611.
Hadden, Jeffrey K. and Anson Shupe, eds 1986. "Introduction." In *Prophetic Religions
    and Politics.* New York: Paragon House, xi–xxix.
Hammond, Phillip E., ed. 1984. "Introduction." In *The Sacred in a Secular Age.*
    Berkeley: University of California Press, 1–6.

McLuhan, Marshall and Quentin Fiore. 1968. *War and Peace in the Global Village.* New York: Bantam Books.

Parsons, Talcott. 1978. *Action Theory and the Human Condition.* New York: The Free Press.

Robertson, Roland. 1984. "The Sacred and the World System." In *The Sacred in a Secular Age,* Phillip E. Hammond, ed. Berkeley: University of California Press, 347–58.

Robertson, Roland and JoAnn Chirico. 1985. "Humanity, Globalization, and Worldwide Religious Resurgence: A Theoretical Explanation." *Sociological Analysis* 46, 219–42.

Wallerstein, Immanuel. 1983. "Crisis: The World-Economy, the Movements, and the Ideologies." In *Crisis in the World System,* Albert Bergesen, ed. Beverly Hills: Sage Press, 21–36.

Wallerstein, Immanuel. 1974a. *The Modern World System.* New York: Academic Press.

Wallerstein, Immanuel. 1974b. "The Rise and Future Demise of the World Capitalist System: Concepts for Comparative Analysis." Comparative Studies in Society and History 16, 387–415.

PART I
THE POLITICS OF WORLD-TRANSFORMING RELIGION

1
A Theory of Prophetic Religion and Politics

Theodore E. Long

CONTEMPORARY SCHOLARSHIP on religion and politics has relied on the assumption that religious prophecy issues within change-oriented political movements challenge existing authorities by promoting a radically new social order. The assumption is sufficiently strong that the attribution of "prophetic" status to religious movements usually hinges on whether they undertake such political action. To that extent, political challenge has become the defining characteristic of prophetic religion.

That view highlights a very important connection between religion and society, but it is faulty on two counts. First, it reduces prophetic religion to its political function, thereby diminishing the religious character of prophecy and its rich yield in other spheres of life. Second, the assumption of such a link between prophecy and politics disregards their multi-faceted interaction, which varies according to empirical contingency. Our conventional understanding has thus impoverished our understanding of prophecy and politics alike.

To better appreciate the rich character of religious prophecy requires a reconception of the idea independent of politics. To specify more precisely and completely its connection to politics requires both a theory and comparative empirical analysis of prophecy and politics throughout the world. Based on a careful reinterpretation of Weber's work, I have recently offered a new formulation of the concept of prophecy (Long 1986) as a first step toward enhancing our understanding of prophetic religion and political action. In this paper I use that concept to begin the task of building a theory that identifies and explains the main contours of their relationship, a task Weber himself never undertook.

I will employ a deductive strategy for the most part, with a view toward

3

constructing a set of theoretical propositions that account for the empirical variation in the relation of prophecy to the political order. The theory seeks to account for three sets of dependent variables: (a) the formation of political interests; (b) the initiation of political activity; and (c) the production of political consequences. We can understand such phenomena, I suggest, as the product of two sets of independent variables: (a) societal conditions and (b) characteristics of prophetic religion.

After working through the general propositions, I use them to develop some hypotheses regarding the historic possibilities of prophecy. As a guide to the interpretation of prophetic politics through history and across societies, the theory suggests several distinct possibilities for prophecy in the modern world: the rise of global prophecy, especially in advanced societies; the rationalization of prophecy arising in established religious institutions; and media claims-making by outsiders with few other resources.

The Concept of Prophecy

A brief review of the reconstructed concept of prophecy will serve as a stepping stone to a theory of prophetic religion and politics (Long 1986). It will make clear how prophecy differs from politics and why we need a theory relating the two. In addition, it will help us identify what such a theory needs to explain and what assumptions we can (and cannot) make in building such an explanation. Finally, that review will yield some clues as to the factors that influence the relation of prophecy and politics and how they bear on it.

The conventional interpretation of Weber's classic analysis (Weber 1947, 1952, 1963, 1978) took prophecy to be a special form of organizational leadership that arises at the margins of society in time of crisis as a politically revolutionary force. That view overextended Weber's conception in two ways. First, it mistook his use of prophecy as an example of charismatic authority for a prototype of charismatic authority. Second, it extended his specific historic example of the politically engaged Hebrew prophets of *Ancient Judaism* to a universal pattern.

On the contrary, Weber understood prophecy more precisely as a religious phenomenon of personal charisma. The focal task of the prophet is to proclaim or demonstrate a divine message in the hope of submitting all of human life to a transcendent system of meaning. If the prophet gains authority, it is most often religious, not political. If the message leaves an impact on society, it is most often in its culture, not its political institutions. Under certain conditions, personal charisma might be converted to political authority or religious efforts might be extended to the political realm. Such extensions of prophecy are not automatic, however, and we cannot assume they will occur.

Neither can we automatically assume that prophecy represents a challenging force arising, in times of internal crisis, from the margins of society to reconstitute the social order. To be sure, that is one pattern of prophecy, but the evidence both from Weber and from recent scholarship shows other possibilities as well. Prophets may also arise in times of peace and order, from within established institutions, in response to global intersocietal currents, or as an expression of or resource for building social solidarity. That does not negate Weber's claim that prophecy is a revolutionary phenomenon, but it does recognize that prophetic revolutions are usually cultural, not organizational. They disrupt established patterns by withdrawing consent from accepted values and aligning themselves with an autonomous realm of divine meaning, not by political challenge.

Defining prophecy simply as *the charismatic proclamation/demonstration of divine claims and judgments on human life or institutions by one who feels called to that mission* forces us to treat its engagement with politics as only one of several possible lines of action open to it. Whether and how it enters politics will thus depend on variable empirical conditions and processes, some of which have already been anticipated by Weber. For example, the social origin and location of prophecy, which we once took for granted, can now be understood as variables influencing its course. My task in this paper, then, is to specify the most important of those variables and how they affect the interaction of prophecy and politics.

Political Possibilities of Prophetic Religion

The first step toward that end is to define the political possibilities available to prophetic religion. In doing so, we must be careful to observe the distinction between social action and politics in religion's engagement with the world. Social action is the more general of the two, referring to the mobilization of resources to influence the course of profane social life. The resources for such action may be of any sort—economic, military, political, educational, even religious—and religious social action may be directed to any realm of life, not just the political. For religion, any effort to affect the world would count as social action.

Politics is one specific form of social action that centers on conflict over collective decisions. As S.E. Finer stipulates, politics is what people do when they are confronted by the predicament of having to choose a common line of action from among alternatives perceived to be mutually exclusive (1971). The predicament arises even when someone proposes that we make such a choice at all for that forces the group to consent to choosing or not. The contradictory alternatives need not be logical; social and personal antagonisms may also define positions as mutually exclusive and generate political conflict over the issue of whose choice rather than what choice prevails. Stated somewhat more broadly than Finer, we may thus define politics as the activity of determining a common policy from among conflicting alternatives.

Politics includes three elements for which a theory must account: interests, action, and consequences. Political interests are the most elusive, including both objective and subjective components. By "objective" I mean the object of action or attention, not the truth or reality of things. When religious groups seek to achieve a political objective by influencing decisions about collective policy, they can be said to have political interests. Such aims are "objective" in the sense that their object(s) can in principle be identified and measured empirically, whether or not they exist as yet.

To say the above implicates the subjective side of political interests, which is that they must be formulated as such to count as interests. In part, that stipulation is a methodological necessity to avoid undisciplined attributions of interests by observers. More than that, however, the formulation of interests has substantive import because it is a political act; to formulate political interests is to focus attention and intent on them, creating some impetus toward political action. Political interests are thus formulations of political objectives for action.

Both the political object and the type of interest religion takes in it vary in ways relevant for our theory. First, the object(s) of interest may be cultural or organizational, economic or governmental/legal. Though the political life of advanced societies is centered in governmental and legal institutions, they have not been so dominant in other eras and they have no monopoly on politics even now. Second, prophetic religion may enter politics to promote change or to prevent it. In addition, change efforts themselves vary, some being directed toward implementing something new, others seeking to eliminate something that already exists. Notice that each kind of interest—change or prevention—may involve political challenge or political alliance with established groups, according to their interest in religion's political objective.

Political action is the mobilization and use of resources to achieve political interests. I have employed the term "resources" where others would use "power" to avoid some crucial ambiguities embedded in the latter. Resources are measurable realities not ineffable potentialities, and they exist independent of their use, not because they are used, as in some versions of "power." As such, the type(s) and amount of resources are independent variables conditioning prophetic political action (see below). By including the "mobilization" of resources as part of political action, I mean to distinguish that as a separate form of action, not part of the origination and development of the resources for prophetic politics, which is another issue. Here mobilization is the gathering of existing resources for political use.

Without claiming to be exhaustive or logically pure about the matter, I will consider three types of resource usage in political action: claims-making, contending, and ruling. Claims-making (Spector and Kitsuse 1977) is simply asserting one's interest in the political realm. Such activity is not limited merely to defining problems and issues or setting the agenda; it also includes arguing one's case, persuading others, and so forth. Contending is engaging in combat about political interests; not just asserting one's own interest but competing with others over those interests. Ruling, in turn, may involve contention, but adds the element of decision to the equation. Those who rule are those who decide matters, not just those who win decisions. Rule may or may not be legitimate; what matters is that political decisions are made and carried out.

Finally, consider the political consequences of prophetic religion's activity. While they may be quite diverse, we can begin to organize their possible variations in terms similar to those used to characterize political interests. The first variable of interest here is thus a simple one: are there observable political consequences or not, and of what magnitude? Second, if there are consequences, then it is important to know where they are located—as in culture or social organization, in economic or governmental institutions, or close or distant in space and time. Third, we must observe the type of consequence produced—changes in society by introducing new elements or eliminating old ones, or the prevention of change.

The prevention of change is much more difficult to treat as a consequence than as an interest. When it actually does occur, it may go unrecognized because nothing changes, which helps explain why change-oriented prophecy is more prominent in people's minds than "preventive" prophecy. Prevention may also be overblown, for its claims are difficult to verify. In principle, though, "prevention" can be decomposed into specific acts and conditions— such as legislative votes or battles—that can be compared with prophetic objectives to determine success and assigned social cause to determine efficacy, just like change.

A clear developmental logic connects interests, action, and consequences, but such development is not automatic or necessary. We generally assume that consequences result from actions taken to produce them, which in turn emerge from the articulation of political interests. We also tend to believe, though perhaps less surely, that in politics, interests naturally yield action, and action yields consequences. Such developments are frequent enough to lend credence to those beliefs, but not frequent enough for us to count on such logic, especially in the case of prophetic religion. Weber made clear, for example, that the Israelite prophets had political relevance even without political aims and that their interests and actions frequently did not generate the next stage of action or consequence. In addition, prophecy is an effervescent phenomenon that can have "revolutionary" consequences in the profane sphere even without becoming politically active. And we must recognize that the logic may even be reversed in some instances, as when interests are formulated in the wake of action.

Determinants of Prophetic Political Action

I turn now to the task of elaborating the conditions under which prophetic religions will become involved in politics, how they do so, and with what results. Unless otherwise specified, I assume that prophecy has taken shape already as a religious phenomenon, which may or may not become political. My approach will be to identify the main independent variables bearing on prophetic politics and to trace the implications of each one for the development of political interests, action, and consequences by prophetic religion in a series of formal propositions.

I will consider two main sets of independent variables: (a) societal conditions, and (b) characteristics of prophecy itself. The first set highlights the different political tendencies of prophecy in more or less developed societies, suggesting that religion may be more overtly political but less influential in more modern societies. The second set emphasizes differences in interest, action, and consequences among prophetic movements themselves, suggesting that the specific political course of prophecy results from its own particular social and religious interests and opportunities. These variables do not explain the internal workings of prophetic political activity, but they do define its main aggregate patterns.

Except for the orienting principles just mentioned, there is no master idea that guides the theory throughout. I note where independent variables are relevant to one another, but for the most part, I seek to discern the specific effects on prophecy we might expect from each variable, given the nature of the variable, of prophecy, and of ordinary social processes. Space limitations prevent a full exploration of how combinations of independent variables might affect prophetic politics or of how all possible variations in prophetic politics might be explained. Those tasks await another occasion.

Societal Conditions. Five societal variables would appear to make an important contribution to the course prophecy takes in society: (a) the degree of institutional differentiation, particularly of religion; (b) the degree of religious pluralism; (c) the degree of religious liberty; (d) the degree of rationalization; and (e) the degree of societal crisis.

1. Differentiation is the most basic factor, for it determines the relevance of the other four. Where religion is not differentiated, religious pluralism, liberty, and rationalization are moot points. The degree of crisis may still vary but it would not affect prophecy in any distinctive way. The limiting case, where religion is undifferentiated, should have an interesting configuration, which can be summarized as follows:

1.1 When religion is undifferentiated from society, prophetic religion will always be engaged in the politics of the society.
1.2 The political interests of undifferentiated prophecy are cultural and usually aim to strengthen existing sacred/religious meaning systems.
1.3 The political action of undifferentiated prophecy will involve either

     claims-making or ruling, but not contending, which arises in differentiated societies. Both types of activity will focus on religious interests.

1.4 Undifferentiated prophecy has a relatively high probability of producing political consequences in the cultural realm but a low probability in the realm of social organization, by virtue of its interest in submitting life to a religious world-view. Accordingly, it will be most likely to preserve existing world-views, less likely to build new ones, least likely to eliminate existing ones.

Differentiation simultaneously opens up some political opportunities for prophetic religion and closes off some. Prophecy loses its automatic connection and relevance to the profane sphere of life, but it also becomes an identifiable political force that may articulate specific political interests. In short, institutional differentiation will simultaneously stimulate ideological differentiation and separate prophecy from the profane realm of activity.

1.5 Compared to undifferentiated societies, prophecy in differentiated societies will be less likely to become involved in societal politics, especially in political action, and is thereby also less likely to produce political consequences.

1.6 Differentiated prophecy is more likely than before, though not predominantly so, to adopt organizational interests, simply because it has an independent social apparatus of its own to advance and protect.

1.7 Differentiated prophecy is also more likely to be change-oriented for its differentiation generates interests independent from and opposed to profane meaning systems.

1.8 Undifferentiated prophecy will still act politically by claims-making and ruling but it will also engage in contending action in relation to other institutions and realms of society.

1.9 In differentiated societies, prophecy will have political consequences less frequently and more inconsistently, those outcomes now depending on prophecy's position and success in social conflict.

    2. It is in the context of differentiation that religious pluralism may exercise influence on prophetic religion's political action. By pluralism I refer to the degree to which there is market dominance or competition among religious groups. An established church would exemplify market dominance, while pluralism would be high when no established church existed and many religious groups competed freely for adherents and influence. Situations of market dominance simulate undifferentiated societies in a differentiated social structure, so we should expect the propositions above to apply in tandem. There is one point that can be added regarding the object of political action in nonpluralistic societies:

2.1 In nonpluralistic societies, a high proportion of prophetic political action takes government and legal institutions as the object of its interest and action.

Increasing pluralism creates a new situation for prophecy—it must compete for religious attention as well as for political credibility. More of its energy is centered on proclaiming its religious message, which must contend with competitors, secular and religious. And the amount and variety of competition is only increased when it does enter the political realm.

2.2 The greater the pluralism, the less likely it is that prophetic religion will formulate political interests, concentrating instead on religious matters.
2.3 In pluralistic societies, the political interests prophecy does formulate will include a variety of objects and will be more likely to emphasize the creation of new cultures, whatever the realm.
2.4 The greater the pluralism, the more prophetic political action will entail claims-making and contending rather than ruling.
2.5 The greater the pluralism, the less likely is prophetic religion to have political consequences.

3. Religious liberty is another variable that gains relevance in differentiated societies and produces special effects primarily for one value of the variable. In societies where religious groups enjoy political liberty, the pattern of pluralistic societies would seem to hold. But where religious liberty is denied, pluralism matters much less, except perhaps for marginal differentiation among religious groups. What matters more is the right to practice one's religion, which is constantly at issue.

3.1 When religious liberty is denied, prophetic religion will be entangled in politics automatically.
3.2 Political interests under those conditions will focus on changing political organization by eliminating limits on religious freedom.
3.3 Political activities undertaken by prophetic religion will center on claims-making almost entirely.
3.4 Prophetic religion in societies without religious liberty rarely will have political consequences. When it does have consequences, most often they will be simply to prevent harm to religious activity.

4. The rationalization of society disengages prophetic religion from political action in many ways, but it also intensifies prophetic politics. The key to that double phenomenon lays in the fact that charismatic prophecy and calculating

rationalism are alien to one another. Neither credits the other, and their relations tend to be distant or power-oriented when they are engaged.

4.1 The greater the rationalization of society, the less prophetic religion will undertake political action, for it will be encapsulated in the "nonrational" religious realm. When it does act politically, it will do so more likely in less rationalized areas of society.

4.2 In highly rationalized societies, prophetic religion's political interests will seek radical cultural change in order to reorganize life on religious principles.

4.3 In highly rationalized societies, prophetic political activity will consist of claims-making almost entirely, for "prophets" will be blocked from contending or ruling.

4.4 The greater the rationalization, the less the chance that prophetic religion will have any political consequences.

5. The degree of societal crisis is the final societal determinant of prophetic political action to be considered here. Generally speaking, crisis is a time when things can be taken for granted no longer, for such reasons as danger, threat, lapses, disorganization, or anomie. It may have objective social referents, but it is defined first by the perception of society's members.

The conventional idea of prophecy credited crisis as the seedbed of prophetic challenges to social order, and there is some truth to that. Apart from the matter of prophecy's origin, which may be various, crisis does seem to call forth prophetic political action to a greater extent than more tranquil times, without regard to the specific type of society in question. And it makes sense to suggest that in a pinch, prophecy more likely will seek and more likely be called to rule. But there is also reason to believe that prophecy's response to crisis is often protective, to conserve social order and its cultural traditions.

5.1 The greater the societal crisis, the more likely that prophecy will become involved in politics.

5.2 In times of crisis, prophetic political interests will center on the preservation of culture, not so much on change; on government and law more than other realms of action.

5.3 In times of crisis, prophetic political activity will tend more toward ruling, less toward claims-making and contending, for its claim to transcendent authority is more plausible and useful to profane society.

5.4 The greater the societal crisis, the more likely is prophecy to have political consequences, for it can supply some of what is missing: certainty and inspiration. Those consequences are most likely to be located in the realm of political culture.

Characteristics of Prophetic Religion. A number of variable features of prophetic religion itself condition its political action: (a) the level of organization
and institutionalization; (b) its social resources; (c) its social location; and
(d) its type of religious orientation.

6. The level of organization in prophetic movements can take at least three
values. The lowest level of organization consists of a charismatic prophet
alone. An intermediate level is when that prophet has gained a group of
followers who grant the prophet charismatic authority. The highest level of
organization for a prophetic movement is when it has built some formal apparatus and heads toward institutionalization. At that point, of course, it is
in the process of changing from prophecy to something else. Even before
religion loses its prophetic character though, its organization has considerable
impact on its political action.

    6.1 The lower the level of organization, the more likely that prophetic
        political interests will center on culture; the greater the organization,
        the more the interests will center on social organization.
    6.2 In general, the level of organization and the amount of political action
        by prophetic religion are positively related.
    6.3 As organization increases, prophecy extends its action and seeks greater
        political influence. At the lowest level of organization, prophetic po-
        litical activity is most likely to involve claims-making; at intermediate
        levels, contending; and at the highest levels, efforts to rule.
    6.4 The political consequences of prophetic religion vary directly with the
        level of organization. What consequences prophetic religion has will
        follow its political interests.

7. As with any movement, the resources available to prophetic religion
will define its political possibilities. We must remember, however, that resources are not automatically used so they only define possibilities, not determine action. In addition, prophecy always has normative resources for it
specializes in symbols, world-views, and ideals. Here I am concerned with
other social resources, four in particular: people, money and property, physical
or military force, and media of communication. These resources have little
bearing on whether or not prophecy forms political interests, but they will
affect the type of interests formed as well as the political activity and consequences of prophecy. After one general proposition, I will treat each resource
separately.

    7.1 In general, the greater the social resources of prophecy, the more likely
        prophecy will become political.
    7.2 When prophecy has few social resources other than normative and
        symbolic ones, it is most likely to emphasize cultural interests.

7.3 The greater the number of people supporting a prophetic movement, the more likely that the movement will emphasize organizational interests regarding government and contending political action.

7.4 The greater the money and property held by a prophetic movement, the more likely the movement will adopt organizational and economic interests and emphasize ruling action.

7.5 The greater the physical or military force controlled by prophetic religion, the more likely the religion will hold governmental or legal interests (cultural and organizational) and to engage in ruling political action.

7.6 The greater the media resources of prophetic movements, the more likely that they will develop interests in political culture and act primarily by claims-making and contending.

7.7 In general, the greater its social resources, the more likely that prophecy will have political consequences.

8. The social location of prophecy would seem to have some bearing on its political action. There are two realms in which prophecy can be located, social and religious. Both can be described in terms of the establishment and outsiders. Socially, that distinction can be applied to the origins and current social position of prophets and their followers in both the social class and associational patterns of society. Those closer to the top and center, respectively, are more established; those closer to the bottom or fringes are more likely outsiders.

Religiously, the distinction applies to the classic types of religious groups: church, denomination, sect, and cult. Prophetic movements are not churches or denominations, but they may be carried by them—what we might call "establishment prophecy." Outside of the establishment, prophecy that gains adherents may take form as a dissident sect or as an innovative cult (Stark and Bainbridge 1985). Differences in the political action of prophecy carried by churches and denominations are probably few, except as they reflect differences relating to pluralism. The major differences are between established social and religious locations and outsiders.

8.1 Establishment prophecy is much more likely to enter politics, to adopt protective, organizational interests, to act by ruling (occasionally contending), and to produce political consequences than are prophetic outsiders.

8.2 When they do enter politics, prophetic outsiders are more likely to adopt an interest in change and to act by claims-making, with some contending activity as well.

8.3 Prophetic sects are more likely to take an interest in organizational change, cults in cultural change.

8.4 Outsiders in the social class system are more likely to take an interest in economic issues, outsiders form associational patterns in governmental or legal issues.

9. The religious orientations of prophecy can be summarized in Weber's (1963, 1978) classic typologies of this-worldly vs. other-worldly, ascetic vs. mystic, and ethical vs. exemplary prophecy. Their influence on the political action of prophecy follows a consistent general pattern, but we can anticipate differences in their bearing on specific dependent variables.

9.1 This-worldly, ascetic, and ethical prophetic movements are more likely to engage in societal politics.
9.2 This-worldly prophecy is more likely to adopt organizational interests; otherworldly, more cultural interests.
9.3 Ethical prophecy is more likely to adopt an interest in social change; exemplary prophecy, in preserving social traditions.
9.4 Ascetic prophecy is more likely than mystical prophecy to engage political interests in direct political action.

Historic Possibilities of Prophecy

Just as limitations of space prevent my developing a full rationale and defense for the above propositions, they do not permit an elaboration of their implications for the fate and direction of prophecy in the modern world. I would like to illustrate the potential fruitfulness of those principles, however, by pointing to three trends in prophetic politics that may be inferred by applying some of these propositions to contemporary circumstances.

The context for such considerations is a rather widespread view that the possibilities of prophecy have been exhausted in the modern world. The very success of prophecy in the propogation of world religions and the building of great civilizations appears to have led to its own demise. As the great modernizing civilizations eclipse "traditionalist periods" where "charisma is *the* great revolutionary force" (Weber 1978, 245), the more irrelevant, implausible, and impotent charismatic prophecy would appear to be. Indeed, as Swatos (1981) has pointed out, Weber's own analysis offers little hope that any true charismatic revolution can develop in modern society.

Once we abandon some of the presumptive baggage carried by the concept of prophecy and develop a careful analysis of prophecy's empirical variation, the historic possibilities of prophecy do not appear so dismal. To be sure, prophecy today may take different forms and relevance than in the great traditionalist periods, but it has sufficient opportunities in the modern world that it may even flourish.

Global Prophetic Politics. There is one pattern that may actually prolong the traditionalist prophetic tradition in the modern world, that being the rise of global prophecy. Traditionalist societies in the world today, of course, may experience prophetic movements similar to earlier ones. But in speaking of global prophecy, I refer more to prophecy that is directed toward a global order of peoples and nations that may arise especially from the advanced rationalized societies.

If we consider the societies of the world as a system, the world appears to be a traditional social formation reminiscent of the Israelite confederacy of tribes. Its operation is particularistic and even personalistic, eschewing the rationalism that tends to discourage prophecy. There is a nascent global culture incorporating notions of human rights but it does not yet enjoy a deep common allegiance among the world's peoples.

Such a setting could well provide the locus for a renewal of prophetic political action in advanced societies. As they become more and more rationalized, prophecy within those societies comes to be encapsulated more and more in the religious realm. One way for prophecy to regain societal relevance would be to enter politics on a traditionalist global stage. It need not become political, of course, but if it does, there is a good chance it will focus on global issues of cultural meaning. That may be one of the few arenas in which transcendent claims would still be honored widely, and the opportunity for culture building are substantial indeed.

Rational Prophets and Media Claims-Makers. Other possibilities for prophecy to flourish and gain political relevance arise from the distribution of resources for prophecy and its social location, which today supports two distinctive and opposing trends. As I suggested above, established prophecy is more likely to act politically and produce political consequences, largely because the substantial resources of established persons and institutions give it interests and power. Accordingly, we should expect more prophetic politics to emanate from those establishment centers. Many have suggested that charisma can infect reason. We might expect then that reason could also claim prophetic charisma, at least to the point of producing hybrids, such as reinvigorated "natural law" ethical theories. In this way, the character of prophetic politics might be shifted away from the "politics of unreason" to a more calculating political proclamation of rational prophecy.

But consider also the type of resources contemporary prophetic movements outside the establishment are likely to be able to muster. Most social resources take time and a modicum of success to accumulate, but almost every prophetic movement can gain some access to the mass media of communication, which connect prophets both to potential converts and to political debate. Notice, however, that when prophets use the mass media, they tend to concentrate on claims-making activity, promoting a variety of absolutist agendas on the airwaves. In that respect, we would expect the politics of unreason to increase and intensify, the very opposite direction from that which rationalized prophets would take political debate.

There is every reason to believe that these trends will develop side by side. Examples of each will compete for political influence, and the two tendencies may even compete for influence within prophetic movements. While the rational prophets move to develop practical plans for implementing divine commands in societal organization, the media claimants will raise sound and fury about basic cultural issues. Even as the rationalizers effect tangible political consequences from their action, those promoting prophecy through the media certainly have the capacity to alter in nonrational ways the political environment within which others act.

Those hypotheses, of course, presume the validity of the theoretical propositions developed earlier. Unlike the poet's license, the theorist's is much more limited, and my speculations may have already exceeded the legal limit. Before pursuing more speculations, then, our discipline calls us back to review the empirical support for these various propositions. Whatever the verdict of that analysis, such efforts will sharpen and deepen our understanding of prophetic politics considerably.

References

Durkheim, Emile. 1961. *The Elementary Forms of the Religious Life*. New York: Collier.

Finer, S. E. 1971. *Comparative Government*. New York: Basic.

Long, Theodore E. 1986. Prophecy, Charisma and Politics: Reinterpreting the Weberian Thesis." In *Prophetic Religion and Politics*, Jeffrey K. Hadden and Anson Shupe, eds. New York: Paragon House.

Spector, Malcolm and John I. Kitsuse. 1977. *Constructing Social Problems*. Menlo Park, CA: Cummings.

Stark, Rodney and William Sims Baimbridge. 1985. *The Future of Religion: Secularization, Revival and Cult Formation*. Berkeley: University of California Press.

Swatos, William H. Jr. 1981. "The Disenchantment of Charisma: A Weberian Assessment of Revolution in a Rationalized World." *Sociological Analysis* 42, 119–36.

Weber, Max. 1978. *Economy and Society: An Outline of Interpretive Sociology*, G. Roth and C. Wittich, eds. Berkeley: University of California Press.

Weber, Max. 1963. *The Sociology of Religion*, E. Fischoff, trans. Boston: Beacon.

Weber, Max. 1952. *Ancient Judaism*, H. Gerth and D. Martindale, trans. New York: Free Press.

Weber, Max. 1947. *The Theory of Social and Economic Organization*, A.M. Henderson and T. Parsons, trans. New York: Free Press.

2

Kingdoms of Heaven on Earth: New Religious Movements and Political Orders

Eileen Barker

IN THIS PAPER I want to look at some of the ways in which new religious movements envisage the political order—what it is, what it should be, and how the new order ought to be achieved. Political order will be defined rather widely to refer not merely to the political apparatus or the type of rule (democracy, totalitarianism, theocracy, etc.) to be found within a society, but also to the general culture and structure that encompasses a moral order and that could (in theory at least) be imposed by a ruling group. No attempt will be made to cover the whole range of ideas found within the new religions, nor will any attempt be made to consider the actual changes that the new religions might make in the political order. This essay is, in fact, part of a much wider study of the changes that new religious movements wish to implement, and some of the tensions and "socio-illogics" that are inherent in their efforts to bring about a new world order.[1] What will be attempted here is an introduction to the diversity that is to be found between and within the movements in their accounts of (1) what is wrong with the present social order, (2) why these wrongs exist, (3) what a future order should look like, (4) how we ought to proceed if the new order is to be established. In conclusion I look at some of the changes that are wrought in kingdom builders themselves.

Basic Orientations to the World

There is probably no more useful introduction to the movement's general orientation towards the world and its political orders than Roy Wallis' three ideal types of new religions as world-affirming, world-accommodating and world-rejecting movements. It is with reference to these that some preliminary observations can be made.

Not all new religious movements want to change the political order. There are some that are fairly content with (or indifferent to) it as it is. These fall into what Wallis calls the "world-accommodating" category in which "religion is not construed as a primarily social matter; rather, it provides solace or stimulation to personal, interior life."[2] This is a category that is comprised chiefly of groups which fall under such general headings as Neo-Pentecostalism and the Charismatic Renewal Movement, but also, Wallis suggests, of some non-Christian groups such as Subud, or the Aetherius Society. He also includes Western versions of the Soka Gakkai (Nichiren Shoshu) in this type.

It might be assumed that movements falling into the second of Wallis' categories, "world-affirming" new religions, would also be uninterested in changing the political order as "the beliefs of these movements are essentially individualistic. The source of suffering, of disability, of unhappiness, lies within oneself rather than in the social structure."[3] Movements that Wallis places in this category (such as est, Transcendental Meditation, and Scientology) are frequently bracketed as members of the Human Potential movement, or labelled quasi- or para-religious movements. It is, however, often the socialization of the individual, itself dependent upon the moral order or social structure, that will be seen as the cause of the source of suffering. Although many of Wallis' world-affirming movements make the claim that they are helping the individual to cope with the situation as it is, many will also claim that they either can or will transform the world. Within this category, "producing social change is dependent upon producing individual change,"[4] but, in fact, several of the movements (the Church of Scientology being an obvious example) have attempted to change at least some aspects of the political order.[5]

Wallis' third type, the "world-rejecting" new religion, is exemplified by movements such as the Unification Church, the International Society for Krishna Consciousness (ISKCON), the Children of God (now sometimes called the Family of Love), the Manson Family, and Jim Jones' People's Temple. The world-rejecting movement "is much more recognizably religious than the world-affirming type:"

> The world-rejecting movement expects that the millennium will shortly commence or that the movement will sweep the world, and, when all have become members or when they are in a majority, or when they have become guides and counsellors to kings and presidents, then a new world-order will

begin, a simpler, more loving, more humane and more spiritual order in which the old evils and mistakes will be eradicated, and utopia will have begun.[6]

It is groups of this type that are likely to be the focus of most attention in an account of new religions and the political order.

Having performed a useful service in distinguishing these initial orientations, Wallis' types tend either to be too crude or to lead to Procrusteanism when one goes into the subject in further detail. In what follows, I have abandoned his categories, for they no longer seem to be helpful in accounting for the diversity that is to be found within the various types, or explaining why some movements, ostensibly belonging to different types, share certain characteristics.

What's the Matter With What We've Got?

Starting from the assumption that those who wish to change the political order believe that the existing order is not "up to scratch," let us look at some accounts of what is perceived to be the matter with the present order.

World-accommodating and world-rejecting movements, but also some world-accepting movements such as the Church of Scientology, usually declare secular humanism to be one of the most evil forces in the current world. It is not, perhaps, surprising that the more fervently religious the movement, the more likely it is to decry the fact that the present order does not have God at its apex. Which God, gods, or deities ought to be running the society is, of course, dependent upon the movement—as is the means by which the transcendental authority is to be revealed to its subjects.

Many of the movements pronounce against the materialism of modern society. In some cases, particularly in the Human Potential Movement or Nichiren Shoshu, this amounts to little more than a generalized way of saying that material comforts are not necessarily to be regarded as bad in and of themselves, but that there is not enough religiosity and/or spirituality. A movement like ISKCON, however, sees a concern with the material aspects not only of society, but also of oneself, to be deplorable—a sentiment summed up in the title of a book about the movement: *I Am Not My Body.*[7]

Some community-type groups, such as the Findhorn or Bugbrooke communes, espouse a back-to-the-land ethic coupled with vegetarianism and/or a belief in "natural" or "organic" foods, and a prohibition on drugs or alcohol. However, for many, economic, scientific and technological advances are to be applauded—so long, that is, as they are used for the "proper" purposes.

Some of the movements, such as the Children of God, are strongly opposed to the capitalism of modern Western society. Other movements declare that they are not necessarily against capitalism, but would prefer a fairer distribution of the wealth it produces. The Unification Church teaches that Satan, who is conceived of in anthropomorphic terms, is at the root of communism, and that he is using communism in his attempt to take over the rest of the world. Although some lip service is usually paid to the desirability of democracy, many of the movements (e.g. ISKCON, Ananda Marga, the Unification Church, and the Church of Scientology) have, on occasion, declared that democracy has become either inoperative or endangered, and that this is frequently evidenced by the persecution of religious minorities such as themselves.

Racial, and often sexual discrimination is a bone of contention in several of the movements. As might be expected, this is especially the case in those movements in which there is a sizable membership of people of a disadvantaged race. In some instances the movement will have been indigenous to the disadvantaged community—the Rastafarians see the society in which they live (and which they refer to as "Babylon") as fundamentally the exploitation of blacks by whites; in other instances (such as the People's Temple) the founder has been white but his advocacy of a society enjoying racial equality has had an appeal to poor blacks. The Unification Church, with its Korean leader, proclaims that men and women of all races must become unified, but its teachings indicate that some cultures are, at least at this point in history, in a purer "position" than others. The Manson Family was openly racist, and "Mo letters" (the literature of the Children of God) contain a large number of virulently anti-Semitic statements.

Perhaps the area of complaint in the present moral order about which there is the greatest diversity of opinion is that of sexual relations, and the roles of women and the family. On the one hand, there are movements such as the Unification Church and ISKCON that regard the lack of moral fiber in the country as being largely due to the self-indulgent gratification of sexual desires that is to be found in the generally promiscuous behavior of young (and older) people, and the breakdown of family life as evidenced by the high divorce rate in America and other Western countries. On the other hand, we find the Children of God, the Manson Family, or the Rajneeshees declaring that part of the trouble with modern civilization is its uptight attitude towards sex, and we find the Children of God and the Raelians viewing the family as a pernicious institution.

Why Is the World in the State It Is?

For a religious movement, the question, "Why is the world not as it should be?" could be a question that requires some sort of a theodicy for at least part of its answer. For Unificationists, their concern with pornography, promiscuity, and the state of the family is explained by the Fall, which is seen as the result of Adam and Eve's misuse of the most powerful of all forces: love. Satan seduced Eve, then Eve persuaded Adam to have a sexual relationship with her before they had matured sufficiently to be blessed in marriage by God. This act of disobedience resulted in their union being centered on Satan rather than on God, and their children and their childrens' children being tainted throughout history with fallen nature (the Unificationist equivalent of original sin).[8]

The concept of original sin takes a variety of forms. Movements that are of a more fundamentalist persuasion tend to stress the willfulness of men in denying God's laws. An example is to be found in an article in *The Plain Truth* (a publication of Herbert Armstrong's Worldwide Church of God):

> Human beings, as a whole, haven't wanted the Creator "meddling" with their lives. He has been dismissed from the supervision of their affairs . . .
>
> God's universe runs on law. God's natural and spiritual laws are a fact of life. Violations exact fearsome penalties. But man would rather reap the consequences than submit to the way of God. Hence the carnage of the 20th century.[9]

The Soka Gakkai see the world's problems arising out of our refusal to realize the correctness of and the need for the Buddhism of Nichiren:

> The root cause for the confusion of a nation is attributed to the disturbance of Buddhist gods. Buddhist gods here signify thought. When the right way of thinking is ignored, prejudiced views and ideologies begin to be accepted by the general public. . . . When thought becomes chaotic, the people fall into disorder, and as they are disturbed, their country becomes agitated. Thus the nation goes into ruin and the race suffers misery.[10]

His Divine Grace, A. C. Bhaktivedanta Swami Prabhupada, the founder of ISKCON, taught his followers that men and women have lost true Krishna consciousness because the desires of their physical bodies distort their spiritual souls, which originally emanated from Lord Krishna himself. Alternately, Scientologists believe that men and women have suffered many wounds and done things that they would rather forget about, not only in this life, but also in previous incarnations. There has been a long-term, descending spiral of aberration during which harmful accretions from the past ("engrams") prevent the essential, spiritual self (the "Thetan") from being realized.

A more secular version of this kind of explanation is given to those who undergo the est experience. This is not altogether surprising, as Werner Erhard went through five Scientology levels and received about seventy hours of auditing. But a not dissimilar account also comes from Bhagwan Rajneesh, who teaches that the world's problems are due to the ego that men and women acquire through social conditioning from the time of their births. As people learn to play the roles that society expects them to adopt in the "appropriate" manner, they acquire false needs that conflict with their true, individual selves.

Generally speaking, religious movements are unlikely to blame secular

structures for the state that the world is in, but some of those of a more
Marxian persuasion will point to power structures or economic systems.
Ananda Marga, for example, declares:

> Capitalism is directly responsible for the needless starvation of countless
> thousands of persons (including approximately 50 to 100 thousand children)
> every day. Although there are some good features of the socialist nations, we
> also find major failures of socialism today. In particular, the Soviet Bloc countries
> maintain their territory as huge prisons.[11]

What Should the New Order Look Like?

Theological concepts such as the millennium, apocalypse, armageddon, and
even *agape* are not always—perhaps not ever—easy to translate unambiguously
into secular realities. Considering how fervently many of the movements want
to change the society in which they find themselves, one might be forgiven
for remarking that there is a disappointing paucity of blueprints for the future.
There are, however, enough generalizations available to indicate that the directions various movements would take in their remedying of the world's ills
are by no means identical, or even similar—even when there is a correspon-
dence of views as to what those ills happen to be. (It is, incidentally, interesting
that a movement that does go some way towards laying down plans for the
political order also states that fixed policies may be unsuitable to guide the
society for long: "Trying to fix 'utopian' policies is foolishness because problems are an inherent part of life—without which development could not occur."[12] It is, perhaps, also interesting that this movement [Ananda Marga]
declares that it is not a religion, despite the fact that it would be considerably
easier for the sociologist to classify it as such than it would be in the cases
of other movements, such as the Church of Scientology, which insist that
they are religions.)

There is a wide divergence of opinion concerning the extent to which the
future order should in fact be ordered. Movements like ISKCON and the
Unification Church are quite clear that some sort of hierarchical, even authoritarian, organization is necessary; other movements decry the thought of
any structures. It is, however, worthy of note that many of these latter movements (Rajneeshism being an example) have developed just as strong power
and communication structures within their own organizations as are to be
found in movements advocating strong structural control. Ananda Marga,
which has a very highly structured organization, advocates the maximum
decentralization of economic power as one of its chief policies. It, like many
other movements, also lays great stress on the importance of freedom. For
example, the first of the fundamental objectives proclaimed by its political
arm, PROUT (PROgressive Utilization Theory), is, "Total freedom of all
kinds of psychic and private expression. Opportunities for intellectual, edu-

cational, and all-round development must be freely available to all." A second objective is that, "Financial accumulation must be limited by establishing a maximum ceiling for property ownership and annual income."[13]

The Unification Church is quite clear that it wants to establish a theocracy— a God-centered society that will accept and live by the divine principles revealed to Sun Myung Moon. The movement's aim is to establish God's Kingdom of Heaven on Earth—to restore mankind and the rest of creation to the state originally intended by God. It is not always clear exactly what the Kingdom of Heaven will look like—at least, it is not clear from the published works available to the rank-and-file membership of the movement. While I was conducting in-depth interviews with Moonies, I found no difficulty in getting them to talk to me on a wide range of questions, many of which I had, initially, been nervous about asking. There was, however, one question that seemed to stump almost all of my interviewees, "What changes would you bring about if you were to be made Prime Minister tomorrow?" When I asked Moonies to describe what they thought the New Age would look like, most supplied rather abstract generalizations: everyone would love each other, there would be trust between people and cultures, children would be happy, crime, and in particular pornography, would be completely eradicated. On being pressed, a few gave some more practical details—we would no longer need passports; everyone would study the movement's "Bible," the *Divine Principle,* at school. One happy response came when, on being told that the sun would shine all day long, I had asked what would happen to the crops, "Oh, that's all right," I was told, "it will rain at night!"

Some details do emerge, however. The *Divine Principle* makes it quite clear that the the Kingdom of Heaven on Earth involves not merely spiritual, but, just as importantly, physical restoration. The *Principle* offers a complicated interpretation of history that claims to reveal that the Messiah is on the earth at the present time. Unificationists do, in fact, believe that this is the office to which Moon has been appointed. They also believe that Jesus was appointed to that role, but that he was killed before he could complete his mission (of getting married and founding the ideal family), and that he was, therefore, able to offer only spiritual, not physical, salvation to the world. Moon, through his marriage to his present wife in 1960, succeeded, it is believed, in laying this crucially important foundation for the physical restoration of the Kingdom of Heaven on Earth. The basic unit of the restored society will be (can now be) the ideal "four position foundation" family that Adam and Eve (and Jesus and his wife) were meant to have founded. This will consist of a husband and his wife, joined together in a God-centered relationship, and their children, who will be born without the taint of original sin.

The ISKCON vision of the future is similar to Moon's in that it is one in which life will be lived both for and through a deity—in this case, Lord Krishna. Both movements believe that the time is now ripe for a great transformation, but the ISKCON vision is less concerned with physical restoration, is less apocalyptic and in some ways less optimistic. Unlike the Moonies, who believe that God and his followers will be able to bring about a state in which Satan is overcome and everyone will be able to reach a state of perfection, Krishna devotees believe that evil will always be with us. Krishna devotees believe that the world, currently in a state of turmoil and decline, is nearing the end of the materialistic age of Kali-Yuga. But the time scale for ISKCON is infinite and changes occur only gradually, over hundreds of years. There is little of the immediacy and urgency that there is with the Unification Church and some of the other new religions, such as the Children of God, which expects its apocalypse before the end of the century. For Krishna devotees, the new age will be one of peace, love, and unity—and in this case that means one in which Krishna consciousness is experienced by all.

The nuclear arms race has led millions of people, not just those who belong to the new religious movements, to fear that there may not actually be a future order—of any kind. Some movements prophesy that it is more than likely that there will be a nuclear armageddon. (Bhagwan Rajneesh has prophesied that the threat of AIDS eradicating the populations of the world is only marginally less likely than the nuclear holocaust.) Those movements that are somewhat more optimistic are likely to make a point of saying that there will be peace and security in their new order.

So far as the position of women is concerned, a few of the Human Potential, world-affirming groups take a near-feminist stance, and female sannyasins have risen higher in the Rajneeshee hierarchy than any men (except, of course, for the Bhagwan himself). Ananda Marga declares that, "women are one of the most exploited groups in the society, mentally, physically and economically." Its projects include a "Progressive Women's Spiritual Association" and programs "run by sisters for sisters" to help raise their consciousnesses. The Summit Lighthouse, the largest of the "I Am" groups, has been led by Elizabeth Clare Prophet since her husband Mark died in 1973. Dada Lekhraj, the founder of the Brahma Kumaris (the daughters of Brahma), believed that women were "intrinsically of a more religious nature and more trustworthy" and the movement sees itself primarily as a women's movement (about nine hundred of the one thousand "dedicated" are women); all the present leaders are women—not that men do not play an important role, carrying out such menial chores as shopping for food, seeing to the furnishings or dealing with problems of rent (in such matters the Sisters confess themselves "not only helpless, but also unwilling to devote time which they feel they could more profitably spend on spiritual matters").[14]

On the whole, however, feminists who are looking for a Brave New World of equal opportunities would be ill-advised to pin their hopes on the new religions' political maneuverings—particularly if the movement had its origins in the East. Movements such as ISKCON have a very clear belief that women,

although undoubtedly of intrinsic value in themselves, are meant to serve
and look after men. The Unification Church has an "equal but different"
policy. It was Eve who was responsible for the Fall, and the *Divine Principle*
explains quite clearly that it is men who are in the "subject position" and,
other things being equal, women should be expected to obey them. (In practice, however, women have held fairly high positions and had considerable
power and influence within the movement; there are even a few Unificationist
feminists who have questioned some of the more chauvinistic assumptions
of the teachings.)

How Is the New Order To Be Brought About?

It is probably safe to say that the greatest leap of faith for most of the membership of these movements is the acceptance that the methods which are
advocated could actually achieve the end that is promised—or, more cautiously, promised on the condition that people (especially the enlightened
followers) do what is required of them. Some of the visions of the new order
would seem to be well beyond the possibility of achievement by mere mortals,
requiring as they do an apparent change in the laws (as we know them) of
nature—including meteorology. It might be argued that some of the other
changes would demand irrevocable laws of human nature and/or unnegotiable
principles of social order also to be changed. What we are interested in here,
however, is what the members of the new religions believe they can achieve—
albeit with, on occasion, supernatural aid.

The methods that the movements advocate in order to achieve their earthly
goals can be divided into two main categories: spiritual and practical. Spiritual
methods include meditation and prayer; practical methods include collecting
money, gaining new recruits, and, not quite the same thing, persuading people
in positions of power to see things from the movements' point of view. Some
activities (such as rituals that have a practical effect—the Unification mass
weddings would be an example) might fall into either category. Another kind
of distinction, which is closely connected but not entirely coterminous with
the spiritual/practical one, is that between personal changes in individual consciousness and structural and/or cultural changes. The movement may concentrate on changing individual members of the movement; it may try to
produce a group with world-changing potential; it may turn its attentions
outside the movement on people in general at a grass-roots level; or it may
concentrate on those whom it perceives as being in positions of power or
influence. Most movements will proceed on more than one of these fronts.

Some social scientists might well be of the opinion that changes in the
individual are irrelevant as far as changes in the "political order" are concerned,
and therefore irrelevant to our present concern. However, this would be to
ignore or to pass judgment on the belief of the membership of many of the

new religions (and indeed of much of contemporary Christendom) that it is the changing of men (and, perhaps, women), and not that of structures, that will bring about the real revolution in society—that will result in a genuine change in the political order. Even movements such as Ananda Marga, which make quite concrete structural proposals (cooperatization, separation of economic and administrative powers, the elimination of prison punishment systems, insane asylums and lonely old people's homes, and fairly detailed plans about elections and voting), can be found laying stress primarily upon changing the individual:

> The most crucial factor for humanly harnessing the vast technological powers and giving increasingly meaningful direction to society is the development of consciousness and broad-mindedness amongst the maximum of the population.[15]

And, to some extent at least, even the social scientist must admit that despite the fact that neither the Church of Scientology nor ISKCON advocates any particular structural changes in society, a world run by Scientologists would look very different from one run by Krishna devotees. Both Scientologists and Krishna devotees believe in order—that is, neither advocates the anarchy one might expect from the teachings (though not the organizational practices) of, say, Bhagwan Rajneesh. And both Scientologists and Krishna devotees believe that they are on their way to creating a better, if not ideal, world, in which people are able to develop their true selves, despite the fact that there is a considerable divergence between their respective concepts of the true self and the techniques required for its realization.

The Church of Scientology promises that there is, with Dianetics and Scientology, "Hope for Survival—Hope for You; Hope for Your Career; Hope for Your Family; Hope for This Planet." It advertises "The Technology of How to Change Conditions," and, upon inspection, one discovers that the technology is one that "offers the *individual* the opportunity to become more aware, to change undesirable conditions, and to improve one's enjoyment of life" (emphasis added). For Scientologists the underlying philosophy is that, whatever the structures, it is necessary to make sure that people in positions of authority are sane and intelligent (which the technologies of Dianetics and Scientology can make them), and that people are educated properly (through the beliefs and practices of Dianetics and Scientology). Furthermore, the Scientologists have long been active in advocating that there should be free access to all information. Once this is accomplished and their techniques are universally employed, there will be no wars because people running the world will be sane, intelligent, informed, and educated enough to sort out their differences around a table. There will be no crime because the properly educated public will subscribe to decent ethical standards and will understand the futility, stupidity, and wrongness of trying to get something for nothing. People will, moreover, not only be happy to produce goods that are of value, but will also be more concerned with the higher, spiritual aspects of life.

For the ISKCON membership, what is necessary is that the devotee should develop not his intelligence or mental capacities, but his spiritual awareness of Krishna and Krishna's central role in the total order of things. This is to be achieved, at least in part, by not indulging the physical body in sensual satisfactions and through correct devotion to Krishna. Devotees abstain from meat and all intoxicants such as drugs and alcohol and lead celibate lives (except for the procreation of children within marriage).

While Krishnas, Moonies, and Margiis lead strictly ascetic lives, and while Scientologists and Divine Light Mission premies lead fairly unremarkable lives in so far as their personal habits are concerned, the Rajneesh sannyasins are encouraged to enjoy completely uninhibited sexual relationships with anyone at any time should they feel so inclined (as long, that is, as careful precautions are taken to prevent the spread of sexually transmitted diseases). Members of Synanon have been encouraged to swap partners at regular intervals, and the Children of God are inveigled into becoming "Hookers for Jesus" and indulging in "flirty fishing" (using sex for proselytization).

From a sociological perspective, some of the techniques for self-improvement can be seen as having a positive consequence for "getting things done." Most obviously the fostering of concepts such as duty, responsibility and, above all, obedience to one's leader can ensure that a controllable work force may be mobilized. The Unificationists are explicit about the practical functions of obedience. Over and above the fact that learning to be obedient is good for the development of the individual, it is also pointed out that if everyone were to do just what he thought was right, then we would never get anywhere. If, however, we obey our leader's commands, we can get somewhere—and should the leader, on occasion, happen to be wrong, we should still follow him because eventually it will be obvious that he was wrong (God will show him his mistake), and, the group, having learned its lesson, will be able to progress, still united, from strength to strength. The *Divine Principle* provides a further concept that has practical consequences for the movement: indemnity. The teachings explain that if a bad action has been carried out in the past, then a good action can, as it were, cancel out the bad one. The more unpleasant and difficult the task, the more indemnity is involved, and the more the performer has contributed to the restoration process.

Throughout the ages, and throughout contemporary Christendom, millions of people have believed and still do believe in the efficacy of prayer in changing and/or influencing natural, personal and/or political events. Members of the new religions are no exception; many spend hours in prayer every day in the hope of bringing about a better world. Members of the Unification Church are given, or give themselves, "prayer conditions" that can last for days or even weeks (praying in relays). These may be for very specific purposes (such as the attempt to influence the outcome of Moon's appeal against his prison sentence).

Other "techniques," such as chanting and meditation, may be less familiar within a Western context yet have long been employed in Eastern religions. Perhaps the best-known chant to have come from the East in recent years is that of the ISKCON mantra:

Hare Krishna, Hare Krishna,
Krishna Krishna, Hare Hare,
Hare Rama, Hare Rama,
Rama Rama, Hare Hare.

Devotees believe that through their continuous repetition of the name of the deity, not only does the chanter become more Krishna conscious, but Krishna himself is incarnated through the very utterance of his name. The Ananda Marga has been less visible than ISKCON in its chanting, but twice a day the margii will repeat the mantra, "Baba Nam Kevalam," which was given to them by their leader, Srii Srii Anandamurti. The daily practice of chanting "Nam-myoho-renge-kyo" is at the very heart of the belief system of Nichiren Shoshu Buddhism. Performing the chant has, it is claimed, well-nigh miraculous effects; testimony upon testimony proclaims not only how the chanter is spiritually uplifted, but also how he or she consequently succeeds in business, has better health, and enjoys more satisfying relationships with the rest of the world. It is, moreover, believed that the benefit of practice is not a selfish practice:

It spreads outwards to one's family and society as supported by the concept that man is in no way separate from his environment.[16]

Yogic practices vary according to the full range bequeathed by Eastern cultures and, correspondingly, the effects that they have, or are believed to have, cover a wide span of interests. Techniques of meditation range from the quiet concentration observed by the Brahma Kumaris to the vigorously physical exercises of Dynamic or Kundalini meditation practiced by the Rajneeshees. Some of the movements believe that changes will come about through the effect of a "critical mass" meditating, as in the case of the Science of Creative Intelligence (Transcendental Meditation) or World Goodwill, which is an offshoot of the Arcane School; others commit themselves to a particular endeavor—as in the case of est's Hunger Project, which collects large amounts of money, not to feed the hungry, but to raise people's consciousness that starvation and malnutrition must be eliminated.

Yet other techniques used by movements in the hope of influencing the world—and, indeed, the cosmos—include those of an esoteric nature, such as are practiced by the Emin Foundation and numerous occult, pagan, and magic groups. "It is the destiny of man to build the Heavenly Jerusalem on Earth. . . . It is the aim of the occultist, in consort with all men of good will, to bring about this heavenly fact into earthly reality."[17] The rituals performed by modern witches and magicians are believed to invoke very real and powerful forces to this end. Cleansing rituals of a more familiar kind are also assumed by many groups to have a greater effect than merely purifying the individual concerned. Raëlians believe that, after publicizing the Elohim's revolutionary message of love, that we have to learn the practice of "Sensual Meditation," so as to elevate humanity's level of consciousness, responsibility, and harmony. We will then be ready for the Elohim (our Fathers from Space) to come to this planet, and so we must build a temple/embassy, ready to receive them, as near Jerusalem as possible.

There can be no doubt that the age of science has not created a population immune to the belief that society and the world order could be significantly altered by practices that have not appeared susceptible to empirical investigation, let alone to any kind of objective proof that they could lead to the results that are claimed for them.

Not all the methods employed by the new movements in their efforts to bring about a new social order are as person-centered as those that have just been mentioned. Some of the movements have started to create the new order within the existing order by living in ashrams, or, more adventurously, in quasi-self-sufficient communes: the Findhorn and Bugbrooke experiments have already been mentioned, and of course Jonestown would be another example. Less tragically, but no less dramatically, there has been the recent collapse of Rajneeshpuram, the ranch in Oregon to which the Rajneeshees moved when they left their earlier commune in Poona. ISKCON has a thriving community, New Vrindaban, in West Virginia, where the devotees have already constructed a considerable part of a vast complex of temples and other buildings that are destined to serve as the center of pilgrimage for the worship of Krishna in the West.

Another kind of social practice that is internal to the movements concerned, but which is seen as a positive move in the direction of overcoming racial and class barriers, consists of the cross-cultural marriages within the Unification Church and intercaste marriages within the Ananda Marga.

Turning attention to those outside the movements, efforts have been made to alleviate hunger and poverty by programs such as AMURT (the Ananda Marga Universal Relief Team), the Unification Church's International Relief Friendship Foundation, or ISKCON's provision of free vegetarian meals for the needy. Nearly all such ventures have, however, tended to be limited in their scope. At a slightly different grass-roots level, members of the Unification

Church also work in what is known as their "Home Church" area; in addition to their specific "mission," fund-raising, and "witnessing" for new members, the Moonies have (in principle) a "parish" of three hundred and sixty people whom they visit, offering to help around the house, shop, baby-sit, or mow the lawn.

Generally speaking, the new religions seem unlikely to hold out any hope of achieving any radical transformation—at least in the required direction—through democratic government. Indeed, many of the movements make a point of distancing themselves from party politics. The ISKCON guru in charge of South Africa was recently quoted as saying, "We are not necessarily in favor of one man one vote in South Africa and we're not necessarily not in favor."[18] It is not uncommon to hear members of the movements explain that nothing can be done "through the normal channels," as politicians are impotent or corrupt. The movement that has achieved the most successful "conventional" position in politics is undoubtedly the Soka Gakkai that controls, although it is officially separate from, the third largest political party in Japan, the *Komeito* (the Clean Government Party). In the West, perhaps the most direct involvement in party politics by a member of a new religion was the election, in 1986, of a member of the Unification Church to the French Parliament as a representative of the *Rassemblement National,* a coalition of right-wing groups led by Le Pen, the leader of *Le Front National.*

More frequently, campaigns are fought on specific issues: the Soka Gakkai has been responsible for numerous campaigns to foster world peace; the Church of Scientology is constantly campaigning for freedom of information and the ending of certain psychiatric practices; and the Unification Church has campaigned against pornography and in support of the Nicaraguan contras.

It is the Unification Church that has received the greatest amount of publicity and scrutiny of its attempts to transform the existing order. There is no space to list all the methods that it has employed to this end but, as an all-out attack on the social scene from a comparatively small organization (the number of full-time Moonies in the West does not ever exceed four figures), the movement has made an impressive impact. Its actual achievement in terms of its stated goals is, of course, another matter. The most striking strategy of the movement is the number and range of fronts on which it has proceeded. It has founded and funded political organizations (such as the Freedom Leadership Foundation and CAUSA) that are specifically devoted to attacking communism. Many other projects, such as the publication of a number of daily newspapers around the world, including *The Washington Times,* have helped the movement to disseminate its views on world affairs. The movement has also established a network of like-minded people in various fields, who, while not necessarily having much sympathy with Sun Myung Moon or his followers, have come to know each other and are now able to work together on various projects that happen to be in accord with the political aspirations of the movement. Much of this "networking" has been accomplished through the hospitality that the Unification Church has extended to notables at dinners, receptions, and, most importantly, conferences. Conferences have been sponsored by the movement for scientists and other academics, including sociologists of religion, theologians, ministers of religion, lawyers, journalists, the military, and both local and national politicians.

Sometimes it seems that conferences are the most popular method the new religions employ in their attempts to bring about a new world order. The Church of Scientology has organized a series of conferences concerned especially with religious freedom; the Foundation of Universal Unity (the Divine Light Emissaries) has held several conferences on the subject of science and spirituality; the Soka Gakkai, as already intimated, is continually sponsoring meetings, lectures, and publications, mainly on the topic of peace; and the Brahma Kumaris have held numerous conferences around the world, again, most often on the subject of peace. In January, 1986, the Bhaktivedanta Institute (founded, like ISKCON, by Prabupadha) sponsored a World Congress on the Synthesis of Science and Religion. The list could continue, but what can be noticed is that recurrent themes at such meetings have been peace, moral and spiritual awareness, the importance of absolute values and absolute truth, and the desire to unify or to create some kind of synthesis between science and religion. It is also the case that the conferences are usually well-publicized, that Nobel Laureates and other important people are "honored guests"; even if the rest of the world is unimpressed with the outcome of such meetings, many of the members themselves seem to find a confirmation that they really are achieving something when their conferences manage to draw the apparent support of such eminent people to promote the kingdom-building efforts of their movement.

What Happens to the Kingdom Builders?

It would be a mistake to think that all the members of any one new religion have exactly the same understanding of what the content of a future order will be, or how it is to be achieved. Furthermore, the movements themselves have changed over the past two decades or so—in some cases, quite dramatically. Most of the early American members of the Unification Church were expecting an apocalyptic event to take place in 1967.[19] With the passage of the years, impending dates of immanence have continued to have a crucial significance, but the understanding of the changes to be expected by each successive date, although still dramatic, seems at least to an outsider to have become progressively less apocalyptic.

At the beginning of the last section, I suggested that the real crunch of faith for much of the membership of the new religions lays in accepting the connection between a visionary, but as yet invisible, goal and the means ad-

connection between a visionary, but as yet invisible, goal and the means advocated for achieving that goal. Thus far, I have been generalizing in order to paint a broad picture that indicated variety between the movements. In this final section, I draw primarily from my study of the Unification Church in an attempt to distinguish between four different types of "Kingdom builders" that can be found within a single movement. Less intensive research into some of the other movements suggests that the types are not peculiar to the Unification Church but are also to be found in other movements, especially, but not exclusively, other world-rejecting movements. (Naturally, not every individual will fit neatly into one or other of the types. Some straddle two adjacent views, and others sometimes appear to vacillate between apparently contradictory positions.) Several Kingdom builders have "progressed" from one type to another—there was, for example, the Moonie who told me:

> When I first joined, I thought that if I stuck around long enough I would be there among the chosen when God waved His magic wand. Now I realize that if anyone is going to build the Kingdom of Heaven on earth it's got to be people like me.

And there was the Divine Light Mission premie who said:

> I think you'll find a lot of premies have changed. I feel that—well, it's difficult to express, but I feel that I've "taken my own power back"—if you can understand: I'm no longer waiting for Maharaj Ji to perform a miracle—I realize that I've just got to do what's right in my own life and get on with it.

The first of the ideal types of Kingdom builders, which has a large (but possibly diminishing) membership at the rank-and-file level, consists of those whom I shall call "magic-wanders." They accept unquestioningly that whatever they are doing is making a direct contribution to the restoration of the Kingdom of Heaven. They believe that their Messiah knows exactly what has to be done, and that all the magic-wander has to do is to have faith, and to raise funds, witness, indemnify, or whatever he or she is instructed to do to the utmost of his or her ability. If the Kingdom of Heaven were not to materialize, it would not be because there was anything wrong with the vision or the method, but because people had not had sufficient faith or been sufficiently diligent in following Moon's instructions. Man's faith and obedience may falter, but the truths revealed by the *Principle* and the Messiah are absolute. Within this category, there can be found a wide range of sophistication. For some, the beliefs are worked out as a systematic and practical theology; for others, there seems to be little but a superstitious acceptance. People of this type are unlikely to be affected by setbacks; apparently contrary evidence is more likely to reinforce their convictions by being interpreted as a sign that Satan is getting worried. But magic-wanders can also "snap" suddenly out of their faith—possibly as a result of deprogramming.

The second type of Kingdom builders is one that has become increasingly common with the passage of time and the passing of dates that were expected to herald changes that have obviously not materialized. Members of this type believe that Moon is indeed the Messiah, but that there is not going to be an apocalyptic change so much as a gradual development towards the new order. The Unification Church is thought to be moving in the right direction (that is, according to the *Divine Principle*), but it is accepted that the members, including perhaps Moon, do not have a precise blueprint for the Kingdom of Heaven. It is suspected that a certain amount of trial and error is inevitable in the restoration process; mistakes may be made on occasion but, so long as the members stick together and try to stay within the guidelines laid down by the *Principle*, progress will be made and the Kingdom will eventually be established—or at least, we shall have got a lot nearer to the restoration than we are at the moment. For members in this category, personal responsibility extends to checking that the methods employed appear to be moving society in the direction of the Kingdom of Heaven. If it appears that the connection is too tenuous, then this type of Moonie might, after a period of doubt, deliberation, and soul searching, decide to leave the movement.

Members of the third type of Kingdom builders have quite severe reservations about the efficacy of the means. On the one hand, they may believe that the new age could be realized, but they are uncertain about the methods being used—all that they can do is hope and pray that there is some connection, because the Unification Church seems to them to be the only movement making a really serious attempt. They may, on the other hand, be skeptical about the possibility of there ever being a Kingdom of Heaven, but they find more to admire and like within the movement than they find in the outside society. They feel that the standards of the movement are higher and more desirable than any to be found elsewhere. Members of this type tend to be those in positions of some responsibility or else, possibly, employed in a mission that can be seen to be of a positive (non-materialistic) value in and of itself.

The final type does not, strictly speaking, contain Kingdom builders. It consists of a group of apostates who have ceased to remain committed to life in the movement. They may still accept the truth of the *Divine Principle*, but they have become unconvinced that Unificationists are truly living up to the *Principle*. They may even believe that the practices employed by the movement are contrary to its avowed principles. It may be that the consequences of attempting to build the Kingdom of Heaven are seen as counterproductive, that the means do not justify the end, or, perhaps, that the leaders can no longer command their respect. Or they may feel that the means the movement are employing are not getting anywhere—that, despite the remarkable accomplishments of the movement since its inauguration thirty years ago, the Kingdom of Heaven does not seem to be coming any closer. A further possibility is that the *Principle* itself is rejected.

The fact that it has defectors is worrying for any movement, but it presents movements that aspire to build the Kingdom of Heaven on earth with a far more threatening situation than the loss of a few Kingdom builders. The fundamental problem for the Unification movement is that there are those who have had the opportunity of hearing the revelations contained in the *Divine Principle,* and yet are not willing to follow its call. Unification theology does stress that there are certain key figures who play (or have played) crucially important roles in the restoration process, and members have tended to think of themselves as being in a special position as Kingdom builders. But the theology also teaches that the Messiah's mission can fail if he is not accepted and followed by members of society as a whole (as happened in the case of Jesus). The Kingdom cannot be truly established unless everyone, not just the chosen few, turns to a God-centered life as defined by the Messiah. There are those in the movement who remain convinced that if only everyone could hear the *Principle* and see the Church in action, they would become convinced of the truth of its message.

The plain fact is that ninety percent of those who have attended Unification workshops do not join the movement. There is also a high voluntary defection rate among members who have spent some time in the movement but who, for one reason or another, have decided that they no longer want to be Kingdom builders in obedience to Moon.[20] It is hard to see how the movement can overcome such disillusionment and/or skepticism, especially when it states that it is fighting against totalitarian regimes such as those of atheistic socialism in order to establish a God-centered, democratic theocracy (assuming this not to be a contradiction in terms) in which everyone is free and responsible for his or her own decisions. Even if the new order were to be established, there always must be a question about just how stable it could be, as even children born without the taint of original sin can, according to the *Divine Principle,* still "fall" before reaching a stage of perfection—as the original Fall, which presumably occurred in the best of all possible orders, would bear witness.

"How would you control anti-social dissidents?" This is indeed one of the questions that might be asked of all those who believe that they have the techniques, truths, insights, or what-have-you that will change people's hearts and minds as a means to achieving a new political order. There tends to be little in the movements' literature that addresses such a question. It is, moreover, a question that most of the movements would prefer to define as irrelevant, in so far as they believe that proper knowledge/education/socialization would obviate the need for mental institutions or prisons, except, perhaps, for the pathologically violent. I have, however, been told by a Scientologist that if, in the new order, someone insists on not behaving in a social manner, they would need to be "rehabilitated." I have been told by more than one Moonie that if someone were to persist in not accepting the truth of the *Divine Principle*, then they would have to be put in a mental hospital—because they could not be really sane if they were to reject what is, so obviously, the truth. It should, however, be stressed that there are other Scientologists and other Moonies who would strongly disagree with such diagnoses. Several Moonies now insist that it is by no means required that everyone should be a Unificationist and that, just so long as a "critical mass" is established, it will not have disastrous effects if some people do fall. It has furthermore been argued that once the world is really God-centered, there will no longer be any need for the Unification Church to exist.

It is not clear that such apparent accommodations are quite as accommodating as they may at first appear, but there can be no doubt that during recent years there have been several noticeable changes in the interpretation of the degree of exclusivity and absolutism involved in the visionary new orders and the means of achieving them.[21] There is no space to examine the content of and reasons for such revisions in this essay, but it might be suggested that such an analysis could provide some of the reasons why visions of new political orders frequently undergo radical revisions as the religions become less new.[22] Hopes of establishing the Kingdom of Heaven on Earth may be appealing in the short run, but are far less easy to maintain in the long term than is the hope of a Kingdom of Heaven—in Heaven.

Earthly Kingdoms: Some Concluding Remarks

This essay has concentrated almost entirely on the ways in which the new religions view the political order. Ways in which the movements have been viewed and treated by the political order have been discussed elsewhere,[23] but it should be noted that the reactions that the movements have elicited from society would seem to be out of all proportion to their numerical strength. The actual numbers of people seriously involved in any one of the new religions is very small. Neither of what are the two most visible of the movements, the Unification Church and ISKCON, can boast as many as ten thousand full-time members in the West; most of the other "world-rejecting" movements have only a few hundred members or less. Although large membership figures are claimed for some of the "world-affirming" movements, these rarely have more than a few hundred who are fully committed. Most Scientologists, est graduates, TM meditators, or Rajneeshees might more usefully be thought of as "clients" who attend some courses but otherwise lead lives that are relatively independent of the movements and their political and/or ideological aspirations.

Furthermore, it is difficult to account for societal reaction in terms of the actual success that any of the new religions have enjoyed in their attempts to establish new political orders, or even in terms of any real threat that they have posed to the existing order. The Manson murders in 1969 and the Jonestown suicides in 1978 certainly shocked the world, but they could hardly be said to have changed it. There are numerous lobbies that have far more political influence than any new religion. The more conventional forms of religion affect the political order as both conservative and radical forces to an extent that makes the most successful efforts of the new religions pale into insignificance. Of course, the reactions have certain implications as far as the First Amendment in the U.S., and church-state relations elsewhere, are concerned; the new religions seem to have been highly successful in testing the bounds of tolerance and of acceptable behavior. But plenty of other groups, subgroups and individuals are constantly performing this function, which is hardly the same as establishing the kind of new order that one might expect of a Kingdom of Heaven.

If, indeed, one were to select two facts that seem to emerge most clearly from an overview of beliefs to be found among the new religions, these might be, first, that most of the dissatisfactions and many of the hopes expressed by the new religions are also expressed by other members of society, including the members of many of the more conventional churches; and, second, that there is no unanimous view held by the new religions—many of their beliefs are directly in opposition to each other.

While there is a general agreement that the Kingdom of Heaven on Earth is to be a place in which the present evils have disappeared and people will be good, happy, and full of love, there is a paucity of blueprints describing what the Kingdom of Heaven will look like in more specific terms. The nearer descriptions of the Kingdom come to practical detail, the clearer it becomes that not only the movements, but also the individual members within each movement, are likely to have their own particular picture. In fact, the more specific these pictures are, the more likely it is that they will become incompatible with each other.

It is not only members of the new religions who find it easier to point out what is wrong with a present order than it is to detail the preferable alternative. Kingdom builders tend, however, to be characterized by both their pessimism concerning the present order and their optimism that a fundamental change for the better can take place. Sometimes it is believed that essentially evil (or contaminated) humans will change into essentially perfect human beings who will, therefore, live in a heavenly society; sometimes it is that an essentially evil (constraining) society will change into an essentially heavenly (liberating) society that will, therefore, allow the perfect individual to emerge.[24]

It is obvious enough that we should expect the methods being employed in establishing the new order to vary according to differences in beliefs about what is wrong, what caused the wrong, and what the new order should look like. It is not all that obvious, however, that the different methods are clearly correlated with the different beliefs. The more radical the expected change, the less obvious (to outsiders) the relationship between the means and the ends appears to become, although the connection between some quite modest ends and the methods employed to reach them may also stretch the credibility of some non-believers. While it might seem that "spiritual" methods, such as prayer or chanting, are less easily refutable, and therefore less likely to result in disillusionment and/or defection, it is the more mundane methods, such as fund-raising and recruiting new members, that can show positive and quantifiable results which can convince members that they are really contributing in a tangible and visible way towards the establishment of the Kingdom of Heaven on Earth—even when they are unsure of what contribution the money or the new believers are to make.

There have been too few longitudinal studies to be able to make any convincing generalizations about the changes that the movements themselves have undergone.[25] What knowledge we have from contemporary and historical studies does, however, suggest that it would be foolish to expect any movement to stick unswervingly to one path or even to one direction for long. Within the Unification Church alone, it has been possible to see changes in emphasis from inward-looking to outward-looking change, between spiritual and practical methods, between apocalyptic expectation and piecemeal social engineering. It has also been suggested that many of the members have passed from belief in a radical change, being brought about largely by supernatural means, to a hope for far more modest improvements in society, being brought about largely through direct involvement in the community.

Nothing that has been said should be taken to suggest that members of the new religions may not change their character, their personality, or their immediate environment quite radically; nor yet is it denied that the presence of the movements may not make some difference to the political order of the society within which they find themselves. It is also possible that the creation of a structure of obedient followers, willing to carry out their leader's orders and/or to comply with suggestions from immediate superiors, could in certain circumstances build up a not insignificant force for change.[26]

None the less, the enormous diversity and the fact that the numbers involved are so small make the chances of the new religions having a radical effect on the political order in a modern, pluralistic society seem rather unlikely, at least in the immediate future. It is even possible that the very existence of the new religions acts, somewhat paradoxically, to prevent radical unrest in the political order by channelling the attention and activities of disillusioned and discontented members of society into a relatively ineffectual arena. It is not being suggested that the new religions are the opiate of the masses. Life in a new religious movement is rarely a bed of roses, and the new religions do not, on the whole, appeal to the masses—but they do appeal to some of the people who might, in different circumstances, be leading the masses.[27]

Herein lies a final irony. It is, in other words, possible, that, taken as a whole, the new religions, by promising more than conventional institutions, actually achieve less in their attempts to establish Kingdoms of Heaven on Earth.

Notes

1. I would like to thank the Nuffield Foundation of Great Britain for a grant to help with the research from which this paper is drawn. The more general analysis is to be found in Eileen Barker, *Armageddon and Aquarius: New Religions in Contemporary Christendom,* Manchester University Press, 1987.
2. Roy Wallis, *The Elementary Forms of the Religious Life* (London: Routledge & Kegan Paul, 1984), 34.
3. Ibid., 24.
4. Ibid.
5. Frances Westley, *The Complex Forms of the Religious Life* (Decatur, GA: Scholars Press, 1983).
6. Wallis, *Elementary Forms,* 9.
7. Angela Burr, *I Am Not My Body: A Study of the International Hare Krishna Sect* (New Dehli: Vikas, 1984).
8. *Divine Principle* (Washington, DC: Holy Spirit Association for the Unification of World Christianity, 1973).
9. John Ross Schroeder, "Why Doesn't God Do Something?" *The Plain Truth* (June 1986), 8.
10. Daisaku Ikeda, *Lectures on Buddhism,* 2 vols. (Tokyo: Seikyo Press, 1962, 279, quoted in Daniel A. Metraux, "The Soka Gakkai's Search for the Realization of the World of *Rissho Ankokuron,*" *Japanese Journal of Religious Studies* (1986) 13/1:38-9).
11. *A New Ideology for a New ERA,* PROUT leaflet, A.2.
12. Ibid.
13. Ibid.
14. Vieda Skultans, "The Brahma Kumaris and the Role of Women," 3 mimeographed paper n.d. See also *Brahma, The Father of Humanity,* a booklet produced by the Brahma Kumaris, n.d.
15. PROUT, *New Ideology,* 3.
16. *U.K. Express,* NSUK, 1982, 11.
17. T.M. Luhrman, "Witchcraft, Morality and Magic in Contemporary London," *International Journal of Moral and Social Studies.* 1:1 (Spring 1986).
18. *The London Standard,* May 12, 1986.
19. See John Lofland, *Doomsday Cult: A Study of Conversion, Proselytization, and Maintenance of Faith* (New York: Irvington, Enlarged edition 1977).
20. See Eileen Barker, *The Making of a Moonie: Brainwashing or Choice?* (Oxford: Blackwell, 1984).

21. For an elaboration of this point see Eileen Barker, "Defection from the Unification Church: Rates of Membership Turnover and Their Consequences," in David G. Bromley, ed. *Falling from the Faith: The Causes, Course and Consequences of Religious Disaffiliation* (Beverly Hills, CA & London: Sage), in press.
22. Note that "old religions" may not be involved in attempts to establish new political orders, Liberation Theology and the Jihad being but two obvious examples.
23. Eileen Barker, "The British Right to Discriminate" in *Church-State Relations: Tensions and Transitions*, Thomas Robbins and Roland Robertson, eds. (New Brunswick, NJ & London: Transaction, 1986) (also in *Society*, Vol. 21 (May/June 1984 34–41); "Tolerant Discrimination: Church, State and the New Religions," in *Religion, State and Society in Modern Britain*, Paul Badham, ed. (New York: Paragon House & London: Macmillan), in press. See also James Beckford, *Cult Controversies* (London: Tavistock, 1985) for an account of reactions from French and German political orders to the new religions; and for a review of some United States reactions, see Anson D. Shupe, Jr. and David G. Bromley, *The New Vigilantes: Deprogrammers, Anti-Cultists, and the New Religions* (Beverly Hills, CA: Sage, 1980) and Thomas Robbins, "New Religious Movements, Brainwashing and Deprogramming: The View from the Law Journals: A Review Essay and Survey." *Religious Studies Review* Vol. 11 (October) 1985, 361–370.
24. See Thomas J. Bernard, *The Consensus-Conflict Debate: Form and Content in Social Theories* (New York: Columbia University Press, 1983), for an interesting discussion concerning the different assumptions that theorists make about the individual and the state.
25. Roy Wallis' analysis of the transformation of Dianetics into the Church of Scientology is still one of the best available studies; see *inter alia* his *The Road to Total Freedom* (London: Heinemann, 1976). But it is also helpful to compare Lofland, *Doomsday Cult* with David G. Bromley and Anson D. Shupe, Jr., *"Moonies" in America: Cult, Church, and Crusade* (Beverly Hills, CA & London: Sage, 1979) and with Barker, *Making of a Moonie*, 1984; and to compare Stillson Judah, *Hare Krishna and the Counterculture* (New York: Wiley, 1974) with Burke Rochford, *Hare Krishna in America* (New Brunswick, NJ: Rutgers University Press, 1985).
26. The conspiracy theory elaborated by Stephen Knight in his account of the 'P2' case suggests certain sinister possibilities of building up a secret network comprised of people in important positions throughout society. See his *The Brotherhood: The Secret World of the Freemasons* (London: Granada, 1984). There is no evidence that such an organization has been created by any of the new religions, but it is undoubtedly the case that several of the movements have attempted, and have had some success in contacting and making friends in "high places" in several parts of the world. The furor that has greeted such attempts does however suggest that, at least insofar as they are publicly recognized (which is perhaps to beg the crucial question), such efforts have not greatly furthered the implementation of a new political order.
27. It is possible that certain aspects of the Halevy thesis (that Methodism played a role in preventing the revolutions and crises of the Europe of the late eighteenth and early nineteenth century occurring in England) could be used to illuminate and elaborate this suggestion. See Elie Halevy, *A History of the English People in 1815*, translated by E. I. Watkin and D. A. Barker (London: T. Fisher Unwin, 1927). For a good discussion of the Halevy thesis, see Michael Hill, *A Sociology of Religion* (London: Heinemann, 1973).

3
Mormon Assimilation and Politics: Toward a Theory of Mormon Church Involvement in National U.S. Politics*

Armand L. Mauss and M. Gerald Bradford

AS THE MEMBERSHIP of the Church of Jesus Christ of Latter-day Saints (Mormon Church) in the United States approaches five million (plus another million or so elsewhere), thereby ranking it among the eight largest American denominations, it is inevitable that Mormon political power, actual or potential, should become a matter of interest to observers of the political scene. Such interest was of course heightened during the recent national battle over the Equal Rights Amendment when strategic interventions by Mormon leaders apparently proved a major factor in the failure of some of the states to ratify that amendment. Yet one is hard put to think of other instances of national political intervention by the Mormon Church or its leaders in the twentieth century. There have been some, of course, but they have been surprisingly few, little noted, and not long remembered, except by specialists. The common image of the Mormon Church as arch-conservative is attributable mainly to its well-publicized opposition to the ERA, as well as to its irrepressible and strident (but hardly representative) apostle, Ezra Taft Benson (now President

*In the preparation of this paper, we wish to acknowledge with gratitude the support of the resources and clerical staff of the Hutchins Center for the Study of Democratic Institutions at the University of California, Santa Barbara. Bradford is Administrative Director of the Center, and Mauss was in residence there on sabbatical leave during 1985.

40

of the Church). Almost totally forgotten are the days when Mormons (even more so than today's "Moonies") were widely regarded in the U.S. as a dangerous, licentious, theocratic, politically separatist, unpatriotic, and un-American cult (Bromley and Shupe 1981, especially chap. 8; Davis 1960; Hampshire and Beckford 1983). Scarcely better remembered are the almost monotonously trendy voting patterns of Utahns and of Mormons generally throughout the twentieth century, or the consistently anti-militaristic public pronouncements of church leaders all the way down to their 1981 opposition to the western basing of the MX missile system (Firmage 1983; Gottlieb and Wiley 1984, chap. 3). In short, the history of Mormon Church involvement in national politics is both more sparse and more complex than one might believe initially.

We hasten to add that we would not so characterize Mormon political involvement in the state of Utah, or even in some neighboring states like Nevada (Croft 1985; Richardson 1984). One would expect (and the historical record makes clear) that formal and informal, public and covert interventions by the Mormon leadership in Utah politics are common and pervasive. How could it be otherwise in a state where nearly three-fourths of the population, and probably even more of its elite, are Mormon? Would we expect Catholic church leaders to remain on the political sidelines in Boston or Detroit? Or Baptist leaders in the states of the Bible Belt? The top Mormon leadership in Utah has intervened in political struggles over issues there ranging from liquor laws and pornography to legislative reapportionment and urban renewal (Alexander 1986; Gottlieb and Wiley 1984, chap. 3; Croft 1985; Quinn 1983). All of that seems understandable enough as a simple matter of wanting to control the cultural, civic, and moral environment of the Mormon heartland. Precisely because it is so understandable, it is a lot less interesting than trying to explain Mormon political exertions outside the heartland in the nation at large. We do not mean in any way to deny the importance of the church in Utah politics, and we acknowledge that the line between Utah and national politics is sometimes rather thin. Nevertheless, the intended focus of this essay is upon the church's involvement in national political issues during the twentieth century. We are thus leaving aside also the potentially important international political implications of the increasing Mormon presence outside North America.

Factors and Predispositions Affecting Church Political Involvements

Presumably, political initiatives by the Mormon Church, or any other organization, do not take place at random or in a vacuum. Among the factors determining the forms and occasions of political intervention would be: 1) ideology, 2) internal polity and governance, and 3) the nature of the relationship between the church and the surrounding society. Since we regard the third of these as providing the major theoretical thrust of our essay, we will consider it shortly in some detail. Let us first, however, briefly discuss the other two factors.

There is little in Mormon doctrine, or in its ideology that bears upon national political issues. In common with most other religions, Mormonism favors a non-militaristic foreign policy that would "renounce war and proclaim peace" (Clark 1975, 89–91). The treatment of the theme of war in the *Book of Mormon* leaves the clear implication that pacifism is respected but not required, and that when war is fought at all it must be completely defensive in purpose and must keep bloodshed to a minimum (LDS Church 1981a, Alma, chaps. 43–55; see also Firmage 1983, and Quinn 1983, 1984, 1985). Where domestic policy is concerned, Mormon doctrine does carry some implications for the themes of order, property, individual rights, and the state, according to Janosik (1951), but with much room for flexibility in interpretation and practical application.

As an empirical matter, church leaders have tended to characterize as "moral issues" those national political controversies on which they have spoken out, as distinguished from "political issues" per se. That is not, of course, a valid distinction to a social scientist who understands all public controversies as ultimately political by definition regardless of their content or substance. Yet we can make certain ideological inferences from what church leaders have considered important enough to deem "moral issues" requiring them to take a stand. By far the most important of these would fit under the rubric of "family morality," including matters of sex and reproduction, child care, and women's roles. (Indeed, one might characterize Mormon political involvements as "family politics.") Besides family, Mormon teachings on the "Word of Wisdom" (a health code requiring abstinence from alcohol, tobacco, and caffeine) and on "free agency" have been cited by church leaders as ideological bases for their political policy positions. Finally, while the history of Mormonism is rather ambivalent on "separation of church and state," its official scriptures and pronouncements sound Jeffersonian enough (Cannon et al. 1962; LDS Church 1981a, Alma 4:18; 1981b 134:9; Clark 1970, 152–154; 1975, 155–157; Firmage 1981; Mann 1967; Williams 1981). Yet Jefferson's "wall of separation" has at times been transformed by Mormon leaders into a "fortress wall" requiring quasi-theocratic control on the inside in order to keep outside Babylon well at bay. That is, the leaders have seemed much more concerned with keeping State out of Church than the other way around.

If the ideological context is only a partial explanation for Mormon political involvements, church polity and governance too seem to play an ambiguous role. On the one hand, Mormon church organization has all the appearance of a very "tight ship." The President of the church is regarded as a Prophet in the Old Testament tradition; and especially when, with his two counselors in the First Presidency, he speaks "ex cathedra" (though that term is not used by Mormons), loyal church members are inclined to obey. There is, however, no tradition of infallibility in Mormonism, and there is some question about the legitimacy of the Prophet's pronouncements on purely secular matters, these being rare in any case. The church is hierarchically organized, with a communication and command network that reaches all the way down to the family level (Johnson 1979). Mobilization for political or other purposes can thus be very thorough and rapid (Gottlieb and Wiley 1984), though such has by no means always proved effective, especially at the national level. There is little in the way of formal arrangements for the upward flow of communication and participation in decision making, but the "pulse" can be taken at the grass-roots level in informal ways. Rifts in social and political values between the leadership and the laity, so often found in other denominations, are not common in Mormonism, since the lay priesthood, even at the very top, is recruited from the same professional and bourgeois occupations held (or aspired to) by the church constituency as a whole (Davies 1963).

Despite the appearance of homogeneity and organizational efficiency suggested by this brief description of ecclesiastical polity, it does not by any means add up to a monolithic and disciplined political bloc (Alexander 1986; Croft 1985; Jonas 1969; Miles 1978). Since the days of Brigham Young, Mormon prophetic charisma has been pretty well routinized in the office of Prophet, rather than in the man, and rarely has a twentieth century prophet publicly taken a position independently of his colleagues in the First Presidency and Quorum of the Twelve Apostles. This collegial basis for prophetic leadership is inherently conservative in process, if not in substance. Important decisions of any kind, especially those affecting the church's relations with the outside, are not made without virtual unanimity among the First Presidency and apostles. Decisions that are highly controversial or divisive among those presiding brethren are simply postponed until consensus can be achieved, which in some cases never occurs. This is certainly one of the reasons that the Mormon Church has shown such reluctance historically to endorse political parties or candidates officially, preferring instead a variety of informal and sub rosa interventions in those few elections that for some reason have been seen as crucial by particularly powerful church leaders (Alexander 1986; Croft 1985). And, incidentally, such cases have backfired on the leaders as often as not, as Mormon voters (and legislators) have not only voted in the opposite way but have sometimes even criticized church intervention (Croft 1985).

As Mormons joined the two-party system with the entry of the state of Utah into the Union near the turn of the century, prominent church leaders could be found in both political parties. At first, those church leaders with strong political commitments often spoke out on political issues and candidates, or even ran for high political office themselves on a strictly individual basis (Alexander 1986). This of course meant that rank-and-file church mem-

bers were occasionally treated to the spectacle of public, and sometimes ac-
rimonious, political disagreements among those whom they had been taught
to revere as spiritual leaders. Exciting as that spectacle may have been, it did
little to enhance prophetic charisma.

Early on, therefore, the prophets, apostles, and certain other top-ranking
leaders holding church-wide office were called upon by the President of the
Church to submit to a pact whereby none of them would run for political
office or accept high political appointment without the concurrence of his
colleagues. After a considerable struggle, all of the general authorities of the
church submitted, except for one apostle who was subsequently dropped from
the Quorum of Twelve Apostles (Lyman 1985). In the spirit of that policy,
high church leaders have usually been very private about their own partisan
preferences, though it would appear that they have been mostly Republican,
especially since the New Deal. Yet even in the very recent past, one can point
to Democrats in high places, including the First Presidency itself (Gottlieb
and Wiley 1984; Williams 1966). Every effort has been made to avoid the
appearance of any sort of alliance between the church and any party or any
ideological pressure group. Individual church leaders who violate this policy,
as Apostle Benson has occasionally done, are likely to find themselves in hot
water with the First Presidency and to have their public initiatives subsequently
neutralized by the polite but pointed counter-initiatives of one or more des-
ignated colleagues (Croft 1985; Williams 1966). Brinkerhoff *et al.* (1985)
are undoubtedly correct in characterizing the posture of the church leadership
as essentially one of "religious pragmatism" that is either apolitical or else
just too complex politically to characterize in simple Left vs. Right terms.

Yet Mormon leaders are not disinterested in political issues or contests
that impinge in some way upon church prerogatives or values. We have already
referred to their considerable interest in Utah politics, even if not so often
in national politics. The responsibility for keeping watch on the political scene
has usually been delegated to a small committee of apostles containing some
representation from both major political parties. During the past decade or
so, this has been known as the Special Affairs Committee, which presumably
makes recommendations to the leadership and then carries out such overt or
covert political action as the leadership directs. The Special Affairs Committee
was heavily involved, for instance, in the campaign against ERA (Gottlieb
and Wiley 1984; White 1983).

We see a Mormon polity, which, on the one hand, is hierarchical and well
organized, with collective collegial control over the political activities of individual church leaders, and with a Special Affairs Committee as its political
eyes and ears (and perhaps fingers!). Yet, on the other hand, the political
effectiveness of this leadership is constrained by its own dependence upon
collegial consensus, by its commitment to partisan even-handedness, or at
least the appearance thereof, and by its manifestly shaky control over the

voting tendencies of the church membership. But this is not the end of the complexity. To speak of "church involvement" in national politics, requires an operational definition both of "church," in this context, and of "involvement." Just what constitutes "involvement" in politics, as we are using the term here? And when is such involvement by Mormon leaders to be understood as "church" involvement? We have left such definitional questions to this stage in our paper because their discussion requires some understanding of the polity that we have just outlined. Ultimately these will have to be our own operational definitions, for none are given officially by the church, as far as we know.

The most unequivocal form of official church expression is a letter signed by the First Presidency (the President/Prophet and his two counselors), or any other action taken publicly and in concert by these three powerful leaders. Sometimes one of the three will act or speak for the entire Presidency, especially in cases of severe illness or debilitation on the part(s) of the other(s). Initiatives and statements by the Special Affairs Committee or by the Public Communications Department (the church's public relations bureau) can also be presumed "official," since it is extremely unlikely that either of those agencies would act on anything important without the approval of the First Presidency. Beyond such formal occasions and expressions, it is difficult to be sure what constitutes official church action, overtly or covertly. If an individual apostle gives a politically loaded speech, or writes on church stationery to legislators, or makes politically strategic telephone calls, is he speaking for himself or for the church? And does it matter whether his speech is given in a conference of the church? Such individual initiatives, even by people in high places, have been subsequently modified, neutralized, or countermanded often enough that we are not usually warranted in taking them as "official" without other substantial evidence of First Presidency backing. Thus, we will not be considering such individual involvements in politics as official "church involvement" for purposes of this paper.

Even when done "officially," though, what actions would constitute "involvement" in the national political process by the Mormon Church? Clearly we would have to include here all of the usual forms of intervention designed to exert pressure in favor of one outcome over others in the political process: lobbying (whether in person, by telephone, or by mail), raising and contributing funds, organizing or supporting pressure groups, and the like. But what about public statements in person or in print? Here again, assumptions of intent toward political ends are problematic. One has to consider the national, social, and political context in which a statement is promulgated, the audience to whom the statement is directed, the level of abstraction at which a political issue seems to be addressed in the statement, and certain other characteristics of the statement and of its rhetoric, as well as its source.

In summary, then, while it may seem obvious to say that any church involvement in politics is going to be a composite function somehow of Mormon doctrine, values, polity, governance, and internal cross-pressures, that turns out to be a very complex observation when it comes to cases. Furthermore, it is not always easy to decide what constitutes "political involvement" and when it is to be considered official "church" involvement as opposed to personal initiatives by the more assertive individuals in the hierarchy. There is another element in the equation, however, which may introduce still more complexity, but which may help us to make sense out of the history of twentieth century Mormon interventions in national politics. We refer to the nature of the church's relationship to the surrounding American society. We propose that this relationship, more than any other consideration, determines which doctrines and values will be brought into the service of which kinds of political interventions at what levels of the hierarchy. In order for this proposition to be understandable, we must first review briefly our general theoretical orientation.

Mormonism, Identity, and Assimilation

As has been proposed elsewhere (Mauss 1982), the history of Mormonism as a relatively new religious movement can be understood in large part as a case study of success in resisting annihilation through either assimilation or repression, the twin perils that typically face every new movement (Mauss 1971, 1975). Deviant new movements of all kinds are subjected to various social control measures by the host society in an effort to "tame" them. If movements resist such pressures too long or too vigorously, they face "the predicament of disrepute" and run the risk of persecution and repression to the point of annihilation. This was the Mormon predicament during most of the nineteenth century. On the other hand, if new movements succumb to social control pressures and inducements too much, too soon, or too ardently, they face "the predicament of respectability" and run the risk of total assimilation. This predicament seems to have characterized the Mormon movement during the first half of the twentieth century. Thus, in its relationship with the host society, a movement might be conceptualized as moving one way or the other on a continuum between the two poles of total repression and total assimilation, these two poles simply offering alternative modes of oblivion.

Successful and durable movements, like Mormonism, seem to have in common an ability to oscillate back and forth indefinitely within a fairly narrow segment in the center of this continuum, maintaining an optimum state of tension with the surrounding society. Thus, in the 1880s and 1890s, when federal occupation and "reconstruction" in Utah loomed as a genuine threat, the Mormons finally abandoned their most deviant subcultural traits and spent the next several decades trying to live down the nineteenth century and cope with "the predicament of disrepute." Their efforts proved extraordinarily successful, in general, and by midcentury they faced "the predicament of respectability." That is, they had become such well assimilated Americans culturally, economically, and politically that they were beginning to lose their unique identity. During the last two or three decades, however, there is evidence that the Mormons are backing away from their long-standing assimilationist posture and starting to assert once again a claim to being "a peculiar people," somewhat in opposition to popular trends and values in the U.S. (Mauss 1982).

It is our theoretical position here that Mormon interventions into national U.S. politics can be understood in large part as a reflection of the historical phase in which the church finds itself vis-à-vis the assimilation process. When the church is in an assimilationist phase (i.e., coping with the predicament of disrepute), it can be expected to assert itself politically in line with major national trends (if at all), and in doing so to draw upon theological and ideological values widely shared with the rest of the nation rather than those peculiar to Mormonism. Furthermore, church political interventions during the assimilationist phase will tend to be more "soft" than "hard" (i.e., more in the nature of formal and informal public statements, rather than of lobbying, organizing, etc.). The object is to show the country that Mormons are "normal" and are good American citizens.

On the other hand, when the church turns back toward a quest for a more unique identity (i.e., coping with the predicament of respectability), its political posture and interventions will tend more often to be in opposition to popular national trends, to draw upon theological and ideological values less widely shared in the nation as a whole, and to include more heavy-handed methods exerted from high places. Thus, it is neither theological commitments nor imperatives of organization and governance that, in and of themselves, determine the occasions and nature of church political involvements. Rather, elements both of theology and of organization will be flexibly and selectively pressed into the service of political stances that express the current phase or "predicament" of the church's relationship with American society. Of course, these phases are not so sharply divided in empirical reality that they can be treated as totally discrete, like yard lines on a football field, but they do tend to be dominated by church policies that emphasize either assimilationism or particularism, respectively. Let us illustrate this theoretical perspective with a brief historical review.

Mormons and National Politics Since Utah Statehood

The Assimilationist Period: 1895–1960 (approximately). This period began with Utah entering the Union as a state (officially 1896) after having officially (if not actually) abandoned polygamy, theocracy, and anti-capitalist economic experiments. Once the church finally settled on a policy of *rapprochement* with the United States, it was almost as though someone had flipped a switch, as a succession of Mormon presidents led the church deliberately toward increasing "Americanization" (Alexander 1986; Davies 1968; Larson 1971; Leone 1979; Lyman 1986). The first part of that period, up into the 1920s, was a transitional period, as Alexander (1986) and Shipps (1967) have pointed out, with the church "feeling its way" around shoals of actual and potential political embarrassment on the way toward the open seas of respectability. Chief among these shoals were the humiliating struggles over the seating in Congress of Utah's first elected Representative (Roberts in 1896) and Senator (Smoot in 1902). In this political context, the church could ill afford any more political isolation or suspicions of political deviance. Accordingly, the church's political interventions during this period were generally in close harmony with regnant national trends, including those associated with the ferment of the Progressive Movement.

The first national political issue to face the Mormons at the beginning of their Americanization was the Spanish-American War (1898). After a vigorous internal debate, and despite the misgivings of some prominent leaders based on a long tradition of Mormon aloofness from the unrighteous wars of gentile America, the church leadership finally endorsed the war effort and urged Mormon boys to enlist (Quinn 1984).[1] Similarly, in both world wars, the Mormon leadership followed national public opinion, beginning with an aloof and isolationist posture as the wars broke out overseas, but joining the patriotic mainstream in support of the war effort once the U.S. became involved.[2] Initial reluctance about the two "anti-Communist" wars in Korea and Southeast Asia was not so apparent, as church leaders spoke out in favor of patriotism in both of those conflicts.[3] It is also true that in all of these wars the church leaders have publicly expressed a favorable disposition toward those Mormons or others who found a basis in their religion for conscientious objection, while making clear that Mormonism did not require it, a cautious position also in basic conformity to national public opinion.[4]

In domestic political issues too, whenever the church leaders have taken an official position up to midcentury or so, it has tended to reflect an assimilation to national trends more than a peculiarly Mormon outlook. The century opened, indeed, with the development of a good old-fashioned American political machine in Utah, as the President of the Church, Joseph F. Smith, in close alliance with Senator Reed Smoot, became in effect the local "boss" of the Republican Party, and derivately of Utah politics (Alexander 1986; Gottlieb and Wiley 1984). This relationship with a major party was understood by the Mormon leadership as an important vehicle of national acceptance and respectability, and deference to that relationship clearly influenced church political stands on Prohibition and on the League of Nations. The origins of the Prohibition Movement reached back into the nineteenth century, but the campaign for a constitutional amendment really gained momentum after 1908 in Utah and elsewhere. For several years, until 1916, President Joseph F. Smith was opposed to a national constitutional amendment, in line with the stand of the Republican Party in general, and the national prohibition campaign did not receive the support of the Mormon Church, despite the latter's own commitment to total abstinence. Finally, when support for national prohibition crystallized among President Smith's colleagues in the hierarchy, and this support, in turn, clearly converged with the emerging national consensus, the church publicly threw its support behind the 18th Amendment.[5]

The next president of the church, Heber J. Grant (served 1918–1945), was uncomfortable with the role of political boss and had political preferences more Democratic than Republican until the advent of the New Deal. Thus Utah after World War I became more of a truly two-party state (Alexander 1986; Gottlieb and Wiley 1984). As President Grant assumed the reins of leadership, he found himself in the midst of the controversy over U.S. Senate ratification of the League of Nations treaty. He personally favored the treaty and said so publicly, but not officially. His colleagues in the hierarchy were divided on the issue, mostly along party lines. He sternly denounced the efforts of his Republican colleagues to marshal biblical and Mormon scriptures in opposition to the League, and urged church members to give the issue their most earnest reflection. Yet the church never took an official position and remained as divided on the issue as was the nation in general.[6]

Another great issue of the Progressive Era was feminism and female suffrage. The church position here again converged nicely with the national consensus that eventually ratified the nineteenth Amendment. Utah as a federal territory had had female suffrage since 1870 (mostly with the ulterior motive of doubling the size of the Mormon voting bloc there, according to critics). Such a motive, however, would not explain the later inclusion of female suffrage in the "assimilationist" state constitution of Utah, nor the extensive and sustained support of the Mormon leadership, male and female, for the national feminist movement throughout the nineteenth century and all the way up through ratification of women's suffrage in 1920—and this, ironically, despite the institution of polygamy (Alexander 1970, 1986; Allen and Leonard 1976; Arrington and Bitton 1979; Beecher 1982; Beeton 1978).

The Depression had the same economic and political impact in Utah that it had elsewhere in the nation, including the Democratic landslides of the 1930s and 1940s. The New Deal era opened with repeal of national Prohibition via the twenty-first Amendment in 1933. Utah ironically became the thirty-sixth state to ratify this amendment, fulfilling the constitutional requirement for ratification by three-fourths of the states at that time. The First Presidency had issued a statement opposing repeal, which obviously proved ineffectual, and the church leadership generally did not otherwise assert itself into this campaign, presumably counting on its ability to control liquor laws in Utah in any case.[7] Led by President Grant, much of the Mormon hierarchy during the 1930s and 1940s opposed the New Deal and the elected officials identified with it, even if they were Mormon (e.g., Senator Elbert Thomas). Yet this period saw not only continuing grass-roots support among Mormons for the Democratic Party but also a continuation of the exodus (begun in the Smoot years) to Washington, D.C., as many educated young Mormons began to find positions in New Deal programs and agencies (Gottlieb and Wiley 1984). Aside from occasional public statements and a few initiatives like the new church welfare program, intended to obviate the need for New Deal programs among Mormons, the church leadership did little to resist national political trends. President Grant was genuinely committed to achieving national respectability for the Mormon Church, and he seems to have been quite reluctant to raise the spectre of resurrected theocracy by conspicuous interventions into the political process, except in a very few instances when he personally cared very deeply (Alexander 1986; Croft 1985; Gottlieb and Wiley 1984).

During the last decade of President Grant's administration, when he was very advanced in years, he took on J. Reuben Clark as one of his counselors in the First Presidency. A distinguished international law expert and diplomat, Clark had served Republican administrations as Undersecretary of State and as Ambassador to Mexico, a post that he reluctantly left for his new church calling. Clark quickly became the church's chief spokesman in political matters, though his initiatives were mostly limited to Utah politics (Lythgoe 1982; Quinn 1983; Williams 1966). In national politics, Clark was conservative but not in an ideological or nationalistic way. When left-wing parties began making some inroads in the nation during the 1930s and 1940s, Clark, representing the First Presidency, would occasionally warn the church to avoid these counterfeit versions of early Mormon communitarianism, especially the Communist Party.[8] In so doing, he was well within the mainstream of American public opinion, of course. At the end of World War II, Clark, on behalf of the First Presidency, issued one of the most eloquent anti-militarist and anti-nationalist statements in print as part of a critique of Universal Compulsory Military Training then being considered as national policy.[9] At the time (1946), such a statement would seem to have been also in some accord with war-weary public opinion, but shortly thereafter the outbreak of the Cold War and the Korean War made the issue moot.

The beginning of the 1950s brought to power the Eisenhower Administration in Washington, D.C. (1953), and the administration of David O. McKay in Salt Lake City (1951). Still in an assimilationist posture, the Mormon hierarchy was pleased to contribute one of its number to the new federal administration as Secretary of Agriculture, Ezra Taft Benson, the first Mormon ever named to a cabinet post. Despite that Republican connection to the

Quorum of Twelve Apostles, President McKay during the elections of the 1950s occasionally assured the world that the church was politically neutral (Croft 1985; Williams 1966). Furthermore, when Apostle Benson would wax too partisan or extreme in his public statements during visits to Utah, President McKay was inclined to send out the eloquent Apostle Hugh B. Brown, newly installed counselor in the First Presidency, and a Democrat, to neutralize Benson's partisanship (Mann 1967; Williams 1966).

In short, as we review the history of Mormon national political involvements from Utah statehood to about 1960, we can see that, with the possible exception of the issue of Prohibition repeal, all of these involvements were reflections of popular national trends, whether in matters of war and peace, the establishment of Prohibition, or women's suffrage. None of the involvements, furthermore, constituted strenuous interventions such as lobbying, organizing, or fund-raising. Whenever the hierarchy was displeased by political developments, such as the repeal of Prohibition or the encroachments of the New Deal, it would limit itself to a single public statement, and otherwise leave the political process alone. During most of this time, members of both major parties were prominently represented in the hierarchy, and Mormon voters were about evenly divided between the two parties (Mauss 1972). Official church policy thus wisely maintained strict partisan neutrality, as a rule, and the church intervened only rarely in national political issues of any kind during a period of more than sixty years (Williams 1966).

All of this bespeaks an overriding interest in normalizing relationships with the rest of the nation and accepting a high degree of assimilation. Such a posture cannot be explained by resort to Mormon doctrines or values, since these have been invoked on behalf of both war and peace, on behalf of both feminism and (more recently) anti-feminism, and were kept on "the back burner" during much of the early Prohibition campaign. Nor can these earlier political involvements of the church be attributed to organizational imperatives, discipline, efficiency, or other matters of polity, for the church showed considerable flexibility and lack of organizational discipline in a number of respects. We believe that all of this adds up to support for our general thesis that the church's political involvements were primarily a reflection of its coping with the overarching predicament of disrepute inherited from the nineteenth century and a desire for assimilation and respectability.[10]

The Turn toward Particularism: 1960 to the Present. Since about 1960, we can see signs that the Mormon Church has begun to turn away somewhat from a general drift toward assimilation. We have discussed in some detail elsewhere how this turn has been reflected in the Mormon subculture generally at both the official level and the folk level (Mauss 1982). Here we are concerned with its political manifestations. In general, it is as though the Mormon Church feels that it has gained enough respectability to risk some reassertion of values or doctrines that are somewhat deviant; indeed, there seems to be a sense of a new predicament in relationships with the surrounding American society—namely, the predicament of respectability. How can the church appear to be so fully "American" and yet lay claim to a unique or special heritage, mission, or identity? This predicament has been well noted by two recent studies of the Mormon movement (Leone 1979; Shepherd and Shepherd 1984), both of which recognize the emerging, as well as historical, need for Mormonism to distinguish itself by taking stands in opposition to something. We interpret the same phenomenon as an indication that the Mormon movement has recently been entering a new stage in its relationship with American society, whether self-consciously or not. In this stage, the church, while not altogether rejecting assimilation and respectability, nevertheless looks for new ways to assert itself against dominant cultural and political trends in order to prevent its total assimilation and concomitant loss of identity. Its very survival as a separate subculture depends upon this cyclical turn toward particularism at historical intervals. When this particularism expresses itself politically, it will, of course, draw selectively and strategically upon the accumulated values and doctrines of Mormonism, and it will try to mobilize the polity and its organizational resources as needed. Yet, we contend, the main imperative will be the need to assert its uniqueness vis-à-vis American society, and not the integrity of doctrine or polity, as such.

This theoretical premise, we believe, makes more understandable the extraordinary political involvement of the Mormon Church in recent years in the national controversies surrounding various feminist issues, such as the Equal Rights Amendment and abortion. Mormon doctrines and values can be and have been invoked on either side of these two issues, and there is simply no compelling doctrinal basis for the church's present position. Nor can one see any imperatives arising from concerns over organization or polity, except perhaps in relation to women and the priesthood, though that concern has never been cited in connection with the church's political positions. Church doctrines and scriptures can as readily be cited in favor of total legal equality for women as against it; and, as we have seen, the church was very supportive early in this century of women's suffrage and of equality for the sexes more generally. On the abortion issue too, Mormonism lacks any explicit basis in dogma (such as that in Roman Catholicism) about when a fetus becomes a "living soul." There is ample basis, indeed, for drawing the inference that Mormonism does not consider the spirit as having entered a new body until after parturition: stillbirths are not treated as having lived, for purposes of church records, and church policy permits abortion in the cases of threat to the mother's life and pregnancy from rape or incest—in which cases the fetuses would presumably have the same theological status as any others (Bush 1985).

The ideological basis, then, for the Mormon positions on equal rights and on abortion is not entirely clear or unambiguous, but it seems to come out of a broader and somewhat nebulous "pro-family" ideology that has been evolving in Mormon culture, and that has been characterized as more "Victorian" than Mormon in origin (Foster 1979; Hansen 1981).[11] That same general ideology is probably the context for the church viewpoint on pornography and homosexuality. The point is not that this ideology is somehow inauthentic in Mormonism, but only that it is not a necessary or inevitable derivative of Mormon doctrine or scripture.

There is no doubt about the strenuous and official political involvements of the Mormon Church in resisting some of the main goals of the feminist movement in the United States, especially a liberal abortion policy and the ERA. We can see these involvements, for example, in the Nevada legislative history of both abortion and equal rights policy (Richardson and Fox 1972, 1975; Richardson 1984); in the church's participation in the International Women's Year meetings of 1975–76 in various states (Gottlieb and Wiley 1984, chap. 7; Huefner 1978; White 1983); and in the campaign over the Equal Rights Amendment in several states, from 1976 onward, the latter apparently being the first instance of an organized national lobbying campaign by the Mormon Church.[12] In most of these cases, the church went far beyond public statements by the First Presidency in asserting its political preferences. It resorted to lobbying and pressuring legislators; to mobilizing public opinion through grass-roots campaigns utilizing church facilities and organizational networks; to the raising and disbursing of funds for political purposes, sometimes via front groups; and to joining forces with other special interest groups (Gottlieb and Wiley 1984; White 1983). Directed primarily by the Special Affairs Committee, these initiatives must certainly have had the approval, if not the instigation, of the First Presidency.

While nothing else seems to have drawn quite the same political exertions by the church as these "family issues" of the 1970s and 1980s, there were a few other issues in the 1960s that are relevant to our discussion. One of these was the brief campaign in the U.S. Congress during 1965–66 to overturn Section 14b of the Taft–Hartley Act, a campaign that ultimately failed. It is Section 14b that permits states to pass their own "right-to-work" laws and thus prevent closed-shop labor agreements. Citing the venerable LDS principle of free agency, the First Presidency intervened in these congressional deliberations overtly, on the side of keeping 14b in the law. All Mormons in the legislative delegations to both houses, whether from Utah or not, were contacted personally and urged to vote in favor of keeping 14b.[13] In this matter, the First Presidency may well have been motivated by the personal economic values of most of the hierarchy, and/or by its own vision of what was best for the economy of Utah, which has traditionally not favored organized labor. In any case, this fairly heavy-handed intervention in national politics represented a departure from the more insecure assimilationist posture of the past.[14]

In most other respects, church political initiatives of the past quarter century have been limited to official statements, keeping the church close to the main-stream or assimilationist postures of the past. Presumably out of a concern that the public demeanor of Apostle Benson and others may have identified the church too closely with right-wing causes in the public mind, the First Presidency in 1963, and again in 1966, disavowed any connection with or-ganizations like the John Birch Society and warned church members against political extremism of the right or left.[15] In response to concerns beginning to be expressed in the 1960s that the church's internal racial policies were inimical to the goals of the rising civil rights movement, the First Presidency, in 1963, and again in 1969, issued statements in opposition to racial dis-crimination and in favor of full civil rights for all citizens in the public arena, without, however, offering much hope for change in the church's own racial policies (Bush and Mauss 1984; McMurrin 1979). Indeed, in line with the theoretical orientation of this paper, we would be inclined, along with Leone (1979) and the Shepherds (1984), to see much of the reluctance of the church in changing its racial policies as attributable to an assertion of its own right to be "peculiar" and to depend on its own modern revelations, rather than upon popular trends. When the racial restrictions on priesthood access were finally dropped by revelation in 1978, there had been no significant outside public pressure for several years (Mauss 1981).

The most recent intervention of any consequence by the church into na-tional politics was its widely publicized criticism of the proposal by the Reagan Administration to station MX missiles in Utah and Nevada. As far as we know, that intervention consisted of no more than a statement by the First Presidency, which cited a long-standing church tradition in opposition to militarism and noted the irony of putting weapons of war in the homeland of a people dedicated to propagating the gospel of peace. Coming in the wake of the horrifying disclosures of the high price paid by many residents of Utah and Nevada for the atomic testing done in their area during the 1950s, the First Presidency's position on MX is understandable enough, and it does not represent a strenuous assertion by the church of a deviant political viewpoint (Hildreth 1982). Still, the church did demonstrate a willingness to assert itself, out of its own identity and sense of mission, in opposition even to a national administration that has been very friendly to Mormons.[16]

Conclusion

It has been the main contention of this paper that involvements by the Mor-mon Church in national U.S. politics for the most part can be understood more by reference to whether or not the church is in an assimilationist cycle vis-à-vis American society, than by reference to doctrine or to polity. The evidence suggests that whatever the nature of doctrine or polity, these can be mobilized selectively and strategically in support of those political interventions deemed most helpful in promoting the survival and success of the church as a movement. Thus, during the first several decades of this century, when survival and success required an assimilationist policy in the church's posture toward the nation, political interventions in the nation's affairs were mild in form and generally in conformity with dominant national trends. Since about 1960, when maintenance of the church's identity has seemed to require a more particularistic resistance to assimilation, church leaders have shown much more inclination to stand against national trends, as in the issues of race relations, abortion, the ERA, and perhaps right-to-work, and a willingness also to resort to political interventions of more heavy-handed kinds. Not all political interventions by the church in recent years can be thus explained, perhaps, but most of them can.[17]

We would offer the concluding observation that some social scientists (e.g., Shupe and Heinerman 1985), noting similarities in the social and political values of Mormons and conservative Christians, have speculated on the prospects for a political alliance of Mormons with the New Christian Right, including the Moral Majority. In agreement with Brinkerhoff, et al. (1985), we would tend to discount such prospects, especially in light of our contention in this paper. While it is true that there are similarities in values between Mormons and the Moral Majority, there are also several important differences, and neither side feels much kinship with the other for historical, as well as theological, reasons. Beyond that, we see Mormon political interventions since 1960 as reflecting not so much a value-congruity with the Moral Majority as an attempt to assert its own uniqueness in American society, a point that would obviously be lost by even the appearance of an alliance with the New Christian Right.[18]

Notes

1. Prior to the twentieth century, the church bound itself to ecclesiastical authorities, not civil authorities, in questions of war and conscientious objection. According to historian D. Michael Quinn, the church followed the dictates of Section 98 of the *Doctrine and Covenants* and adopted and practiced a policy of "selective pacifism," in effect breaching the tenets of the twelfth Article of Faith. Section 98 of the *Doctrine and Covenants* reads in part: ". . . renounce war and proclaim peace . . . this is the law that I gave unto mine ancients, that they should not go into battle against any nation . . . save I, the Lord, commanded them. And if any nation . . . should proclaim war against them they should first lift a standard of peace unto the people, nation, or tongue; and if that people did not accept the offering of peace, neither the second nor the third time, they should bring these testimonies before the Lord; then I, the Lord, would give unto them a com-

mandment, and justify them in going out to battle . . ." (LDS Church 1981b, 98:16, 33–37). The twelfth Article of Faith holds: "We believe in being subject to kings, presidents, rulers, and magistrates, in obeying, honoring, and sustaining the law" (LDS Church 1981c, 61). The church position came to reflect the twelfth Article rather than *Doctrine and Covenants* 98 with the onset of the Spanish–American War in 1898. The First Presidency came out in favor of the U.S. position on this war in a letter dated April 28, 1898, sent to Utah Governor Heber M. Wells (Clark 1966, 299). Their position was also made public the same day in an article published in the *Deseret Weekly* (Quinn 1984, 1985).

2. Prior to the outbreak of World War I, church president Joseph F. Smith condemned both the British and the Germans. However, when the U.S. entered the conflict in 1917, the church supported the national war effort. In an address to General Conference, April 1917 (the very day the U.S. declared war), President Joseph F. Smith stated the new church position (Clark 1971,50–52, 61–62).

   World War II was initially condemned by some general authorities as an "unholy war." The First Presidency issued a "Message on World Peace" at the October, 1939, General Conference to this effect. Copies of the message as published in the *Deseret News*, October 14, 1939, were sent to leading and influential officials in Washington (Clark 1975, 89–91). Some even raised the question of whether or not the church as a whole ought to take a conscientious objection stand on the general question of involvement in the war. However, the church finally settled on its by then long-standing position that conscientious objection was not the rule of the church (Quinn 1985).

   Near the first part of the war, the church issued, over the signatures of the First Presidency, a major policy statement during the April, 1942, General Conference, reaffirming its 1898 policy on war. During this whole period the church still repeatedly "renounced war" in general (Clark 1975, 116–119, 139–140, 157–163, 182–183, 189, 216–217, 219).

3. An important exception to this general sentiment was expressed by President J. Reuben Clark, Jr., in a letter to Senator Henry Dworshak, dated May 17, 1954. He not only feared the consequences of U.S. involvement in Indo-China but felt the greatest danger to the country rested in the increasingly popular opinion that the U.S. was destined to dictate to and rule the world (Quinn 1985).

   On May 24, 1969, however, the First Presidency issued a statement supporting the country's involvement in the Vietnam War. A particular factor guiding the church's decision in this instance may have been a desire to avoid jeopardizing its already fragile and restricted arrangement with the U.S. government over draft deferment allotments granted the church for missionaries during the war (Quinn 1985). Earlier, during the Korean War, the church had maintained its position of opposing war but nevertheless answering the country's call. It supported this so-called "police action" but also came out again in support of conscientious objection. This was the subject of an editorial in the *Deseret News*, June 25, 1951 (Quinn 1985). For additional references to the church's position on wars during this century, see Allen and Leonard 1976, 437, 490–491, 506, 541–547; Arrington and Bitton 1979, 251; Firmage 1983; Quinn 1983; Walker 1982.

4. In the late 1960s, there was evidence that the church was beginning to modify

somewhat its previous position permissive of conscientious objection. In reply to an inquiry about the status of members who took the position of conscientious objection, the First Presidency instructed its secretary, Joseph Anderson, to state that membership in the church did not automatically make one a conscientious objector. However, existing laws provided for this stance, and the church had no objection if a member availed himself, on a personal basis, of exemption from military service (Quinn 1985). But then in General Conference in April, 1968, Elder (Apostle) Boyd K. Packer came out unqualifiedly in opposition to conscientious objection. Three years later, however, the First Presidency again instructed its secretary to state the position of the church on this topic, namely that worthy members, who otherwise were conscientious objectors, were entitled to full fellowship in the church (Quinn 1985). This would appear to be the official policy of the church on this issue at the present time.

5. The temperance movement was one of the longest reform movements in this country's history. Almost from the outset, the church had been in opposition to "strong drink" (LDS Church 1981b, Sec. 89). For decades prior to Prohibition, the church had opposed the sale and use of alcoholic beverages. With the onset of the Prohibition Era in American politics in the early 1900s, the church was faced with the question of which of three options to support: 1) a national prohibition amendment, 2) state prohibition laws, or 3) state laws allowing local options for each community.

Church President Joseph F. Smith and Utah Senator Reed Smoot initially favored the third option. They seemingly took this position fearing that church support of statewide prohibition would alienate many of the Senator's supporters and jeopardize his seat in the U.S. Senate. Also, they did not want to give the appearance of the church controlling state politics to its own ends. Hence a statewide prohibition bill was defeated and later bills were vetoed by Utah Governor William Spry, a Mormon. Church Elders Heber J. Grant, George A. Smith, and David O. McKay, and Presiding Bishop Charles W. Nibley, however, were all in favor of state prohibition. They supported a local option bill that was passed in 1911 and urged all Utah communities to adopt the law, in anticipation of passage of a statewide bill.

By 1916, President Joseph F. Smith reversed his position and the church then supported statewide prohibition and even nationwide prohibition. In 1917, Utah became the forty-first "dry state." In 1919, the national Prohibition Amendment passed, with full church support, and took effect in January, 1920.

6. An April 10, 1919, editorial in the *Deseret News*, signed by the First Presidency, called for support of a "peace day" and for wide discussion within the church of the League of Nations (Allen 1973). In a stake conference address in Salt Lake City on September 21, 1919, President Grant personally endorsed the idea of the treaty and came out in opposition to those who suggested that the scriptures of the church were in opposition to an endeavor such as the League of Nations. By implication it was also suggested that proponents of the treaty were not to invoke the scriptures in defense of their position. (Clark 1971, 137–142.)

The October, 1919, General Conference of the church devoted a considerable amount of time to discussion of the treaty, but it took no official position on the issue. The treaty was ultimately defeated by the U.S. Senate.

7. By 1928, the conflict between the so-called "wets and drys" had become a central issue in American politics, and national sentiment was growing to repeal Prohibition. The First Presidency last addressed this issue in their December, 1933, Christmas message. They reasserted their view that repeal of Prohibition should have little or no effect upon members, who were still expected to conform to church standards in avoiding alcoholic beverages (Clark 1971, 338–340; see also Allen and Leonard 1976, 487–488, 513; Arrington and Bitton 1979, 248–249; Shepherd and Shepherd 1984, 58, 186).

8. In 1936, during the Great Depression, at a time when the U.S. Communist Party was becoming increasingly influential in the country, the First Presidency, upon learning of members joining the Communist Party, issued a "warning" statement (Clark 1975, 16–18). The rationale for the church taking a position on this issue seems clear enough. The First Presidency perceived the Communist movement in America as not only a threat to democratic institutions and to the Constitution, but also wished to emphasize that this political ideology did not represent a contemporary version of the church's long-standing communitarian ideals traditionally referred to as the "United Order."

This 1936 statement was followed by a First Presidency message at the outbreak of World War II, April 6, 1942, again warning members against Communist influences in the country and distancing the church and its welfare policies and practices from this ideology (Clark 1975, 151).

9. The First Presidency sent this statement in the form of a letter, dated December 14, 1945, to the congressional delegation from Utah (Clark 1975, 239–242). On June 28, 1946, in a letter to all stake presidents and bishops, the First Presidency suggested that those church officials who wished to write to their respective congressional representatives in opposition to this pending legislation ought to do so by formally endorsing the December 14, 1945 statement. The proposed military legislation was, however, eventually passed into law (Quinn 1985).

10. One of our esteemed critics (Williams 1985) has assessed our theoretical framework here as successfully explaining church political interventions only about half of the time. He finds as particularly counterindicative to our framework the opposition of the church leaders to Franklin D. Roosevelt and to the repeal of Prohibition, both of which set those leaders against the national (and Utah) public consensus in the ostensibly "assimilationist" 1930s. He finds further that our framework understates the importance of the church's economic and political self-interest in such instances as protective tariffs, opposition to the closed union shop, initial opposition to airline deregulation, and the successful opposition to MX missile basing.

In response, we would say that we have not meant to ignore either the personal political preferences of certain powerful church leaders or their perceptions of the political and economic interests of the church. What we have tried to do, rather, is to consider all of these in the more macrocosmic context of the ongoing struggle of Mormons as a people to maintain the optimum balance between assimilation and peculiarity. Viewed from this more abstract perspective, the "wishes of the Brethren," while always important, are not necessarily determinant. They can be muted, modified, or augmented by such other considerations as the amount of internal resistance from dissenting colleagues in the leadership or from church folk more generally, as well as by external pressure from the national political and economic establishment. Thus it is the over-all thrust of corporate responses to the environment over fairly long periods of time that must provide the basis for our generalizations. During the 1930s, for example, while there is no doubt about the opposition of the First Presidency of the Church both to Franklin D. Roosevelt and to repeal of Prohibition, we would argue that such opposition was neither well sustained nor strongly asserted in the face of the "assimilationist" posture of the general church membership, which was strongly in line with the national consensus on both repeal and the New Deal.

Some of the issues of economic policy are complicated by the difficulty of distinguishing "church" interest from Utah and regional interests (as with tariff and labor policy), which are likely to become even less identical as church membership increases in other regions of North America. Furthermore, the initiatives of the church leaders in the cases of the closed shop (Taft–Hartley 14b) and airline deregulation were feeble, transitory, and ineffective. In general, such political opposition to national trends as occurred in the Mormon leadership during the first (assimilationist) half of the twentieth century would pale in intensity by comparison with the later ERA campaign or with the church political posture of the nineteenth century.

11. Since its first pronouncements in the late nineteenth century, the church has maintained a fairly consistent position on the question of abortion and on the conditions under which it is permissible. This position was again reiterated as recently as the April 1985, General Conference by the newly appointed Apostle Russell M. Nelson (Nelson 1985). As noted, the church's position on this point does not derive from a doctrine fixing the time when the spirit enters the body, but seems to be based on the general recognition of the fetus as a form of human life, presumably from the time of conception, and the taking of this human life as a most serious transgression, if not a kind of murder (Keller 1985; Nelson 1985). Although we have not been able to document whether the church, on the basis of this particular view on abortion, has ever supported any specific national legislation on the issue, it would not be surprising to find the church taking such a stand in the future, should a given piece of proposed legislation fit the particular requirements mandated by the church's position on the issue. This is a position that is actually very similar to public policy in most U.S. states prior to *Roe v. Wade* in 1973. (For additional references on this point, see Bush 1976, 1985; Hill 1981; Oliphant 1981; Richardson and Fox 1972, 1975; Sherlock 1981.)

12. As a context for the gradually developing opposition to the ERA by Mormon leaders, it is important to recall that the "Age of Aquarius" (the 1960s) was widely perceived by Mormons and others to have seriously undermined traditional family values with its celebration of sexual and other kinds of "liberation." The new and vocal women's movement was looked upon with suspicion as a product of the same social crisis. There is reason to believe also that church opposition to the ERA was stiffened by alarm over the efforts of federal agencies to interpret existing civil rights statutes (which did not even have constitutional status) as

disallowing Brigham Young University administrative control over the living arrangements (and thus sex lives) of its students. The church had little to say about ERA during the early 1970s, though Belle Spafford (Relief Society President, 1945–1974, and President of the National Council of Women, 1968–1970) found herself sometimes having to defend the traditional place of women in Mormonism.

In December 1974, the new president of the Relief Society, Barbara Smith, sought to reconcile differing views on the role of women within the church and also attempted to position the church appropriately in reference to the national women's movement and the proposed Equal Rights Amendment. Her December 12, 1974, address at the University of Utah was the first statement on what was to become the church's official position on the ERA (Winder 1980). On October 22, 1976, the First Presidency issued its official position in an editorial in the *Deseret News*. In May, 1978, when ERA supporters formally petitioned Congress to extend the deadline for ratification to 1986, the First Presidency responded with a statement (dated May 25, 1978), reaffirming its position and coming out in opposition to extension (Winder 1980). Later in the same year, the church addressed the question some critics had raised, namely that the ERA was a political issue on which the church should remain silent. The First Presidency, in an interview published in the *Deseret News* on August 26, 1978, reaffirmed its view that the issue was a "moral" one on which the church should take a stand. Finally, on October 12, 1978, when Congress extended the deadline for ratification of the amendment to June 30, 1983, the First Presidency again issued an official statement on the topic (Winder 1980). (For additional references on this issue, see Shepherd and Shepherd 1984, 38–39, 206–207; Arrington and Bitton 1979, 234–240; Richardson 1984; Huefner 1978; Oliphant 1981; White 1983.)

13. Utah, in 1965, was one of nineteen states with right-to-work laws on their books. On June 22, 1965, the First Presidency sent a letter to all Mormon members of Congress reiterating the church's position in favor of voluntary unionism and expressing their hope that the Congress would take no action to alter the present laws (Mangum 1968).

More controversy seems to have been raised over the manner in which the First Presidency chose to make public their opposition to changing the law than to the substance of their argument. Their letter was sent only to Mormon members of Congress rather than to all members or to relevant members of select committees, and the letter did not make sufficiently clear that it was expressing only the opinions of the presiding brethren, not necessarily based on divine revelation. The manner in which the church acted in this case raised the fundamental question of what church policy and procedure ought to be in such dealings, and whether speaking out on a specific piece of legislation pending before Congress, regardless of the subject matter, might not have cast the church in the position of crossing the mythic line between church and state. Opponents of the church's position on this issue charged that the church in this case was really motivated by regional economic interests, trying to induce corporations to relocate in Utah through keeping wages low. (See also Davies 1968; Frederickson and Stevens 1968.)

14. There are references (Croft 1985) to the effect that the First Presidency in 1977

wrote to key members of Congress voicing its opposition to proposed legislation that would deregulate the airline industry. Presumably their reason for taking this stand was the fear that such a move would curtail airline service into Utah and hence hamper the church's missionary program. If this action in fact was taken, it would be another instance in which the church chose to speak out on a specific piece of legislation. We have not been able to document this claim, however. Nor have we been able to document a reference to the claim that the First Presidency seemingly reversed itself on this point by issuing a statement sometime in the early 1980s in favor of airline deregulation in conjunction with airport development in Salt Lake City (Gottlieb and Wiley 1984, 117).

15. As a corollary to the church's position in opposition to the extremism of Communism, the church has also taken a position on political ideologies of the extreme right, starting in the mid-1960s, particularly during and after the general presidential elections of 1964. The first statement to this effect was made public January 3, 1963, in an editorial in the *Deseret News* (Williams 1981). Three years later, just prior to April General Conference, at a time when some general authorities were endorsing certain right-wing individuals and groups in the country; and some church members were using church facilities to promote their own partisan politics; and when the John Birch Society was attempting to get the church to endorse its activities, the *Church News* ran an editorial, again disavowing the church's association or involvement with any political groups or ideologies, left or right. (Williams 1966; see also Allen and Leonard 1976, 619.)

16. One of the first public statements by a general church authority on the whole question of arms buildup and the uses of nuclear weapons was made by Elder J. Reuben Clark, Jr., shortly after World War II. President Clark had opposed the war as a pacifist, and opposed all forms of militarism. In a General Conference address in October, 1946, he spoke critically about the dropping of the atomic bomb on Japan (Blais 1984; Quinn 1983, 211–213; 1985). As far as can be determined, the general authorities have never modified Elder Clark's remarks during the intervening decades. On May 5, 1981, the First Presidency issued a statement on the proposed basing of MX missiles in Utah and Nevada. While the thrust of the statement centered on concerns over the physical, social, economic, and human survival problems inherent in the MX missile system, the statement reaffirmed the church's long-standing opposition to the arms buildup and stated once again the church's position that world peace will come only through the increased influence of the Gospel of Jesus Christ (Firmage 1983). This topic was addressed in the First Presidency's Christmas message of 1980 and again in their 1981 Easter message. Five years earlier, President Kimball, in an article in the *Ensign,* had criticized the too easy equation of national defense with weaponry (Firmage 1983). The Defense Department eventually abandoned plans to base the MX missile in Utah and Nevada (See Gottlieb and Wiley 1984; Hildreth 1982.).

17. Critic J.D. Williams (1985), again, has pointed to the "reactionary" stance of the church in recent years on race and feminist issues as instances of the triumph of ideology and personal political commitments over good sense among the church leadership. He thus accuses us once again of playing down these ideological and

political factors in our theoretical effort to emphasize the recent Mormon quest for peculiarity in the face of the "predicament of respectability." Why, he asks, would church leaders take such obviously "irrational" stands on "grave national issues" just for the sake of "looking peculiar"? Surely they must have been driven simply by their own political and ideological preferences. How else could the church leaders justify "ignoring (legitimate) claims to economic and social justice" and thus jeopardizing the proselytizing efforts of the church?

Our reply is both empirical and theoretical. As an empirical matter, one can hardly make the case that conservative Mormon social policies of any kind have hampered the missionary work of the church, given the high conversion rates in recent decades among both men and women (and even among blacks once they became an explicit focus of proselytizing in 1978). Of course, one would expect a conservative church image to attract converts from some constituencies but not others (a point addressed in Mauss 1982).

As a theoretical matter, we must point again to the implications of our having chosen the fairly abstract and macrocosmic perspective employed here. While it does not require us to ignore the personal ideologies, politics, or motives of church leaders, neither does it require us to pass our own value judgments on those things, as Williams apparently feels obliged to do. Rather, our framework poses the question in a way that is an alternative (but not necessarily superior) to the way in which critics like Williams may pose it. Instead of trying to understand the "reactionary perversity" of church leaders in light of their own putative beliefs and motives, we pose the question this way: What corporate or collective imperatives might explain the apparent need of the church leadership to take strong and enduring stands athwart the national consensus (as in the case of the racial and feminist issues)? Our theory suggests the answer that an internal, collective, subcultural need (shared by both leaders and members) was felt to reassert the church's claim to transcendental uniqueness in the face of generations of assimilation. Where the race issue was concerned, for example, it seems clear that the church was more concerned with protecting the charisma of the office of prophet from the appearance of expedient political compromise than with enforcing the ideological preferences of certain church leaders (Mauss 1981). A related explanation suggests itself for the feminist issue.

18. Interestingly enough, in unintended complementarity to the position of this paper, Speer (1984) argues that the political postures of the New Christian Right are also attributable in large part to the degree of accommodation to American society by Evangelicals. He finds rather a different outcome of accommodation for Evangelicals from that which we have postulated for Mormons, which tends also to strengthen our concluding point here that Mormons and the New Christian Right are "coming at" politics in the U.S. from somewhat different directions.

References

Alexander, T. G. 1986. *Mormonism in Transition: A History of the Latter-day Saints, 1890–1930*. Urbana and Chicago: University of Illinois Press. (Chapters 2, 3, 5, and 12 are especially relevant here.)

Alexander, T. G. 1970. "An Experiment in Progressive Legislation: The Granting of Woman Suffrage in Utah in 1870." *Utah Historical Quarterly* 38: 20–30.

Allen, J. B. 1973. "Personal Faith and Public Policy: Some Timely Observation on the League of Nations Controversy in Utah." *B.Y.U. Studies* 14(1): 77–98.

Allen, J. B. and Leonard, G. M. 1976. *The Story of the Latter-day Saints.* Salt Lake City: Deseret Book Co.

Arrington, L. J. and Bitton, D. 1979. *The Mormon Experience: A History of the Latter-day Saints.* New York: A.A. Knopf.

Beecher, M. U. 1982. "The 'Leading Sisters': A Female Hierarchy in 19th Century Mormon Society." *Journal of Mormon History* 9: 25–39.

Beeton, B. 1978. "Woman Suffrage in Territorial Utah." *Utah Historical Quarterly* 46: 100–120.

Blais, P. 1984. "The Enduring Paradox: Mormon Attitudes Toward War and Peace." *Dialogue: A Journal of Mormon Thought* 17(4): 61–73.

Brinkerhoff, M. B., J. C. Jacob, and M. M. Mackie. 1985. "Mormonism and the Moral Majority Make Strange Bed-Fellows?: An Exploratory Critique." Paper presented at the annual meeting of the Pacific Sociological Association, Albuquerque, NM.

Bromley, D. G. and A. D. Shupe, Jr. 1981. *Strange Gods: The Great American Cult Scare.* Boston: Beacon Press.

Bush, L. E. Jr. 1985. "Ethical Issues in Reproductive Medicine: A Mormon Perspective." *Dialogue: A Journal of Mormon Thought* 18(2): 40–66.

Bush, L. E. Jr. 1976. "Birth Control Among the Mormons: Introduction to an Insistent Question." *Dialogue: A Journal of Mormon Thought* 10(2): 12–44.

Bush, L. E. Jr. and Mauss, A. L. 1984. *Neither White nor Black: Mormon Scholars Encounter the Race Issue in a Universal Church.* Salt Lake City: Signature Books.

Cannon, M., R. Bushman, Q. McKay, R. Wirthlin and G. Magnum. 1962. "What is the Proper Role of the Latter-day Saint with Respect to the Constitution?" *B.Y.U. Studies* 4: 151–77.

Clark, J. R. 1975. *Messages of the First Presidency,* Vol. 6. Salt Lake City: Bookcraft, Inc.

Clark, J. R. 1971. *Messages of the First Presidency,* Vol. 5. Salt Lake City: Bookcraft, Inc.

Clark, J. R. 1970. *Messages of the First Presidency,* Vol. 4. Salt Lake City: Bookcraft, Inc.

Clark, J. R. 1966. *Messages of the First Presidency,* Vol. 3. Salt Lake City: Bookcraft, Inc.

Croft, Q. M. 1985. *The Influence of the L.D.S. Church on Utah Politics, 1945–1984.* Ph.D. Dissertation, University of Utah.

Davies, J. K. 1968. "The Accommodation of Mormonism and Political-Economic Reality." *Dialogue: A Journal of Mormon Thought* 3(1): 42–54.

Davies, J. K. 1963. "The Mormon Church: Its Middle Class Propensities." *Review of Religious Research* 4: 84–95.

Davis, D. B. 1960. "Some Themes of Counter-Subversion: An Analysis of Anti-Masonic, Anti-Catholic, and Anti-Mormon Literature." *Mississippi Valley Historical Review* 47: 205–24.

Firmage, E. B. 1983. "Allegiance and Stewardship: Holy War, Just War, and the

Mormon Tradition in the Nuclear Age." *Dialogue: A Journal of Mormon Thought* 16(1): 47–61.

Firmage, E. B. 1981. "A Church Cannot Stand Silent in the Midst of Moral Decay." *Sunstone* 6(4): 37–39.

Foster, L. 1979. "From Frontier Activism to Neo-Victorian Domesticity: Mormon Women in the 19th and 20th Centuries." *Journal of Mormon History* 6: 3–21.

Frederickson, H. G. and A. J. Stevens. 1968. "The Mormon Congressman and the Line Between Church and State." *Dialogue: A Journal of Mormon Thought* 3(2): 121–29.

Gottlieb, R. and P. Wiley. 1984. *America's Saints: The Rise of Mormon Power.* New York: G.P. Putman's Sons.

Hampshire, A. P. and J. A. Beckford. 1983. "Religious Sects and the Concept of Deviance: The Mormons and the Moonies." *British Journal of Sociology* 34(2): 208–29.

Hansen, K. J. 1981. *Mormonism and the American Experience.* Chicago: University of Chicago Press.

Hildreth, S. A. 1982. "The First Presidency Statement on MX in Perspective." *B.Y.U. Studies* 22(2): 215–25.

Hill, D. G., Jr. 1981. "Abortion Politics and Policy: The Beginning of Actual Human Life." *Sunstone* 6(4): 25–27.

Huefner, D. S. 1978. "Church and Politics at the Utah IWY Conference." *Dialogue: A Journal of Mormon Thought* 11(1): 58–75.

Janosik, G. E. 1951. *Political Theory of the Mormon Church.* Ph.D. dissertation, University of Pennsylvania.

Johnson, F. R. 1979. "The Mormon Church as a Central Command System." *Review of Social Economics* 37(1): 79–94.

Jonas, F. H. 1969. "Utah the Different State." In *Politics in the American West*, F.H. Jonas, ed. Salt Lake City: University of Utah Press.

Keller, J. E. 1985. "When Does the Spirit Enter the Body?" *Sunstone* 10(3): 42–44.

Larson, G. O. 1971. *The "Americanization" of Utah for Statehood.* San Marino, CA: Huntington Library.

L.D.S. Church. 1981a. *Book of Mormon.* Salt Lake City: Church of Jesus Christ of Latter-day Saints.

L.D.S. Church. 1981b. *Doctrine and Covenants.* Salt Lake City: Church of Jesus Christ of Latter-day Saints.

L.D.S. Church. 1981c. *Pearl of Great Price.* Salt Lake City: Church of Jesus Christ of Latter-day Saints.

Leone, M. P. 1979. *Roots of Modern Mormonism.* Cambridge, MA: Harvard University Press.

Lyman, E. L. 1985. "The Alienation of an Apostle from his Church: The Moses Thatcher Case." *Dialogue: A Journal of Mormon Thought* 18(2): 67–91.

——— 1986. *Political Deliverance: The Mormon Quest for Utah Statehood.* Champaign, IL: University of Illinois Press.

Lythgoe, D. L. 1982. *Let 'Em Holler: A Political Biography of J. Bracken Lee.* Salt Lake City: Utah State Historical Society.

McMurrin, S. M. 1979. "A Note on the 1963 Civil Rights Statement." *Dialogue: A Journal of Mormon Thought* 12(2): 60–63.

Mangum, G. L. 1968. "The Church and Collective Bargaining in American Society." *Dialogue: A Journal of Mormon Thought* 3(2): 106–11.

Mann, D. E. 1967. "Mormon Attitudes Toward the Political Roles of Church Leaders." *Dialogue: A Journal of Mormon Thought* 2(2): 32–48.

Mauss, A. L. 1982. "The Angel and the Beehive: The Mormon Quest for Peculiarity and the Struggle with Secularization." Lecture delivered under the auspices of the Charles Redd Center for Western Studies at Brigham Young University, November, 1982. A condensed version appeared in *BYU Today*, August, 1983.

Mauss, A. L. 1981. "The Fading of the Pharoahs' Curse: The Decline and Fall of the Priesthood Ban against Blacks in the Mormon Church." *Dialogue: A Journal of Mormon Thought* 14(3): 10–45.

Mauss, A. L. 1975. *Social Problems as Social Movements*. Philadelphia: J. B. Lippincott.

Mauss, A. L. 1972. "Moderation in All Things: Political and Social Outlooks of Modern Urban Mormons." *Dialogue: A Journal of Mormon Thought* 7(1): 57–69.

Mauss, A. L. 1971. "On Being Strangled by the Stars and Stripes: The New Left, the Old Left, and the Natural History of American Radical Movements." *Journal of Social Issues* 27(1): 183–202.

Miles, A. O. 1978. *Mormon Voting Behavior and Political Attitudes*. Ph.D. Dissertation, University of Utah.

Nelson, R. M. 1985. "Reverence for Life." *The Ensign* 15(5): 11–14. (Official L.D.S. Church monthly magazine.)

Oliphant, L. C. 1981. "Is There an ERA-Abortion Connection?" *Dialogue: A Journal of Mormon Thought* 14(1): 65–72.

Quinn, D. M. 1985. "Conscientious Objectors or Christian Soldiers? The Latter-day Saint Position on Militarism." *Sunstone* 10(3): 15–23.·

Quinn, D. M. 1984. "The Mormon Church and the Spanish-American War: An End to Selective Pacifism." *Dialogue: A Journal of Mormon Thought* 17(4): 11–30.

Quinn, D. M. 1983. *J. Reuben Clark: The Church Years*. Provo, Utah: Brigham Young University Press.

Richardson, J. T. 1984. "The 'Old Right' in Action: Mormon and Catholic Involvement in an Equal Rights Amendment Referendum." In *New Christian Politics*, D. G. Bromley and A. D. Shupe, Jr., eds. Macon, GA: Mercer University Press, 213–33.

Richardson, J. T. and S. W. Fox. 1975. "Religion and Voting on Abortion Reform: A Follow-up Study." *Journal for the Scientific Study of Religion* 14(2): 159–64.

Richardson, J. T. and S. W. Fox. 1972. "Religious Affiliation as a Predictor of Voting Behavior in Abortion Reform Legislation." *Journal for the Scientific Study of Religion* 11(4): 347–59.

Shepard, Gordon and Gary Shepard. 1984. *A Kingdom Transformed: Themes in the Development of Mormonism*. Salt Lake City: University of Utah Press.

Sherlock, R. 1981. "Abortion Politics and Policy: A Deafening Silence in the Church." *Sunstone* 6(4): 17–19.

Shipps, J. B. 1967. "Utah Comes of Age Politically: A Study of the State's Politics in the Early Years of the 20th Century." *Utah Historical Quarterly* 35: 91–111.

Shupe, A. and J. Heinerman. 1985. "Mormonism and the New Christian Right: An Emerging Coalition?" *Review of Religious Research* 27(2): 146–157.

Speer, J. A. 1984. "The New Christian Right and Its Parent Company: A Study of Political Contrasts." In New Christian Politics, D. G. Bromley and A. D. Shupe, Jr., eds. Macon, GA: Mercer University Press, 19–40.

Walker, R. W. 1982. "Sheaves, Bucklers and the State: Mormon Leaders Respond to the Dilemmas of War." *Sunstone* 7(4): 43–56.

White, O. K. 1983. "Overt and Covert Politics: The Mormon Church's Anti-ERA Campaign in Virginia." *Virginia Social Science Journal* 18 (Winter).

Williams, J. D. 1985. "Critique of 'Mormon Assimilation and Politics' " (Mauss and Mradford). Presented at the annual Sunstone Symposium, Salt Lake City, August.

Williams, J. D. 1981. "In a Democracy, Church Interference is Dangerous." *Sunstone* 6(4): 36, 40–44.

Williams, J. D. 1966. "Separation of Church and State in Mormon Theory and Practice." *Dialogue: A Journal of Mormon Thought* 1(2): 30–54.

Winder, L. 1980. "LDS Position on the ERA: An Historical View." *Exponent II* 6 (Winter): 6–7.

4
State-Within-A-State Diplomacy: Mormon Missionary Efforts in Communist and Islamic Countries

Anson Shupe and John Heinerman

CHRISTIAN MISSIONIZING in the past has been indivisibly linked to political force: from the Roman Catholic friars who accompanied the Spanish conquistadors into Central and South America to the nineteenth century China missionaries who joined with European troops against the T'ai-Ping Christian revolutions. Christian missionaries have traditionally strode arm-in-arm with the military across the portals of countless Third World cultures, accustomed to sharing in the hegemony of resulting Western-style "modernization."

However, since World War II not all cultures have been as helpless as those in the Third World once were in the face of "missionary invasions." They often do not want their values and allegiances transformed. Some modern nation-states, particularly Marxist-Leninist and Islamic ones, have even formally decreed themselves atheistic and/or "off limits" to Western Christian missionaries. Despite differences in the amount of toleration for traditions and sometimes imported sectarian religions, the general communist policy is to "discourage" (through bureaucratic harrassment, legal restraints, and outright persecution) religious "dissenters" within their populations (Fletcher 1981; Lane 1978; Powell 1975; Kline 1968). No Communist country explicitly encourages religious proselytization by any group, internal or otherwise

(Pankhurst 1986). Likewise, many Islamic nations legally forbid proselytization by other faiths.

Yet in recent years one particular sectarian religious group has been making unique inroads against the hegemony of "state" atheism and "state" Islam. Here we examine the recent activities of the Church of Jesus Christ of Latter-day Saints (the Mormons) in a number of communist and Islamic societies. Within the past two decades the LDS Church has acted as a "state-within-a-state" in conducting negotiations with both types of countries with which the United States government has had inconsistent diplomatic relations. The purpose of these negotiations has been to open up these societies to Mormon missionizing. Indeed, in some instances the LDS Church has accomplished goals that U.S. diplomacy either could not or did so only with great difficulty. After identifying recent efforts to establish branches of the LDS Church in several Eastern European and Middle Eastern countries as well as the People's Republic of China, we will indicate some underlying conditions of the Utah-based sect's success.[1]

The Decision To Penetrate Communism

Currently the LDS Church is aggressively seeking footholds (in terms of establishing missions and, where possible, constructing temples and churches) in communist countries. This development is ironic for two reasons. First, as Pankhurst (1986) and others have noted, the anti-religious policies of Eastern European and Asian regimes represent a common thread running through otherwise diverse national populations and styles of communism. Second, the LDS Church's public posture since World War II has been vehemently anti-communist. Though Joseph Smith and Brigham Young certainly never heard of Karl Marx, post-World War II Church leaders have literally and insistently equated communism with satanism. For example, in 1942 Church President David O. McKay and other members of the First Presidency (the President and his two counselors) officially declared at a session of the semiannual General Conference:

> Communism destroys man's God-given free agency . . . Latter-day Saints cannot be true to their faith and lend aid, encouragement, or sympathy to any of these false philosophies. They will prove snares to their feet (Brough 1975, 77).

One of McKay's counselors, J. Reuben Clark, Jr., reportedly stated that communism "would destroy our American Constitutional government" and that "to support Communism is treasonable to our free institutions. . . ." Church members were called upon to "completely eschew Communism in any shape or form." Years later Church President Harold B. Lee warned against "false prophets and christs" deceiving people in countries like Russia "under the label of politicians or of social planners or so-called economists. . . ." More recently, Apostle Bruce R. McConkie (1966, 151) wrote that communism "necessarily is a dictatorship of the severest and most ruthless type." Church President Ezra Taft Benson, the Church's premier anti-communist, suggested in 1977, while an Apostle, that not just the teachings but the very discussion of communism be banned at Brigham Young University.

Yet during this same time, behind the strident rhetoric, Mormon leaders have been privately shifting their thinking about dealing with communism. It has been a gradual but steady process over the past thirty years. As early as October 1945 Church President George Albert Smith (LDS 1980, 108) stated:

> I look upon Russia as one of the most fruitful fields for the teaching of the gospel of Jesus Christ. And if I am not mistaken, it will not be long before the people who are there will desire to know something about this work which has reformed the lives of so many people.

Despite their public condemnations of communism during the Cold War of the 1950s, Mormon leaders were at the same time (without benefit of publicity) actually courting good will and concessions from those same countries. A case of such contradictions was President David O. McKay, who requested right-winger W. Cleon Skousen to write the hostile *The Naked Communist* (Iler 1978, 26) and who was repeatedly on record as denouncing any contact with communists. Yet McKay hosted a Soviet delegation in Salt Lake City in 1955. One of the Soviet party, the son-in-law of the U.S.S.R. Premier Nikita Khruschev, recalled McKay's persistent inquiries about purchasing land in the Soviet Union on which the Church could build a mission headquarters:

> The head of the [Mormon] church, its president Mr. McKay, kept on asking during our visit, "Isn't it at all possible to buy in the Soviet Union, at least five acres of land and begin preaching there our Mormonism?" Naturally we answered Mr. McKay that the land in the Soviet Union belongs to the people and is not for sale (Adjoubey 1956).

But it was not until the late 1970s that the LDS Church began an earnest campaign to open up communist nations for missionizing and to extend its influence. On repeated occasions the Council of the Twelve Apostles met and discussed the best strategy for tackling this unique crusade. After some time they selected Brigham Young University, their "cultural and educational showpiece" at Provo, Utah, as the vehicle to launch it. Specifically, they planned to work through the school's music and dance groups that regularly perform internationally. BYU touring cultural groups became a valuable vehicle enabling the LDS Church to find entry through both Iron and Bamboo

curtains, permitting various Church leaders and representatives to gain legitimate, cordial entrance into countries that would otherwise deny visas to
such leaders if they tried to enter simply on their own Church credentials.
In 1982 the chairperson of the BYU Dance Department said in an interview:

> Getting into places like this [an Iron Curtain Country] is hard enough, let
> alone for an Apostle. The Brethren are able to take advantage of the situation
> here at the Y because we are always invited as an educational and cultural in-
> stitution, NOT as a religious one. By accompanying our groups, the brethren
> can act as official representatives for the religious organization behind the school
> which we're from. You'd be surprised how many doors this had opened for us
> in Iron Curtain Bloc countries, where the Church could never have gone oth-
> erwise except for our song-and-dance groups from the Y. We are known
> throughout all of Europe as being THE popular university from America when
> it comes to folk dancing and folk singing. We've capitalized on our popularity
> there and especially in Asia to create an enormous amount of good will for the
> Church and its leaders.[2]

There was some initial opposition, not surprisingly, from that bastion of
conservatism, Ezra Taft Benson. Apostle Benson at first adamantly refused
to send young Mormons out to communist nations, but he was outvoted
and outnumbered in the Council of the Twelve. Later he also became attuned
to the changing "drift" of his fellow apostles.[3]

Mormons Penetrate the Iron Curtain. While many American Protestant denominations during the late 1970s and early 1980s had to be content with
smuggling religious literature and other paraphernalia into communist countries where their adherents had to exist underground, the LDS Church trium-
phantly entered through the front door and at the invitation of Communist
officials. From 1977 to 1981 no less than five touring groups from BYU
performed in Poland. In August 1977, Church President Spencer W. Kimball
himself visited Warsaw and dedicated that land for the preaching of the Restored Gospel, an event downplayed by the local press. In 1979 alone, BYU's
American Folk Dancers troupe performed before hundreds of thousands of
spectators in Romania, Czechoslovakia, Hungary, Poland, and the Soviet
Union. They spent two full days before television cameras in Bucharest and
Moscow on ninety-minute specials for the national networks of both countries.
Romania's special was aired three separate times on the same day (August
23, the Romanian equivalent of America's Fourth of July). Central Soviet
Television aired its documentary on the youthful dancing Mormons across
eleven time zones to an estimated 150 million viewers in the U.S.S.R. (*Church
News* October 6, 1979, 13).

The Mormons took the Eastern Bloc communist countries by storm. Their
success encouraged Church leaders to continue these efforts. In 1981, Gordon

B. Hinckley, Second Counselor to Church President Spencer W. Kimball, accompanied the Young Ambassadors, a BYU music/dance group, to cities such as Bucharest (Romania), Belgrade and Zogreb (Yugoslavia), and Moscow, Kiev, and Leningrad (U.S.S.R.). Again, Central Soviet Television taped them, this time for a full half-hour program. They were interviewed by Young Communist Radio and Radio Moscow as well. In addition, *Soviet Life* magazine (a major English-language propaganda organ) ran a very positive article on their group and on Brigham Young University. Douglas Tobler, a BYU history professor who acted as tour manager, boasted that the students acted in "a John the Baptist function in preparing these nations for the message of the gospel" (*Church News* June 20, 1981, 4). At the same time, Gordon B. Hinckley went on to meet privately with several Soviet government officials—the first time that any Mormon leader had ever met with representatives of the U.S.S.R. in that country. Out of that initial contact came a meeting one year later between LDS Apostle Thomas S. Monson and communist leaders in East Germany (the Soviet Union's closest Communist Bloc ally). The result: in May 1983, the LDS Church was permitted to conduct ground-breaking ceremonies for not only a stake center but also a temple in Freiberg, East Germany.[4] This event marked the first time that an American Protestant group had ever been allowed to build a religious house of worship in a Communist Bloc country.

Mormons Penetrate the Bamboo Curtain. While Mormon public relations victories behind the Iron Curtain and the granting of permission to begin constructing a temple in a communist country are impressive, they may not be as significant in the years ahead as the bridges the Mormon Church is building to the People's Republic of China. It is a complicated story but one that should make envious all other American religious groups with hopes of someday reopening missions in China. What follows is a condensed chronology of events that have transpired between LDS leaders and political representatives of The People's Republic of China during the last decade (1976–1984).

In early September 1976, Dr. Paul Hyer, Professor of Chinese at BYU, was dispatched by Church and BYU officials to the People's Republic of China. Hyer had just finished important diplomatic work for the church and the university in the Soviet Union and the People's Republic of Mongolia. In China he was to represent the LDS Church at the funeral of Chairman Mao Tse-tung. Hyer was given an official welcome and had the opportunity to confer with assorted dignitaries. It is worth noting that Dr. Hyer was the only representative from any American denomination present at Mao's funeral.[5]

On January 1, 1979, the United States and the People's Republic of China officially reestablished diplomatic ties after several decades of hostile relationships. On March 30 of that year, according to a *Church News* article (April 7), Church President Spencer W. Kimball told a group of Regional Representatives at a special closed session in the Church Office Building at Salt Lake City:

> It appears that the time is not too distant when the gospel might be preached to the people of China. Long have we looked forward to the day when the great populous country of China would enter into the family of nations studying the gospel of Christ. We have been conducting Mandarin classes in every meetinghouse in Hong Kong since September 29, 1978. Chinese children should be taught to save and put aside funds to prepare to serve in China. The door to China is starting to open.

About the same time various Church leaders conferred privately with Idaho's Senator Frank Church, chairman of the Senate Foreign Relations Committee, for U.S. government permission to send a group of Mormon students from BYU to the People's Republic of China. Permission was granted. As a result, the Young Ambassadors troupe, accompanied by no less than an Apostle from the Council of the Twelve, James E. Faust, was the first group from a major American university to be allowed to entertain inside China since 1949. The Chinese were impressed by the students' uniform clean-cut appearances, enthusiasm, and statements to the effect that like the Chinese they as Mormons also believed in strong family ties and honoring their ancestors. One Chinese official reportedly commented: "These students must be the finest in American youth" (Housen 1979, 10).

Apostle Faust's status in the LDS Church was downplayed to the Chinese, but he went along for a theologically important reason. He was not there simply to lend dignity or importance to the troupe but rather to fulfill another mission. In 1921, David O. McKay, then an apostle in the Council of the Twelve, and Apostle Hugh J. Cannon had also journeyed to China. Within the walls of the Forbidden City in Peking, in the Pavilion of a Thousand Springs, the two Mormon elders dedicated the entire country of China for the preaching of the Restored Gospel. On instructions from the First Presidency, Apostle Faust in 1979 conducted a special prophetic prayer—in the presence of his hosts and colleagues—on precisely the same spot, using vague religious allusions that confused Chinese interpreters but that were perfectly clear to the Mormons; the McKay mission's dedication of importing Mormonism to China was reaffirmed.[6]

In 1980 the Peking government invited the Young Ambassadors to return. This time they were accompanied by Gordon B. Hinckley, second counselor to the First Presidency. He too visited the identical spot prayed over in the Forbidden City by both the 1921 mission elders and Apostle James E. Faust with a prayer of his own (Hinckley 1980, 4).

By 1981 the BYU International Folk Dancers were received with the pomp and ceremony usually reserved for visiting political dignitaries. On this occasion Apostle Boyd K. Packer went along to do some politicking. The students performed in China's most prestigious theater, The Red Tower Theater. A massive crowd, including hundreds of Communist Party officials, attended (*Church News* June 20, 1981, 4).

By now such good-will overtures were beginning to show prospects of reciprocity. In early 1981 the ambassador of the People's Republic of China to the United States met with Church President Spencer W. Kimball during a two-day visit to Salt Lake City. He also addressed BYU faculty members and students, spoke with members of the Mormon Tabernacle Choir, visited the Granite Mountain genealogical vaults, and conferred with other Church leaders (*Church News* August 23, 1980, 4).

The next year Apostle Neal Maxwell, a former CIA employee, accompanied the Lamanite Generation, a BYU dance-and-music ensemble consisting of Native American LDS converts, to China.

The year 1983 marked more serious efforts by Church leaders to expand relationships with the Chinese government. The practice of having high-ranking Church officials traveling with the musical groups began to reap dividends. Two apostles, Howard H. Hunter and Bruce R. McConkie, went along with the BYU International Folk Dancers and the Young Ambassadors, respectively. They used the opportunity to continue discussions with Chinese leaders. Significantly, that year relations between Peking and Washington had cooled quite a bit as the result of a United States decision to continue selling arms to Taiwan. Several U.S. government-sponsored tour groups involving college-age young adults from across the country were cancelled by the Chinese in retaliation—but not the Mormon tours.

In January 1984, Zhao Ziyang, the first communist Chinese premier to visit American soil since 1949, stopped off in Hawaii on his way to Washington, D.C. to confer with President Ronald Reagan. After touring Pearl Harbor, his next stop was at the Mormon-owned village of Laie, on the island of Oahu. He met with Apostle Marvin J. Ashton and officials from BYU—Hawaii and from the Mormon-owned Polynesian Cultural Center. Ashton raised several proposals for an educational-cultural exchange program coordinated by BYU (and utilizing low-key missionary tactics, though he did not mention these). Ashton had previously instructed everyone present not to discuss any religious topics. By the end of the meeting a number of mutual complements were exchanged. Mormon prospects seemed brighter than ever.[7]

The Mormon mission to China is still just beginning. There is no way yet to know how the Peking government places the LDS Church within America's plurality of religions, or if the Chinese know they are being subtly proselytized as they are being entertained. Meanwhile the Church is earnest about employing such future cultural trips as wedges to open the Chinese door (the

Mormons' metaphor) to LDS missionary work. The Director of the Office of Performance Scheduling at BYU spoke frankly about this crusade in China:

> We've acquired many valuable political allies there. And we've been able to discuss a lot about our religion. The way we work it usually is to lead into a discussion, first of all, about our groups. Then we steer the conversations towards our school here. Finally, we link it up with our chief sponsor, which is the Church. And that leads us into a discussion about Joseph Smith and the first principles of the Restored Gospel. Our young people are given intensive orientation before they ever go. Someone from Salt Lake from the International Mission Office comes down and gives them a good pep talk.[8]

There are some Mormon leaders who hold enormous hopes for a future Mormon–Chinese relationship. And there are various Mormons working to keep a Mormon presence in U.S.–China relations. For example, LDS member Jon M. Huntsman, Jr. was press coordinator for President Ronald Reagan's April 25–30, 1984, visit to China, according to a May 13, 1984, article in the *Deseret News*. That same month, Dr. Russell M. Nelson, the heart surgeon newly appointed to apostleship on the Council of the Twelve, travelled to China for a two-month visit in order to teach Chinese medical authorities complex techniques of heart bypass surgery. As one reporter on Salt Lake City's KUVY Television "Newswatch" program on April 9, 1984, described this trip, "His knowledge of world health conditions as well as his international travels will greatly contribute to his opening the bamboo curtain for future missionary work."

Just as European converts pumped fresh blood into the LDS Church after 1840 during the great immigration to Salt Lake City, so Church leaders have looked both to the Third World and to Chinese Asia in recent years for the souls to produce dramatic growth. Some have referred to China as an awesome "sleeping giant to the truth" and "the next great missionary harvest." Given the Chinese government's recent relaxation of anti-religious policies and even cautious encouragement of some religious bodies (Flinn 1986), prospects for the growth of a Mormon Mission in China, and subsequent evolution and accommodation, are excellent.

Mormonism and the Political Hegemony of Communist Regimes

There are two remarkable qualities about the Mormon Church's efforts to woo communist governments, aside from its early diplomatic victories and the lack of publicity given them outside the Church. First, the Church's still prevalent anti-communist stance that it adopts in public, and the shrill rightist rhetoric of some of its leaders, contrast strikingly with the conciliatory style of its overseas mission ventures in communist countries. Second, and perhaps more impressive, the Mormon–communist connection has been undertaken at the Church's initiative almost totally independent of the U.S. government. This has undoubtedly proven a strength, given the Church's ability to maintain good relations with foreign powers even as tensions between governments rise and fall.

Successful Mormon diplomacy with countries such as the People's Republic of China, where conversions are still basically insignificant in number, and the Church's success in increasing membership in countries such as the German Democratic Republic, where construction of a temple was recently begun with official blessings,[9] can be explained by the fundamental problems of stabilization and legitimacy that continue to plague communist regimes, particularly in Eastern Europe. Pankhurst (1986) observes:

> The periodic political upheavals in Eastern Europe indicate that the region is still not politically stabilized, and the competition between the state/parties and the religious groups plays a central role in this stability. Such instability reflects the inadequate institutionalization of the regimes and, consequently, their inability over time to pursue consistently a long-term development strategy.

Pankhurst regards religious groups under such circumstances as engaged in basically an interest group form of competition. Since the Marxist–Leninist political model (in Pankhurst's words) "requires that the ruling communist party be unchallenged by other parties, movements, or interest groups," those religions that have their roots in the pre-communist culture of a given country pose a challenge. They represent different symbolic systems with alternate sources of legitimacy. Nevertheless, Pankhurst suggested that religions will tend to support the legitimacy claims of communist regimes in the long run not only because they ultimately must accommodate out of self-preservation but also because their adherents share with the communists a sense of nation-building destiny.

But why then should the Mormons (as "outsiders") show every sign of being able to thrive in a communist regime, as they certainly have done recently in the German Democratic Republic, once they have "gotten a foot in the door" and been permitted to exist? One answer is that it is because there is a critical way in which the presence of Mormon adherents contributes to the stabilization/legitimation problems faced by communist regimes. Mormon theology is post-millennial, and the theme of a coming "time of troubles" (i.e., civil strife and societal/governmental breakdown) prior to Christ's return to earth is popular among both LDS leaders and believers (see Heinerman and Shupe 1985, chap. 2). Democratic government, and particularly religious freedom (as in the First Amendment to the U.S. Constitution), are regarded as divine gifts provided for the cultivation of the Restored Gospel, but they are only temporary, if useful, things. Christ's return will usher in a theocracy that will render all other ideologies irrelevant. Thus no government or ideology can command ultimate loyalty, for in the near future they will disappear. The result of this expectation is that Mormonism has become well-nigh synonymous with patriotism, conservatism, civility, and law-abidingness, not just in the United States but also in whatever cultures it happens to locate. Mormonism has the ability to adopt to various political systems and "render unto Caesar what is Caesar's" because it respects its own internal channels of authority and prophecies of doom for the "Gentile" world so well. It flourishes best in liberal democracies, but it can also survive in tyrannies.

For example, in Germany of the 1930s the Latter-day Saints weathered the Nazi *reich* with the same mixed fortunes as most Germans. Some rank-and-file members as well as Church leaders supported Hitler and even promoted Nazi ideology in meeting houses (Dixon 1972; Keele and Tobler 1980).

Alfred C. Rees, president of the East German LDS mission from 1937 to 1939, apparently "tried to win Nazi sympathy by professing admiration for the Party's accomplishment" with an article he wrote for the official Nazi newspaper *Völkiche Beobachter*. In it he compared the strength of the German people after World War I with the Utah pioneers' tenacity. (Rees also praised the German government for its condemnation of the use of tobacco and alcohol by youth.) Rees' article was reprinted and distributed as a tract by Mormon missionaries, a large swastika printed on its front cover. Other Mormons resisted the Nazis and were martyred, some excommunicated beforehand to distance them from more patriotic or fearful Saints. But most Saints coped as best they could, not wishing to confront their government and certainly not flaunting their otherwise strong identity with the Israelites of the Old Testament. The average Mormon was also an average German, with the same national pride and misgivings that grew as the war progressed.

Further support for the pan-national (or ultimately the *non-national*) nature of Mormonism comes from that wartime period. Young American Mormon men caught up in the compulsory draft received information packets from the LDS Church that advised them that, though they might unknowingly or inadvertently find themselves in battle shooting at and killing European Mormons, they were to do their duty to their own government, with no moral penalty. In a letter to Hugh B. Brown, a member of the LDS First Presidency during the Vietnam War, one Mormon sociologist summed up the earlier war's "Message of the First Presidency" issued by a Servicemen's Committee that released American Mormon soldiers from the onus of killing Axis Mormons:

> The implication, which the First Presidency even made explicit, is that a young man has an obligation to do whatever his government orders. If he is drafted into military service, he must go regardless of whether his government

is Fascist, Communist, or Democratic. If his government orders him to kill, even a fellow Latter-day Saint whom it has defined as an enemy, he is under obligation to execute its commands. However, the young man is absolved from any moral responsibility because the government officials, who supposedly are responsible for the war, must bear the judgment of God for each individual's actions who is following their command (White 1967).

Thus, in regimes where religious institutions tend to be stubbornly indissolvable remnants of pre-communist culture and can even serve as rallying points for dissent (Borowski 1986), a religious sect that makes its peace with the status quo and exhorts members' compliance with civil authority is an asset for stabilization and, at least ostensibly, affirms regime legitimacy. (The extent to which the mayor of Freiberg and city council members who attended the groundbreaking ceremony for an LDS temple and stake center in that city were familiar with post-millennial Mormon theology is unknown but most likely limited.)

This guarantee of accommodation is precisely the argument that LDS representatives made to Polish officials on one occasion. Robert Gottlieb and Peter Wiley, in *America's Saints: The Rise of Mormon Power* (1984, 153), recount:

> In an interview with church radio station KBYU, David Kennedy, the church's ambassador at large, spoke of the delicate negotiations that took place with the Polish government prior to the establishment of a church mission in that country. The Mormons, Kennedy promised, would not only stay out of opposition politics, but would provide, at least indirectly, support for the government. "There is nothing that says you have to be a democrat (with a small d) in order to be a Mormon," Kennedy declared. Explaining to the Polish government the significance of the Twelfth Article of Faith, Kennedy told the Polish authorities that Polish Mormons would be taught to be "good citizens," to uphold their government and sustain the country's work ethic.

In fact, Kennedy, as Secretary of the Treasury under Richard Nixon, used his public office to "help maintain and support the Mormon presence" in various countries when he helped one Third World foreign minister obtain a loan in exchange for tolerance of LDS missionaries in the latter's country.

Mormon citizens in communist regimes reinforce, by their conformity, regime norms. Their accommodationist tendencies are much easier to tolerate, from any Marxist government's perspective, than their sometimes more militant fellow religionists. Moreover, in countries accused of violating human rights and religious liberties, the Mormons can be pointed to as evidence that such charges are baseless or exaggerated. They are the exceptions used to dismiss the rule.

In addition to reinforcing regime norms, moreover, the wealth of the LDS Church can also be used as a lever to gain entry into communist societies.

Since the early 1980s Church leaders have contributed movies and services such as drilling wells in Somalia, as well as in Senegal and Zimbawbe through AFRICARE, a private voluntary organization. In 1985 the Church raised $440,000 from special "fasts" (in which members contribute the cost of one skipped meal) for communist Ethiopia, spending $382,000 of it on a dam project near Geddobar. Altogether the Church has pledged $1.1 million to help build the dam. Said the Director of International Development for AF-RICARE:

> By the Church taking such an active interest in what we are doing, it's helped to create a tremendous feeling of goodwill relations between them and various government officials in these different countries. I know that top communist party officials in Addis Abba [Ethiopia] have experienced a considerable change of heart towards outside religions coming in to help them simply by the work the LDS Church has already done there. They seem to like the Mormons a lot.[10]

Mormon Inroads Within Islamic Countries

Islamic nations, like communist ones, often explicitly and legally discourage Christianity by prohibiting its missionizing activities. Yet the LDS Church has shown a history of interest in converting Moslems, and Church observers have repeatedly noticed at least surface resemblences between their own movement and Islam.

Similar strategies have been used in politically and economically unstable countries like Nigeria, where the LDS Church's Thrasher Children's Research Fund sets up village health "demonstration projects" ostensibly to improve hygiene, nutrition, and immunization among villagers, then uses these locales as centers from which spread specially selected missionaries.[11]

Because it cannot negotiate for footholds, as it has in communist societies, the LDS Church has moved cautiously in Islamic countries, working indirectly through its media subsidiary Bonneville International. This Church-owned corporation typically offers local television-radio stations in such countries its low-key Home-Front series of upbeat, pro-family messages as well as others dealing with health and hygiene. The strategy is to generate public sympathy and good will for the Church as a positive social influence before attempting either a formal mission locally or further public relations work. According to a vice-president of Internal Public Relations for Bonneville Media Productions this strategy has brought good results in Chile (which now ranks fourth in the world for the most Mormon stakes, or dioceses), the Dominican Republic, Peru, Brazil, and Mexico. Currently such a "stepwise" approach of initially innocuous media presentations followed by later formal mission establishment is underway in sixty-eight countries, including Saudi Arabia, Libya, Egypt, Jordan, and Israel.[12]

Personalized mission work for the LDS Church in Islamic countries has, on occasion, attempted to jump ahead of media-generated official and public good will. The resistance of Islamic countries, with better established state-encouraged religious institutions than communist regions, has resulted in less hospitable reactions. Former Mormon missionaries have reported the sometimes disastrous results of their efforts. One agricultural expert now retired from Utah State University had been sent to Somalia with eleven other (predominantly LDS) colleagues to establish an agricultural extension there in 1981. The LDS Church requested that they carry with them missionary tracts and other recruitment materials. Successful missionary efforts came to the attention of Somalian officials, who later expelled the agricultural experts.[13]

Saudi Arabia has been an especially intense target of LDS mission work, in part with the assistance of the influential arms-dealing Khashoggi family, that is heavily involved in Utah real estate development (see Heinerman and Shupe 1985, 233–35; Gottlieb and Wiley 1984, 45). In mid-1986 the Church had an estimated 1200–1600 members in that country in sixteen wards and branches in such areas as Riyadh, Jeddah, Al-Khorar, Pahahran, Abqatq, and Ras tanora. In April, 1984 through ARAMCO (the Arabian–American Oil Corporation) Mormon company employees obtained necessary entry documents for Church Apostle Boyd K. Packer and (later) an Elder of the Church's First Quorum of the Seventy (its major policy-making bureaucratic apparatus). These leaders were brought into the country as consultants to ARAMCO for dedications and other religious ceremonies connected with missionizing. The Saudis were unaware of this.

The Mormon mission in the Kingdom of Saudi Arabia had been growing, particularly among other foreign oil employees, but also among Saudis. (Said the Mormon Bishop of Riyahd in an interview: "I had more missionary success in two years there than I had during my entire time in San Francisco.")[14] After a growing casualness in conversion attempts and such telltale signs as baptisms of new members in the Red Sea, the government eventually became aware that Mormons were violating Saudi law. In 1985 Saudi police conducted a series of raids and arrested and detained several dozen Mormon ARAMCO employees and their families, confiscating religious tracts, copies of the *Book of Mormon*, and organizational charts of stake/ward leaders and members. After interrogations and sometimes harsh treatment in prisons, most of these Church members were unceremoniously deported.[15] Relations between the LDS Church and the Saudi regime were later "smoothed out," however, by David Kennedy who flew to Riyadh in early winter 1986 as a representative of the American-Arab Council (of which the LDS Church is highly supportive).

There are other "connections" or "vehicles" to the Middle East for the LDS Church, such as AMIDEAST (the American–Middle East Educational Training Services, Inc.) whose current president is a devout and active Mormon, and who works closely with Brigham Young University officials to promote LDS Church interests with Islamic countries.[16] But the point is best made in summary: as in other fields of endeavor, LDS Church members are expected to use their vocational statuses to further Church mission work, regardless of a particular locale's restrictions.

Conclusion

Mormonism is currently the fastest growing religion in the United States as well as worldwide. Between 1970 and 1980 it doubled its membership. In this article we have pointed to one reason: the group's persistent, tenacious, sometimes pragmatic, missionizing.

There is every reason to believe that in the near-future the LDS Church's missionizing zeal will not soon fade and therefore that we will see additional attempts to establish local outposts, if not full-fledged branches, in communist and Islamic societies ordinarily considered inhospitable to Western Christianity. The combination of low-key Fabian-style diplomacy, a world view that justifies daily accommodation to regimes that are believed (by Mormons) to have no long-term survival or to regimes that have not yet resolved internal problems of stability, and a willingness to circumvent (at risk) laws on proselytizing, makes such a prediction highly probable.

Notes

1. Missionizing and Mormonism (i.e., the faith of members of the Church of Jesus Christ of Latter-day Saints headquartered in Salt Lake City, Utah) are virtually synonymous. Since an initial printing of 5,000 copies of the *Book of Mormon* in 1830, the Church still publishes as many as three million copies a year in languages as diverse as Polish, Norwegian, Samoan, and Korean. Along with the Bible, the *Book of Mormon* is unquestionably one of the most widely distributed books in history. One rough estimate of the number of total copies ever printed hovers at more than twenty-one million (Knight 1980, 6).

   Despite its large families (Utah currently has the highest birthrate of any state in North America), the LDS Church relies heavily on missionary contacts for its phenomenal growth. These contacts come in various forms: from responses to Church advertisements in magazines (such as *Reader's Digest*) and on television (the well-known Home-Front series of appealing family-oriented spots); from visitors' sign-in lists at the Salt Lake City Temple Square historical cities and similar regional facilities; from attendance at LDS Church-sponsored seminars and pageants; and from the relatives and friends of current members (Seggar and Kuntz 1972; Stark and Bainbridge 1980).

   The worldwide Mormon missionary program is well-known. Young men 19–

20 years old (and increasingly young women of the same age) spend two to four months at the Church's Missionary Training Center adjacent to the campus of Brigham Young University in Provo, Utah. Besides intensive foreign language training, prospective missionaries undergo indoctrination in public relations skills, and in strategies for making contacts, gaining entry, and maintaining rapport with contacts.

2. Interview with the Chairperson of the Dance Department, Brigham Young University, Provo, Utah, January 16, 1982.
3. Interview with the Director of the Office of Performance Scheduling, Brigham Young University, Provo, Utah, January 16, 1982.
4. Ibid.
5. Based on interviews with Paul Hyer in Salt Lake City, Utah, 1980; and an interview with Spencer J. Palmer, Department of Languages, University of Utah, Salt Lake City, Utah, January 18, 1984.
6. Palmer. Ibid.
7. This information was obtained from several sources: Doug Curran, Mike Foley, and Reg Schwenke, "Through Open Doors . . ." *Church News* (January 15, 1984, 8–10); Sheri L. Dew, "As Elder Statesman." *This People* (March/April, 1984, 22–9); and an interview with J. Elliot Cameron, President of Brigham Young University, January 16, 1984.
8. See note 3.
9. According to the article "Temple Begun In Freiberg," (*Church News*, May 15, 1983, 5), the groundbreaking ceremony for the temple and stake center was attended by not only various Church leaders from Europe and the United States but also the mayor and representatives of the Freiberg city council.
10. Interview with Joseph Kennedy, Director of International Development for AFRICARE, Washington, D.C., June 17, 1986.
11. Interview with Edwin Q. Cannon, Executive Secretary of the LDS Church International Mission Office, Salt Lake City, December 15, 1983.
12. Interview with Walter Cannells, Vice-President of International Public Relations, Bonneville Media Productions, by telephone, May 20, 1985.
13. Interview with Paul Grimshaw, Salt Lake North Mission, Salt Lake City, Utah, May 15, 1986.
14. Interview with LDS Bishop Wayne Sehlberg, Riyadh, Saudi Arabia, by telephone, May 7, 1986.
15. Interviews with Dean Bagley, former ARAMCO employee, at Star Valley, Wyoming, and with LDS Bishop Wayne Sehlberg, Riyadh, Saudi Arabia, by telephone, both May 7, 1986.
16. Interviews with AMIDEAST staff members, Spring 1986, Washington, DC.

References

Adjoubey, Alexv. 1956. *The Silver Cat, Or Travels in America* (Moscow, USSR). (A portion of the English translation was discovered in the Frank Moss Papers,

Box 245, Folder 22, in Western Americana Section of the Marriott Library in the University of Utah Library, Salt Lake City.)

Blane, Andrew. 1977. "Protestant Sectarians and Modernization in the Soviet Union." In *Religion and Modernization in the Soviet Union*, Dennis J. Dunn, ed. Boulder, CO: Westview Press, 382–407.

Borowski, Karol H. 1986. "Religion and Politics in Modern Poland." In *Prophetic Religions and Politics*, Jeffrey K. Hadden and Anson Shupe, eds. New York: Paragon House, 221–32.

Brough, R. Clayton. 1975. *His Servants Speak*. Bountiful, UT: Horizon Publishers.

Church News. "Touring Groups Touch Hearts." June 20, 1981: 4.

Church News. "Chinese Ambassador Visits Utah." January 17, 1981: 5.

Church News. "Y Dancers Honored." October 6, 1979: 13.

Church News. "Door to China May Be Opening." April 7, 1979: 3.

Dixon, Joseph M. 1972. "Mormons in the Third Reich, 1933–45." *Dialogue: A Journal of Mormon Thought* 7 (Spring).

Fletcher, William C. 1981. *Soviet Believers*. Lawrence, KS: The Regents Press of Kansas.

Flinn, Frank K. 1986. "Prophetic Christianity and the Future of China." In *Prophetic Religions and Politics*, Jeffrey K. Hadden and Anson Shupe, eds. New York: Paragon House, 307–28.

Gottlieb, Robert and Peter Wiley. 1984. *America's Saints: The Rise of Mormon Power*. New York: G.P. Putnam's Sons.

Heinerman, John and Anson Shupe. 1985. *The Mormon Corporate Empire*. Boston: Beacon Press.

Hinckley, Gordon B. 1980. "China Hosts BYU Performing Group." *Church News* (August 23), 4.

Housen, Lynne Hollstein. 1979. "Y Students a Success in China." *Daily Universe* (August 11), 10.

Iler, John R. 1978. "Cleon Skousen Retires, Reviews Many Careers." *Monday Magazine* (April 17).

Keele, Alan F. and Douglass F. Tobler. 1980. "The Fuhrer's New Clothes: Helmuth Hubener and the Mormons in the Third Reich." *Sunstone* 5:27.

Kline, George L. 1968. *Religion and Anti-Religious Thought in Russia*. Chicago: University of Chicago Press.

Knight, Hal. 1980. "Book of Mormon is Woven into the Basic Threads of Restored Gospel." *Church News* (January 5), 6.

Lane, Christel. 1978. *Christian Religion in the Soviet Union*. Winchester: MA: George Allen and Unwin, Ltd.

L.D.S. 1980. *My Kingdom Shall Roll Forth*. Salt Lake City: The Church of Jesus Christ of Latter-day Saints.

McConkie, Bruce R. 1966. *Mormon Doctrine*. Salt Lake City: Bookcraft, Inc.

Pankhurst, Jerry G. 1986. "Comparative Perspective on Religion and Regime in Eastern Europe and the Soviet Union." In *Prophetic Religions and Politics*, Jeffrey K. Hadden and Anson Shupe, eds. New York: Paragon House, 272–306.

Powell, David E. 1975. *Anti-Religious Propaganda in the Soviet Union: A Study of Mass Persuasion*. Cambridge, MA: MIT Press.

Seggar, John and Philip Kentz. 1972. "Conversion: Evolution of a Step-like Process for Problem-Solving." *Review of Religious Research* (Spring), 178–84.

Stark, Rodney and William Sims Bainbridge. 1980. "Networks of Faith: Interpersonal Bonds and Recruitment to Cults and Sects." *American Journal of Sociology* 85: 1386–87.

White, O. Kendall Jr. 1967. Letter to LDS President High B. Brown. Salt Lake City, UT: October 30.

PART II
Varieties of Liberation Theology

5

The Role and Response of the Catholic Church in the Redemocratization of Brazil

Thomas C. Bruneau

DURING THE LAST DECADE of military rule in Brazil the Catholic Church adopted a commitment in terms of a preferential option for the poor. Since at least 1975 the Church has been outspoken in criticizing the military regime that came to power in 1964 and the model of development it promoted. In accord with this criticism the Church created organizations, programs, and movements favoring the interests of the lower classes and formulated alternative perspectives on the future of Brazilian society and politics.

Today the Church has reached a critical juncture in its role in politics and society due to events in Brazil as well as in the Vatican. In Brazil the political transition is in the process of consolidating the civilian regime. The political landscape remains somewhat unclear regarding the political party system and alliances, but the transition seems certain to continue. The Catholic Church, meanwhile, is under the vigorous (though stern) leadership of Pope John Paul II, who is implementing a particular vision of the Church that can be understood only with reference to his background in Poland and his perception of the current state of world Catholicism.

This implementation was clear in the Extraordinary Synod of Bishops held in late November and early December 1985, which assessed twenty years of the Second Vatican Council. Its evaluation of the Council is positive, but the themes, particularly on the Mystery of the Church, clearly reflect the Pope's priorities. The influence of the Vatican in the particular case of the Church in Brazil is more apparent now than at any time since shortly after the separation of Church and state in 1889. It was manifested in the Pope's twelve-day visit to Brazil in 1980 and extensive meetings with Brazilian bishops since. These meetings included those with three archbishops in September 1984, at the time of Frei Leonardo Boff's hearing at the Sacred Congregation for the Doctrine of the Faith; some of Boff's work was condemned and he was ordered to refrain from public activity. Undoubtedly, the most important meeting to date was in early March 1986 when the Pope and key members of the Roman Curia met with the five Brazilian cardinals, the Presidency of the National Conference of Brazilian Bishops (CNBB), and the bishops heading the fourteen regional divisions of the CNBB. During the week-long meeting in Rome most of the key issues dealing with the Theology of Liberation, relations between the Vatican and the Brazilian Church, and the structures of the Brazilian Church were covered.

It is my hypothesis that the political role defined and implemented by the Church during the military regime will change. At the same time the Church will not disappear from the social and political scene in Brazil. This hypothesis is based on a review of a variety of events and processes as well as my understanding of the dynamics of this large, complex, and central institution in Brazil. My purpose in this article is to analyze why this role will change, but first a brief review of this role and my understanding of the dynamics of the Church is necessary.[1]

The Importance of Commitment and Role

Virtually all Brazilian and foreign students of the Church in Brazil agree that the institution has played an important role in society and politics during the past decade. Further, it is a role that contrasts with the past, when the Church intentionally and unintentionally supported the status quo, as has indeed been the case for most of the modern history of the Church in other Latin American countries. In the context of the Brazilian military regime, particularly between 1969 and 1978, civil society was repressed while the regime promoted economic growth and eliminated internal opposition to its policies. Consequently, political parties and intermediary groups were either done away with or tightly constrained and freedom of expression was abolished. During this period, the economy and society changed substantially, but no legitimate and structured means were allowed for the representation of interests for the vast majority of the population (Santos 1985).

In this context the Church became the institutional opponent to the regime and the results of the economic model it promoted. The Church filled a role that was missing due to the divorce between the state and the nation. This was important as the Church possesses considerable institutional weight and can bring to bear impressive resources, many of which have their origins abroad. The Brazilian Church, with 353 bishops, is the second largest hierarchy (after Italy and before the U.S.); it has 13,000 priests and 38,000 nuns, 10,000 "works" and probably 80,000 Basic Christian Communities (CEBs), and the largest Catholic population in the world with some ninety percent of the 130 million person population declaring themselves Catholic. This large institution is extremely well coordinated by the CNBB, and to a lesser extent by the Conference of Brazilian Religious (CRB). The CNBB has in the past decade been unified and its coordination has been in the direction of an active and progressive role in society and politics. This role is in line with the "preferential option of the poor" that was formally adopted by the Latin American Episcopal Conference (CELAM) at the meeting in Medellín in 1968 and reaffirmed in Puebla in 1979. However, while the adoption of this position remained formal and without practical significance in many of the Latin American churches, in Brazil it was implemented to a very large extent.

A fairly substantial literature on the Church in Brazil exists, so it is probably not necessary to review the statements, organizations, and movements here (Bruneau 1985a, Paiva 1985). Briefly stated, the Church has sought to implement a view of society derived from its transcendental image and in stark contrast to the goals and programs of the regime. This has involved: extensive statements and other public documents by the bishops and clergy; the founding and promotion of organizations and movements for the benefit of the lower classes and others prejudiced by the regime and its economic model; promotion of the CEBs; and stimulation of a great variety of programs. In most cases these statements and movements have involved not only a specific sector of the Church but the institution as such throughout its many levels and in most parts of the country. Implementation has indeed varied from diocese to diocese but, during the last decade at least, there has been substantial internal unity on an active and progressive sociopolitical role.

In contrast to other times and places in the history of the Church, in Brazil the institution has been unequivocably supportive during the last decade of participation and democracy. Further, the Church has played a role in the current political transition. There were a variety of means through which the Church participated in and even at times led the movement for a return to liberal democracy. This time it has witnessed increased popular participation. Since at least 1977 the CNBB has issued documents stressing the importance of participation and democracy and denouncing the lack of popular involvement in the affairs of government. In 1985 and 1986 these demands focused on popular participation in the formulation of a new Constitution. In the most complicated period of the transition—1983 and 1984—the bishops

jointly and individually sent letters and telegrams to Congress and other entities emphasizing the importance of direct presidential elections. In September
of 1984 the CNBB sponsored a fast for the return of direct presidential elections or at least a more representative Electoral College. Also in 1984, the
bishops criticized the government's use of power in the documents of the
National Campanha da Fraternidade.

In statements and documents the Church, particularly at the level of the
bishops in the CNBB, came out clearly in favor of democratic participation
and the return of a democratic regime. Through the CEBs the Church also
encouraged and sponsored a form of "empowerment" where groups of people
from lower economic strata are encouraged to become aware, organize, and
make demands. Since this involves up to four million people, this could result
in an important momentum in society. This momentum was given a particular
orientation through the preparation of slides, documents, and pamphlets specifically designed for political education. These materials were prepared at
the national level, in the CNBB, as well as in a number of dioceses, and were
distributed widely throughout the whole country. In terms of a campaign,
then, the Church was very much involved in criticizing the non-democratic
nature of the regime, encouraging participation, and assigning value to democracy that would not remain formal but would also result in social change.

Did this involvement have an impact? In some of my past research on the
Church in Brazil I found through the use of a sample survey that the Church
lacked influence in its general approach to the laity, although through the
CEBs it could generate influence. On balance I would conclude that the
Church has played an important role in the political transition in Brazil. One
source suggests that one of the reasons for the political opening was the
intention by the regime to remove justification for the Church, and a few
other organizations, to act in a political way.[2] In broader terms, the Church's
role was important in delegitimating the military regime; in creating a network
of organizations and informal contacts that provided an umbrella for political
action and encouraged a variety of individuals and groups to become involved;
in the mobilization and political education promoted through the CEBs; and
in the specific statements on participation and democracy. This importance
is better understood by a brief review of a few points of the Brazilian transition
that have made it unique in the current process of political transitions in
Southern Europe and parts of the Third World.

The Political Transition

The Brazilian transition is unique in terms of the length of time involved
and its complexity. Unlike its counterparts in Argentina, Greece, and Portugal
which were caused by defeat, or anticipated defeat, in wars, the Brazilian
transition was initiated in 1974 by a regime that was strong, unified, and
still enjoying high rates of economic growth. This transition bears the most

resemblance to the process in Spain, where the old regime initiated a process whereby a new democratic regime could be established. A substantial literature on the Brazilian transition exists as well as a reasonably high degree of agreement on the motivations of the regime in its initiation and the reactive, if dynamic, role of the opposition in pushing it ahead (Diniz 1985; Figueiredo and Cheibub 1982; Bruneau 1985b).

Most important, however, is the fact that, after almost ten years of a controlled political opening in which the stages and timetable were set largely by the regime, the government ultimately lost control. The critically important process of presidential succession, which had been the main focus of the regime and the main reason for its *casuísmos*, slipped out of control when the candidate of the opposition PMDB—Tancredo Neves—was elected in the electoral college on January 15, 1985, with 480 votes to the government candidate's 180 votes. It was clear that the lack of interest and ability on the part of the incumbent President João Figueiredo was an important factor contributing to the government's loss of control. Equally important, however, was the popular mobilization in favor of direct presidential elections in early 1984 and the increasing perception by large sectors of the population that the regime founded with considerable popular support in 1964 was now illegitimate, because it was not elected democratically and because it was unable to deal with the major social and economic crisis faced since 1981. The mobilization and perception of illegitimacy assisted in the fragmentation of the government party, the PDS, which allowed for the triumph of Neves in the electoral college. Thus the planned political opening escaped the plans and control of the government. While direct elections were not held in selecting the new President, it was clear that he was a popular candidate and represented the hopes and aspirations of the majority of the population. This became particularly clear at his untimely illness and death when the whole country identified with his suffering.

The role of the Church in the transition was to emphasize the lack of legitimacy of a government that was unable to resolve the economic and social crisis, to promote popular mobilization, or to give value to participation and democracy. The Church not only played a key role in the transition but also helped to define the agenda for a new regime, which would have to pay more attention to issues of poverty and to the agrarian situation. Whether the Church was the key actor in the transition is impossible to say, as civil society became so active in 1983 and 1984 and the political parties began to play more central roles in the political process. Aside from the political parties, it does seem clear that the Church played a more direct role in the political transition than any other organization or movement in society.

The Church and Politics in a New Context

Today, in contrast to the situation during most of the twenty-one years of the military regime, relations between the Church and the government, particularly at the national level, are very good. Tancredo Neves met with the leadership of the CNBB in August 1984, and again in late February, after his election. President Sarney visited the CNBB in June of 1985 as the first president to do so since the CNBB was founded in 1952. There have since been visits by government ministers to the CNBB and ongoing communications between the CNBB and the government. Relations are good and there is extensive dialogue.

It must be noted, however (and I will return to this point later), that cordial relations and dialogue do not necessarily result in success in terms of policies. For example, an individual who had the confidence of the Church, Nélson Ribeiro, was selected and then retained in the cabinet shuffle of early 1986 as the Minister of Agrarian Reform, yet the law itself (Plano Nacional de Reforma Agrária) was much less than the Church had anticipated. In the area of popular participation in the selection of a Constituent Assembly, the Church preferred the election of an Assembly different from the Congress on the assumption it would attract a different type of candidate than traditional politicians. The Government's proposal, however, which was subsequently adopted by the Congress in November, 1985, gave the Congress elected in November 1986 the power of a Constituent Assembly. In sum, in two areas of concern to the Church—agrarian reform and popular participation in politics—the policies adopted by the government have not met the expectations of the Church.[3]

In one area the Church's demands have been supported by the government, but this case illustrates the complexities involved in the issue of the Church and politics in the democratic regime. In February 1986, President Sarney banned the Jean-Luc Godard film, *Je Vous Salue, Marie,* which the Church had found offensive. The precise link between the Church's request that it not be shown and the President's decision to veto the film is unclear. The result has been not only its prohibition but also dissent within the Church, even among the hierarchy, over censorship and extensive attacks on the Church by some sectors of the media and intellectuals.[4]

I assume that the liberal democratic regime in Brazil will become consolidated and not collapse to a populism on the left or a military regime on the right. But it will be a consolidation within the traditions of Brazil—meaning capitalist and elitist—and in line with the length of time and peculiarities of the transition itself. Even with the increased mobilization in 1983 and 1984 in Brazil the lower class is still not mobilized and is poorly organized. The mechanisms of control and co-optation continue even with the ongoing formation of parties and pressure groups. It is within this political context of continuity and elitist control that the Church will operate, and it is also likely to remain a context of continuing large scale social inequality and misery.

Because of the anticipated continuity in control and inequality, some in the Church stress that there has in fact been very little change with the transition. For them the only change is that the dictatorship of the generals has been replaced by a dictatorship of businessmen. While there is a certain amount of truth in this assertion, it is far too simplistic. Even the mere presence of the forms of liberal democracy are likely to have a large impact on the political role of the Church. Before analyzing this likely impact it may be useful to make a number of observations on why politics might be relevant for the Church, and vice versa.

Religion and Politics

The Church in Latin America has always played a political role. Since it was established coterminously with the founding of these societies and was integrated with the state through the patronage system, the Church used the resources of the state to establish the faith and was in turn used by the state for legitimacy and for implementing government programs. During the history of modern Brazil the Church played a role at critical political junctures. In some instances it was less important and more reactive than any other institution (1889 and 1946), whereas at other points it was active and probably made an impact (1934 and 1964). This choice of dates is significant for in the former two a republic was either established or reestablished, whereas in the latter two the Church provided, at least initially, support for authoritarian regimes. Most recently, as noted above, the Church, which initially supported the military regime, had by 1976 come into active opposition and was the main institutional opponent of the regime. My analysis of this process of change in the Church sees the Church as a complex international institution that seeks to maintain and increase influence in changing environments. However, I have emphasized that the Church is not just any institution but rather one with a transcendental mission.

This point is very important, for with the current focus on the political role of the Church in Latin America, or religion and politics anywhere for that matter, there is a tendency to analyze the religious institution in terms of secular institutions. Analysts have employed different orientations, with some seeing the Church changing to regain lost ground and others viewing it in Gramscian terms, as a class struggle within the Church and the people ("o povo") taking control. What these interpretations have in common is a model of the Church as a secular institution much like a business organization or political party (Paiva 1985). I have attempted to clarify my approach to analysis by drawing on the concept of charisma in order to complete an institutional analysis of the dynamics of the Church. It should be noted that the Extraordinary Synod of Bishops in late 1985 gave particular stress to a concept that is very close to Pope John Paul II's view of the Church as Mystery. That is, the Church is not only a secular institution, devoid of its mystery, but is infused by the Holy Spirit and has a unique calling in the world (Bruneau 1985a).

The relevance of these observations is important. As a social scientist I am clearly most interested in the Church as an institution and particularly in its political involvement in society. However, even if we have no belief in the charisma or "spirit" of the Church, this aspect must be stressed in order to analyze the dynamics of the institution. For members of the Church, and clearly for the elite composed of clergy and bishops, the charisma or mystery should be foremost. If this is overlooked a number of important dimensions fall short, including the following: the core beliefs of the faith that tend to promote unity even while there are serious disagreements over particular political questions; the stress on continuity of the 2,000-year history of the institution that "relativizes" many current issues; the ability to stress different parts of the overall message depending on the context; and the formal commitment to a pastoral for all classes and societies, precisely that which makes the Church "Catholic."

Clearly these emphases receive different attention depending on the time and the national context, but they nonetheless remain relevant. My particular purpose in calling attention to them here is to suggest that our understanding of the institution will be incomplete, even in its political role, if we do not always remember that the Church is fundamentally a religious institution. For my purposes I am interested in its political role (and I suspect that some in it may hold similar ideas, but as activists), but its dynamic can never be understood apart from its transcendental basis, that is, its Mystery. The relevance of these observations here is to serve as a warning: the dynamics of the Church as an institution are not those of an institution whose basis is secular and national.

In analyzing the likelihood of an ongoing active and progressive role by the Church in Brazilian politics a number of dimensions must be considered. Specifically there are six main dimensions of varying importance and on different levels of abstraction. Indeed, some become relevant only when others are also included. It is clear to me from my research on the beginning of change in the Church in the 1950s as well as a review of the current activities that the role of the CNBB is fundamental. Without it the progressive role would never have been initiated; likewise, if its orientation changes this role will be greatly diminished. Brazil is a modern nation-state and important dynamics work at the national level. The Church's structure is a holdover from the Middle Ages, with bishops and dioceses in a country and the supreme Pontiff in Rome. Without a national organization that promotes other national organizations—the CNBB and appendages—this national dynamic will be lost. Isolated efforts at diocesan levels could continue but the overall momentum would not be maintained. For this reason the CNBB is at the center of my analysis. I should hasten to add, however, that while I think it certain that the scope and activity of the political role of the Church will diminish as the civilian regime becomes consolidated, it will not disappear completely, given the history of the Church in Brazil and the extent of its involvement in society.

Open and Pluralistic Politics

During the twenty-one years of the military regime there were substantial variations in the degree to which the regime allowed open discussion, and the organization and action of political parties and movements. The regime was under the tutelage of the military, which made the key political decisions and imposed them on society. During the period 1969–74 the level of repression was high and torture common; it seemed as though the military, utilizing the doctrine of national security as a justification, sought to impose a totalitarian system in Brazil (Comblin 1977).

It was in this context of repression, torture, and very tight control over civil society that the Church defined and implemented its extensive role in politics. The initial stimulus in doing so was to defend its own members—bishops, clergy, nuns and lay activists—from the government's repression. That it had to defend them indicated that the Church had already begun to adopt a progressive orientation, as was indeed the case through the CNBB from the mid-1950s.

In the context of repression the Church was the only institution in Brazil with enough autonomy, largely because of its charisma and international links, that could successfully oppose the military regime (Bruneau 1974). In defending elements in the Church against repression, the priests and bishops came to a new awareness of the problems and inequalities of Brazilian society and their criticisms became stronger and more pointed. Having adopted a progressive discourse, the Church was then frequently faced with having to support people who were being oppressed by the government or back down, thereby indicating that they were not serious. In the overwhelming number of cases the Church supported these people and in turn suffered increased repression.[5] By the late 1970s the Church, at the level of the CNBB and in probably one-half of the 245 dioceses, acted in line with the progressive discourse, which was then further elaborated in close contact and involvement with this dynamic and repressed society. The Church during the last half of the military regime became the voice of those without a voice and was very active in defending the poor and others hurt in the political and economic processes of a rapidly changing Brazil.

Today the political, if not the social, context is very different. The military regime has ended in disrepute, six main political parties are active at the national level and dozens at the local level, the Communist parties have been legalized, pressure groups are forming apace, and there is no government censorship of the media. While passing through a unique transition in which there is still no direct election for the presidency, for all purposes Brazil is functioning as a democratic regime. Clearly it is an elitist political system with tremendous social and economic inequalities, but it is still a democratic regime with much pluralism. In this context the Church is no longer the voice of those without voice, but rather one among many demanding social change. For instance, in the Plenary for Popular Participation in the Constituent Assembly, the CNBB is one of forty organizations involved; admittedly probably twenty percent of the other organizations were founded in or by the Church, but the point is that they now exist and work on their own.[6]

In this political context what is the justification for continued Church involvement in political issues? While the Church does possess a large and extensive institutional structure in Brazil it is nonetheless limited, considering the size of the country and the population. Further, it is no secret that religious influence is weak in Brazil, with the vast majority of the ninety percent declared Catholic population either not practicing at all or involved in other forms of religion not directly linked to the Church, such as popular religiosity or the various forms of Spiritualism.[7] The Church clearly has its religious work cut out for it. Therefore, how can it justify the commitment of scarce resources for political activities when parties and pressure groups now operate freely? One might respond in one of two ways: that the situation has not changed dramatically in this new dictatorship of businessmen, or that religion and politics cannot be so easily separated in the mission of the Church. It seems clear that these arguments are not convincing for the Church, with its transcendental mission, which adopted its suppletive mission in a particular context. This point is recognized by the CNBB:

> "This transformation [political transition] imposes on the Church a profound reflection concerning its suppletive function that she assumed during a period when the people were without intermediaries for the defense of their rights and interests and found themselves unprepared before the arbitrariness of the State" (CNBB 1984, 21).

The pressure is now reversed: from being called upon to be involved in politics in defense of the people and their interests to reconsider what the contribution of the Church will be as one of several entities involved with the concerns of the people. Whereas in the past the Church was attacked for its progressive political role by government officials, conservatives, and newspapers such as *Jornal do Brasil* and *Estado de São Paulo* and could respond that it had to speak and act as nobody else could or would, this response is no longer possible.

This new pluralism and political activity has another implication that is very important but is difficult to document adequately. My information comes from interviews with people working at the bases, but no sample survey underlies it. During the period of repression, when the Church was the only institution operating in the interests of the poor in most parts of the country, and the only one able to provide an umbrella for the formation of groups and movements, a wide variety of activists became involved in Church-sponsored programs and movements. The question of whether a person was or was not a Catholic was not at issue. Today there are unlimited options for activists in parties, movements, programs, and even the government agencies. These have specific functions that are generally more specialized than those promoted by the Church and are more varied concerning ideologies. There is a perceived tendency, then, for elements in the Church—the pastoral agents—to leave Church activities and enter others. This tends to decrease the momentum of the social and political movements related to the Church and of course gives support to reconsiderations of the hierarchy as to the desirability of the "suppletive function."

Democratic Politics Is Complicated

Not only is there less demand for Church involvement and less pressure from pastoral agents for involvement in political matters, but there is also a very obvious reason for a retraction from the high level of involvement of the recent past. Politics is now extremely complicated. During the military regime there developed an appreciation in the Church that it was by and large without political influence in this "modernizing military regime." On issues of interest to the Church that allowed for evaluation (not to mention those great issues of a better society or a different economy) such as agrarian reform, Indian policy, the imprisonment of priests and religious, and permanent visas for Church personnel from abroad, it was obvious that the Church had little influence in the military regime. But at least it was fairly obvious who was to blame. The military and their civilian technocrats in this dictatorship held all the power and could be blamed for policies, lack of policies, or the lack of implementation. Responsibility was clear, as was appropriate for a military regime with its clear definition of structure and authority.

Today the political situation is very different. There has been a complicated and somewhat confused transition, yet no clean break with the past. The civilian regime remains tentative two years after its initiation; the extent of power held by civilians in comparison to the military apparatus is not obvious; the political party system is in flux; and there is much negotiation over everything as a constitution is yet to be framed and the period of the president's tenure is not even agreed upon.

The question raised, then, is how to deal with this complicated situation? The civilian government has been keen to dialogue with the Church and to involve it in some programs, such as agrarian reform. As one of my contacts in the hierarchy expressed it: "The projects of the Church and the government are similar." Indeed many of them originated from positions defined by the Church in its criticism of the military regime. But what kind of influence can the Church exercise in this pluralistic regime where the tradition is one of low mobilization and much inequality? This is particularly the case as the Church will have to work as an institution—through the CNBB or the more important archdioceses—and not through individuals. Increasingly, priests and nuns are not allowed to operate in the political parties, and there is unlikely to be much support for a Christian Democratic Party. For the institution to operate in this context requires agreement and unity on the goals and on the means. By their very nature political issues in a democratic regime are not clear; some win and some lose but the game goes on. It is simply not clear as in the military regime where issues could easily be painted in black and white terms. There is, then, the question of internal unity in the Church over political issues.

On some issues such as moral questions unity should logically be easier to achieve. However, the case of the Godard film and the divisions within even the hierarchy indicate caution on this matter as well. Even if agreement is possible there may be a more serious problem, which is co-optation of the Church by the government. Most of the important social and economic issues were defined by the Church over the past decade. The government can take these up now and attempt to involve the Church in their resolution. At the minimum, the government can use the moral support of the Church to resist criticism.

But there are bound to be problems and criticism. How to exercise influence but not be co-opted in the process? The Church has gained its autonomy from the state and upper classes during the past decade or so and must be very careful now to avoid losing it. This has been pointed out by one of the more astute advisors of the bishops in warning against "tacit co-optation" and has been reiterated by the President of the CNBB in terms of maintaining a critical and objective attitude.[8] But any political action in this complicated context can be questioned. It is very possible that unity within the Church will be seriously threatened and the only solution is to draw back from political involvement.

The Unity of the CNBB

While implementation of Church policies takes place in the dioceses, parishes, CEBs, and a variety of movements, there is no question that the CNBB has played the fundamental role in defining a progressive position for the Church and implementing it through a myriad of programs. The CNBB allows the Church to avoid the isolation of the dioceses and to respond at the national level to national problems. As it is difficult to conceive of problems that are not of a national scope in centralized and modern Brazil, the ability to respond at this level is important. Just as there is a national capital—Brasília—so there is a national organization of the Church—the CNBB. Without it there would be only the 243 dioceses and the archdiocese of Brasília would be in no legal position (according to Canon law) to speak for the rest of the Church. It might be noted that both the first and now the second archbishop of Brasília are politically conservative; certainly with them there would be no progressive orientation on political issues.

The CNBB operates extremely efficiently with an impressive bureaucratic nucleus and a high degree of participation by the bishops. There are annual General Assemblies, with an attendance of almost 300 bishops, in which all the key issues and documents are discussed and voted. Among the important decision-making bodies between the Assemblies are the Episcopal Pastoral Commission, composed of eight bishops, which meets monthly for several days, and the Permanent Council that is composed of these eight, the three-bishop Presidency, and fourteen bishops heading the regional divisions. These twenty five represent almost ten percent of the Assembly. All of the positions are elected in the General Assemblies and all of the bishops who have not retired are entitled to vote. It is true that the CNBB has been under progressive leadership since 1970 but it is hard to accept the criticism that often emerges in the more conservative press that the CNBB is run by a cabal of leftists.[9] Associated with the CNBB in varying degrees of proximity are twenty one organizations. Among these are the Indian Missionary Council, the Workers' Pastoral Commission, and the Land Pastoral Commission. Through these and ad hoc organizations, the CNBB maintains a high level of involvement in troubled sectors of society.

Even with the mechanisms for participation and elections for all positions, there has always been a vocal minority of bishops who have opposed the CNBB on sociopolitical issues. Of late these issues have centered on the Theology of Liberation and the role of the CEBs. While officially the CNBB is supposed to serve as the communications link with Rome, in fact a number of the bishops in the CNBB have established their own links and have tended to undermine the work of the CNBB.

It should be stressed that the official status of episcopal conferences is unclear within Canon Law and the structure of the Church. According to the Cardinal-Prefect of the Sacred Congregation for the Doctrine of the Faith, Joseph Ratzinger, ". . . the episcopal conferences do not possess a theological basis, do not constitute part of the indispensible structure of the Church . . . ; they have only a practical and concrete function (Ratzinger and Messori 1985, 40)." According to Ratzinger their role is very limited and they cannot act in the name of all the bishops unless all have agreed. Further, "No Episcopal Conference has as such a teaching mission: their documents do not have a specific value, but the value of consensus which is attributed to them by the individual bishops (Ratzinger and Messori 1985, 41)." In the Final Report of the Extraordinary Synod of Bishops the references to episcopal conferences are ambiguous. "There is no one who doubts their pastoral usefulness, indeed even their necessity in modern times. In an episcopal conference the bishops of one nation or of one territory exercise their pastoral role jointly." However, this observation is followed by references to "the inalienable responsibility of individual bishops toward the universal church and their own particular church."[10] Here the universal church is Rome and the particular church is the diocese. Finally, it is recommended that a theological study of the status of the episcopal conferences be made particularly concerning their doctrinal teaching authority.

In sum, the theological basis of conferences such as the CNBB is not agreed upon, and the Cardinal-Prefect of the most important Congregation, a theologian and archbishop appointed to this position by Pope John Paul II, thinks they have no theological basis.

Internal dissent and tensions have increased in the CNBB and a certain polarization appears to be taking place. This was clear at the twenty-third General Assembly of the CNBB held in April 1985. In dealing with the theme of "Christian Liberty and Liberation" they were unable to achieve consensus on a document. Rather, they published a "Letter to Pastoral Agents and Communities" in which they point out the positive and negative aspects of their pastoral work. This was more of an undigested list than anything else, and the fact of disagreement, tensions, and conflicts comes out very clearly.[11]

I believe that with the decrease in external conflict and with the military regime now defunct, internal conflict over sociopolitical issues will increase. With the perception that there is less need for the Church to assume political positions and act on them, and with the inherent complexity of civilian politics, there will be an increase in conflict. Thus either the CNBB will assume very moderate positions, which will tend to allow its co-optation, or it will seek to continue past positions and commitments, which will result in more conflict. Of course another alternative is that the CNBB will pull back from positions and commitments dealing with political issues. I think the last alternative is most likely, considering that the Vatican is obviously concerned with the Church in Brazil.

The Universal Church

While some students of the Catholic Church in Brazil tend to neglect it, the fact is that the Church everywhere is part of the Universal Church, with its center in Rome. A national Church, particularly one as large, important, and well-organized through the CNBB as the Brazilian, can enjoy a good deal of independence. Ultimately, however, Rome can exert control if it wishes.

The relationship between Rome during the papacy of John Paul II and the Brazilian Church is complex. On the one hand, there is a certain polarization due to the silencing of the theologian Leonardo Boff from May 1985 until April 1986, the prohibition of an international program sponsored by the CNBB, and the prohibition of folk masses. The polarization has also been encouraged by the reaction of groups of Brazilian theologians, particularly in the Boff case.[12] On the other hand, there are reports of dialogue, cooperation, and understanding when the Brazilian bishops have made their five-yearly *ad limina* meetings and when the Presidency of the CNBB has met with the Pope.

That the Pope is concerned with the Church in Brazil is obvious, given the size of the Catholic population, the number of bishops, the extent of innovations in theology and structures, and its active sociopolitical involvement. The Pope made a twelve-day visit to Brazil in mid-1980 and has been in close contact ever since. To highlight this concern are the examples of two recent meetings. In July 1985 the Presidency of the CNBB and the members of the Episcopal Council on Doctrine met in Rome with the Pope, the Sacred Congregation for the Doctrine of the Faith, and the Sacred Congregation for Bishops. The topics dealt with included the Boff case, Theology of Liberation, communications between Brazilian bishops and Rome, and the publications of Catholic publishing houses.[13]

During the week of 10–15 March, 1986, the Pope called to Rome the Presidency of the CNBB, the five Brazilian cardinals, and the bishops in charge of the fourteen regions of the CNBB. This was an unprecedented event for the Brazilian Church and almost unprecedented in recent Church history. The topics included the CNBB, the Theology of Liberation, and Church unity. A key theme of the Pope's presentation was the importance of the present moment for the Church in Brazil when democracy has returned but many social and moral problems continue. Further, he emphasized the specific mission of the Church, which is not to replace politicians, union leaders, sociologists, economists, etc.[14] While the two meetings appear to have been amiable, the message was clear: The Church in Brazil is part of the Universal Church and the role of this Church is primarily religious unless conditions are such that the Church is called upon for a suppletive role. These conditions have now passed in Brazil.

In addition to the communications and meetings in Rome there is an even more concrete means whereby the Vatican is seeking a reorientation of the Brazilian Church. In all of the nominations to archbishoprics for the last several years the individuals appointed were not particularly conservative politically but nor were they progressive. Rather, they have been known for their pastoral concerns in more strictly religious terms. These sees include Brasília, Goiânia, Olinda-Recife, and Pôrto Alegre. Moreover, in two of these the previous archbishops were clearly progressive in political terms. Even if, as some in the hierarchy have pointed out to me, these archbishops "evolve" a bit in the new contexts, nevertheless their orientations are predominantly pastoral. If such appointments continue in this vein, then the episcopacy will gradually adopt a coloration different from the present. In line with this orientation are scattered events such as the pastoral visit, in May 1984, by the Sacred Congregation for Catholic Education to the Seminary in São Paulo, increased control over Catholic universities and publishers, and the proposal for a universal catechism. In sum, the tendency from Rome seems to be clearly in the direction of less sociopolitical involvement.

Theology of Liberation

I am not convinced that the Church in Brazil required the Theology of Liberation to develop its active and progressive role in society. It seems to me that institutional dynamics, particularly the conflict with the state, and a reliance on a social doctrine would have been enough for the definition of a new role. Further, whereas there are theologians of this orientation in most countries of Latin America, the institutional Church is active and progressive in only a few. However, this theology has been elaborated, has been widely taught to bishops and others in Brazil, and has been utilized in the justification of the Church's role in society.

It should be noted that there is not one but at least four formulations of this theology.[15] Even with this variety it remains for some the crucial statement on the commitment and role of the Church, whereas for others it embodies all that is wrong with this role. For the latter group it is a lightning rod calling attention to radicalization and the dangers of Marxism. This topic has become all the more heated due to the silencing of Leonardo Boff, which we are told had nothing to do with the theology, and the Ratzinger document of August 1984, "Instruction on Certain Aspects of the 'Theology of Liberation'."[16] We might note now that the final document from the Extraordinary Synod of Bishops gave support to the principle of prophetic denunciation of poverty and oppression.

The main issue in this heated debate is the extent to which the Theology of Liberation draws on Marxism in its analysis of society and politics and whether one can utilize some elements of Marxism without adopting the whole perspective.[17] It is likely this debate will continue for some time, but meanwhile this theology remains predominant in Brazil. Two of the three major Catholic publishing houses (Vozes de Petropolis and Edições Paulinas) are heavily oriented in this direction. Vozes also publishes the *Revista Católica Brasileira* and *SEDOC* and is the Brazilian publishing house for the proposed fifty-two volume Summa of Theology of Liberation that is intended as a synthesis of this theology from the basis of the poor and Christian communities. It should be noted that the influence of this group in Brazil is very strong. They were able to prevent the publication of Ratzinger's book with a major publishing house; its circulation was thus decreased.[18]

From all evidence it seems that the Theology of Liberation is alive and thriving in Brazil. The commitment of those involved is clear and their intelligence and productivity impressive. Some of the best minds in the Brazilian Church are involved, and much of the seminary orientation is within this perspective. There are, however, some indications that the influence of this theology is beginning to wane. My evidence on this controversial point comes from pastoral agents and theologians who consider that the theology has already given all it can and no longer has a resonance in the present context of Brazil, or in other more developed South American countries, for that matter.

This theology was elaborated in a situation not only of poverty, misery, and injustice but also repressive dictatorships in which Marxism, with its analysis of class conflict and the promise of revolution, seemed appealing. Today most of South America is involved in a political transition. While injustice does indeed continue, the dictatorships, at least for the moment, have passed. In this context the discourse of most of the Left has been seriously moderated for fear of a polarization encouraging the return of the military. Communist parties have been legalized, and previously alienated elements have become involved in government. While Marxist analysis may remain predominant in some academic circles its broader appeal is limited in this present context. Insofar as the Theology of Liberation draws on these Marxist categories its appeal also seems likely to diminish. I find it particularly significant that one of the most highly respected philosophers in Brazil, Pe. Henrique Lima Vaz, who had a crucial role in the original formulation of the Theology of Liberation in Brazil, is now a very strong critic of it for its utopianism based on the putative scientific approach of Marxism. If a thinker with the capacity and background of Pe. Vaz is critical of the present formulations of this theology, it would seem that its continued intellectual appeal is likely to be restricted.

The Theology of Liberation achieved great influence and international attention not only because it seemed appropriate for a certain time and context but also because traditional Thomistic theology apparently had little to say to this particular context. Today there are efforts to create a more "authentic" Liberation Theology that may or may not replace this theology. There are also efforts in Rome with the Pontifical Council for Culture and in Brazil to elaborate a Theology of Culture and Faith (Azevedo 1982). The idea behind this effort is to elaborate a theology that will allow the Church to adapt to varying conditions, now so diverse even within Latin America. The theme is inculturation, and it is worth noting that it received attention at the Extraordinary Synod of Bishops.

There are, then, a variety of efforts to formulate theology beyond the present lines of the Theology of Liberation. Undoubtedly its present intellectual hegemony will diminish as will its application with the future publication of a common catechism which will serve as a point of reference for national and regional churches.

Basic Christian Communities

The discussion so far in this article has focused overwhelmingly on the bishops and particularly on the CNBB. In opposing my analysis, which suggests the Church will pull back from an active and progressive sociopolitical role, a critic might suggest that the movement at the bases is such that the Institutional Church will not be able to change course. The support for this argument would have the CEBs as a key component.

These CEBs have received a great deal of attention in Latin America, particularly in Brazil. They have been a priority of the CNBB for many years as well as for dioceses throughout the country. They embody the preferential option for the poor, as their members are most often the rural poor and those on the periphery of the large cities. They hold obvious sociopolitical implications, and we are told they also "reinvent" the Church. They are not only part of the Church but also a new way of being Church.

Brazil probably has in excess of 80,000 of these CEBs, and they are in many ways a defining characteristic of this progressive and innovating Church (Boff 1977). If the expectations of some of the members of the CEBs and most of their proponents are fulfilled there should be sufficient momentum, through the link between the CEBs at the bases of society and the Church of which they are a form of being, to keep the Church heavily involved in all realms of political activity to which the bases are exposed.

There is much written on the CEBs in terms of theology, documents on particular experiences, and anticipated results regarding Church and society. There is, however, little empirical research that would allow us to comment on the momentum and capacity of these CEBs. There are, however, some observations that can be made on the basis of available materials that put in question the viability of their momentum for keeping the institutional Church involved.

In his very useful and thorough study of the CEBs, Marcello Azevedo (1982, 225–53) has shown that they can be included within at least five models of the Church. The significance of this observation is that the CEBs do not require a particular form of Church to be legitimate and play a role. There is, then, no need for them to "reinvent" the Church, as they are compatible with a variety of common views of the nature of the Church. If this is the case, then there should be no particular pressure or momentum leading to a particular model of Church with extensive sociopolitical involvement. Also, this observation relativizes the Theology of Liberation for the CEBs as this is not the only theology that legitimates them in the Church.

Undoubtedly the most sophisticated empirical analysis for the CEBs is the Ph.D. thesis of W. E. Hewitt (1985) dealing with a variety of CEBs in the Archdiocese of São Paulo. Hewitt drew a sample from a number of regions and applied questionnaires containing items on internal and external variables.

His overall finding goes against the anticipated results from a perspective derived from the Theology of Liberation that would emphasize the initiatives and mobilization of the members. Rather, he found that the single most important determinant of the group orientation and structure of the CEBs was the quality of the group's ties to the institutional Church. It was the Church, then, rather than a momentum or involvement at the bases that determined their behavior. At the minimum this raises serious questions as to the ability of the CEBs to reinvent the Church as well as to maintain the momentum of involvement in sociopolitical issues.

It is important to note that the institutional Church has begun to bring the CEBs under closer episcopal supervision. Between 1975 and 1981 there were four national meetings of CEB members, theologians, social scientists, and bishops. These meetings were not held under any particular auspices and provided for some the spectre of the "popular church" of Nicaragua (Kloppenburg 1983). The Permanent Council of the CNBB decided in late 1982 to define more clearly the responsibility for the meetings and to emphasize the ecclesiastical links between the CEBs and the institutional Church. The next meeting of the CEBs was held in Ceará in July 1983 with the participation of thirty bishops and the emphasis was on integration and cooperation between base and elite.[19] Thus, rather than the CEBs reinventing the Church, the episcopacy is monitoring and defining the area of operation of these movements. It is likely that the CEBs will remain important, even a defining characteristic of the Brazilian Church, but based on what research we have and recent events it is unlikely they will have the momentum to provide the orientation for the institutional Church. More likely they will be but one element of the pastoral, one that is appropriate for the lower class in the rural areas and the periphery of the large cities.

Structures for Lay Involvements?

If the above analysis is correct, the institutional Church will tend to pull back from active involvement in sociopolitical issues. The emphasis must be on the institutional as it adopted such an active and progressive role during the last decade. The norm since the Second Vatican Council has been on the Church as the people of God participating in society and politics but in the context of the military dictatorship. Now the emphasis seems to focus on the laity and its involvement so that the institutional Church can redefine its role.[20] This may be difficult, however, for there are few organizations or movements for the laity beyond the CEBs, which are primarily for the lower class. There are some older groups such as the Cursilhos and the Encontros de Casais com Cristo and new groups such as Comunione e Liberazione, but these are still limited in their appeal. Nothing yet exists on the scale of Catholic Action of the 1950s and early 1960s that has had such an impact on the Brazilian Church.[21]

During the past decade a pastoral specifically for the middle class has been neglected in the Church's implementation of the preferential option for the poor. In my interviews I found a general awareness of the need for some new approach to the laity and for new structure, but so far few concrete plans. This is not to say that there have not been sacraments and even schools for the middle class, and in archdioceses such as Rio de Janeiro a focus on the middle class, but in general little has been done to prepare this laity to assume a role that is likely to be vacated by the institutional Church. It seems particularly important now to motivate and prepare the laity for these tasks in line with the past and present orientation of the Church. Otherwise it will be all the more difficult to extricate the institutional Church from extensive involvements since, if it does pull back, much of the involvement of the past decade or so is likely to collapse.

Conclusion

The commitment and involvement of the Catholic Church in political issues during the past decade has been extensive, active, and progressive. Today this momentum continues and for some it is probably difficult to envision their Church in any other perspective. There are however important processes at work in Brazilian politics and in the Universal Church that seem likely to encourage a redefinition of Church commitments and actions. It is likely the shift will be gradual, providing polarization can be minimized, and will be in the direction of a more pastoral approach. My use of the term pastoral will not be acceptable to all but it does in fact seem obvious that issues dealing with state power, coercion, and political parties will be avoided. The Church will continue to operate on some fundamental questions concerning institutional interest and doctrine such as education, the family, and the right to life but more as a pressure group than an institution, and it will limit the issues in order to maintain unity and moral authority.

Notes

1. The materials for this article, consisting of documents and interviews, were collected in November and December 1985 and February and March 1986 with support of the Fulbright Commission in the form of a research grant.
2. José de Souza Martins, A Igreja Face à Política Agrária do Estado, in *Vanilda Paiva*, 1985, 121. Here he refers to General Golbery and a speech in 1979.
3. In the report on President Sarney's visit to the CNBB the *Folha de São Paulo* summarized the views of eleven bishops at the CNBB on the issues of the agrarian reform, Constituent Assembly, and National pact, June 26, 1985. In November the Episcopal Pastoral Commission sent a note to all the bishops, published and

given to President Sarney, in which they criticize the government for its lack of sufficient progress in these three areas. The document can be found in the *Folha de São Paulo* November 2, 1985.

4. According to the *Folha de São Paulo,* February 5, 1986, the President gave in to demands of the Church. *See* this issue of the paper for various criticisms of the government and the Church including dissent by bishop Dom Mauro Morelli.

5. This repression has been documented in Centro Ecumênico de Documentação e Informação, Repressão à Igreja no Brasil: Reflexo de uma Situação de Opressão (1968–1978). Rio de Janeiro: CEDI, 1978.

6. The Plenário Pró-Participação Popular na Constituinte publishes a newsletter on its events and participants. I took these figures from no. 7 of July 1985. For the Church's position on the Constituinte see CNBB, *Igreja e Constituinte: Subsídios para Reflexão e Ação Pastoral* (Brasília: CNBB, 1985).

7. For an analysis of religious influence see Bruneau (1982). That there is wide awareness of this fact is indicated by the CNBB publication, *Bibliographia sobre Religiosidade Popular* (São Paulo: Paulinas, 1981).

8. For the warning on "tacit co-optation" see Pe. Fernando B. de Ávila, O Momento Nacional e a Presença da Igreja, *Síntese,* 34 (1985), 21. The warning on maintaining a critical and objective attitude was given by Dom Ivo Lorscheiter at the 23rd General Assembly of the CNBB in April 1985. See CNBB, *Comunicado Mensal,* no. 388 (April 30, 1985), 299. Co-optation is suggested in the reporting by the *Folha de São Paulo* reporting on the meeting between the Presidency of the CNBB and President Sarney following the critical statement issued by the Episcopal Pastoral Commission on 1 November dealing with the lack of progress in three areas. *Folha de São Paulo,* November 2, 1985.

9. This view is common in the *Jornal do Brasil, Estado de São Paulo,* and *Jornal da Tarde.* The archive of the *Estado de São Paulo* was very useful in allowing me to review the reporting on the Church during the past five years. Through the CNBB's *Comunicado Mensal* I was able to verify the debate and voting on virtually all issues in the General Assemblies.

10. *New York Times,* December 8, 1985.

11. CNBB, *Carta aos agentes de pastoral e às comunidades* (São Paulo: Paulinas, 1985). The disagreement is clear in the popular reporting—*Folha de São Paulo,* April 14, 1985 and in the discussion reproduced in the *Comunicado Mensal* no. 388.

12. Two polemic documents in this regard are Coletive da Libertação, *Fé e Política: O Reino de Deus Sofre Violência* (São Paulo: Icone Editora, 1985) on the Boff case and José Oscar Beozzo, organizer, *O Vaticano II e a Igreja Latino-Americana* (São Paulo: Paulinas, 1985) on Cardinal Ratzinger and the Extraordinary Synod of Bishops.

13. This meeting was reported on in *Comunicado Mensal,* no. 391, July 31, 1985, 836.

14. I have used the reports from the *Folha de São Paulo* for the week of March 10–17, 1985 for my information on the meetings and statements.

15. These four are defined by Cardinal Aloisio Lorscheider in *Comunicado Mensal,* no. 388, April 30, 1985, 379–81.

16. That the Boff case had nothing to do with the Theology of Liberation was one

of the points in the meeting in July 1985 in Rome of the Brazilian bishops with the Sacred Congregation for the Doctrine of the Faith. See *Comunicado Mensal* no. 391, July 31, 1985, 836.

17. It seems worth pointing out that Cardinal Ratzinger in his document on the Theology of Liberation deals only with that variety where a Marxist option has been made. Does this mean there are no others or are there and they are no problem? This is not dealt with in his document. See Ratzinger and V. Messori, 1985: 135.

18. The book was published by Editora Pedagógica e Universitária Ltda., which is a minor publishing house. The media in the week of March 17 suggest the 52 volumes will not be published by Vozes without passing through theologians from the Vatican. See, e.g., *Folha de São Paulo* March 20, 1986.

19. The Permanent Council document was published as CNBB, *Comunidades Eclesiais de Base na Igreja do Brasil* (São Paulo: Paulinas, 1982). A report on the meeting was published by Frei Leonardo Boff, "CEBs: a Igreja inteira na base," *Revista Eclesiástica Brasileira* vol. 43 (September 1983), 459–70.

20. This theme was highlighted by the President of the CNBB, Dom Ivo Lorscheiter, in interviews to the press in December 1984. See for instance *Estado de São Paulo*, December 30, 1984. He also stated this point at the 24 General Assembly of the CNBB in April 1985. *Comunicado Mensal,* no. 388 (30 April 1985), 299.

21. This point was made by one of the more important laywomen, Marina Bandeira, to the bishops. See Ibid, 290.

References

Azevedo, Macello de Carvalho, S. J. 1982. *Inculturation and the Challenges of Modernity.* Rome: Pontifical Gregorian University.

Boff, Leonardo. 1977. *Eclesiogênese: As Comunidades de Base Reinventam a Igreja.* Petroloes: Vozes.

Bruneau, Thomas C. 1985a. "Church and Politics in Brazil: The Genesis of Change." *Journal of Latin American Studies* (November).

Bruneau, Thomas C. 1985b. "Brazil After Tancredo." *Third World Quarterly* 7 (October).

Bruneau, Thomas C. 1982. *The Church in Brazil: The Politics of Religion.* Austin: University of Texas Press.

Bruneau, Thomas C. 1974. *The Political Transformation of the Brazilian Catholic Church.* Cambridge: Cambridge University Press.

CNBB (National Conference of Brazilian Bishops). 1984. *Diretrizes Gerais da Açaõ Pastoral de Igreja no Brasil, 1983–1986.* 7th ed. São Paulo: Paulinas.

Comblin, José. 1977. *A Ideologia da Segurança Nacional: Oder Militar na America Latina.* A. Veiga Fillio, trans. Rio de Janeiro: Civilizaçao Brasileira.

Diniz, Eli. 1985. "A Transição Politica no Brasil: Uma Revaliacao da Dinâmica de Abertura." *Dados* 28: 329–46.

Figueiredo, Marcus Maria and José Antonia Borges Cheibub. 1982. "A Abertura

Politica de 1973 a 1981: Inventário de um Dabate." *Boletim Informativo e Bibliografico de Ciencias Sociais* 14.

Hewitt, W. E. 1985. "The Structure and Orientation of Comunidades Eclesiasis de Base (CEBs) in the Archdiocese of São Paulo." Ph.D. dissertation, Department of Sociology, McMaster University, Hamilton, Ontario, Canada.

Kloppenburg, Dom Bouventura. 1983. *Igreja Popular*. Rio de Janeiro: Editora Agir.

Paiva, Vanilda. 1985. "A Igreja Moderna no Brasil." In *Igrejã e Questão Agrãria*, Vanilda Paiva, ed. São Paulo: Edicoes Loyola, 52–67.

Ratzinger, Joseph and Vittorio Messori. 1985. *A Fé em Crise? O Cardeal Ratzinger se Interroga*. Padre Fernando José Guimaraes, trans. São Paulo: Editora Pedagogica e Universitária.

dos Santos, Wanderley Guilherme. 1985. "A Pós-'Revolucão' Brasileira. In *Brasil, Sociedade Democratica*, Helio Jaguariba et al., eds. Rio de Janeiro: José Olumpio Editora, 223–336.

6

Nicaragua: The Struggle For The Church

Michael Dodson

THE SMALL CENTRAL AMERICAN NATION of Nicaragua has occupied a prominent place on the stage of international politics in recent years. In a replay of events from the 1920s, one sees that it was United States foreign policy that made this so. Specifically, it was the U.S. reaction to the popular uprising, led by the Sandinista National Liberation Front (FSLN), that overthrew the U.S.-backed regime of Anastasio Somoza Debayle in July 1979. At the time of its defeat that government was the longest running dictatorship in the Americas. But its moral decadence and political bankruptcy in the eyes of the Nicaraguan people, not to mention in the views of its neighbors throughout the hemisphere, had seriously eroded the regime's credibility. Therefore, despite severe repression, it was overthrown through an extraordinary effort of mass mobilization among the Nicaraguan people. The popular insurrection brought to power a revolutionary government that was suspicious of U.S. intentions and determined to achieve a measure of independence with respect to U.S. foreign policy.

The Nicaraguan Revolution occurred almost simultaneously with the fall of the Shah in Iran. These two stalwart Third World allies of the United States fell nearly at the same time. In each instance the new government was vocally anti-American. These perceived foreign policy failures of the Carter administration contributed to the rightward shift in American politics leading to a Republican victory in 1980. The Reagan administration came into office already convinced that the Nicaraguan Revolution was Marxist and therefore a threat to the security of the Americas. Resisting the spread of that revolution became a top foreign policy priority, thrusting Nicaragua to the center stage of world events.

Nicaragua has been defined by U.S. leaders as a textbook case of the dangers

110

of Marxist revolution. Attempts have been made to sustain this interpretation by asserting that the Nicaraguan Revolution is antireligious and hostile to the church. The underlying presumption is that Marxist revolutions are necessarily antithetical to religion. Therefore, any political conflict in Nicaragua that concerns the church must be due to government persecution of the church. By circular logic the inferred persecution is then offered as evidence that the Nicaraguan Revolution is Marxist and so a threat to hemispheric security.

This syllogism has a satisfying logical coherence if one accepts all of its assumptions uncritically. It may be solidly grounded in the experience of the church in the Soviet Union and much of Eastern Europe. However, it cannot easily be grounded in the Nicaraguan experience because it ignores a crucial difference between Eastern Europe, for example, and Central America. In the former an orthodox brand of Soviet Marxism was imposed through the dominating presence of the Red Army at the close of the Second World War. Those "revolutionary" governments did not depend on church support to establish their legitimacy with the populace. Throughout Central America, however, the church played a prominent role in delegitimizing repressive regimes. Since the late 1960s, a revolution in thought and pastoral practice of the Central American Catholic Church has been a prominent stimulus to demands for political change.

In Central America religious ferment and reorientation has led to the mobilization of many poor people at the grass-roots. New interpretations of faith, new styles of pastoral work, and new forms of religious community developed since the Second Vatican Council (1962–65) have stimulated once-quiescent Christians to organize and to demand a restructuring of the social order (Cleary 1985). Under the impetus of this change in Catholicism, Christians played a key role not only in support of the Nicaraguan Revolution but also in revolutionary movements elsewhere in Central America. In this way the church has been a significant source of demands for democratization that, in the context of Central America, have had a revolutionary impact. The Nicaraguan Revolution itself was distinguished by the deep involvement of Christians whose commitment to the struggle was motivated by religious faith.[1] This presence has been acknowledged at the highest levels of the revolutionary movement. For example, Comandante Tomás Borge, the only surviving founder of the FSLN, has said of the Nicaraguan church:

> . . . our church has not been a church that is detached from the people. . . . We know of other historical experiences where the church divorced itself completely from the poor. In our country the church is linked to the peasants and the workers . . . even if it be in strictly religious terrain . . . both organized and unorganized Christians participated in all aspects of the revolutionary struggle that brought the Sandinista Front to power. Many, indeed, came to the revolutionary process through Christian organizations (Tamayo 1983).

The revolutionary government has now been in power for nine years. The church is caught up in the revolutionary process and also in the counter-revolution that has been organized against it. The church is also divided within itself over how to respond to the revolution, while much of the political controversy in the country centers on the church. Yet religious activity flourishes, punctuated by a noisy religious dialogue in which the members of a society that takes its religion seriously are talking among themselves in a relatively uninhibited way for the first time in five decades. Religion is not the primary preoccupation of the government, but it is a central concern in the lives of Nicaraguans. Mass is celebrated regularly in hundreds of churches in Managua and throughout the country, with high attendance. Church buildings that were damaged or destroyed during the war have been rebuilt and are scenes of daily activity.[2]

In short, organized religion in Nicaragua is a vibrant part of daily life and represents a potent social and political force within the country. The FSLN is well aware of this and not only has acknowledged the right of religious freedom but has sought to accord the church a significant place in the political order. Some of these measures, which have failed to produce harmony between church and government, will be discussed below. What must be said at the outset is that the church in Nicaragua today vividly reflects the paradox of religious change in a revolutionary setting. Contradictory images of the church abound and divergent views of its present role and future prospects are put forward, even by church people themselves. The church seems to grow ever more sharply divided. Why this is so, how it has come about, and what it portends for the future of the church in a revolutionary society are the themes taken up below.

The Two Churches of the Insurrection

In order to understand the Nicaraguan church today, it is necessary to take account of the different ways that the church reacted to the insurrectionary struggle, while recognizing that it is composed of diverse groups that have different theological assumptions and pastoral orientations. We must also remember that the norm of Latin American history has been for church and state to march across the political stage together. Even if it was a weak partner, the church tended to cleave to established power in order to secure its own interests, both religious and temporal.[3] Consequently, when traditional regimes were challenged by revolutionary movements, the church also came under attack. The anti-church attitudes of the Cuban revolutionaries and the even more intense anticlericalism of the Mexican Revolution illustrates this relationship (Quirk 1973).

The Nicaraguan experience is intriguing because the church itself was changing its understanding of important Christian values. The postconciliar church in Nicaragua, as elsewhere in Latin America, became increasingly critical of the country's inegalitarian society and the political repression required to maintain it. Thus, the church was changing even as the opposition movement was forming. When the insurrection broke out in the fall of 1978, many in the church were prepared to endorse the right of the people to rebel; some were even prepared to join that rebellion as combatants. Rather than a target of the Nicaraguan Revolution, the church was one of its guiding forces, with all levels of the church represented in the popular struggle.[4]

However, this panorama of church involvement should not be mistaken for unity of perspective and commitment to the building of a revolutionary society. From the Archdiocese of Managua to rural Christian Base Communities (CEBs), from bishops to priests to laity, Nicaraguan Catholics were united only in opposition to the final, brutal repressions of the dictatorship. Apart from this vital but temporary bond, important differences marked the religious and political attitudes of the diverse groups that comprise the Nicaraguan Catholic Church. We must sort out these differences, which have been pushed to the surface by the strains of redefining the church's mission in a revolutionary society.

The Nicaraguan bishops issued a pastoral letter in June 1979 that upheld the right of an oppressed people to defend itself against tyranny.[5] Although issued at a time when Somoza's fall already seemed certain, the letter was interpreted by many Nicaraguans as a sign of episcopal solidarity with the revolutionary process. Such public support of popular rebellion was unprecedented in Latin American history. But what did the letter really imply about the bishops' attitude toward the revolution? It was progressive in that the hierarchy declared publicly its defense of human rights in the face of indiscriminate bombing of the civilian population. However, we cannot infer from the letter an episcopal commitment to support the Revolution.

Two weeks after the triumph of the Revolution the bishops issued a statement of reflections to be read in all parishes which warrants comment for two reasons. First, since the hierarchy had kept their distance from the physical struggle, the FSLN, which had mobilized the insurrection, was for them an unclearly defined political force. Second, the tone of the text suggested that at the very outset of the revolution the bishops feared that the new government would be indifferent or even hostile to the church. This point can be illustrated briefly.

The text of July 31 began by proclaiming "a new era in our history has begun," and by acknowledging "the necessity of pressing substantial changes in our sociopolitical structures." But it proceeded immediately to talk of "anxieties and fears" among the people, and of "genuine perplexities" regarding the ideological aspects and organization of the new government. At this time the FSLN had scarcely begun to reorganize the political system. Moreover, the text spoke of *not* putting rights and freedoms into practice and, taking up the theme of reeducating the Nicaraguan people, warned against any tendency "to impose something foreign." Much of the document was preoccupied with the future of religion, referring critically to power systems that try to block God out of the life of a society. It also asserted that "spiritual values and self-determination are not negotiable," and concluded with a quotation from Pope John Paul II which declared that "without Christ, persons do not understand who they are, nor what is their true . . . Destiny."[6]

This tentative, fearful approach contrasted sharply with a joint statement issued at about the same time by the National Confederation of Religious of Nicaragua (CONFER), a Catholic organization, and the Evangelical Ecumenical Pastoral Group, which was Protestant. Their statement expressed "immense joy" at the inauguration of a new era and described this rejoicing attitude as widespread. It said, in part:

> God has truly passed over Nicaragua with his arm of might and freedom. There are many signs of his wonderful presence among our people: the thirst for justice of the poor and oppressed; the presence and great courage of women in the struggle; the examples of unity, hospitality, and comradeship; the responsibility with which the Nicaraguans have assumed the task of reconstruction; the great generosity in victory; . . .
>
> We realize what this great Nicaraguan Revolution means for the church in all the world, especially in Latin America. God is calling us to give the best of our energies and our lives to be a part of this process of reconstruction, illuminating it with our faith in Jesus Christ.[7]

This strongly upbeat perspective on the Revolution and the church's future within it was also echoed by a large gathering of CEBs and church people working at the grassroots level who met in Managua during September 1979, to reflect on the lessons of the insurrection and to discuss ways to project a Christian presence into the revolutionary process.[8]

On November 17, 1979, the Nicaraguan bishops issued an historic and much celebrated Pastoral Letter entitled "Christian Commitment for a New Nicaragua." This letter represented a high point of hierarchical optimism about the Revolution. It also recognized the authentic Christian work of the CEBs and invited active dialogue between them and the hierarchy. Potentially divisive issues were only implicit in this text. On the one hand, the letter explicitly recognized the depth of Christian involvement in the revolutionary process and appeared to accept its justification. It acknowledged the FSLN as the nation's leading political force and granted that dramatic changes in society would be made. The bishops endorsed a socialism that was democratic and produced "justice, solidarity, peace and freedom. . . ." The document even embraced "a dynamic class struggle that produces a just transformation of the social structure. . . ." In doing so it adopted some of the most theologically progressive positions of Vatican II and of the Latin American bishops' meetings at Medellín and Puebla. It saw that the Nicaraguan Revolution "implies the renunciation of old ways of thinking and behaving," that the church must "present the appearance of poverty" and "act as the natural ally of the poor."[9]

On the other hand, this Pastoral Letter also referred to the "concerns and fears" of many Nicaraguans. It mentioned abuse, negligence, and demagoguery; it referred obliquely to "various forces" that "contributed generously to the historic process" and worried that they would be prevented from contributing further.[10] The letter did not specify what these forces were, but one might infer that they were the middle and upper classes to which the church was traditionally close and which it had a continuing obligation to serve pastorally.

What is clear is that this document foreshadowed nascent conflict within the church, specifically between hierarchy and base. It anticipated a schism that became highly conflictual in subsequent years by demanding that the base be in communion with the hierarchy, and by asserting that the church could not be involved in providing political and economic solutions for Nicaragua. In these statements lay seeds of the bishops' disaffection from the FSLN as well as potential for rupture between the hierarchy and those sectors within the church that sought active participation in the Revolution.

Initial Approaches to the Revolution

As Nicaragua looked to the future in late 1979 it faced formidable challenges that complicated still further the inherently difficult tasks of nation-building. The near collapse of the Nicaraguan economy during the war meant that the FSLN had to revitalize the economy quickly, in particular the agricultural sector. But economic revival had to be accommodated to agrarian reform, which was a major goal of the Revolution. The destruction of the hated National Guard meant the necessity to build a new national army. New political and administrative institutions had to be created and a viable foreign policy based on the principle of non-alignment had to be worked out in the face of deepening hostility from the United States and, within less than two years, a growing U.S.-sponsored counterrevolutionary war based in neighboring Honduras (Black 1981, 121–22).

How did the church respond to the tumult these tasks necessitated and work to establish its place in the new society? The church was not left to its own devices to meet this challenge. In January 1980 the leadership of the Latin American Bishops Conference (CELAM) met with the Nicaraguan bishops in San José, Costa Rica, and agreed to offer "fraternal assistance" to the Nicaraguan church. Based on the assumption that the Nicaraguan church lacked the basic resources to carry out a pastoral program, CELAM committed itself to establish courses on Puebla and courses in catechesis, to distribute bibles and CELAM publications, and to assist in developing a pastoral plan.[11] At least some of the bishops welcomed this CELAM overture enthusiastically.

However, while some bishops welcomed the initiative, it was not happily received by Christians at the grassroots level, as indicated in a formal response issued by Managua-based CEBs. They objected to the fact that those closest to the unfolding reality in Nicaragua, Christians such as themselves, had not been consulted about the Church's pastoral needs, or about the best use of resources to meet them. They insisted that some of the resources mentioned were in fact already present in the Nicaraguan church. They also pointed to the Literacy Crusade then being mobilized by the government to combat illiteracy and wondered why leaders of CELAM had taken no account of it. To Christians at the grassroots this sudden concern for Nicaragua on the part of CELAM and their own bishops reflected a "missionary mentality" that was inappropriate in a revolutionary society, where pastoral work should reflect the people's own historical experience (Revelas 1980, 2–3). The CEBs also questioned the motives behind CELAM intervention.

We are less concerned with the validity of those suspicions than with their existence and with what this foretold of future conflict. Early in the Revolution the bishops turned to external sources of support and influence for their church. These sources were at the highest level of the Latin American church and were far removed from the day-to-day experience of the country; they were sources that had no experience with the popular insurrection that had so profoundly shaped the way many Nicaraguans understood their faith. As the hierarchy continued to look to such sources for support rather than to draw on their own resources and indigenous experience, they failed to build a sense of community that could bind all sectors of the church together.

Divergence among groups within the church was propelled from the other direction as well. Immediately after the Triumph, in 1979, Catholic priests and Protestant pastors founded the Antonio Valdivieso Center (CAV) to foster contact between the government and the church and to encourage Christian involvement in the tasks of revolutionary reconstruction. Working in concert with the Central American Historical Institute, based in Managua's Jesuit university, and with a Catholic lay organization known as the Center for Rural Education and Development, the CAV gave Christians, both lay and clerical, a substantial presence in the Revolution. These organizations facilitated a linking of Christians at the grassroots with a pro-revolutionary leadership within the church. It also gave these elements of the church extensive contacts with Christians outside Nicaragua. In the course of time, however, these groups came increasingly into conflict with the hierarchy, so that the relationship that evolved between hierarchy and base was more competitive and conflictual than complementary and unifying (Dodson 1986, 43).

In May 1980, without warning or prior consultation, the hierarchy told the four Nicaraguan priests who occupied key positions in the government to resign their posts. The priests, who brought needed skills to a government that was acutely short on skilled human resources, urged dialogue to seek an acceptable basis for their service to the nation. This issue was to simmer for the next four years with the Archbishop of Managua, Miguel Obando y Bravo, spearheading the effort to remove these priests from their positions in a Sandinista government. Sensing concern within the church hierarchy about the intentions and direction of the Revolution, the FSLN issued a lengthy position paper on the religious question in its party newspaper, *Barricada*, on October 7, 1980.

The "Official Communique Concerning Religion" went out of its way to praise the church for its role in the liberation of Nicaragua. It also committed the government to a guarantee of religious freedom calling it an "inalienable human right."[12] At the same time, the communique promised to assure conditions under which all manner of religious celebrations could be carried out and urged that they be kept free from the taint of politics. This assertion indicated a concern on the part of the FSLN that religious events might be used to attack the Revolution. So, at the end of the first year, diverse positions were forming among lay groups in church and state that reflected a measure of mutual suspicion. While seeking accommodation, the Sandinistas were wary of the church leadership. For their part, the bishops certainly were suspicious of the FSLN. But the bishops were also suspicious of the groups at the grassroots that showed enthusiasm for the Revolution. In due course the hierarchy became estranged from both the government and the church's own grassroots.

The bishops' swift reply to the FSLN communique was combative in attitude and argumentative in style. The overall effect was to impute totalitarian tendencies to the government and to imply a latent hostility toward religion. The reply criticized totalitarians because they orchestrate a false participation that merely manipulates social groups. Against this tendency the bishops declared that Nicaraguans "must demand a *conscious and deliberate participation,* as free men, not as slaves (emphasis in original).[13] The reply went on to talk in general terms of "an ideology" that rejects religious values and undermines religious belief. It implied that the priests serving in the government had been lured into service with "flattery and sinecures," and suggested that the government they served was "extremist."[14] In short, the bishops' reaction to the communique made clear that they distrusted the motives of the FSLN, they expected the church to suffer under a Sandinista government, and therefore they approached the unfolding revolution in a resistant frame of mind. This approach was based on assumptions or generic concerns about the nature of Marxism, revolution, and mass mobilization, rather than on specific actions the government had taken against the church, for at this juncture the FSLN had adopted a solicitous and conciliatory approach toward the church.

Competing Visions of Church and State

By the end of 1980, with the Revolution still less than two years old, the
action of highly motivated groups in the Nicaraguan church had begun to
reveal a potentially deep schism within the institution. At issue were competing
visions of the church's proper role in a revolutionary society. Underpinning
these competing visions were divergent theologies and ecclesiologies. At the
grassroots were clergy and lay Christians who embraced a theology of liberation that rooted pastoral action in the social conditions and political struggles of the poor. For them the church was most closely identified with the
"people of God," the majority in Nicaragua who struggled to achieve their
rightful dignity. On the other hand, key members of the Episcopal Conference
of Nicaraguan Bishops operated with a more traditional theology that sought
to transcend social class identification and placed a much stronger emphasis
on the spiritual role of the church. Moreover, their view of the church stressed
the importance of the hierarchical structure of the institution and demanded
strict obedience to authority. The following discussion will show how these
groups came into increasing conflict with one another, and how this intra-
church conflict spilled over into church–state conflict, at times giving church–
state tensions a level of bitterness that is so often associated with political
disagreements that are reinforced by religious sentiments.

The bishops' reply to the FSLN statement on religion was followed shortly
by a pastoral letter entitled "Jesus Christ and the Unity of His Church in
Nicaragua," which repeated the need to "arm" the faithful against the materialist ideologies being propagated by the new government; it also praised
the CELAM-sponsored programs then being implemented, while chastizing
Christians who were not submitting themselves fully to the authority of the
bishops. The letter accused these disobedient Christians of trying to create
a "parallel magisterium" within the church.[15] In adopting this posture the
bishops succeeded in making church unity, which they defined as unquestioning obedience to church authority, the major issue in church life. This
posture was bound to produce conflict because it meant that Christians at
the grassroots would have to draw back from active participation in the programs of national reconstruction then being advanced by the revolutionary
government. Yet such drawing back meant forsaking their newly developed
theological principles.

Under the leadership of Archbishop Obando, the Episcopal Conference
now aggressively undertook to promote its own pastoral agenda for Nicaragua.
The nation's seminary was reopened and Mexican priests were brought in to
provide instruction. Two religious movements associated with a highly spir-
itualist, otherworldly, and socially conservative form of worship, the "char-
ismatics" and the "cursillos de cristianidad," were revived and actively promoted. A Catholic parents' association also was established and in the

archdiocese of Managua a Diocesan Lay Commission was set up to link each parish to the Curia and to the bishop. The Commission then served as an instrument for implementing diocesan plans at the parish level. Structually, it represented an effort to recentralize control within the institutional church. To parish priests and lay Christians attempting to work in harmony with the revolution, it seemed an effort to pre-empt local initiatives and impose on all parishes the pastoral strategy of the bishops. That strategy encouraged Christians at the grassroots to avoid participation in FSLN programs and projects.[16]

In mid-1981 a CELAM team, consisting of five Latin American bishops, visited Nicaragua as part of a fact-finding mission in Central America. The team interviewed the bishops at length and also met with government leaders. Its subsequent report portrayed the Nicaraguan church as divided in the following terms: "Those faithful to the [revolutionary] process and critics of the church, on one side; and those faithful to the church and critical of the process on the other."[17] The report asserted that the Institutional Church was beginning to be held hostage by small groups within its midst, assisted by the government. At the same time, it claimed, a majority in the church disagreed with this radical minority, preferring that the church situate itself "above" the revolutionary process, exercising a critical role vis-à-vis government programs.

Practical actions taken by the hierarchy in the second half of 1981 and in 1982, particularly in the Archdiocese of Managua, reflected the perspective offered in the CELAM report. In the name of church unity the hierarchy began to move against priests and religious whose pastoral work was deemed divisive. These moves, which often were made without consulting those affected, were sometimes accompanied by conflict that exacerbated division rather than increased unity.

Some examples will illustrate. The parish priest of San Judas, a poor barrio in Managua, was removed in this way, and the Sisters of the Assumption were ordered to move out of the parish house. In August 1981 a bitter controversy raged for weeks over Archbishop Obando's removal of Father Manuel Batalla from the parish of the Sacred Heart in the barrio of Monseñor Lezcano. The Superior of the Dominican Order traveled to Nicaragua to urge dialogue in the matter. Meanwhile, parishioners occupied the parish church, demanding the priest's reinstatement while curia spokesmen insisted on the bishop's right and duty to remove him for the sake of parish unity.[18]

There have been numerous other cases of such interventions to remove priests or religious considered disruptive to diocesan pastoral programs. Often these actions have affected foreign clergy and religious, as in each of the above cases. Similarly affected in 1981 were Jesuit priests Luis Medrano and Otilio Miranda who also worked in poor barrios of Managua. Father Pedro Belzúnegui, who worked in Tipitapa, a poor Managua suburb, was replaced by the Archbishop while he was out of the country.[19] In July 1982, Obando removed from the poor barrio of Santa Rosa Father José Arias Caldera, who had been parish priest there since 1974. Father Arias was known for his frequent protection of young combatants during the popular insurrection and was quite popular in his parish. Upon receiving notice of his removal, parishioners gathered at the church to hold a prayer vigil. While they were assembled, the auxiliary bishop of the archdiocese arrived, announcing that he had come not to initiate a dialogue, which the parishioners had requested, but to revoke the sanctuary. His efforts to do so led to a scuffle in which the bishop was pushed and fell. Father Arias accepted the transfer imposed upon him but the indignant parishioners demanded that the hierarchy take them into account in its decisions. The Archbishop's answer was to excommunicate all those involved in the incident with Monseñor Vivas and place the parish church under interdict so that religious services could not be held there.[20]

The intra-church conflicts described above arose directly from a clash of pastoral strategies. In this sense, they were intramural in nature. At the same time, they carried implicit political connotations because the parishes intervened and the clergy removed were in all instances associated with support for the programs of the Revolution. Concurrent with these events was an ongoing disagreement over the presence of priests in the Sandinista government. From the very beginning, priests occupied important positions, including those of Foreign Minister, Minister of Culture, and Director of the Literacy Campaign. On the grounds that the Revolution needed skills that these highly trained individuals could provide, their government service had been accepted by the hierarchy. However, shortly after the resignation of two prominent non-Sandinistas from the governing junta in May 1980, an unsigned letter bearing the seal of the Episcopal Conference was sent to each priest demanding his immediate resignation from the government. The letter warned that if the priests failed to do so they would be considered "in open rebellion . . . to legitimate ecclesiastical authority. . . ."[21]

There followed a protracted period of public controversy that placed great strain on church unity. At least one bishop publicly disavowed the letter while Christians at the grassroots vigorously urged dialogue rather than ultimata. In late June a national assembly of CEBs with over 600 delegates in attendance appealed directly to the bishops to meet with the priests and seek a compromise arguing that the emergency conditions that made their services necessary still prevailed. In support of this initiative, delegates from a national meeting of Nicaraguan clergy called upon the Papal Nuncio to mediate the dispute.[22] Finally, in mid-July, the hierarchy agreed to meet with the priests and their discussions produced a temporary resolution of the conflict. The bishops agreed that the national emergency had not ended and the priests agreed not to exercise their sacerdotal functions during their tenure in office. Just as importantly, these meetings produced a commission that was set up to facilitate dialogue between the hierarchy and the government.[23] With periodic inter-ruptions, these formal links of communication between the government and the church hierarchy have remained in place ever since. These channels of dialogue have not eliminated tensions and hostility, but they may well have prevented a complete rupture between church and state.

Efforts on the part of the Nicaraguan government to maintain dialogue with church officials who are outspokenly hostile to the FSLN and its policies reflect an unusual determination to preserve the integrity of organized religion in a revolutionary society. The good will of both the church and the gov-ernment was severely tested during Pope John Paul's subsequent visit to Cen-tral America in Spring, 1983.

The Papal Visit and Its Aftermath

The Vatican showed keen interest in the Nicaraguan church following the Triumph of the Revolution. For their part, the Nicaraguan bishops traveled to Rome frequently to seek advice, support, or intervention in local church matters. During the first two years of the Revolution the Vatican acted with restraint, urging dialogue on the issue of priests in government, and refusing to join in the bishops' demand for their resignations. On June 29, 1982, however, the Pope intervened directly with a letter addressed to the Catholic bishops of Nicaragua, in which he urged the church to be a "sign and in-strument of unity in the nation." The path to unity, he asserted, was for all Christians to accept a "union of mind and heart, respect and obedience, . . . sentiment and action with the bishop." He went on to speak of the "absurd and perilous" character of a popular, or people's church. While recognizing that a "church born of the people" was authentically religious, the Pope insisted that it was dangerous and out of keeping with Christ's plan of salvation.[24] Thus, he condemned such a popular church and exhorted all Nicaraguan Catholics to close ranks in strict obedience to their bishops. This was the theme that the Pope emphasized during his visit to Nicaragua on March 4, 1983.

During his historic trip through Central America, the Pope referred to himself as an emissary of peace and also insisted that his visit was strictly pastoral and not political. But the region was already deeply politicized by the prevailing popular struggles and most Central Americans were looking for signs that the Pope sympathized with their partisan views. All understood that what the Pope had to say was of potential political significance. It is fair to say that many Nicaraguans, according to whether they supported or op-posed the course of the Revolution, hoped to receive some sign that the Holy Father approved or rejected the Nicaraguan Revolution.

Elaborate preparations were made for the Papal visit, but the tensions between church and state made cooperation between the government and the hierarchy difficult. Again, both the government and the Episcopal Conference sent delegations to Rome to "brief" the Pope and to prepare the way for his visit. The government wished to establish clear guidelines for the itinerary in order to assure strict security measures. Moreover, with the country then enduring external aggression, the government viewed the Papal mission of peace as especially pertinent to Nicaragua. The bishops, however, sought to minimize any political message the visit might carry. This led to conflict when the bishops tried to insist, as a condition of the Papal visit, that the priests resign from the government, and that the Pope be officially the guest of church leaders rather than of the government (Zinser 1983, 11). As writers throughout Latin America have pointed out, this last condition would have distinguished Nicaragua from all other stops on the Papal itinerary, where he was consistently met by heads of state without accusations of undue partisanship. Had government leaders not been involved, their absence could have allowed opponents of the Revolution to characterize the Sandinistas as indifferent or hostile to the church (Allas 1983, 40–45).

Pope John Paul II spent less than twelve hours on Nicaraguan soil. The most widely reported event that marked his arrival was his apparent rebuff of Ernesto Cardenal, one of the priests occupying a ministerial post. Unnoticed by the press or the Pope, Sandinista leaders and the bishops present embraced and shook hands at the initiative of Comandante Tomás Borge, to the applause of onlookers. The gesture seemed to symbolize the unity that had been the watchword of the Papal visit.[25] Unfortunately, far from healing existing divisions, succeeding events exacerbated them. Here attention will be focused on the Mass celebrated in Managua's 19th of July Plaza that afternoon. The crowd exceeded 500,000, or about twenty percent of the Nicaraguan population, and included more than half of the nation's clergy. Those unable to attend watched the Mass on television. When the Pope arrived, dozens of doves were released into the air to symbolize the country's intense desire for peace while the people waved Sandinista, Nicaraguan, and Papal flags.

Archbishop Obando y Bravo opened the Mass with a welcoming speech that focused on the Pope's controversial letter of June 1982. He went on to share an anecdote that compared John Paul's visit to Nicaragua with the visit of Pope John XXIII to the cell of an Italian prisoner who was eventually freed due to Papal intervention. The anecdote seemed to suggest that Nicaraguans also were imprisoned, awaiting liberation at the hands of the Holy Father.[26] Even if the analogy seemed fitting to the archbishop, it struck a harshly discordant note on this occasion for two reasons. First, it hardly represented the views of many ordinary Nicaraguans in the Pope's audience. Second, it violated the hierarchy's own policy of keeping the visit pastoral and spiritual rather than partisanly political.

The Pope's homily elaborated at great length on the theme of Church unity.[27] The text was highly abstract, and in his manner of delivery the Pope at times seemed distant, at other times emphatic and lecturing. At first his remarks were accompanied by frequent applause from the crowd, but gradually a mood of restlessness developed. Probably few listeners could at first see the point of the address. Eventually, however, they did discern that the Holy Father seemed to be accusing those who supported the Revolution of being unfaithful to the church. He insisted vehemently that church unity required strict obedience to the bishops, and repeated the harsh criticisms of CEBs and other Christian groups supportive of the Revolution that he had made the previous summer. In his speech the Pope used the word "unity" fourteen times; he spoke of peace only once, and that was in response to the growing chants for peace within the crowd that had begun to interrupt the homily about half an hour after the Pope began reading from his prepared text.

What ensued was a spontaneous reaction from the Pope's audience. Impatient for him to speak directly to their specific national situation, groups began to shout, chant, and sing, including, in the end, members of the FSLN leadership who had initially tried to restrain the crowd. The Pope's response to this growing tumult was to repeat the single word "silencio!" Gradually the crowd quieted sufficiently for the Pope to conclude the Mass. He was, however, visibly estranged from his audience—indeed, he had never established rapport with it—and when the Mass was concluded he left the stage hurriedly and without the warm and effusive farewell greetings that usually mark his large, open-air Masses. As he departed, the strains of the FSLN Hymn could be heard in the background.

No aspect of the Pope's Central American trip has been more widely commented on than the stopover in Nicaragua. Much of that commentary, particularly in the United States, was sharply critical of the Sandinistas for allegedly trying to sabotage the visit. It can be argued that this judgment is unfair without necessarily absolving the government of all responsibility. It must be said, however, that the key to the misunderstandings generated by the Papal visit lay within the church itself, and did not come primarily from the government. The institutional church already was divided when the Sandinistas came to power, not for political but for religious reasons. In the general euphoria of the Triumph, the divisions were scarcely noticed.

The Nicaraguan church was a remote outpost of the Roman church prior to the Insurrection. It was woefully understaffed and dependent on foreign clergy. Many of these foreign clergy (but including prominent Nicaraguans as well) were deeply influenced by post-Medellín theology. Their efforts to implement that theology nurtured the grassroots Christian mobilization that played such an important role in the struggle to overthrow Somoza. A unique conjuncture of events brought Christians and secular revolutionaries together in Nicaragua to produce a revolution without precedent in the history of either Latin America or of the Catholic Church.

But this revolution also coincided with a gathering counter-revolution in

Catholicism that involves backing away from the more socially radical implications of liberation theology and a reassertion of hierarchical authority and centralized control. Nicaragua has been a prime testing ground for the clash of these competing tendencies. In 1979, at the onset of the Insurrection, Archbishop Obando could not get a hearing at Puebla, and indeed was not even invited to attend. Since the Triumph, the Nicaraguan church has become a focal point of concern. The essence of that concern was exemplified in the Pope's approach to his Nicaraguan visit. He displayed little interest in the war (he ignored the mothers of victims of the *contras* who stood before him during the Mass), he showed little awareness that many Christians were proud of Nicaragua's revolution and identified themselves with it, and he directly attacked the very religious organizations that had given vitality to their faith in the darkest moments of the preceding decade. In place of these things he offered them only unquestioning obedience to bishops who distrusted the Revolution and sought to distance themselves from it.

While the Pope merely ignored the religious and political issues of concern to many Nicaraguans during his visit, the Nicaraguan hierarchy has addressed those issues vigorously. In August 1983, they stoutly condemned the bill on patriotic military service that was then being debated in the Council of State. As in other controversial cases, this letter was unsigned and was later repudiated by at least two bishops. What fanned the flames of division was the letter's call for young men to resist the draft as a matter of "conscientious objection" (Dodson 1986, 46). This letter was seen both by the FSLN and by many Nicaraguan Christians as a partisan attack on the war effort and therefore on the Revolution.

This view was reinforced when the hierarchy published a pastoral letter during Holy Week in 1984 calling for direct negotiations with the *contras*. This is the most sensitive issue in Nicaragua today and the position adopted in the letter directed criticism only at the FSLN and Christian supporters. Indeed, it described the latter as having "abandoned ecclesiastical unity and surrendered to tenets of a materialistic ideology" (Dodson 1986, 47). Far from promoting reconciliation, this letter exacerbated mutual suspicions between the church hierarchy and the government, and furthered the estrangement between hierarchy and base.

It is consistent with the positions described above that the bishops did not show support for the electoral process carried out in summer and fall of 1984. Archbishop Obando and the president of the Episcopal Conference, Bishop Pablo Vega, strongly supported the abstentionist position taken by the Coordinadora, a group of rightist political parties and interest groups that refused, with considerable U.S. encouragement, to participate in the election. Their views were extensively reported in *La Prensa*, the conservative opposition newspaper. Indeed, during the campaign Archbishop Obando told a group of U.S. businessmen that he and the Archdiocese "had been actively involved in efforts to secure the removal of the FSLN government."[28]

Conclusion

Conflict over religion in revolutionary Nicaragua is not the product of a campaign of persecution against the church, organized by the FSLN and motivated by *a priori* assumptions as to the reactionary nature of religion. U.S. policy makers and even some Nicaraguan church leaders have made this claim repeatedly, but the evidence shows that the Sandinista government has taken a conciliatory approach toward the church. Most of the clashes between the government and the church have involved the Archbishop of Managua, who has increasingly identified himself with the counter-revolution, or with priests under his jurisdiction.

The more important conflicts over religion in Nicaragua are within the church itself. They stem from the deep politicization of the church that has its roots in post-Medellín reforms. In Nicaragua the pastoral experiments stimulated by Medellín led to a revitalization in the life of the church. Christian Base Communities were the focal point of this revival, bringing hitherto neglected campesinos and urban poor into active engagement with the church. Because the spread of this prophetic Christianity coincided with the rise of popular organizations and mass resistance to the Somoza regime, it produced a sizable body of Christians at the grassroots who supported the Revolution. Because CEBs flourished without much supervision from the hierarchy, after the Triumph their very autonomy was a challenge to the bishops. In the course of the Revolution, these two legacies have become mutually reinforcing, exacerbated by the efforts of external actors to politicize the church still further.

The church experience in Nicaragua demonstrates one set of political consequences that can result from the systematic implementation of the "preferential option for the poor." Such implementation can lead to democratizing trends within the church itself. In turn, mobilization and empowerment of the poor within the church can stimulate and reinforce revolutionary political demands in an authoritarian society. The Institutional Church is seriously discomfited by this train of events. On one level, it makes even moderates within the church hierarchy uncomfortable because it releases a political enthusiasm at the grassroots that threatens to pull the church too far into partisan political struggles. In Nicaragua this seems to such church people to mean being either for or against the Revolution, but not neutral. Most bishops, and probably many clergy too, prefer to think of the church as above partisan politics. Hence, their vision of the church as transcending partisan divisions, uniting all classes and factions into the single body of Christ, is directly challenged by this development.

On the more strictly religious level, the Nicaraguan experience threatens the hierarchical principle of the Catholic Church and the centralized control it implies. In Nicaragua the CEB experience did not so much enable the hierarchy to speak for the poor as it enabled the poor to speak for themselves. This led to a demand for dialogue within the church that accorded a strong measure of dignity and respect to the laity at the grassroots. Here I would argue that the Revolution aggravated an intra-church problem, not because of state interference but because of the example set by the revolutionary process. That process modeled and encouraged mass mobilization and popular demand-making. It was easy to construe allegiance to such a revolution as a direct challenge to the bishops' authority over the faithful. The repeated instances of conflict between the hierarchy and the grassroots discussed in this essay demonstrate my point.

The question for Nicaragua, then, and by extrapolation for the rest of Latin America, is whether the competing visions of the church generated by Medellín can be reconciled without a loss of vitality and without driving away those lay Christian activists among the poor who were produced by the pastoral initiatives of the last generation.

Notes

1. "Pope Speaks Out in Nicaragua Despite Heavy Government Control." *The News,* Mexico City (March 5, 1983), 1 and 6.
2. These assertions are based on the author's personal observations during repeated visits to Nicaragua since 1980.
3. Perhaps the most analytically rigorous and informative treatment of this theme is the widely influential study by Ivan Vallier (1967).
4. An excellent source on the history of church involvement in the Nicaraguan Revolution is: *Nicarauac* (Revista del Ministerio de Cultura de Nicaragua), Año 2: 5 (Abril–Junio 1981), 1–196.
5. "Justificó Obando y Bravo el Derecho del Pueblo Nicaragüense a Rebelarse." Editorial de *New York Times,* published in *Excelsior* (March 7, 1983) 34.
6. "Nicaraguan Bishops Speak to Catholics and All Nicaraguans." *LADOC,* United States Catholic Conference, Washington, DC, 10: 2 (November–December 1979), 20–23.
7. Ibid., "Nicaraguan Religious Groups: Message of Joy and Gratitude," 24–26.
8. *Fe cristiana y revolución Sandinista en Nicaragua* (Managua: Instituto Histroico Centoamerican, 1980).
9. "Carta Pastoral del Episcopado Nicaraguense." In *Los Cristianos están con la revolución* (San José: Deparmento Ecuménico de Investigaciones), Cuadernos, No. 2 (1980), 15–31.
10. Ibid.
11. *Nicaragua: La Hora de los desafíós* (Lima: Centro de Estudios y Publicaciones, 1981), 64 and 97–100.
12. "Comunicado Oficial de la Dirección Nacional de F.S.L.N. Sobre la Religion." Barricada (7 de octubre de 1981), 3. This communique has been reproduced often. For instance, it can be found in *Nicarauac,* Año 2: 5 (Abril–Junio 1981), 93–97.
13. *Nicaragua: la hora de los desafíos,* 113–124.

14. Ibid.
15. Ibid., 130–135.
16. Interview with Father Antonio Castro, Managua, June 3, 1983.
17. "Nicaragua." CELAM Report on the Church in Central America, (n.d.), 58–68.
18. See articles in *El Nuevo Diario*, August 19, 20, 24, and 27; *La Prensa*, August 24, 25, 27; *Barricada*, August 20, 26, 1981.
19. "Problems within the Church in Nicaragua," *Envío*, No. 4 (Managua: Instituto Histórico Centroamericano, September 1981), 2.
20. *Amanecer*, No. 12 (Septiembre 1982), 4–5.
21. *Amanecer*, No. 2 (Agosto 1981), 8.
22. "Informe de la Mision," 55.
23. Ibid., 57.
24. *Amanecer*, No. 13 (Octubre 1982), 3–4. See also Hynds (1982:8).
25. "Juan Pablo II en Nicaragua," *Envio*, No. 21 (March 1983), Instituto Histórico Centroamericano, 7–20.
26. The author was not present at the Papal Mass in Managua but has seen a videotape of the Mass and discussed the events with Nicaraguans who did attend.
27. "Juan Pablo II en Nicaragua," 15.
28. "The Electoral Process in Nicaragua: Domestic and International Influences." The Report of the Latin American Studies Association Delegation to Observe the Nicaraguan General Election of November 4, 1984 (Austin: LASA Secrerariat), 1–35.

References

Allas, Tomas Gerardo. 1983. "Conflicto de poderes clérigos—Estado ante la proximidad de la visita papal." *Proceso* 7 (February 28).
Black, George. 1981. *Triumph of the People*. London: Zed Press.
Cleary, Edward L. 1985. *Crisis and Change: The Church in Latin America Today*. Maryknoll, NY: Orbis Books.
Dodson, Michael. 1986. "The Politics of Religion in Revolutionary Nicaragua." *Annals of the American Academy of Political and Social Science* 483 (January).
Hynds, Patricia. 1982. "The Catholic Church in Nicaragua." *Central America Update* IV (November).
Quirk, Robert E. 1973. *The Mexican Revolution and the Catholic Church, 1910–1929*. Bloomington: Indiana University Press.
Revelas, José. 1980. "López Trujillo enviá conquistadores: el clero local, firme en el gobierno." *Proceso* (May 26): 2–3.
Tamaya, Juan O. 1983. "Church Consolidates: Its Position as Sole Non-Sandinista Power." *Miami Herald* (April 12).
Vallier, Ivan. 1967. "Religious Elites: Differentiation and Development in Latin American Catholicism." *Elites in Latin America*, Seymour M. Lipset and Aldo Solari, eds. Cambridge: Oxford University Press.
Zinser, Adolfo Aguilar. 1983. "El acierto del Papa." *Uno Mas Uno* (February 20).

7

Liberation Theology and the Concept of Human Rights

William R. Garrett

LIBERATION THEOLOGY as it has developed in Latin America and other Third World contexts, especially in Africa and Asia, carries with it a bold affirmation of human freedom and a claim to the right of self-determination on the part of exploited classes. While initially this assertion of human liberties might appear to be consonant with the human rights tradition that was launched by the assertion of God-given rights in the American Declaration of Independence and the subsequent Bill of Rights, the French Declaration of the Rights of Man and Citizens, or the United Nations Declaration of Human Rights, liberation theologians actually subscribe to a quite different conception of human rights than that which endorses a notion of universal, inalienable prerogatives reserved for individuals and which governmental functionaries cannot in equity violate. What accounts for the difference between these two affirmations of human liberties is the appropriation of a Marxist theoretical infrastructure by liberation theologians. This infrastructure in their theological confession places the interests of the people above those of the individual and lodges the right to determine what are the "needs of the people" in the hands of an elite group who represent the vanguard of the exploited classes.

To establish this basic thesis, I shall need to demonstrate, first, what are the central features of the classical human rights tradition and, second, the sort of rights theory embraced by Marxist-oriented theologians within the cadres of Latin American and other Third World national groups who have joined forces with the liberationist perspective. At the conclusion of this comparative analysis, I shall propose that a differing set of consequences arise from defining human rights in an individualistic or collective sense.

The Tradition of Inalienable Human Rights

In a previous essay (Garrett 1985), the history and intellectual sources of the tradition of inalienable human rights have been treated extensively. Rather than repeat that analysis here, I shall state in summary form the conclusions of which supporting argumentation and documentation are contained elsewhere. Those findings include the following: the natural law theories appropriated from Stoicism by medieval churchmen were integrated into the teachings of the Roman Catholic Church as a basis for the church's social ethic (Troeltsch 1931)—especially after the papal revolution in the eleventh to thirteenth centuries, when canon law was codified and rationalized (Berman 1983). Embedded in these natural law formulations was a theory of individual rights, familial organization, the nature of the state, economic regulations, and principles for the proper order of slavery. For the most part, individual rights were relatively underdeveloped, for the primary concern—especially among lawyers trained in canon law—was the interrelation between the church as a corporation and the state as a countervailing institutional, corporate structure. The school of secular natural law—which ranged from the thought of Gerson to Grotius, Althusius, and Pufendorf to the social contract theories of Rousseau and Locke—also failed to produce a fully developed construct of individual rights. Hence, the first assertion of a God-given human right to freedom of religion, an assertion that later developed into a whole panoply of human rights, including the rights to freedom of assembly, free press, trial by a jury of one's peers, etc., was propounded by Roger Williams in colonial Massachusetts. Almost at the same time, the Levellers during the English Civil War (Woodhouse [1938] 1974) laid claim to a set of rights remarkably similar to Williams', and later in eighteenth-century America the Baptist lawyer-minister Issac Backus developed a corresponding notion of divinely ordained human liberties that government could not alienate without doing violence to the will of God.

The American revolution provided the occasion when the principles of Lockean political philosophy, as delineated by Jefferson especially, were fused with the notions of inalienable natural rights that had been carried into the political experience of the new nation of the United States by the lower status groups comprised of separatist, evangelical Calvinists of Baptist or Congregational affiliations. The result was to effect a set of constitutional guarantees that declared as self-evident that certain individual prerogatives were beyond the purview of governmental encroachment, namely, the rights to free exercise of religion, freedom of the press and of free speech, the right to assembly, the option of trial by jury, the right to due process of law. All of these rights were, of course, borne out of the experience of dissenter and separatist groups who had not been accorded such liberties in the colonial administrations dominated by the elites of the Standing Order churches.

Once Jefferson and the other Founding Fathers made common cause with the lower status evangelicals in the colonial period, the dye was cast for the subsequent constitutional direction taken by American legal development. The individual rights articulated in the Bill of Rights became part of that taken-for-granted reality that all Americans regarded as the proper state of affairs. In point of fact, however, this taken-for-granted set of prerogatives was quite different from the freedoms that prevailed in England, prerogatives that were only in effect when they had been granted by Parliament and which could, consequently, be withdrawn by Parliament at any time. New World political theorists held out for an inviolate notion of human rights that stood in sharp contrast, therefore, to the sort of liberties claimed by their English cousins across the Atlantic.

The successful prosecution of the American and French Revolutions resulted in the institutionalization of the inalienable human rights theory. Since the 1780s, therefore, these ideas have endured as a seminal contribution to the legal–political tradition of Western civilization. Although the Jellinek (1901) thesis—which asserted that the French Declaration of the Rights of Man and Citizens was patterned after the bills of rights contained in colonial constitutions in America—still appears to be essentially correct, the fact remains that, once the notion of inalienable human rights was introduced into the mainstream of political philosophy in the West under joint Franco-American auspices, these declarations have remained the model for all subsequent human rights covenants, including the United Nations' (1964) Universal Declaration of Human Rights adopted by the General Assembly in 1948.

Several significant sociological features inhere in the sort of human rights theory that devolved from the Franco-American version of divinely ordained liberties. The first is that, precisely because these rights were held to be God-given, it was individuals who enjoyed a connection with deity and not governments. The state was regarded in both America and France as the product of a secular social contract with no warrant from or linkage to the sacred realm. A second ramification was that, because these guarantees of rights were divinely ordained, governments should not seek to infringe upon them. This was clearly an effort to vouchsafe certain prerogatives from political adjudication. And finally, these rights were regarded, precisely because they were divinely ordained for humankind in general, as universally bestowed on all persons, regardless of age, sex, race, religion, or any other cultural trait or distinction. To be sure, this implication has not always been honored in the realm of empirical, sociopolitical life. Blacks were defined as three-fifths a man in the Constitution of the United States for census purposes and only later acquired the benefits of those rights enjoyed by whites. Women, too, have experienced a deferred recognition of their legitimate rights in American social life. The imperfections of the political systems introduced in the United States and other Western nations, however, do not alter the fundamental fact that the universal implications of this human rights position were implicit in its formulation from the beginning. And, indeed, it is precisely this universal feature that has been most problematic for societies which embrace a Marxist-Leninist perspective.

The Marxist Alternative to the Human Rights Perspective

In a previous essay (Garrett 1986), the argument was advanced that from Rousseau to Marx to contemporary liberation theologians there has emerged a political stance that has been described as totalitarian democracy (Talmon 1960). Succinctly put, this point of view is committed to democratic liberties, but it insists that freedom must be attained collectively; that is, everyone must freely will the same thing and act in concert with respect to attaining the common good. By contrast, the liberal approach consists of individual en-franchisement with its trial-and-error method of political endeavor and the absence of systematically legitimated coercion insofar as attaining social harmony is concerned. That argument is extended in this essay to suggest that the totalitarian democratic stance is a consequence, in part, of the rejection of a universal notion of human rights. To establish this claim, we need first to examine the thought of Rousseau, then Marx, and finally, in the following section of this essay, the theological reflections of a selected group of liberation theologians.

In *The Social Contract* of Rousseau, it may be recalled, the author (1954, 19) declared that entry into the original agreement of the social contract—or what Rawls (1971) has called the hypothetical situation—required that persons must experience the total alienation of every one of their rights in order to assure that everyone would enter into the contract on an equal footing and that the burdens of societal existence would be fairly shared by all its members. The demand for the total alienation of all individual rights, however, was counterbalanced by the fact that the collectivity, in effect, became the bearer of rights that could not be alienated, for this would undercut the whole theoretical basis of the Rousseauian model (Althusser 1972). Hence, Rousseau was not opposed to the notion of natural rights as such, but merely to the claim that inalienable rights were the peculiar possession of individuals.

Marx subscribed to a similar point of view, but for somewhat different reasons. In his article, "On The Jewish Question," Marx (1975) launched a scathing criticism of the American and French versions of a universal rights of man. The thrust of his critique was to suggest that both of these versions were essentially bourgeois defenses of property and social position, defenses that do not free man from religion, property, and trade, but free him to participate in religion, property, and trade under an alienated structure of civil society (Ibid., 233). Moreover, Marx (1975, 46, 234) concurred with Rousseau that the preservation of universal natural rights created the basis for the abstract social role of citizens and laid the foundations for political society divorced from authentic community. What both Rousseau and Marx aspired to attain was a civil society populated by *real* man, that is, man who becomes a "species-being" in his or her empirical life and therefore no longer needs political society.

The model that informed the Rousseau-Marxian perspective placed such profound emphasis on the natural, collective nature of community consensus that it plainly left no room for discrete individuals legitimated by any sort of claim to natural rights. Rather, rights enjoyed by individuals were to be those deemed necessary by the collectivity as a whole. Consequently, prerogatives must remain flexible in order to change with the evolving "general will" or the needs of the working class as discerned by the dictatorship of the proletariat that served as their vanguard. All efforts to chisel in stone a system of universal rights would, perforce, frustrate the ongoing transformation of human relations in a dynamic, humane community context. Marx's opposition to the American and French doctrines of inalienable natural rights was not simply a tactical ploy to disparage them as a subterfuge that only barely disguised the vested interests of the bourgeoisie. He also resisted natural rights theory on the more formidable theoretical grounds that such notions were incompatible with the nature of human development that he envisioned as essential for achieving a genuinely free and unalienated society.

The reservations of Marx have been perpetuated in societies committed to a Marxist-Leninist political theory. In a recent comparison of human rights theories in liberal, democratic societies, Marxist social orders, and the traditional culture of India, Max Stackhouse (1984) has demonstrated with great precision the enduring opposition to natural rights theory by contemporary Marxist regimes. The Soviet Union and her satellite countries abstained from approving the United Nations Declaration of Human Rights in 1948. Although approval was given to the Helsinki Accords in 1975 by East Germany, it is not altogether clear how seriously that regime took the items in "basket three" which included an endorsement of such basic liberties as freedom of religion, speech, free press, travel, information, and property. Indeed, it seems quite clear that the early qualms about universal rights have not been overcome in Marxist societies and that the needs of the people still take precedence over the rights held by individuals.

Evidence in support of this view recently became available in a publication of A. Barmenkov (1983) entitled, *Freedom Of Conscience In The USSR*, which identified the official party position on religious liberty and the rights of the Churches. Although the Soviet Constitution explicitly states in Article 52 that citizens enjoy the right to freedom of conscience—as well as the right to unbelief—so long as there is no incitement to hostility on religious grounds, Articles 39 and 59 declare that ". . . the enjoyment of rights and freedoms must not be to the detriment of other citizens' interests" (Barmenkov 1983, 77). The author also draws the familiar distinction between bourgeois guarantees of human liberties and socialist freedoms, wherein the former are dismissed as superficial glosses on upper class interests while the latter represent real liberties without the hypocrisy of liberal, Western democracies.

Indeed, the author (1983, 7) asserts without qualification that "The

U.S.S.R. is the first country to realize in practice the broadest possible freedom of conscience." Nonetheless, Soviet law does prohibit collective prayers and religious processions in public, because the overwhelming majority of people in the U.S.S.R. are atheists. Thus, "(t)he law protects unbelievers from forcible interference by church organizations in their lives" (Ibid., 70). The instrument for effecting this policy is the Council for Religious Affairs. This agency also has the responsibility for registering religious groups, allocating places of worship—since church holdings were forfeited when property was collectivized after the Revolution—and deciding when a religious organization should be terminated or a place of worship closed down (Ibid., 79). Soviet law likewise prohibits religious organizations from operating charities, since the Soviet regime claims that it has long since eliminated poverty, hunger and unemployment. Hence, "(c)harity by individuals and church organizations in these conditions would offend the sense of pride and honour felt by all Soviet citizens" (Ibid., 64). Similarly, religious organizations are prohibited from organizing prayer or other types of meetings for children, teenagers, and women—including Bible schools, literary, needlework, trade schools, or groups to teach religion. Nor are they allowed to arrange sightseeing tours, operate children's playgrounds, or open libraries and reading rooms. In the judgment of the Party, all of these activities have nothing to do with worship and are, therefore, not a proper function for religious groups.

Furthermore, certain religious groups are explicitly identified as fostering anti-socialist sentiments, and therefore should not to be allowed to operate without restriction—such as the Jehovah's Witnesses, Evangelical Baptists, and certain Jewish sects. Citizens must, above all else, recognize their duty to the state and their obligation to further socialist ends. Toward this aim, the government itself has been actively engaged in a propaganda campaign to eradicate religious beliefs from the minds of its citizens. Barmenkov (Ibid., 165) describes the strategy of the state in the following manner:

> It is not a ban on belief in God, nor violence to views and feelings of a religious man but a patient attitude to sincere convictions in matters of faith, making the believer change his mind on the basis of scientific knowledge for his own good, in the name of spiritual emancipation, that is the immutable principle of Soviet state policy toward religion and the major principle of atheist propaganda by scientific means.

It is not my intention in this portrayal of Soviet policy relative to freedom of religion to engage in a reactionary debate with advocates of the Soviet system. Rather, our intention is to demonstrate that this perspective originates from a concern for the collective interest—and is in this regard faithful to Marx—while it simultaneously subordinates the interests of individual believers. What is very much relevant to this discussion, however, is the validity of those charges by Marxist-Leninist regimes that the inalienable right to freedom of conscience upheld by liberal, democratic polities in the West is merely a bourgeois smoke screen for the preservation of religious sentiments that function as a means for further enslaving the working classes. The claim advanced in this analysis is not that Western democracies have always been vigilant in the protection of freedom of conscience, but that this conception of unalienable human rights affords a better protection for individual freedoms than those that place the interests of the collective above those of selves.

Liberation Theology and the Human Rights Tradition

It should be clear from the foregoing discussion that the concept of human rights embraced by liberal, democratic societies in the West differs substantively from the perspective on individual prerogatives endorsed by Marxist-Leninist social orders. What I intend to establish in this section of the essay is that the point of view on the human rights issue common among liberation theologians, primarily in Latin America, is closer to that of the Marxist school than to that doctrine of inalienable rights prominent in the West. I also intend to establish, however, that the reason for the appropriation of the Marxist alternative among Latin American liberationists stems, in large part, from their decision to establish a "solidarity with the poor." Above all else, this decision has severed ties with a point of view that concerns itself with humankind in general. It has resulted in a favored position for a specific class group, namely, the dispossessed of society. While it is not my aim to downplay the miseries, oppression, or insights of the poor, it is my contention that the poor have no greater claim to truth than any other class-based group in society. On this issue, I am in fundamental agreement with Peter Berger (1976) that it is difficult to find any grounds for according to the poor superior wisdom or moral rectitude than that which prevails in other class groups. Indeed, I shall argue below that one does more for the poor by resisting the temptation to relinquish claims to an unalienable and universal system of individual rights.

There can be little doubt any longer—as the editors of *Monthly Review* (1984) have correctly discerned—that liberation theology represents a collaborative effort between religious idea systems and leftist social theory. Theologians and secular Marxists still remain somewhat uneasy about this cooperation, to be sure, and there is considerable truth in Segundo's (1976, 35) claim that those who have produced a theology of liberation in Latin America operate with a "thousand different ways of conceiving and interpreting 'Marxist' thought." My immediate concern is to explore how the appropriation of Marxist categories has influenced the concepts of freedom embedded in liberationist thinking.

Both Gutierrez (1973) and Segundo (1976)—clearly the leading theologians among Latin American liberationists—forthrightly endorse the position that liberation from exploitation is a historical process wherein the content of what it means to be free cannot be expressed prior to or apart from a dynamic engagement in the orthopraxy of struggle against dehumanizing forces. Gutierrez (1973, 32) asserts, for example, that what he means by liberation is not simply a release from poverty or unwholesome living conditions, but a permanent cultural revolution in which the very nature of humankind is constantly being remade. An evolutionary perspective so conceived leaves little room for a concept of human rights with universal validity.

Although Pope John Paul II (1982, 111) has used the language of "the fundamental rights of man" to encourage the acceptance of such individual prerogatives as the ". . . right to life, to security, to work, to a home, to health, to education, to religious expression, both private and public, to participation, and the like," liberation theologians have been reluctant to resistant in according any degree of legitimacy to his pleas. More typical has been the stance of Hugo Assmann (1976, 33–34, 97) that explicitly rejects the models of the French Revolution of 1789 and the Russian Revolution of 1917 as adequate for Latin America. Yet the Marxist presuppositions, rhetoric, and theoretical structure are still affirmed with no corresponding homage paid to the liberal, democratic revolutions of Western culture. The end result is to leave the clear impression that the Marxist program really does inform a great deal of contemporary Latin American theology in a liberatist mode. Comblin (1979, 52–53) reinforces this conviction with his critique of the role of liberalism in Latin America, as does Franz Hinkelammert (1983, 165–193), a German economist and long-time resident of Honduras, who has made common cause with liberation theologians by his virulent critique of "entrepreneurial metaphysics" that he identifies with the works of Locke and others in the natural rights tradition.

The opposition of the church in Latin America to liberalism—by which I mean, in this instance, such liberal precepts as the separation of church and state as well as universal liberties for human beings qua human beings—is not a new phenomenon. As Comblin (1979, 53) quite rightly asserts, "(t)he Catholic Church in Latin America was a political church from the outset, and it has never stopped acting in this role. Its permanent alternatives are: submission of the church to the state and use of the church for the 'realistic' objectives of the state; or the state by the church to achieve its 'mystical' aims." In this regard the Church in Latin America is simply remaining faithful to what was the dominant tradition in Roman Catholicism prior to Vatican II. During his long reign, for example, Pope Leo XIII (1878–1903) set forth what was the official teaching of the church by condemning forthrightly all notions that affirmed an unconditional liberty of conscience and other inherent freedoms to thought, speech, writing, publication, and so forth on the grounds that these liberties were not given to humankind by nature, for such a point of view would absolve the state of serving the Truth and its God (Pope Leo XIII [1888] 1941). To the contrary, the state was urged to forsake such liberal notions and commit itself instead to the propagation of the only true faith as interpreted by the Roman Catholic Church.

Although Vatican II reversed the Church's teaching on these matters, the leaders of the church in Latin America have balked at embracing this portion of the new constitution on the grounds that liberalism constitutes a "trick" devised by first world countries against peoples of the third world. Boff (1979, 145) is typical of those who regard the period from Leo XIII to Vatican II as a period when the church made an uneasy peace with the modern world, a peace that Latin Americans are now wisely sloughing off in favor of a post-modern alternative. Accordingly, the "rights" endorsed by Liberation theologians are those that arise out of the needs and experience of the poor and oppressed classes of society. Solidarity with the exploited classes, Raul Vidales (1979, 54) asserts without qualification, is the only way to avoid "pharisaical universality," that is an abstract affirmation of universal rights that ignores the "structural evils" present in society.

This hermeneutical turn (Assmann 1979, 134) to find the revelation of God in the real-life experience of the poor and exploited classes signifies to Latin American liberationists that the reflection of "grassroots Christians" bears a special authenticity and authority that more abstract and isolated theologies cannot possess. Precisely because it is contextualized in struggles for liberation, the message of the poor carries with it a warrant and legitimacy that is beyond the pale of criticism and objection. With a sort of chiliastic abandon, then, liberation theologians typically assert that the poor will enunciate that freely derived system of rights that will be appropriate to and liberating for all human beings, whether they be oppressed or oppressors.

The thematic of "solidarity with the poor" has recently been fleshed out in several of its more important ramifications by Leonardo and Clodovis Boff (1984, 48) who write:

> The theologian of liberation opts to see social reality from a point of departure in the reality of the poor—opts to analyze processes in the interests of the poor, and to act for liberation in concert with the poor. This is a *political* decision, for it defines the theologian as a social agent, occupying a determined place in a correlation of social forces: a place on the side of the poor and oppressed. At the same time it is an *ethical* option, because it experiences ethical indignation at the scandal of poverty and exploitation. It evinces an interest in the advancement of the poor, which can occur only in the presence of structural change in historico-social reality. Finally, it is an *evangelical* definition: in the gospels the poor are the primary addressees of Jesus' message and constitute the eschatological criterion by which the salvation or erudition of every human being is determined (Matt. 25:35–46).

Clearly, this sort of theological stance runs the risk of romanticizing the religious insights and moral probity of the poor as a particular class group within Latin American social structure. That this sort of danger has become partially realized is evidenced in *The Gospel At Solentiname*, a book compiled by Father Ernesto Cardenal (1984), now the Minister of Culture in Nicaragua, that contains a number of responses by poor farmers and fisherfolk who live on a group of islands in Lake Nicaragua. A variety of Scripture passages were read that produced the following excerpted reflections:

> Felix: "He (Jesus) was coming to liberate the poor. He wasn't coming to liberate the rich. That's why the news had to come to poor people. It was for them most of all. And it's the same now: the new, the word of God always goes to the poor people. Because I believe that the poor people, because of their poverty, always hear the word of God more often than the rich . . ."
>
> *I* (Cardenal) said: "And the rich don't need liberation. What liberation do the rich need!"
>
> William: "The rich need to be liberated from their money."
>
> Felipe: "When the poor get liberated, they'll get liberated too. . . ."
>
> Oscar: "They (the shepherds to whom the birth of Jesus was announced) were like us, poor and in need of a liberator. Because they took care of the animals, but on the other hand they were alone, abandoned by everybody. That's the way we are, humiliated by the rich too. But if somebody comes to tell us that we shouldn't be always serving those rich people like slaves, comes to talk to us about revolution, something like that, then we gradually realize that we too can struggle. . . ."
>
> Felipe: ". . . .The Angel of God could have gone to the King's palace and said to him: 'The Savior has been born.' But the angel didn't go where the king was but where the poor people were, which means that this message is not for the big shots but for the poor little guys, which means the oppressed, which means us. . . ."
>
> And *I* (Cardenal) said: "That's exactly what they said about Jesus. The good news is for the poor, and the only ones who can understand it and comment on it are the poor people, not the great theologians. And it's the poor who are called to announce the news, as Jesus announced it. You would have to make our friend see that Jesus gave thanks to the Father because he had hidden this from the learned and he had revealed it only to the poor and humble. . . ."
>
> Marcelino: "Jesus is present again in the temple announcing the good news, and he does it through the mouth of this poor community. And the scripture that's just been read has been fulfilled right here. . . ."

These spontaneous responses to various passages of Scripture provide exposition that is fresh, perceptive, and immediately relevant to the life situation of the poor folk from whom these sentiments arose. One would have to be callous, indeed, to dismiss these responses as the mindless reactions of peasants to Biblical stories whose meaning is beyond their exegetical capacities. Yet for all the insight that these comments contain, there is a darker, more somber side to their reflections as well. Embedded in their discourse lurk some distressing animosities, including a burning hatred for the rich, a latent anti-intellectualism, and, not least, the ascribing of a messianic role to the poor and oppressed. What plainly does not appear in these comments is a notion of the universal destiny of humankind nor a universal concern for human beings qua human beings. Rather, there is sinuated through this discourse willy-nilly a sort of caste bias against all those who are not perforce a member of the poor and oppressed classes of society.

The outrage that the poor feel with respect to their miserable condition and the venting of this hostility against the rich certainly comes as no surprise. And anyone familiar with the abject poverty of Latin American peasants can surely be sympathetic with their point of view. When this legitimate outrage is translated into a theological program, however, the results are not altogether attractive. Any liberationist cause, whether on behalf of women, blacks, Irish Catholics, or Latin American peasants, runs the risk of elevating its group into a privileged position in relation to humanity as a whole. The unfortunate consequence of such stances is to perpetuate the conditions of inequality, precisely because everyone is not accorded the same rights on the basis of their common humanity. Certain categories of people are necessarily relegated to less than human status in such instances by virtue of their placement in one or another socially defined "out-group." And the overriding tendency is for justice to degenerate into violent retribution wherein the formerly oppressed now become the new oppressors.

No one in a revolutionary situation can give advance assurances, of course, that the struggle will produce a more humane regime than the one currently in place. However, one can subject to close inspection the sort of political structures, legal framework, and normative goals carried by a revolutionary movement in order to develop some provisionary assessments of the likely social consequences to follow from the enactment of a given post-revolutionary order. If adequate safeguards for protecting the interests of minorities or other groups are not in place, then one can reasonably question the propriety of supporting that strategy for ushering in a better world.

A Critical Appraisal of Liberation Theology and the Human Rights Tradition

The foregoing comments provide a backdrop for bringing together several critical observations relative to the tradition of liberation theology in Latin America and its probable consequences for that region, should it successfully achieve its goals. I am not assuming in this evaluation that liberation theologians and their followers possess a full-blown blueprint for the post-revolutionary order. There are sufficient tendencies already evidenced in their writings, however, to draw some cogent deductions about the social patterns likely to ensue from their current conceptions of the Latin American situation and their emerging visions of what the new order in their countries ought to resemble in broad outline, if not in the finer details. Two caveats should be registered at the outset of this enterprise. The first is that I have not assumed *a priori* that all revolutions are inherently evil and should therefore be avoided at all costs. While a number of historians and social theorists (*see* Brinton's classic study, 1965) have compiled a substantial body of evidence that suggests that revolutions typically expend large numbers of lives to effect a circulation of elites, nonetheless, I do agree with Davies (1976, 123) that revolutionary activities may, on occasion, be the only possible recourse for persons committed to greater freedom and justice. The second caveat is that I am not concerned in this instance with engaging in a theological evaluation of liberation theology. Rather, my focus is on the social consequences likely to emerge from the liberationist perspective and its relation to the older tradition of human rights heretofore dominant in Western civilization.

1) The first critical observation pertains to the anti-modern sentiments so deeply entrenched in the liberationist perspective. Two significant factors help account for the distrust of modernity among Latin American liberation theologians. The first is the long colonial experience that delayed the entrance of many societies of Latin America into full participation in modern life until very recently. And the second has to do with the incorporation of neo-colonial dependency theory (Laurentin 1972; Ellison 1983) into the definition of the situation informing most economic and political interpretations of the plight of Latin America. From this perspective, the poverty and exploitation of Latin America peasants stands as a formidable symbol of what modernity encouraged among First World nations. In blaming industrialized nations for the misery prevailing in Latin America, liberationists have also rejected the cultural values and political traditions shaped by modern, bourgeois experience. In the long run, this may well prove to be a serious mistake.

Even so sympathetic a critic of liberation theology as Harvey Cox (1984, 163) cautions against too hasty a jettisoning of the tradition shaped by bourgeois values and theology. While there are aspects of this tradition that are surely subject to criticism and condemnation, Cox urges that the more noble portions of the modern, liberal legacy need to be appropriated and incorporated into whatever economic–political system may be emerging in the post-modern world. It seems altogether clear that what Cox regards as worth salvaging from the modern, liberal ethos is its conceptions of human rights, political freedoms, and individual liberties. These ideals may not always have been achieved in practice, but their noble intent—as well as their partial realization—is certainly worth retaining.

2) The second critical observation with respect to liberation theology follows hard upon the first. This is that, because Latin American Christianity has been predominantly informed by the Roman Catholic communion, it has not been historically open to the human rights tradition that arose pri-

marily out of Protestant sources. Although John Paul II and the post-Vatican II teachings of the church have made common cause with the human rights tradition, the Latin Americans have found it easier to chart their own course independent of a notion of unalienable natural rights. The sort of political-legal freedoms popular among Liberationists has, therefore, carefully avoided association with the more conventional human rights tradition of the West. The church in Latin America is far more comfortable with the sort of thought forms associated with Pope Leo XIII, thought forms that deny the necessity, or even the desirability of the separation of church and state or the need for inviolate guarantees of individual human freedoms. Such a stance is another means of rejecting the modern world and the normative ethos associated with it.

3) A third critical observation relative to liberation theology concerns the strategic decision to identify with the poor and regard the lower classes as the only legitimate source from which religious, political, and legal truth can emerge. The most immediate danger attending this stance is the tendency to regard only one group in society as worthy of human rights. This inevitably creates a social situation in which those who are denied their proper repre-sentation can now claim a special prerogative that redresses their exclusion from access to power and decision making in areas that affect their lives. Any political order today that fails to insure universal rights for all its citizens runs the risk of signing its own death warrant. For the sort of aspirations relative to individual freedoms let loose by modern sentiments are not likely to go away anytime soon. Regimes that claim to be acting only on behalf of the poor and exploited classes may be able to stay in power for a while, but their success will depend quite heavily on how willing their leaders are to use ex-cessive repressive and police measures against those other sectors of society who also claim to have a stake in the ongoing process of societal formation.

With this third observation, then, I come to the heart of this analysis. Essentially, the issue is quite simple and I can couch it in the following terms: are the needs and interests of societal members better served by an inalienable doctrine of human rights or by a concept that regards individual liberties as variable and contingent on the evolving needs of the collectivity as a whole? Because the destiny of so many people in Latin America and elsewhere in the Third World may well hang on the answer to this question, a glib response is wholly inappropriate. Some might suggest from the outset, of course, that the question is merely rhetorical. If one accepts the basic thrust of Barrington Moore's (1967) structural thesis that revolutions that start with the middle classes typically produce democracy, those that originate from above eventuate into fascism, and those that spring out of the lower class result in communism, then talk about which alternative approach to human rights is preferable might appear a superfluous enterprise.

The *Kulturkampf* over human rights principles currently being contested around the globe suggests, however, that some evaluative judgments need to be formulated, even though the matter will certainly not be resolved on the grounds of reason alone. The crucial issue separating the Marxist from the bourgeois-liberal version of human rights, it seems to me, is the commitment to universalism. A human rights platform that excludes particular categories of persons from protection or that reserves the right to withdraw personal freedoms under circumstances deemed expedient by the leadership cadres has structured within it a fatal flaw, a flaw that one can reasonably predict will almost assuredly be abused when a regime finds itself under attack. Legal recognition of universal, inviolate human rights does not guarantee that governments will refrain from taking repressive actions against persons or groups opposing their policies, but such impediments do make it more difficult for political leaders to take arbitrary action against those whom they dislike or distrust. Barrington Moore (1967, 508) has astutely observed, for example, that communist repression, especially in the Soviet Union, has mainly been directed against its own population, while Western liberal societies have typically directed their repression outwards against others in colonial situations or revolutionary movements rather than against their indigenous populations. The general accuracy of this sweeping judgment would appear to suggest that the human rights tradition does proffer a great deal of protection from governmental repression at home, even though it has not been altogether effective in restraining imperialistic practices outside the borders of liberal societies.

Indeed, imperialism in the various forms exhibited by liberal societies constitutes a moral-political scandal precisely because it violates the universal claim that all persons should enjoy a given set of rights by virtue of their very humanity. It is the historical failure of Western societies to respect the human rights of persons outside their borders that has convinced many Latin American intellectuals that the whole human rights tradition is permeated with cant and hypocrisy. One cannot gainsay the fact that the concrete relations between Western liberal societies and the nations of the third world have evidenced hypocrisy, greed, and a callous pursuit of self-interest. Yet, a case can also be made that the creed of universal human rights does provide a basis for a self-critical function that promises greater leverage against all forms of political repression than does its alternative. Self-critical evaluations of particular policies and actions are rendered possible by virtue of the uniform and universal character of the rights claimed by this tradition. This sort of critique becomes problematic when rights themselves are understood as variable and contingent on the existential needs of the people as one finds in the Marxist position on human rights.

The argument developed above is unlikely to change the minds of many deeply committed liberationists. The best that can be hoped for is that certain of the issues pertaining to the human rights controversy have been illuminated.

Although the notion of inalienable human rights is derived from a historically specific religious group couched within a particular configuration of social circumstances, this tradition has, from the outset, pressed toward the universal realization of human liberties. It has experienced considerable success, perhaps most notably in the adoption of the Universal Declaration of Human Rights by the United Nations. Today, the future of this tradition remains very much in doubt. The appropriation of a Marxist approach to human rights by liberation theologians in Latin America and elsewhere may well signal a growing reluctance to embrace the principles of an inalienable, universal scheme of rights among Third World peoples generally. If this should prove to be the case, and if Christian liberationists are in part responsible for this turn of events, then we may be witnessing the development of a profound irony. For it was the Christian tradition that gave rise to the concept of God-given human rights, and it may also be a part of that tradition that is now contributing to its demise.

References

Althusser, Louis. 1972. *Montequieu, Rosseau, Marx*. London: NLB.

Assmann, Hugo. 1976. *Theology for A Nomad Church*. Maryknoll, NY: Orbis Books.

Barmenkov, A. 1983. *Freedom of Conscience in the USSR*. Moscow: Progress Publishers.

Berger, Peter L. 1976. *Pyramids of Sacrifice*. Garden City, NY: Doubleday.

Berman, Harold J. 1983. *Law and Revolution*. Cambridge, MA: Harvard University Press.

Boff, Leonardo. 1979. *Liberating Grace*. Maryknoll, NY: Orbis Books.

Boff, Leonardo and Clodovis. 1984. *Salvation and Liberation*. Maryknoll, NY: Orbis Books.

Brinton, Crane. 1965. *The Anatomy of Revolution*. Rev. and expanded edition. New York: Random House.

Cardenal, Ernesto. 1984. "The Gospel At Solentiname," *Monthly Review* (July/August), 107–20.

Camblin, Jose. 1979. *The Church and the National Security State*. Maryknoll, NY: Orbis Books.

Cox, Harvey. 1984. *Religion in the Secular City*. New York: Simon and Schuster.

Davies, J. G. 1976. *Christians, Politics and Violent Revolution*. Maryknoll, NY: Orbis Books.

Monthly Review Editors. 1984. "Religion and the Left," *Monthly Review* 36: 3 (July/August).

Ellison, Marvin Mahan. 1983. *The Center Cannot Hold*. Washington, DC: University Press of America.

Garrett, William R. 1986. "Religion and the Legitimation of Violence." In *Prophetic Religion and Politics*, Jeffrey K. Hadden and Anson Shupe, eds. New York: Paragon House, 103–22.

Garrett, William R. 1985. "Religion, Law, and the Human Condition." Presidential Address presented at the Annual Meeting of the Association for the Sociology of Religion, August 24, 1985, Washington, DC.

Gutierrez, Gustavo. 1973. *A Liberation of Theology*. Maryknoll, NY: Orbis Books.

Hinkelammert, Franz. 1983. "The Economic Roots of Idolatry: Entrepreneurial Metaphysics." In *The Idols of Death and the God of Life*, Pablo Richard, *et al.*, eds. Maryknoll, NY: Orbis Books, 165–93.

Jellinek, Georg. 1901. *The Declaration of the Rights of Man and Citizens*. New York: Henry Holt and Company.

John Paul II, Pope. 1982. "The Fundamental Rights of Man." In *The Pope and Revolution*, Quentin L. Quade, ed. Washington, DC: Ethics and Public Policy Center, 108–12.

Laurentin, Rene. 1972. *Liberation, Development and Salvation*. Maryknoll, NY: Orbis Books.

Leo XIII, Pope. {1888} 1941. *Liberatas Humana*. New York: Paulist Press.

Marx, Karl. 1975. *Karl Marx: Early Writings*. New York: Random House.

Moore, Barrington Jr., 1967. *Social Origins of Dictatorship and Democracy*. Boston: Beacon Press.

Rawls, John. 1971. *A Theory of Justice*. Cambridge, MA: Harvard University Press.

Rousseau, Jean Jacques. 1954. *The Social Contract*. Chicago: Henry Regnery Co.

Segundo, Juan Luis. 1976. *The Liberation of Theology*. Maryknoll, NY: Orbis Books.

Stackhouse, Max L. 1984. *Creeds, Society, and Human Rights*. Grand Rapids, MI: William B. Eerdmanns Publishing Co.

Talmon, J. L. 1960. *The Origins of Totalitarian Democracy*. New York: Praeger.

Troeltsch, Ernst. 1931. *The Social Teachings of the Christian Churches*. London: George Allen and Unwin, Ltd.

United Nations Office of Public Information. 1965. *Everyman's United Nations*. New York: United Nations.

Vidales, Raul. 1979. "Methodological Issues in Liberation Theology." In *Frontiers of Theology in Latin America*, Rosino Gibellini, ed. Maryknoll, NY: Orbis Books, 34–57.

Woodhouse, A. S. P. {1938} 1974. *Puritanism and Liberty*. Chicago: University of Chicago Press.

8

The Influence of Certain Political Movements in South Africa on the Church's Role in the Struggle for Liberation

Bonganjalo Goba

SINCE THE EVENTS of 1976, when the black youths of Soweto decided to confront the oppressive structures of apartheid, the church has been challenged more than ever before to participate in the ongoing struggle for liberation in South Africa. There is a sense in which the political activities of black youths involved in various political organizations that seek to work for radical change have challenged the church to evaluate its specific role within the existing political conflict that prevails in our society. This has not only compelled churches to develop a radical theology, but has forced certain members of the Christian community to be involved and take sides within the political struggles that are ongoing.

The purpose of this paper is to analyze the kind of impact that various political organizations have had on the church's role in trying to dismantle the system of apartheid. My aim is not to measure in a quantifiable fashion this impact but rather to give a critical appraisal of the development of certain theological perceptions about the mission of the church in the South African context.

I am aware that there are serious problems involved in this kind of exercise. Let me mention only a few:

144

(1) We have serious differences within the South African Christian community about the church's role in the political sphere. These differences are not only of a theological nature but reflect our attitudes and commitments about the present political status quo.

(2) A second problem has to do with how as Christians we analyze and understand the political realities of our society as well as ways of engaging in the process of social change.

(3) A third problem has to do with our attitudes and relationships with secular political movements that are involved in the process of social change.

These three areas constitute some of the serious stumbling blocks in any discussion about the political involvement of Christians in programs of social change. But I will focus my attention on those churches that have displayed a strong social commitment to participate in the actual process of political change in South African society, that is, those churches that belong to the South African Council of Churches.

The attempt to analyze the impact of certain political movements on the church's role will require a brief analysis of their (a) ideological perspectives, (b) strategies, and (c) current political significance in the events that are taking place in South Africa at this moment. The movements I wish to analyze are the Black Consciousness Movement, the United Democratic Front, and the National Forum. These movements represent the kind of political activity that has mobilized and sensitized the black masses to engage in the struggle for liberation in South Africa. But before I examine the goals and impact of these movements on the church, let me give a brief historical background of certain political events relevant to their formation.

A Brief Historical Background of the Political Events in the Black Struggle from 1950 to the Present

I believe the political events of the 1950s represent a turning point in the black struggle in South Africa. This was a period of intense repression accompanied by the introduction of certain laws the aim of which was to entrench the political ideology of apartheid, thus depriving blacks of virtually all their political rights. The latent consequence of this was the creation of a mass movement as a strategy to challenge the policy of apartheid.

The passing of the Suppression of Communism Act of 1950 by the white Nationalist regime was a clear attempt to crush black political opposition in the country. This did not just precipitate angry reaction but also forced black political organizations to evaluate their strategies. The Suppression of Communism Act was followed by a series of laws such as the Separate Representation of Voters Act of 1951, the goal of which was to remove blacks, especially the so-called coloureds, from the common voters roll. This also led to the termination of the Native Representative Council. During this period the country also saw the passing of the Bantu Education Act of 1954, which subjected blacks to an inferior kind of educational system.

In response to this denial or breach of rights a number of black political organizations decided to pursue a strategy of mass resistance. On the May 1, 1950, a declaration was passed making this day Freedom Day. Masses were encouraged to stay away from work. An appeal was made to the government by the black political leadership to call a National Convention—but without success. After failing to convince the white regime of the urgency of a National Convention, black political leadership in 1952 organized the Defiance Campaign, in which they called upon the government to repeal the pass laws, the Groups Areas Act, and the Separate Representation Voters Act. But the government refused. On the 26th of June the Defiance Campaign started and by the end of the year, 8000 people had been arrested. In many ways this was the beginning of mass political resistance against the policy of apartheid.

During March, 1952 various executives of political organizations, as a response to the growing political repression in the country, decided to convene a Congress of the People in order to consider the newly created Freedom Charter. After considerable organizing and planning, a Congress of the People was convened on the 25–26 of June in Johannesburg to review this milestone document. About 3000 people attended this historic occasion. Since most readers will not be readily familiar with the contents of the Freedom Charter, it is presented complete in the Appendix.

As repression increased from the government side, the resistance against apartheid intensified, especially after 1956. This led to the banning of major black political movements in the 1960s. Then followed the treason trial in which important black political leaders such as Nelson Mandela were sentenced to life imprisonment. Probably most important about this period is that out of it, for the first time, there emerged a clear commitment to violence as a means to political change especially in acts of sabotage. This commitment to violence has remained problematic in the black community but continues to express itself even in current events in South Africa.

It was during the period of the late 1960s, with intense repression accompanied by a clear absence of strong black political leadership, that the Black Consciousness Movement coalesced under the leadership of Steve Biko. While the issues that confronted the black community in the fifties remained unsolved, the leadership came from black youths, especially students in various black campuses who had a clear commitment to redefining the goals and philosophy of the black struggle. Black Consciousness itself was born out of frustration with white students' liberal politics in the late 1960s, especially within the National Union of South African Students (NUSAS). In the absence of any broad-based black political movement, a number of black students (led by Biko) formed the separatist SASO (the South African Student Organization). The first meeting was organized at Marrianhill in 1968 by Biko and other black student leaders from a number of black campuses around the country. At the SASO's inaugural meeting at Turfloop, Biko was elected president of the organization. From this point onwards black students throughout the country began to disassociate themselves from NUSAS and other white-dominated student organizations.

One of the basic ideas prominent at the inception of SASO was that of self reliance, i.e., a call for black South Africans to determine their own political destiny, accompanied by a severe criticism of white liberalism. There was a very strong rejection among SASO's leaders of ideas associated with integration, non-racialism, assimilation, and trusteeship. At the same time there was a strong, mutually negative reaction coming from the white liberal community as well.

As SASO gained momentum on black campuses and at seminaries, strong emphasis was put on the concept of Black Consciousness or Black Pride. The message of SASO challenged students as well as the black masses to begin defining goals and values for their own liberation struggle. By the 1970s SASO was well established throughout the country. Because of its impact on university campuses and seminaries, SASO gained political significance in the country. To define better SASO's ideology, Biko and other student leaders began to identify black oppression as having serious psychological consequences which had to be exorcised from the psyches of black people. The problem was perceived as one of a profound inferiority complex among the black masses, a product of Western political and cultural imperialism. Because of this inferiority complex, blacks had to rediscover a new sense of identity and new pride through a process of liberation. Part of this process required that blacks have to begin to criticize various aspects of white Western civilization.

This search for a relevant ideological perspective led the leadership of SASO to creative ideas and insights from the African wisdom of the past, wisdom reflected in many African writers and philosophers. Black Consciousness was defined as an attitude of mind, a way of life. Yet this approach was not new. As Gerhard (1979, 272) has observed, "Almost point for point, SASO had arrived anew at the diagnosis and cure originally devised by Lembede and Mda in the 1940s under the rubric of Africanism. But now the diagnosis was more searching and the cure more likely to be found acceptable by significant sections of the African intelligentsia and even the African society at large."

I was actively involved in SASO as a theological student at the Federal Theological Seminary, a commitment that continued even during my ministry in Cape Town, where I had close contact with Steve Biko both as a friend and as a comrade in the black struggle during that time. While it is true that Black Consciousness as a philosophy grew out of our own experience, we were also influenced to a great extent by ideas from a number of African thinkers such as Nkurumah, Nyerere, Fanon, Senghor, as well as some of the thinkers within the black power movement in the United States such as Malcolm X, Stokely Carmichael, Charles Milton and leading black theologian James Cone. Thus the ideology that was being promulgated by SASO in the 1970s had strong similarities to the black nationalist ideology that was promoted by Lembede and Mda in the 1940s.

Nevertheless, I believe SASO developed a unique strategy in order to popularize its campaign of political resistance. This was done by adopting the ideology of a broad-based black nationalism whose goal was to sensitize and politicize the black masses by exposing the existing political contradictions of the South African society. One of the issues that the SASO leadership confronted was discrediting "dummy" political institutions created by the white Nationalist regime. Their leaders tried to discourage blacks from participating in these institutions, but without success. The government went ahead and created the quasi-political institutions of the Urban Community Councillors and the so-called homeland governments, sometimes referred to as Bantustans. These were to become one of the most critical issues in the current political unrest in South Africa. Individuals who have been targets of violence belong to, or are seen to be supporters of, these quasi-political institutions.

In order to organize the masses and move beyond the university campuses, SASO helped launch the Black Peoples Convention in 1971. Drake Koka was elected president of this organization. But BPC could not generate great impact since the leadership was under constant political harrassment, which finally led to its banning. From this period onwards SASO was confronted with many obstacles. Besides political harrassment, there were problems with leadership that led to ineffectiveness. During this difficult period an important role was played by black clergy and theological students in holding various political organizations together. Such an attempt to further solidarity occurred with the Black Renaissance Convention–1974 which also had an impact on the church leadership. As if in recognition of the mounting politicization of black religious leaders, the government in 1975 decided to expropriate the Federal Theological Seminary, one of the largest black ecumenical seminaries in South Africa.

In sum, the impact of SASO as a political organization can be seen in the way it brought about a radical shift in the thinking of black students and youth in general subsequent to the events of 1976. SASO helped to redefine the political nemesis of the black masses more clearly by heightening the racial character of the black struggle. It created an atmosphere of political assertiveness among black youths, well displayed in the trial of the SASO

Nine during 1976 and earlier in 1973, when banning orders were served on Biko and Pityana. The other important contribution that Black Consciousness made in black political thinking was that it encouraged a radical sense of independent political strategizing among black youths. These factors are important when examining the kind of influence the history of South African black liberation has had on the church's role in the current struggle for liberation in South Africa.

The Emergence of the United Democratic Front and National Forum

What is significant about the formation of the United Democratic Front (UDF) and the National Forum is that both these movements were established in the same year, 1983 (the United Democratic Front on August 20, the National Forum on June 11–12). It is important to analyze both these movements in terms of their objectives, strategy, and philosophy. What is also important about these organizations is that they have succeeded in bringing together labor, students, and community organizations in the form of two separate coalitions with the sole purpose of challenging the system of apartheid at a time when there has been an absence of strong political leadership in the black community. Let me begin by giving a brief outline on the formation of the United Democratic Front and then the National Forum.

The United Democratic Front, Its Goals And Strategy. Immediately after the establishment of the President's Council (followed by its proposals for a new constitution of South Africa to initiate the so-called reform process), Dr. Boesak, one of the leading black theologians in South Africa and the president of the World Alliance of Reformed Churches, called for a United Front. In a speech he stated that there was no reason why churches, civic associations, trade unions, student organizations and sports bodies should not unite on the apartheid issue, pool their resources, inform people of the Front, and, on the day of the election, "expose their plans for what they are."

The United Democratic Front came into existence to challenge the Koornhof Bills and the New Apartheid Constitution, the goals of which were to incorporate Coloureds and Indians in the decision-making process while excluding blacks. The main thrust of the UDF was to promote broad political unity and solidarity among all groups who were involved in the struggle against apartheid. The UDF sought to challenge the plans of the President's Council and Koornhof Bills in order to counteract the old tactic of divide-and-rule that was envisaged in this New Constitution. Unquestionably the United Democratic Front has succeeded in providing a strong united platform for major black opposition groups to challenge the system of apartheid, particularly under its so-called New Constitution. To appreciate this point it is important to consider the declaration made by the UDF at its inaugural meeting in Cape Town.

The United Democratic Front Declaration in its essentials does not depart significantly from the message of the Freedom Charter. What is unique, however, is that it is more specifically directed to the rejection of the New Constitution and the Koornhof Bills by organizing the masses at the grassroots level. The significance of the UDF is irrevocably tied to the so-called process of reform initiated by the white South African regime. The reform process has failed to demonstrate a change of heart among the white political elite. What it has succeeded in doing is creating an atmosphere of frustration andpolitical rebellion within the black community. The evidence of this can be seen in the current unrest and escalating violence throughout the country.

The UDF has succeeded in mobilizing the masses for its various campaigns: work stay-aways, sports boycotts, and lately, consumer boycotts. Above all, it successfully organized against the election of Coloured and Indian members to Parliament. Apart from that, it has mobilized student protest against unequal and inferior apartheid educational system. As a result of its impact and effectiveness the present white regime has arrested and charged its leaders with treason, including Dr. Allan Boesak, thus fanning further the fires of rebellion.

It is difficult to summarize the underlying philosophy of the United Democratic Front because it represents a coalition of many labor, student, and community organizations. Unlike the Black Consciousness Movement examined earlier, the UDF does not emphasize in an exclusive fashion the racial character of the struggle. It seeks to promote a democratic vision that unites all the groups committed to the struggle for liberation. This does not mean it has no ideological perspective; rather, it represents ideological perspectives that find expression in the various organizations that are affiliated with it. What the UDF has succeeded in achieving is the organizing of people at the grassroots level, thus providing a formidable base of resistance against apartheid. UDF, through its campaigns and philosophy, will continue to shape future political events for a long time. For UDF represents well-organized political resistance in the black community, something that even the present white regime cannot overcome.

The Emergence of the National Forum. The National Forum was established specifically to challenge the politics of co-option under the new so-called political dispensation. However, its strategy differs from that of the UDF in that the political mobilization of the masses are to be constituted exclusively by the oppressed groups. Its tone is more militant, its leaders concerned that any alliances not be merely marriages of convenience that embrace elements of the ruling class and thereby "sell out" to bourgeois interests. It examines the South African problem from both a class and a race perspective, which is why there is a strong criticism of racial capitalism in the documents of the National Forum.

Thus, unlike the UDF with its broad democratic vision, the National Forum emphasizes the narrower nationalist character of the struggle with the goal of establishing a socialist system. The National Forum has not succeeded in creating a powerful organization capable of mobilizing the masses. Its real success has been its ability to redefine the philosophy of Black Consciousness as in its strongly Marxist-flavored Manifesto of the Azanian People, promulgated at Hammanskraa on June 11–12, 1983.

The Influences of These Movements on the Churches' Role in the Current Liberation Struggle

It is difficult to assess the church's role in the current struggle for liberation in South Africa because past religiously based activism reflects the kind of theological perceptions grounded in church resolutions and theological statements made by Church leaders, not necessarily those of ordinary church members. But this theological orientation, especially among the members of the South African Council of Churches, is beginning to have an impact not only in terms of challenging the ideology of apartheid but also in shaping what ordinary church members think about the role the church should play in South Africa. I do not wish to analyze specifically the period of the 1950s nor examine events surrounding the Christian Institute under the leadership of Dr. Beyers Naude, as these are well-documented elsewhere (de Gruchy 1979). What I want to do here is to begin with an analysis of the Black Consciousness Movement, particularly its impact on the black church leadership and its theological orientation, then move to the United Democratic Front and the National Forum.

If one examines the period of the late 1960s one discovers that the Black Consciousness Movement played a significant role in the development of black theology. Before this, theology in South Africa tended to reflect the dominant theological hermeneutic of the white liberal theologians within the English-speaking churches. In this hermeneutic the South African political reality was understood in terms of racial oppression. In other words the emphasis was on the removal of racial discrimination, but at the cost of failing to analyze and confront the existing political power relations in South Africa. So the basic theological hermeneutic of the English-speaking churches did not really address the problem of political conflict completely.

The real shift in the theological orientation of the young black church leadership of the mainline Protestant churches and the Roman Catholic Church came with the emergence of Black Consciousness in the late 1960s. What the Black Consciousness Movement did in terms of challenging the

black Christian community, particularly its leadership, was to contextualize
their theological approach so as to take seriously the black religious experience.
Theology from this time onwards became associated with the quest for black
liberation. Christian faith became an important medium of resistance against
apartheid. Within the black theology movement, the black church became
an important expression of black protest in the South African context. Allan
Boesak (1979, 101–104) one of the leading black theologians in South Africa,
makes the following observation referring to the role of the church.

> It is within the heat of the struggle that Christians are today especially called
> to be the light of the world. In the midst of the struggle we are called to be
> the embodiment of God's ideal for his broken world. Christians must be there
> to represent God's possibilities for authentic Christian love, meaningful rec-
> onciliation and genuine peace.

The Black Theology Movement that began in the later part of the 1960s,
influenced to a great extent by the Black Consciousness philosophy of Steve
Biko, has created a radical vision of the church. The church within the context
of black theology gains its authenticity as it participates in the ongoing struggle
of the people. This explains why certain church leaders such as Bishop Tutu,
Allan Boesak, and many others have played a prominent role in the political
arena in South Africa. Because of the radical shift in the theological perceptions
especially of the black clergy, the church is becoming more and more involved
in confrontation with the state. The black church, particularly, is seen as the
institution that protects the oppressed and the marginalized. Even those black
radicals who are generally opposed to Christianity acknowledge the important
role that the black church has to play in the current political struggle in South
Africa. Thus, these theological perceptions emerging in South African society
are a response to the political dynamics prevalent there. Yet this theological
response has been effective only because of the ideological base it has received
from the Black Consciousness Movement.

The impact of the United Democratic Front and National Forum in terms
of their underlying objectives are also indivisible from the role certain church
leaders played in the formation of both these movements. The UDF, as a
broad movement of progressive democrats, has promoted theological perceptions that tend to be more open and critical of the racial analysis of the
South African situation. On the other hand those theologians who are sympathetic to the National Forum have tended to support a black theological
perspective, one that highlights the racial–class character of the South African
struggle.

One of the key results of this new radical theological hermeneutic that is
evolving among young leadership of those religious bodies belonging to the
South African Council of Churches has been a clear commitment to participate

in the ongoing political struggle for liberation. This commitment has taken many forms. For example, this black liberation theological perspective has compelled the church to confront the theological justification of apartheid as a heresy. The significance of this confrontation is that it has accentuated the conflict between the church and state in South Africa. Challenging apartheid as a theological heresy has revived the old commitment of groups belonging to the South African Council of Churches to encourage acts of civil disobedience. These have included some of the recent events in South Africa in which some of the prominent church leaders such as Dr. Boesak have been arrested. Apart from this we see a growing involvement of the young black clergy in secular political movements, especially UDF and National Forum. As a result of this some of the church leaders were charged with high treason by the government in 1984 and others are presently under detention.

What this means is that there is now a new commitment to a theological praxis the goal of which is to bring about political transformation inspired by both new ideological perceptions and a re-reading of the Bible. It is clear from the remarks above that the shift in theological orientation is compelling the church to take more direct action in opposing the system of apartheid. This shift in theological orientation is accompanied by a clear willingness on the part of the young black clergy to participate actively in secular political movements. The notion of God siding with the oppressed, reflected particularly in black theology, is leading many black and a few white Christians to support the political movements such as the United Democratic Front and the National Forum.

This shift we can see in the KAIROS Document of 1985, a critical theological study of the current political crisis in South Africa. In the document there is a strong criticism of the state's de facto racist theology, i.e., the kind of theology that supports the status quo. But this statement goes even further in attacking what it refers to as "Church Theology." It criticizes traditional church theology for not being radical enough. It is particularly critical of the way the notion of reconciliation has been used to resolve the current political conflict in South Africa. For example:

> In our situation in South Africa today it would be totally unchristian to plead for reconciliation and peace before the present injustices have been removed. Any such plea plays into the hands of the oppressor by trying to persuade those of us who are oppressed to accept our oppression and to become reconciled to the intolerable crimes that are committed against us. That is not Christian reconciliation, it is sin. It is asking us to become accomplices in our own oppression, to become servants of the devil. No reconciliation is possible in South Africa without justice. (KAIROS Document, 9)

What is unique about this document is that it accuses the present white South African regime of tyranny and challenges the church to consider acts of civil disobedience as the only option available to Christians to challenge the apartheid state. The document goes even far beyond the resolutions made by religious bodies in the past in calling on the church to side with the oppressed. It encourages the church to participate in the political campaigns of the masses as they struggle for their liberation. The church according to this document must offer moral guidance to the struggle of the people, not simply homilies or other-worldly comfort.

In conclusion, the participation of political movements in the struggle for human liberties in South Africa has provided a unique context for the current theological praxis reflected in the statements and actions of certain churches involved in the liberation struggle. This theological praxis reflects the emancipatory interests of the masses. It offers an ongoing attempt by the church to define its role within the struggle.

Appendix
THE FREEDOM CHARTER

"We, the People of South Africa, Declare for all our Country and the World to know:

That South Africa belongs to all who live in it, black and white, and that no government can justly claim authority unless it is based on the will of all the people:
That our people have been robbed of their birthright to land, liberty, and peace by a form of government founded on injustice and inequality:
That our country will never be prosperous or free until all our people live in brotherhood, enjoying equal rights and opportunities:
That only a democratic state based on the will of all the people, can secure to all their birthright without distinction of colour, race, sex or belief:
And therefore, we the people of South Africa, black and white together—equals, countrymen, and brothers—adopt this Freedom Charter. And we pledge ourselves to strive together, sparing neither strength nor courage, until the democratic changes here set out have been won.

The People Shall Govern

Every man and woman shall have the right to vote for and to stand as a candidate for all bodies which make law.

The People Shall Share in the Country's Wealth

The national wealth of our country, the heritage of all South Africans, shall be restored to the people.

All people shall be entitled to take part in the administration of the country.

The rights of the people shall be the same, sex.

All bodies of minority rule, advisory boards, councils and authorities shall be replaced by democratic organs of self-government.

All National Groups Shall Have Equal Rights:

There shall be equal status in the bodies of state, in the courts, and in the schools for all national groups and races.

All people shall have equal rights to use their own languages, and to develop their own folk culture and customs.

All national groups shall be protected by law against insults to their race and national pride.

The preaching and practice of national race or colour discrimination and contempt shall be a punishable crime.

All apartheid laws and practices shall be set aside.

All Shall Be Equal Before The Law:

No one shall be imprisoned, deported, or restricted without a fair trial.

The mineral wealth beneath the soil, the banks and monopoly industry shall be transferred to the ownership of the people as a whole.

All other industry and trade shall be controlled to assist the well-being of the people;

All shall have equal rights to trade where they choose, to manufacture, and to enter all trades, crafts, and professions.

The Land Shall be Shared Among Those Who Work It:

Restriction of land ownership on a racial basis shall be ended and all the land redivided amongst those who work it, to banish famine and land hunger.

The state shall help the peasants with implements, seed, tractors, and dams to save the soil and assist the tillers.

Freedom of movement shall be guaranteed to all who work on the land.

All shall have rights to occupy the land where they choose; People shall not be robbed of their cattle, and forced labour and farm prisons shall be abolished.

There shall be a forty-hour working week, a national minimum wage, paid annual leave, and sick leave for all workers, and maternity leave on full pay for all working mothers.

No one shall be condemned by the order of any Government official.

The courts shall be representative of all the people.

Imprisonment shall be only for serious crimes against the people, and shall aim at re-education not vengeance.

The police force and army shall be open to all on an equal basis and shall be the helpers and the protectors of the people.

All laws which discriminate on grounds of race, colour, or belief shall be repealed.

All Shall Enjoy Equal Human Rights!

The law shall guarantee to all their rights to speak, to organize, to meet together, to preach, to worship, and to educate their children;
The privacy of the house from the police raids shall be protected by law;

All shall be free to travel without restrition from country-side to town, from province to province, and from South Africa abroad;

Pass laws, permits, and all other laws restricting these freedoms shall be abolished.

There Shall Be Work and Security:

Miners, domestic workers, farm workers, and civil servants shall have the same rights as all others who work.

Child labour, compound labour, the lot system and contract labour shall be abolished.

The Doors of Learning and of Culture Shall be Opened:

The Government shall discover, develop and encourage national pride for the enhancement of our cultural life:

All the culture treasures of mankind shall be open to all, by free exchange of books, ideas, and contact with other lands:

The aim of education shall be to teach the youth to love their people and their culture, to honour human brotherhood, liberty, and peace:

Education shall be free, compulsory, universal, and equal for children:

Higher education and technical training shall be opened to all by means of state allowances and scholarships awarded on the basis of merit;

Adult illiteracy shall be ended by a mass state education plan;

Teachers shall have all the rights of other citizens;

All who work shall be free to form trade unions, to elect their officers, and to make wage agreements with their employers:

The state shall recognize the right and duty of all to work and to draw full unemployment benefits:

Men and women of all races shall receive equal pay for equal work:

Unused housing space to be made available to the people, rent and prices to be lowered, food plentiful and no one shall go hungry;

A preventive health scheme shall be run by the state;

Free medical care and hospitalization shall be provided for all, with special care for mothers and young children;

Slums shall be demolished and new suburbs built where all have transport, roads, lighting, playing fields, creches, and social centres;

The aged, the orphans, the disabled, and the sick shall be cared for by the state;

Rest, leisure, and recreation shall be the right of all;

Fenced locations and ghettos shall be abolished, and laws which break up families shall be repealed.

The colour bar in cultural life, sport, and in education shall be abolished.

There Shall be Houses, Security, and Comfort:

All the people shall have the right to live where they choose, to be decently housed, and to bring up their families in comfort and security;

There Shall be Peace and Friendship:

South Africa shall be a fully independent state, which respects the rights and sovereignty of all nations;

South Africa shall strive to maintain world peace and the settlement of all international disputes by negotiations—not war;

Peace and friendship amongst all our people shall be secured by upholding the equal rights, opportunities, and status of all;

The people of the protectorates—Basotholand, Botswanaland, and Swaziland—shall be free to decide for themselves their own future;

The right of all the people of Africa to independence and self-government shall be the basis of close cooperation."

References

Boesak, Allan. 1979. *The Black Church and the Future*. South African Outlook, 101.

Boesak, Allan. 1976. *Farewell to Innocence: A Socio-Ethical Study on Black Theology*. Maryknoll, NY: Orbis Books.

Buthelezi, Manas. 1974. The Relevance of Black Theology. South African Outlook, 198–299.

CIIR. 1985. *Treason Against Apartheid*. London: Catholic Institute for International Relations.

CIIR. 1982. *War and Conscience in South Africa*. London: Catholic Institute for International Relations.

de Gruchy, John. 1979. *The Church Struggle in South Africa*. Grand Rapids, MI: William B. Eerdmans Publishing Company.

Dugard, John. 1980. *A National Strategy for 1980*. South African Institute of Race Relations.

Gerhard, Gail. 1979. *Black Power in South Africa*. Berkeley, CA: University of California Press.

Gill, Robin. 1977. *Theology and Social Structure*. London: Mowbrays.

Goba, Bonganjalo. 1983. "Emerging Theological Perspectives in South Africa." In *Irruption of the Third World Challenge to Theology*. Virginia Fabella and Sorgio Torres, eds. Maryknoll, NY: Orbis Books, 19–29.

Kairos Theologians. 1985. *The Kairos Document*. Brammfontein, South Africa.

Morrel, Muriel. 1971. *Action Reactional Counter-Action*. South African Institute of Race Relations.

PART III
RELIGIOUS MINORITIES AND INTEGRATION

9
Muslims in Communist Nations: The Cases of Albania, Bulgaria, Yugoslavia, and the Soviet Union

Jerry G. Pankhurst

UNQUESTIONABLY TWO of the most dynamic forces on the international scene today are Marxism and Islam. There are many variants of each of these major ideologies, some more strict and totalitarian than others, but seldom do they come together in accommodation or cooperation. Each is too suspicious of the other. There is a tendency in both orientations to unite social identity, faith, and politics, seeing these three as inseparable aspects of a single thrust toward transforming the world. For this reason, the conflict in Afghanistan seems to be somehow fitting, however unjust and unhappy, because it reflects this basic antipathy. By contrast, the idea of a communist mullah seems incongruous, involving too many contradictions. Yet the Afghanistan invasion may well have been partly initiated in order to build a stronger barrier between the communist-controlled Muslims of the Soviet Union and resurgent fundamentalist Islam, especially from the Iranian South.

On the other hand, as Bennigsen (1984a) has suggested, the fifth largest "Muslim power" in the world is the communist Soviet Union with its nearly fifty million ethnic Muslims. There are also major Islamic populations in several other communist nations. Pipes (1983, 337) notes that 10.7 percent of all Muslims live in the communist countries from Yugoslavia to China. How

161

do they get along, and what are the characteristic kinds of relationships between the Muslim groups and communist political authority? How is the seemingly natural opposition between Islam and communism handled by these peoples? What is the future of these relationships? Can there be communist mullahs?

Questions like these may be easier to answer if we possess an adequate conceptual framework within which to pose and address them. The central task of this paper is to provide such a framework. Consideration of the situation of Muslims in four communist countries—Albania, Bulgaria, Yugoslavia, and the Soviet Union—will provide empirical case material for the present discussion. These cases will be examined in the light of my own earlier conceptualizations of general church–state relations in "state atheist nations" (Pankhurst 1983, 1986). By using this conceptual framework to evaluate the situation of Islam in these nations, the special dimensions of the Islamic situation may be identified.

Four Distinct Cases

This study attempts a nomothetic approach to the sociopolitical conditions of Muslims in communist lands. Such an enterprise seeks to improve our understanding of the patterned relationships found within the cases and to identify major dimensions of variation among the cases. The experience in each case is not the same; however, though the specific character of the cases must be kept in mind, the goal here is not to provide a detailed portrait of each of them. Instead, the object is to single out the relationships that are relevant to an understanding of the larger phenomenon of Muslims under communist rule. Since no one case embodies all the range of variation possible in Muslim–communist interaction, the strategy of comparison is a *sine qua non* for the enterprise. In making this comparison and in trying to generalize from these four cases, it is also essential that the limitations that stem from the selection of cases are taken into account.

The general issue of communism and Islam cannot be fully addressed in this paper because of the limited selection of cases to be covered. The four nations chosen for consideration—Albania, Bulgaria, Yugoslavia, and the Soviet Union—are all well-established communist regimes in Eurasia with a predominantly European national elite. Furthermore, the political structures of Bulgaria, Yugoslavia, and the Soviet Union are dominated not only by communists, but also by Slavs, a factor that may influence communist–Muslim interactions in ways not found in non-Slavic settings. These three countries also have Muslim ethnic minorities; only in Albania is the majority of the population (seventy percent) ethnically Muslim.

Besides these four cases, in the "mature" communist nations (that is, those dating from about 1950 or earlier) there are also significant Muslim groups:

in Romania, 272,000 Muslims; Mongolia, 171,000 Muslims; and China, 15,000,000 Muslims (Weekes 1984). Barrett (1982) records small groups of Muslim adherents in Poland and Hungary as well. There are also large Muslim populations in many of the newer communist or Marxist nations, such as Ethiopia, 11,000,000 Muslims; Mozambique, 1,700,000 Muslims; Vietnam, 570,000 Muslims; and Afghanistan, 14,100,000 Muslims. Finally, the more general question of communism and Islam would also have to be addressed with consideration of the communist movements among Muslim populations in non-communist lands.

Recognizing some of the special properties of the comparative cases to be studied, caution must be exercised in making generalizations. However, since these cases are mature nations, each with a large and influential Muslim population, it may be possible to envision parts of the future of less fully developed situations in the experiences covered here.

The unit of analysis in this study is the nation, within which the focus is upon the political interactions between the governing communist groups and the Muslims. Given the relatively disciplined and hierarchically unified political activities within the four communist regimes, seeing the regimes themselves as actors does little to distort their nature, though they differ from each other in important ways. This does not give us license to think that regime policy vis-à-vis Muslims is unchangeable or lacking in dynamism. Regime policy is always the outcome of a political process of debate and weighing of options. It can and does change from time to time and from one specific application to another, even though, in the end, a relatively stable pattern emerges and is applied relatively consistently for some period.

By contrast, frequent reference to the "Islamic population" or to "Muslims" or "the Muslim group" in a given country should not be taken to suggest that such entities are unified like regimes nor themselves actors. There is no overall structural unity of the Muslim population in any of these countries, as will be shown below, and there are major distinctions among sub-groups of Muslims in each country. Such sub-groups are defined by differentiated ethnicity, nationality, language, culture, historical background, and even form of Islamic practice. As will become apparent, internal differentiation among Muslims in a given country also implies somewhat differentiated policy approaches by the regime to the specific region or group. What then unifies each nation's Muslim population, in the end, is only the religion of Islam.

I have previously argued the value of envisioning religious groups and communist regimes (or "state/parties") as interest groups in competition for adherents among the population. In this formulation, an adherent is one who accepts the authority claimed by the interest group, and thus, the competition is essentially one over authority in the system. This approach is derived from the perspective of Ralf Dahrendorf (1959), who also suggests a framework for interpreting the nature of the public's attachments to interests on latent and manifest levels. For present purposes, ethnic or national Muslims in a given country represent a "quasi-group" linked by latent interests to which the religious leadership is appealing for support. Once such interests are acknowledged and acted upon, i.e., made manifest as an interest, the ethnic Muslim can be considered an adherent to the Muslim interest group.

Since the communist state claims authority in areas that Muslim religion might wish to reserve for itself, such as education of children, to become a Muslim adherent involves rejecting the regime in this range of affairs. Some regimes, however, are less totalistic in their claims of authority than are others, and the result is that some Muslim adherents may easily mix their Islamic attachments with communist attachments while those in other countries cannot do so as easily. Among the present cases, Yugoslavia is the least totalistic, Bulgaria and the Soviet Union are in the middle but tending toward the totalistic end of the spectrum, and Albania is at the totalistic extreme.

Further specifications of the situations of Muslims in the four countries can be found in Table 9.1. This table provides population totals for each of the four countries and, in column 1, for the ethnic or national Muslims within them, no matter to which specific ethnic group they may belong. Column 2 gives the percentage of the country's population that possesses a Muslim ethnic or national identification. As such, this category represents the effective quasi-group for the Muslim religious interest groups in a country. Column 3 provides an estimate of the percentage of the country's population who can be considered bona fide followers of the faith of Islam, in whatever variant, as estimated by Barrett (1982). This figure can be understood to represent roughly the proportion of the country's population who are adherents to the Muslim religious interest group. (Two or more ethnic subdivisions may be included in this interest group.) To reiterate, the goal of the interest group is to bring more of the quasi-group members into this interest group category.

As I have previously argued, the potential strength of a religious interest group in a communist country may be increased if the religion is strongly tied to an ethnic identity, as, for example, Roman Catholicism is to Polish national identity. In such cases, both religious and ethnic interests reinforce each other, enlarging the range of manifest interests that can appeal to a population as against the claims of the state/party interest group. Column 4 in Table 9.1 indicates the strength of ethnic or national ties for the Muslims of the given nation. This is a very general estimate for the major groups in the country; it does not apply for a minor group that may be co-resident.

Finally in reference to the format of Table 9.1, column 5 indicates whether or not there are territorial units of the state that are identified with a Muslim ethnic group, and column 6 identifies such units by name if they exist. The presence of Muslim ethnoterritories represents a public acknowledgement by the regime, at least for symbolic purposes, of the right to some degree of self-determination for the ethnic group. Naturally, this need not

TABLE 9.1.
FACTORS INFLUENCING THE SOCIOPOLITICAL STRENGTH OF MUSLIM
GROUPS IN FOUR COMMUNIST NATIONS.

Key
1. Number of Ethnic Muslim Nationals.[a]
2. Percent of Population That Are Ethnic Muslim Nationals.[a]
3. Percent of Population That Are Muslim Religious Adherents.[b]
4. Strength of Ethnic or National Ties. (weak, strong)
5. Are there one or more Muslim ethnoterritories in the nation? (yes, no)
6. Names of Major Ethnoterritories, if any.

1. Number of Muslims Eth./Nat.	2. % of Pop Eth./Nat.	3. % of Pop. Affil.	4. Ethnic or Nat. Tie	5. Ethno- terri- tories?	6. Name(s) of Major Ethnoterritories
ALBANIA	population = 2,900,000[a]				
2,000,000	70.0	20.5	weak	no	
BULGARIA	population = 8,900,000[a]				
1,014,000	11.0	10.6	weak	no	
SOVIET UNION	population = 272,000,000[a]				
46,000,000	17.3	11.3	strong	yes	Uzbek SSR Tadzhik SSR Kirgiz SSR Turkmen SSR Azerbaidzhan SSR Kazakh SSR Checheno -Ingush ASSR Dagestan ASSR Karakalpak ASSR Tatar ASSR etc.
YUGOSLAVIA	population = 22,800,000[a]				
3,700,000	16.0	10.4	strong	yes	Bosnia-Herzegovina Kosovo

NOTES:
   Data is for 1983 and is taken from *Muslim Peoples: A World Ethnographic Survey*, Second Edition, Revised and Expanded, ed. Richard V. Weekes (Westport, Connecticut: Greenwood Press, 1984), from Appendix 1., pp. 882–911. The source of minor arithmetic anomalies in these data could not be located.
   [b]Data is for mid-1980 and is taken from the *World Christian Encyclopedia*, ed. David B. Barrett (New York: Oxford University Press, 1982), from Table 1 of each of the country summaries. Specific page citations by country are as follows: Albania, p.134; Bulgaria, p.199; U.S.S.R., p.689; Yugoslavia, p.753.

refer to specifically religious rights, but the line between ethnic group and religious group prerogatives, as we have already suggested, is a fine one. If there is an ethnoterritory, it provides a forum upon which issues of ethnic interest may be argued, and a claim may be made in that forum that ethnic and religious interests have some commonalities. If the regime is not too strongly antireligious, even direct claims for religious rights may be pursued within the ethnoterritorial structure.

Usually, the existence of a Muslim ethnoterritory indicates a policy decision earlier in a regime's history on how to deal with issues of ethnic and national consciousness. This decision, in turn, was undoubtedly made largely on the basis of two factors: first, the ideological interpretation of the appropriate place for ethnic and religious interests, and second, an assessment of the overall political strength of the ethno-religious group and the apparent means to deal with this alternative claim on authority. In conjunction with this latter factor, then, there is an interactive pattern between the presence of an ethnoterritorial unit and the prior strength of a religio-Ethnic group. That is, if the group is strong today, it is likely already to have an ethnoterritorial base, and if not strong, it is likely not to have had nor ever to get such a base. Without such an ethnoterritory, the group is hindered in pressing its claims for further prerogatives, claims for greater authority for the group in the general system.

A group that is growing in numbers or vigor will be pressing for greater autonomy, i.e., local authority, for its ethnoterritory if it has one. Such is the case for the Muslim Albanians of Kosovo in Yugoslavia and for the major Muslim groups in the U.S.S.R. If a Muslim interest group does not have an ethnoterritorial base, to the extent that it is increasing in numbers or vigor, it will seek to gain one. The strongest such case recently has been the quest of the Soviet Crimean Tartars for reconstitution of their former homeland. Soviet authorities have forbidden them to return to the Crimean Peninsula since World War II, charging them with complicity with the German invaders. Official permission to return, should it come, would indicate some acknowledgement of the legitimate claims of the Crimean Tartars for some degree of group autonomy.

In general, Table 9.1 indicates a fact that should be underscored, that is, the situation of Muslims in communist nations is tightly connected with ethnic conditions in these countries. This is not surprising since religion and ethnicity are usually closely intertwined. In addition, as a way of life as much as a pure theological system, Islam always presents ethnic issues along with religious ones (Pipes 1983, 89–93). However, they are entangled in extremely complex ways for Muslims in these countries.

Regimes and Nations

Though all nominally communist, the four nations in this study are very different in their applications of Marxist principles and their status in the socialist world and the world at large. The Soviet Union, of course, is by far the largest of the four in geographic, economic, population size, and international political power. Being the oldest communist nation and a modern superpower, it serves as a reference point for all other communist regimes. In foreign affairs, it dominates Bulgaria but has not been able to keep Yugoslavia and Albania under its wing. Yugoslavia is a leader of the Non-Aligned Movement and enjoys intense economic, political, and social relations with both communist and non-communist countries. Albania, though apparently undergoing some significant changes since the 1985 death of its long-term Stalinist dictator, Enver Hoxha, remains aloof and isolated from most of the rest of the world. Its biggest trading partner is Yugoslavia; the Albanian economy is the smallest and weakest of the four.

The four regimes are all centralized and bureaucratized, but Yugoslavia has permitted a considerable amount of devolution of authority to its regional levels and the regional elites. This has been necessitated by the strong nationalistic differences between, in particular, the Orthodox Serbs and the Catholic Croats. In a certain sense, the Muslims, who are concentrated in the Republic of Bosnia-Herzegovina and the Autonomous Province of Kosovo, have themselves gained a portion of autonomy as a result of the generalization of concessions made to the stronger Christian nationalities. However, the Serbo-croatian-speaking Bosnian Muslims share such autonomy as they have with co-resident Christian Serbs and Croats, with whom there is an ongoing, though not clear cut, contest for power (Lockwood 1979; Pipes 1983, 275–77).

Though it had been thought that these Muslims might assimilate into either Serb or Croat nationality, or adopt a simple "Yugoslav" ethnic identity, by the late 1960s the regime came to recognize the category "Bosnian Muslim." The Bosnian party had its own reasons to promote this idea. "By expressing its support for the existence of a distinct Muslim nation at this time," Burg (1983, 40–41) states, "the Bosnian party leadership can be seen as attempting to defuse the competition for Muslim allegiance between Serbs and Croats and, by doing so, mobilizing the political support of the Muslim cultural, intellectual, and even religious leadership."

Though some Bosnian Muslims may be losing their Muslim ethnic tie (Meier 1983), in general they seem to be well-established and largely accommodated to the Yugoslav situation. Ramet (1984) outlines a Muslim revival among the Bosnians, and indicates the sources of some friction between the leaders and the regime. However, relations between the Bosnian Muslim religious leaders and the regime are largely stable—there is even some evidence of official support for the Muslim leaders—and Muslims have taken a significant role in the Bosnian party, comprising some one-third of its members (Burg 1983; Irwin 1984).

The second largest groups of Muslim in Yugoslavia—Albanians—find themselves frequently embroiled in a more difficult and conflict-ridden quest for autonomy and self-determination. Nevertheless, there are some avenues through which the struggle for power may be more or less legitimately pursued within established institutions, especially because this group is concentrated in Kosovo, an Autonomous Province within the Republic of Serbia. In 1981, seventy-eight percent of the Kosovo population was Albanian (Baskin 1983). However, Kosovo is the poorest region of Yugoslavia.

Along with demands for greater economic investment in the region and better management by the authorities, the Kosovars have frequently demanded greater autonomy for Kosovo in the form of republic status. They sense that the central authorities view them as second-class citizens not deserving of the status of an autonomous republic. On the extreme, some Albanians have a vision of a "Greater Albania" in which not only current Albania and Kosovo would be united, but so too would portions of Macedonia and Montenegro that have large groups of Albanian residents. These nationalist sentiments are complicated by their connections with the international interaction between Yugoslavia and Albania, though it is not certain that the Albanian leadership is completely happy with the unrest on its borders. Indeed, Enver Hoxha, the late Albanian leader, was on record as calling for republic status for Kosovo *within* Yugoslavia (Baskin 1983).

Since strenuous and sometimes violent outbursts in 1981, Kosovo has been "subject to combined military and police rule under the control of the federal authorities" (Meier 1983, 47). Given the depressed economy of the province, the central government of Yugoslavia has also declared Kosovo to be a special concern of the whole country, not just the focus of local efforts for socioeconomic improvement nor exclusively a Serbian Republic problem. This allegedly means that "The whole country is to take part in an investment program of job-creating industries, inducements to private agriculture, and family-planning education to curb the birth rate" (Bourne 1986b). The attempts by the Kosovo Albanians to gain greater autonomy have also been accompanied by the rise of considerable Serbian unrest aimed against additional Albanian prerogative (Bourne 1986a).

In Yugoslavia, the somewhat decentralized state structure allows for the existence of regional units partially coextensive with ethnic groups. Though they are not formally ethnoterritories (Meier 1983), for Muslim groups, the state structures of Bosnia-Herzegovina and Kosovo provide forums in which ethnic interests can be pursued, even if conflictually as in Kosovo. This is especially possible because the Yugoslav party—formally, the League of Communists of Yugoslavia—is less controlling of other institutions than is the case for the communist parties in the other countries, and also because the party itself includes ethnic divisions of some consequence.

Perhaps numbering nearly as many as Albanian Muslims in Yugoslavia are Muslim Gypsies. However, they apparently pose no special problem for the regime religiously, adapting fairly well to whatever circumstances they encounter. Weekes (1984, 306) notes that the largest Gypsy settlement in the world, almost totally Muslim, is located near Skopje in Yugoslav Macedonia.

The final group of Yugoslav Muslims are of Turkish background. Scattered around the Muslim areas of settlement, they may be adopting the general "Yugoslav Muslim" identification, given its generally non-problematic quality.

All in all, the lesson to be learned from the Yugoslav example seems to be that Islam per se need not be a problem for a communist regime. Granted, Yugoslavia is a peculiar communist regime, and it has no peer among the other mature regimes. Nevertheless, the option it suggests may be one taken up by new Marxist regimes trying to find a means to deal with their situations. In Yugoslavia, many Muslims are active in public life. The problems of Yugoslavia that have been mentioned are not, in the end, religious problems. Instead, they are problems associated with nationalism and national aspirations. It is interesting to note that in a major article on the "crisis in Kosovo" (Baskin 1983), not once is religion, Muslim or Christian, brought up. Instead, the crisis is attributed entirely to ethno-nationalist, socioeconomic, and purely political causes. Surely there is a religious substrate to the problems of Kosovo but it seems clear that this is not the central issue. Muslim religion is much more central in the maintenance of Bosnian Muslim identity and its development. However, so far the Bosnian situation has been fairly manageable for the authorities.

Neither in Albania nor in Bulgaria are there even quasi-legitimate avenues through which to pursue Muslim national or ethnic autonomy. In neither case is there any institutionalized pattern to seek decentralized authority. There are no Muslim centered ethnoterritories upon which a struggle for localized authority can be built, nor do the regimes permit any significant degree of decentralized authority in any case.

There is relatively little information available about Muslims in these two countries, but a general outline is clear. In Albania, the two major Muslim groups, Sunnis and Bektashis, neither of which were attached to any ethnic identity other than Albanian, had engaged in strong cooperative relationships for many years before World War II. Already established before the war, according to Irwin, was the "secular control of the Muslim hierarchy" (1984, 212). After the war, the communist leadership almost immediately seized all church properties and, accusing major religious leaders of collaboration with the enemy and then imprisoning or killing them, installed a compliant set of religious officials. The constitution guaranteed freedom of religion until it was altered in 1976, but religious practice was effectively prohibited from 1967 onward (Tonnies 1982). Muslims were isolated from co-religionists outside the communist bloc who might provide support for any form of resistance to developments.

Though not subject to quite so draconian measures, Muslims in Bulgaria have found themselves the object of a long-term campaign of "Bulgarization."

The apparent goal is to create in Bulgaria a "single-nationality state"—"something southeastern Europe has not known in its 3,000 years of recorded history" (Binder 1985, 158). The regime has pursued this goal in several ways. First, it has both forced (in 1950–51) and encouraged (since 1968) its Turkish minority to return to Turkey. Large numbers have done so (Irwin 1984). Second, for those who stayed, whether Turkish or Slavic Muslim, that is, so-called Pomak, Muslims were forced to change their names to Slavic forms. Pomaks have been gradually forced to change their names for many years, at least since 1970 (Irwin 1984). More recently, ethnic Albanians, Gypsies, and Armenians have been compelled to do the same. A campaign to change Turkish Muslim names to Bulgarian names was carried out during 1984–85 (Binder 1985). Now there is an attempt by the Bulgarian authorities to claim that all Bulgarians came from the same non-Turkish stock, that is, that the Turks never existed in Bulgaria (Kamm 1986).

The Chief Mufti of Bulgaria has claimed that the charges of coercion in connection with these name changes are false. He contends that all the changes were made voluntarily. Furthermore, he claims that these name changes in no way indicate any pressure against the faith ("Bulgarian Chief Mufti Defends State Policy" 1986). Nevertheless, Amnesty International charges that at least 100 ethnic Turks were killed resisting the name changes in 1984–85 and that 250 people were arrested.

In many regards, the Soviet case is the most complex to characterize overall, if for no other reason than that there are no fewer than thirty-eight separate Muslim nationalities within the borders of the U.S.S.R. The ethnoterritorial structure of the Soviet state has provided these groups with a pseudo-legitimate basis upon which to seek national autonomy within the federal system. In fact, many of them have an ethnoterritory bearing their names, whether simply a so-called "Autonomous Oblast" (A.O., e.g., Adygei Autonomous Oblast) or "Autonomous Soviet Socialist Republic" (A.S.S.R., e.g., Karakalpak A.S.S.R.) or even a regular "Soviet Socialist Republic" (S.S.R., e.g., Tadzhik S.S.R.).

Overriding this seeming boon, however, is the strong centralization of the Communist Party of the Soviet Union (CPSU) which places Slavic nationals, and especially Russians, at the pinnacles of power in virtually every area of the society and economy. With this system, even local affairs are under the general supervision of the central elite—ultimately, the Moscow elite—which includes very few ethnic Muslims. Those who are included are subject to the strict discipline of the party in all matters.

Regime Policy and Practice

Whatever the possibilities for local autonomy and the devolution of authority to the Muslim communities, in these four cases the communist regimes all attempt to preserve for themselves an overarching monopoly of power. Extra-party initiatives must be pursued either clandestinely (in Albania) or within very stringent limits (in Bulgaria and the U.S.S.R.) or within the regulated environment of the party-dominated order (in Yugoslavia). Interestingly, it is in Yugoslavia, with the loosest structure, that the largest and most disruptive Muslim protests have occurred.

Except in Albania, ethnic Muslims can pursue strictly secular goals through the party structure as members or as non-party voluntary activists. In this way, they might, for example, seek the preservation of cultural artifacts such as mosques or madrassahs or ethnic art and literature, or they might push for the development of ethnic language media, school curricula, and the like. They cannot legitimately press for the expansion of religious prerogatives.

Regime policies regarding Islamic religion vary greatly in our four cases, with Albania unquestionably having the most restrictive policy. All religious activities, whether Muslim or Christian, have been banned there since the late 1960s. By contrast, neighboring Yugoslavia evidences a comparative openness toward religious activities. Nevertheless, since the 1970s, there has been a tightening of the regulative measures and several instances of direct interference by the state in Muslim affairs. In addition, the number of Muslims in positions of authority has been reduced. This pattern seems to have grown, in the first place, as the impending death of President Tito threatened the breakup of national unity. Muslim nationalist agitation has risen in the midst of the relative liberalism of the regime, and the fragility of the ethnoterritorially structured state has forced the regime to clamp down on any movements that seek regional or ethnic autonomy. More than in any other country, Yugoslavia preserves the multinational separatism and tensions that have been the persistent bane of Balkan state formation efforts.

Bulgaria's situation has certain parallels with that of Yugoslavia, but its regime is not so liberal nor its national unity so fragile as Yugoslavia's. There is no ethnoterritorial political unit dominated numerically by Muslims nor any significant Muslim political authorities. While the state has reached a modus operandi with the national Bulgarian Orthodox Church, an institution that is seen as preserving and stimulating Bulgarian national interests, it has pursued a much more negative policy toward Islam and Muslim believers. Besides the campaign of name-changing discussed above, between 1956–65 there was a major reduction in the number of clergy, and Pomak religious institutions have been suppressed to some degree ever since.

Soviet policy regarding Muslims is conditioned by a range of concerns that are not found so evident in the policies of the other three nations. First, the Soviet regime is very sensitive to the feelings of Muslim leaders in the Third World, and this sensitivity affects domestic policy toward Muslims. This sensitivity arises insofar as the U.S.S.R. aspires to find new clients and trading partners in this part of the globe. However, the issue goes beyond international trade and diplomacy since the Soviets also claim to be, and are seen to be, the exemplar of the value of a Marxist development strategy. Third World leaders, it is correctly assumed, are observing the treatment of Muslims in the U.S.S.R. and drawing conclusions regarding the compatibility of the Marxist patterns with Islamic traditions. Being aware of this "surveillance" from abroad, the Soviet leaders attempt to create a good impression by both making some sincere efforts to address the needs of the traditional Muslim population and by generating propaganda that touts improvements in life among Muslims. As a political, military, and economic superpower, the Soviets have a different perspective on this question than do the regimes of the Albanians, Yugoslavs, or Bulgarians, who stand more as peers than as real or potential patron states for Third World nations.

Historical and geographical characteristics of the Soviet situation also make it distinct from the other three. Historically, most of the Muslim populations of the U.S.S.R. were incorporated into the Russian Empire by the middle of the last century both for reasons of imperium and for the alleged protection of these populations from the imperialistic designs of southern neighbors, especially Turkey and Iran. Though perhaps given disingenuously, the protection provided by the Russians was welcomed in some quarters, and, indeed, there were certain mutual accommodations between the Russians and the Muslims that facilitated the situation for the Muslims. In the other three nations there was neither the imperialistic conquest nor the protective accommodation found in the early Russian situation.

Even so, the Soviets squandered rare Muslim goodwill toward Russians and any possible goodwill toward the Bolshevik Revolution when, in the 1920s and early 1930s, Muslim elites were decimated, and all national communist allies among the Muslim groups were crushed militarily (Bennigsen and Wimbush 1979). This set the stage for the very ambivalent attitude of the Muslim peoples toward the Soviet regime today.

The situation of its Muslim population is a major issue for the Soviet leadership both because of its sheer demographic size, numbering nearly fifty million, and because of the real segregation and regional distinctiveness of this group. In short, to treat this population badly would be to create problems for a very large segment of the nation both numerically and regionally. Since most of the Muslim population is located in the four Central Asian republics, Uzbekistan, Turkmenistan, Tadzhikistan and Kirgizia, plus contiguous Kazakhstan and Azerbaidzhan, this region has required a special policy of economic development coupled with a special political adaptation. At least since World War II, this Muslim region (which henceforth shall be referred to simply as Central Asia) has represented significant development potential for the U.S.S.R. It has valuable natural resources and a population surplus available for induction into the labor force and the military. With the highest fertility in the U.S.S.R., its population represents a great reserve upon which the Soviet economy might draw as it needs labor for its growth. On the other hand, this population is not easily moved into the Soviet economic mainstream, and this is one of the great dilemmas facing Soviet planners (Rywkin 1982).

All of these characteristics of the Soviet Muslim situation suggest its unique dimensions. The importance of this population in the thinking of Soviet leaders has seemingly protected it from excessively strong antireligious measures over the last two decades or so. Hence, in strictly religious terms, the regime has interfered less in the situation than it has in the situations of Christian or Jewish groups. Though a considerable amount of antireligious propaganda aimed at Islamic populations has been published, comparatively little direct action against Islam has been carried out in recent years. Bennigsen (1984b) documents an increase in antireligious propaganda among Muslims since the Iranian Revolution and the Afghanistan invasion.

Co-opting the Muslim "Church"

Elsewhere, I have described how communist regimes maintain certain clear limitations on religious activities, sponsor antireligious propaganda, and support other forms of antireligious pressure. However, I have contended that the major thrust in regime policy today is toward co-opting the religious groups into support of goals being pursued by the regime itself. While the early attempts of the regimes to wipe out religion cannot be denied, the more recent way to deal with this allegedly outmoded and negative phenomenon is to manage it so that, first, it does not grow too strong, and, second, its energies and resources are put to what the regime sees as useful purposes (Pankhurst 1983, 1986). Except for the Albanian case, this pattern seems to apply to Islamic groups as well as Christian and Jewish ones.

Such a form of "management" of a religious group by a communist regime depends upon the regime interrelating in specific ways with the structure of the religious group itself. Most typically, the regime attempts to co-opt the highest leadership of the group and thus control the hierarchical lines of authority of the group. If a group has a weak or non-existent hierarchy, it is more difficult to manage in this way. In such a situation, the regime may try to influence the religious group to establish a stronger vertical structure of authority, as the Soviet regime did with the Baptist church after World War II, for example. If this approach does not work adequately, the regime is forced to be more inventive in its dealings with a religious group. The latter is the case for the relationships of communist regimes with several Protestant groups, and with virtually all Muslim groups.

Muslim groups possess certain structural characteristics that have a great impact upon the means regimes can use to manage them. Besides the general lack of hierarchical authority patterns, there is also a strong horizontal integration of Muslim groups on the local level because of the strong emphasis upon family, kin, and community relations that is sanctified by the religion. Furthermore, there is no denominational structure that would divide a Muslim community in the way Christian communities are divided by denominational affiliations, nor do the individual mosques represent the divisions of class, race, or even theological interpretation that are typical among separate parishes or congregations of Christians, especially within Protestantism.

Figure 9.1 attempts to portray these and other differences between the general Christian variant of relations with communist regimes and the Muslim variant. Each variant summarizes *tendencies* in structural patterns of relationships and is, therefore, more an ideal type than an empirical type. Dark, solid lines indicate strong bonds between actors while lighter dotted lines indicate relatively weaker bonds.

Starting at the bottom of each variant, the solid line across local Muslim communities indicates the strong horizontal integration just discussed, while the dotted line across congregations and parishes indicates the generally greater diversity of specific groups among Christians at this level. In many cases, the local level is not only integrated by family, kin, and community ties, but also by ethnic identities. This is true for many Christian groups (e.g., Armenians, Orthodox Bulgarians, Catholic Poles) and for virtually all Muslims. To the extent it is the case, the regime must cope with the additional set of ethnic variables as it tries to penetrate to the local level of religious groups in order to exert influence there.

The review of cases so far indicates that ethnic ties and religious identifications reinforce each other in all the Muslim groups in the four countries. However, the groups differ as to the effective focus for ethnic ties. The Muslims of Bulgaria do not have an ethnoterritory that can serve as such a focus and are therefore relatively weaker than the Soviet and Yugoslavian Muslims who have ethnoterritories. The Muslims of Albania might want to claim the whole of Albania as their ethnoterritory, but the regime has effectively neutralized this desire through terror and, to some undetermined degree, through defining all religions as the agents of invaders, ruling classes, and oppressors of the true Albanians. In denouncing religion in 1967, Enver Hoxha stated that "The history of our people demonstrates clearly how much suffering, distress, bloodshed, and oppression have been visited upon our people by religion" (as quoted by Irwin 1984, 212–13).

Just above the bottom line of each variant in Figure 9.1 are diagonal lines indicating the relationship between the individuals of the local communities and the clergy. Though some local leaders of Muslim communities gain considerable followings, the general pattern is one of a loose association between the populace and the local and regional leaders of the faith. There is no official clerical status in the Islamic faith, and there is little by way of a hierarchy of authority in the relations between the clergy and the public. Leaders are hon-

FIGURE 9.1
The Structure of co-optative Relationships Between Communist Regimes
and Christian Churches and Between Communist Regimes and Muslim Groups

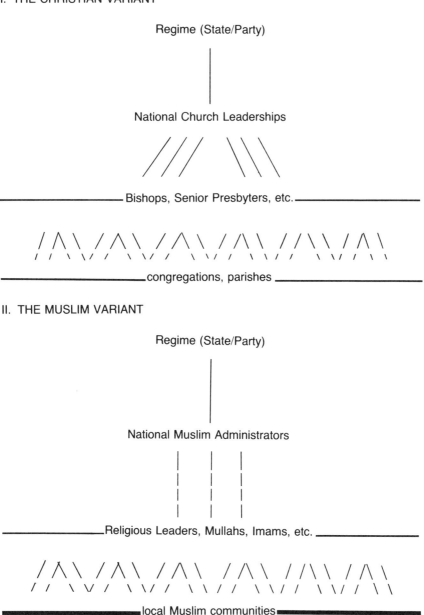

I. THE CHRISTIAN VARIANT

Regime (State/Party)

National Church Leaderships

Bishops, Senior Presbyters, etc.

congregations, parishes

II. THE MUSLIM VARIANT

Regime (State/Party)

National Muslim Administrators

Religious Leaders, Mullahs, Imams, etc.

local Muslim communities

ored for their generally acknowledged wisdom, not for their consecration or church sanction. With the latter, Christian clergy have a stronger status in their churches and may give certain kinds of authoritative directives to their congregations. For this reason, the bonds between the public and the clergy are seen as stronger, and are marked by the heavier and darker lines in Variant I.

This does not, of course, mean that Muslims hold their clergy in disrespect. To the contrary, they are generally ascribed great honor. However, such honor does not carry the active direction that many forms of Christian clergy may exercise over behavior. However, there is a variant of Muslim structure that is apparently becoming increasingly important in exerting an active influence upon followers. This is the Sufi tradition, in which one becomes an adept-follower of a leader and engages in a particular discipline of prayer and other activities (Bennigsen 1984a, 1984b). Broxup (1981, 1983), Critchlow (1984), and other writers have noted the rise in the U.S.S.R. of "Parallel Islam," that is, the unofficial Islam of the Sufi brotherhoods. They believe that it represents a major revival of Islamic faith and a promise of increased strength amongst Muslim groups in the future in the Soviet Union. Though there is some Sufi activity among Bosnian Muslims, Sufism is prevalent among Muslim Albanians in Yugoslavia and may contribute to their autonomist tendencies. As a form of strengthening the bonds between the people and local religious leaders, Sufism may represent an important defense for a Muslim group in a stiff interest group competition.

Moving up to the next higher level in the diagrams, we note that local and regional Muslim leaders are only loosely bound to each other. This is largely the outcome of the non-clerical orientation of most forms of Islam. The leaders tend not to have the kinds of strong organizational interrelationships that are typical among Christian leaders as, for example, between a priest and his bishop or between two priests in the same denomination who meet regularly to review common problems. The horizontal line for "Bishops, Senior Presbyters, etc." might have been darkened except for the already mentioned tendency among Christians to emphasize denominational or ecclesiastical differences among themselves.

The next structural layer is that of the national leaderships of the faiths. The bonds between the regional/local leaders and the national leaders demonstrate a major and consequential difference between the Christian patterns and the Muslim patterns of church-state relations. The theologically justified hierarchical patterns of Christian groups tend to give the national leadership considerable influence over regional and local affairs, and they tend to stimulate a great deal of interaction between the national level and the regional/local leaderships. Hence, the bonds are portrayed as dark, solid lines. The fact that they are diagonal signifies that they represent institutionalized forms of hierarchical relations within the churches.

On the other hand, the Muslim bonds between regional/local leaders and national leaders normally have no such official function nor is the interaction, apparently, nearly as intense as that among the Christian leaders at this level. Thus, the bonds for the Muslim variant are drawn lightly with dots and are vertical and few in number.

Furthermore, it is only with great caution that national leaders among Muslims in communist lands should be mentioned at all. Muslims do not build national Islamic churches, instead they seem to develop national communities of Muslims. That is, the leaders that emerge are not typically given special religious sanction for their leadership. Instead, they enjoy such prestige and honor as they may get by dint of their special personal characteristics and reputation for wisdom and holiness. Such a leader may garner some official functions incidentally, but national officials of Islamic groups may not enjoy such real leadership authority over the people. The individuals usually cited as national Islamic leaders, the chief muftis, are, in fact, essentially government officials. They are to oversee "church"-state affairs for Muslims, but otherwise they have little religious sanction for their positions.

Conclusion

In both Christian and Muslim cases, the bonds between national leaderships and communist regimes is strong. In fact, this is the first and most important part of the co-optative process from the point of view of the regimes. They seek to co-opt the national level leaderships and through them to co-opt the regional and local leaders and, subsequently, through them co-opt the local communities of the faithful. Other things being equal, in a hierarchically organized Christian church this strategy works more or less well as the regime's influence is diffused down the system of clear and solid bonds throughout the church.

In the case of the Muslims, however, it should be apparent why this system of co-optative relationship is much more difficult to effect among Muslims under communism. The national-to-local-level bonds are non-institutionalized and weak. They are not suitable carriers of influence from the regime down to the local communities of believers. Furthermore, even if they were, the strong horizontal integration of Muslims through family, kin, and community ties would counteract any such influence that was not consistent with these localized interests. For these reasons, the co-optation of Muslims by the four communist regimes I have surveyed is generally much more difficult than the co-optation of Christians. As a result, any efforts to influence Muslims must take a different tack than efforts used to influence Christians. What working agreements are finally reached and institutionalized in each country may take intriguing forms.

178 JERRY G. PANKHURST

References

Barrett, David B., ed. 1982. *World Christian Encyclopedia: A Comparative Study of Churches and Religions in the Modern World, A.D. 1900–2000*. New York: Oxford University Press.

Baskin, Mark. 1983. "Crisis in Kosovo." *Problems of Communism* 32: 61–74.

Bellah, Robert. 1970. *Beyond Belief: Essays on Religion in a Post-Traditional World*. New York: Harper and Row.

Bennigsen, Alexandre. 1984a. "Islam and the USSR." *Geopolitique* 7: 53–60.

Bennigsen, Alexandre. 1984b. "Mullahs, Mujahidin and Soviet Muslims." *Problems of Communism* 32: 28–44.

Bennigsen, Alexandre A. and S. Enders Wimbush. 1979. *Muslim National Communism in the Soviet Union: A Revolutionary Strategy for the Colonial World*. Chicago: University of Chicago Press.

Binder, David. 1985. "Going Back: Bulgaria, 20 Years Later." *The New York Times Magazine* (December 8), 154–64.

Bourne, Eric. 1986a. "Tensions among ethnic groups in Yugoslavia begin to boil over." *Christian Science Monitor* (July 28), 10.

Bourne, Eric. 1986b. "Economic woes worsen ethnic tensions in Yugoslavia." *Christian Science Monitor* (July 29), 11.

Broxup, Marie. 1983. "Recent Developments in Soviet Islam." *Religion in Communist Lands* 11: 31–35.

Broxup, Marie. 1981. "Islam and Atheism in the North Caucasus." *Religion in Communist Lands* 9: 40–49.

"Bulgarian Chief Mufti Defends State Policy." 1986. *Keston News Service* 241 (January 9): 17–18.

Burg, Stephen L. 1983. "The Political Integration of Yugoslavia's Muslims: Determinants of Success and Failure." *The Carl Beck Papers in Russian and East European Studies*, Paper No. 203.

Critchlow, James. 1984. "Islam and Nationalism in Soviet Central Asia." In *Religion and Nationalism in Soviet and East European Politics*, Pedro Ramet, ed. Durham, NC: Duke University Press, 104–120.

Dahrendorf, Ralf. 1959. *Class and Class Conflict in Industrial Society*. Stanford, CA: Stanford University Press.

Irwin, Zachary T. 1984. "The Fate of Islam in the Balkans: A Comparison of Four State Policies." In *Religion and Nationalism in Soviet and East European Politics*, Pedro Ramet, ed. Durham, NC: Duke University Press.

Kamm, Henry. 1986. "New Line in Bulgaria: What Turks? Where?" *New York Times* (April 20): 12.

Lockwood, W. G. 1979. "Living Legacy of Ottoman Empire: The Serbo-Croatian Speaking Moslems of Bosnia-Herzegovina." In *The Mutual Effects of the Islamic and Judeo-Christian Worlds: The East European Pattern*, Abraham Ascher, Tibor Alasi-Kun and Bela Kiraly, eds. Brooklyn: Brooklyn College Press, 209–25.

Meier, Viktor. 1983. "Yugoslavia's National Question." *Problems of Communism* 32: 47–60.

Morrison, Peter. 1985. "Islam in China: An Update." *Religion in Communist Lands* 13: 152–55.

Pankhurst, Jerry G. 1986. "A Comparative Perspective on Religion and Regime in Eastern Europe and the Soviet Union." In *Prophetic Religions and Politics,* Jeffrey K. Hadden and Anson Shupe, eds. New York: Paragon House, 272–306.

Pankhurst, Jerry G. 1983. "Religion and Political Process in State Atheist Nations." In *Religion and Communist Society,* Dennis J. Dunn, ed. Berkeley, CA: Berkeley Slavic Specialities, 45–66.

Pipes, Daniel. 1983. In the Path of God: Islam and Political Power. New York: Basic Books.

Ramet, Pedro. 1984. "Religion and Nationalism in Yugoslavia." In *Religion and Nationalism in Soviet and East European Politics,* Pedro Ramet, ed. Durham, NC: Duke University Press, 149–69.

Rywkin, Michael. 1982. *Moscow's Muslim Challenge: Soviet Central Asia.* Armonk, NY: M. E. Sharpe.

Shaw, Ezel Kural. 1975. "The Ottoman Aspects of *Pax Ottomanica:* The Political, Practical and Psychological Aspects of *Pax Ottomanica.*" In *Tolerance and Movements of Religious Dissent in Eastern Europe.* East European Monographs, No. XIII, Bela K. Kiraly, ed. Boulder, CO: East European Quarterly, 165–82.

Tonnies, Bernhard. 1982. "Religious Persecution in Albania." *Religion in Communist Lands* 10: 242–55.

Weekes, Richard V., ed. 1984. Muslim Peoples: A World Ethnographic Survey, 2nd ed. 2 vols. Westport, CT: Greenwood Press.

10

The Roots of Hindu-Muslim Conflict in India: British Colonialism and Religious Revival

K. L. Seshagiri Rao

THE MEETING OF EAST AND WEST in India under the British colonial rule (1803–1947) precipitated a common reaction of the Hindus and Muslims against British domination in the form of religious revivalist movements. India associated Western culture and religion with foreign imperialism. Hindus responded by strengthening their religious traditions through a return to more stringent practices. The Muslims ruled the country from the twelfth century onwards until the British defeated and displaced them towards the end of the eighteenth century. They feared the influence of foreign ideologies and culture on their youth. They attempted to intensify Muslim solidarity. This revivalism engendered a strong demand for self-government in the people.

Revivalism had both good and bad effects though; its most harmful effect was the strong separatist tendencies it caused. Hindus believed that India was their mother country, and rightfully belonged to them. The attempts of the Muslim conquerors to suppress Hinduism did not succeed greatly. Hinduism was firmly entrenched in the culture, and the Hindus constituted a majority of the population. They looked back to the golden age of Hinduism. The Muslims also desired a return to previous conditions, those that had existed when Muslims ruled the country before the British took control. With each religion looking to the past, pride was installed in the hearts of both

180

Hindus and Muslims, resulting in ever-increasing differences between the two communities.

These religious considerations played and continue to play a major role in India. The tense relationship between Hindus and Muslims has long been one of India's major problems. So keen is this problem that it has been said that "the ultimate problem of India is the reconciliation of these two opposing religious groups." Bitter hatreds have gone into the hearts of both communities; they are deep rooted, and stem from a combination of historical, political, religious, and socioeconomic factors. During long periods this bitterness may fall into abeyance among the masses, but sooner or later, a wave of fanatical hatred seems to come back in terrible forms.

The religious causes were the most often immediately responsible for Hindu-Muslim tension. Hinduism is a non-evangelistic, inclusive religious group, rich and ornate in symbolism and religious worship. Islam is evangelistic, exclusive, and austere in its monotheistic devotion. Too much distrust existed between the two groups to permit harmonious relations.

Muslims would slay a cow on certain Muslim festivals, but the cow is sacred in the Hindu religion. The Hindus performed *arati*, involving loud religious music when passing a Muslim mosque where Muslim prayer required silence. Hindus and Muslims lived apart from each other; the Muslims did not fit into Hindu caste society.

One of the most important causes of a widened gulf between the two communities was the introduction by the British government of a system of separate representation of Muslims in legislatures. Though there was a demand for it, the demand was in fact instigated from above. Accordingly, Muslims could stand for election and be elected by Muslim electorates only. This was completely opposed to the democratic principle and the process of unification and integration that had been going on silently in the country for centuries. The separate electorates intensified rivalries between Hindus and Muslims, and created disruption; barriers were created where none existed previously, and the Muslim community was further isolated. The whole fabric of political and social life became vitiated and religion took on political overtones.

Hindu–Muslim unity was a theme most dear to India's great political and religious leader Mahatma Gandhi. Time and again, he placed his life in the balance in an effort to bring about a real peace between these two communities. He was a Hindu reformer who preached and worked for the rights of Muslims. He sought to break down the barriers that kept their hearts apart. His efforts towards reconciliation of the followers of the two religions were misunderstood. He was assassinated by a misguided, fundamentalist Hindu who considered him to be a roadblock to the promotion of Hindu interests.

Gandhi pursued the freedom of his country through nonviolent means. He felt that if a country is torn by internal turmoil, it can never aspire to progress or independence. He saw a great political advantage in the unity of Hindus and Muslims, and felt that it was the way to a successful national feeling as well as the catalyst that would inspire the country to independence. He believed that both Hindus and Muslims must work together for everlasting freedom of India. He sought understanding and friendship with the Muslims: "I was seeking the friendship of good Mussalmans, and was eager to understand the Mussalman mind through contact with their purest and most patriotic representatives."[1]

In Gandhi's mind, *swaraj* or self-rule was invariably associated with Hindu–Muslim unity. He felt that India could not be a nation when Hindus and Muslims fought each other. He felt that they should "shed enmity and accept heart-friendship as an eternal factor of national life."[2] He thought that it would be "irreligious" for Hindus and Muslims to perpetrate violence upon one another. He wanted their energy to be saved to free themselves from British domination.

Gandhi was most successful in joining Hindus and Muslims in the *Khilafat* campaign urging the British to protect the legitimate interests of the Sultan of Turkey. The support of the movement by the Congress directed against Britain's "betrayal of Islam" was of paramount importance to Hindu–Muslim unity. Gandhi espoused the cause and in 1919 suggested direct action against the British because of their refusal of Khilafat demands. The whole of India opposed the regime set up in the dismantled Ottoman empire. Gandhi evoked Hindu sympathy for the cause of Turkey, and in so doing provoked Muslim thankfulness for Hindu support. Gandhi emphatically required that the Hindus ask nothing in return for this support, such as the cessation of the Muslim slaughter of the cow. The masses of Muslims, who had been slow so far to support any nationalistic movement, came forward enthusiastically and joined the Non-Cooperation Movement for Indian independence. It gave both Hindus and Muslims a brief unity in their struggle against the British during 1919–1922.

Gandhi suspended the noncooperation movement in 1922, when some acts of violence erupted in the movement. He was arrested and sentenced to six years in prison. The anti-British Muslim leaders, the Ali brothers, were given two years in prison.

The Khilafat movement lost its cause when the Sultan of Turkey declared that he was no more the Spiritual head of the worldwide Community of the Muslims. After this, the Muslim leaders of India began to speak a different language; they gave up the idea that they could live only under the sufference of either the Hindus or the British. So the sense of unity between the leaders of the Hindu and Muslim communities quickly disappeared. Actually, the great masses of both the communities had never really shared the bonds of unity. Whether out of ignorance or steeped in traditional prejudice, the great majority of two peoples continued in the path of suspicion and hatred. After

1922, the separatist tendencies became augmented with increasing mass re-action.

According to British records, the first Hindu–Muslim riot took place in 1809 at Benares; since then sometimes sporadically, sometimes for longer periods, trouble had been breaking out whenever some irritant to communal feeling cropped up. Only four years before the Moplah rising, in September 1917, there had been mass attacks upon Muslims in Bihar and Utta Pradesh.

The Moplah rebellion had started among the Muslim peasants living in the Malabar region (presently Kerala State) against the Hindu money-lenders and landlords of the area. These riots resulted in a Hindu reactionary feeling causing open hatred of each other. In Kohat, in the Northwest frontier province, the Hindu minorities suffered greatly. Gandhi undertook a twenty-one day fast; he felt that he had not tried hard enough to bring about unity. His fast was to ask God for strength to try harder, and "to expiate his own guilt."

The fast, however, failed to unite the Hindus and Muslims. Gandhi and Shaukat Ali were appointed as a committee of two to investigate the riots and the conditions that gave rise to them. Gandhi arrived at the conclusion that there was no provocation on the part of the Hindus, while Shaukat Ali felt that there was fault on the Hindu side.

Muslims, in general, felt that a unified India with a central government would not treat them fairly. Sir Muhammad Iqbal made this point in his Presidential address to the All-India Muslim League in December 1930: "Is it possible to retain Islam as an ethical ideal and to reject it as a policy in favor of national politics in which religious attitude is not permitted to play a part?"[3] Then Iqbal further observed that the violent Hindu–Muslim feuds might expand to a civil war. He suggested that "in these circumstances, it is obvious that the only way to a peaceful India is a redistribution of the country on the lines of racial, religious, and linguistic affinities."[4] Other Muslims began to see the need for the "Islamic" country, and even Jinnah, a strong advocate for united India at the time, was discouraged by the Hindu attitude.

Muhammad Ali Jinnah entered public life as private secretary to Dadobhai Naoroji of the Indian National Congress. Jinnah represented the moderates in the Indian National Congress. At the time, he felt that Hindu–Muslim unity was the only path to independence, and he shunned the Muslim League and its sectarian goals. He eventually joined the Muslim League in 1913, but he made it affirm that its primary goal was independence of India. Although he recognized the fears of the Muslim population, he felt that through constitutional rights, the safety of Islamic minority could be assured in free India. As late as 1924, Jinnah observed: "The advent of foreign rule and its continuance in India is primarily due to the fact that the people of India, particularly the Hindus and the Muslims, are not united and do not sufficiently trust each other. . . . I am almost inclined to say that India will get dominion responsible government the day Hindus and Muslims are united."

Jinnah shifted positions around 1930; he no longer maintained the philosophy of unity between Hindus and Muslims. Regarding the motives for such a change, speculations have ranged from his concern for Muslim minority to self-interest and envy and jealousy at Gandhi's popularity. In any case, Jinnah expressed his new philosophy thus: "We must think of the interests of our community . . . the Hindus and Muslims must be organized separately, and once they are organized, they will understand each other better." He captured control of the Muslim League and adopted a platform calling for the creation of the separate state of Pakistan.

The plan to create separate nations out of India was launched in 1933. Gandhi thought that "conception of nations based on religion was absurd and repugnant." But a majority of Muslims under the leadership of Mohammed Ali Jinnah came to feel that the Hindus, who composed a three-to-one majority, had no interest in the rights of Muslims, and the only way these rights could be secured was through the creation of a separate Muslim state. Gandhi, who was never anti-Muslim, felt that the Hindus would never usurp the rights of the Muslims and that the creation of a separate state was immoral. Hence towards the final days of the independence struggle, the conflict was not so much between the Indians and the British, but between Hindus and Muslims, with the British more or less acting as mediators.

The Congress Party became predominantly Hindu, thereby alienating Muslims. With the advent of adult suffrage, this alienation spread even to the villages. The process of "self-identification" of the masses with their religious groups and leaders had begun to ferment. Increasing enfranchisement brought increasing disparity between the Hindus and Muslims. Often political leaders of each community would emphasize the mass prejudices that led to discord. The Muslim League became increasingly active and resentful of Hindu power.

The Hindu–Muslim rift was never repaired. At the All Parties Conference in Delhi in February 1938, which was called to write the Indian Constitution, the Hindu–Muslim differences came to the fore. The Muslim nationalist, Mukhtar Ahmed Ansari, advised Gandhi that the Congress should arrive at some agreement with Muslims, but this suggestion was brushed aside at the insistence of Jawaharlal Nehru. The All-India Muslim Conference in Bombay, two months later, decided heavily against both British and Hindu domination. The split between the two communities was never mended and resulted in the conception of two separate states on religious lines.

Hindus and Muslims were not eager to forget centuries-old hatreds. Gandhi knew that it was not easy to bring down the wall of enmity. He wrote: "I had realized early enough in South Africa that there was no genuine friendship between the Hindus and Mussalmans. I never missed a single opportunity to remove obstacles in the way of unity. It was not in my nature to placate anyone by adulation, or at the cost of my self respect. But my South African experiences had convinced me that it would be in the question of Hindu–Muslim unity that my *ahimsa* would be put to its severest test, and that the question presented the widest field for my experiments in *ahimsa*. The conviction is still there. Every moment of my life I realize that God is putting me on my trial."[5]

Gandhi stressed the common bonds, aspirations, and sufferings of the Hindus and Muslims. Both religious groups had been in India for a long time and both deserved a place there. Jinnah stressed the cultural differences between the two communities as well as the history of communal riots; he felt that violence was inevitable. He detested Gandhi's philosophy of non-violence. As Coolidge says: "The Muslims, though in a minority, had been rulers of India before the British, they still regarded themselves as being superiors, encouraged by their religion, which unlike that of the Hindus, claimed to be the only true one. Despite their numerical inferiority, they wanted at least equal status."

As it happened, the Hindu parts of India had been under British domination considerably longer than those parts mainly Muslim, with the consequence that Western education had gone further among the Hindus. Indian civil servants, capitalists, and even lawyers were largely Hindu; while the Muslim, being a late comer to the professions, found the cards stacked against him. Many a Muslim, including at times Jinnah himself, felt that the British were more likely to protect Muslim interests than Congress, in which Muslims were always a minority group.

The conflict continued. Although Gandhi did not want separation, he felt that any such action should be democratic, so that Baluchistan, Sindh, and the Northwest Frontier Province, where Hindus had a majority, should be allowed to vote on their future. Jinnah, realizing that they would vote to remain unified, wanted them to be forced to separate. But Gandhi had no way of pressuring Jinnah; nonviolence and fasting were impossible against him.

The Muslims were more concerned with maintaining their rights than shedding the British; they were prepared to wait. Gandhi and the Hindus were eager for independence, but they needed Muslim support to apply pressure to the British.

The Muslim League played a decisive role in the partition of India, encouraged by the popular gains it made in the elections of 1937. Suddenly leaders of other Muslim factions began joining forces with the League. With religious fervor the fight for an independent "Islamic" state was waged. The League launched propaganda programs that attacked the All-India Congress as unfair to the Muslims, completely Hindu-influenced, and unacceptable to the Islamic people of India. Jinnah had now become President of the Muslim League, and in his speech before the League on March 22, 1940, he outlined his case for an Islamic state. The President stressed the Muslim dissatisfaction with the Indian government's proposals for independence, and demanded that the predominantly Muslim areas in North-West and East India "be grouped to constitute 'Independent States' in which the constituent Units shall be autonomous and sovereign." Also, Jinnah demanded that the Congress take sufficient action in making constitutional provisions that would protect the economic, political, cultural, and religious freedoms of those Muslims living in areas of Hindu majority. To justify his demands for partition, Jinnah emphasized the difference that existed between Hindus and Muslims and that any plan for a united India was not a viable dream. He said that:

> The Hindus and Muslims belong to two different religious philosophies, social customs, literatures. They neither intermarry, nor interdine . . . their aspects of life and views on life are different . . . they have different epics, different heroes and different episodes. . . . To yoke together two such nations under a single state. . . . must lead to growing discontent and final destruction of any fabric that may be so built up for the government of such a state."[6]

In March 1940, the Muslim League passed the Pakistan Resolution, which stated that the unalterable goal for all Indian Muslims was the creation of a sovereign "Islamic" state. This goal of oneness of purpose was exemplified by Jinnah. All his efforts since that day were inspired by one idea—the establishment of Pakistan.

The arrival of World War II proved to have very favorable effects upon the Pakistan movement. The British had to rally Indian support in order that Japan would not overrun that country as it had done in Burma and Malaya. The Muslim League seized the opportunity as the right time to force the British to make certain concessions. The League protested Britain's attempts to impose a wartime central government upon India. Jinnah, knowing that this opposition virtually ruined India's war effort, was able to procure certain guarantees from the British. They agreed to set up plans for self-government in India as soon as the hostilities ended. For this purpose, Churchill sent Stafford Cripps, member of the British War Cabinet, to draw up a plan for home-rule that would be mutually acceptable to all involved. Cripps offered a plan whereby India would be given independence after it had framed a constitution agreeable to all, and if at the time of independence the creation of Pakistan was thought necessary by the government, then the Muslims could have their "Islamic" state. The Cripps Proposal was turned down by both parties, Hindus and Muslims, as unfair, for each felt that it gave too much to the opposition. The Cripps Proposal had a worsening effect upon the internal struggle in India. Positions became more solidified. Mahatma Gandhi and the Congress became more resolute in their demands for withdrawal of British rule and transference of power to the All-India Congress. The Muslim League strengthened its insistence for a Pakistan as the only acceptable course of action. Both parties, sensing the British urgency for solving the problem, felt confident in obtaining their goals. Muslims felt further encouraged as some members of the Congress weakened in their demand for a unified India and felt that concession to the League's demands was the wisest move. On May 2, 1942, Shri Rajagopalachari introduced before the All-India Congress a resolution in support of Pakistan, but it was defeated, 120 to 15. The Hindus argued that partition would ruin India, and that neither of the nations would be able to survive for lack of power. But the Muslim League saw that an "Islamic" state was a necessary step toward achieving power status.

From 1940–1947, the League carried out an extensive propaganda campaign that was designed to convince Britain that unity was impossible and to force the Congress, through threats and actual violence, to concede to partition. The League reiterated its claims that Muslims had ruled prior to the British, and that the Congress was a Hindu organization and that a central government would mean Hindu rule and Muslim subjugation. Further, it asserted that India had never been one nation, but had a history of many factions and no unity, so that it would be a travesty to impose a central government upon all Indians. The Muslims under Jinnah threatened that, if they were not allowed to pursue their own religion in their Islamic state, force would be used.

The British attempted again to resolve the question of unity between the two factions. With World War II drawing to a close, the allied war aims were to concede self-determination to all nations. So the British called together the main factions of India, including Gandhi and Jinnah. This conference met at Simla on June 25, 1945. The British proposal, called the Wavell Plan, hoped to form a coalition government and, more importantly, to allow the major parties to negotiate informally and to reach an agreement. The Simla Conference failed for two main reasons. First, the British refused to agree to the League's demand that it was the sole representative of Indian Muslims and that Jinnah be recognized as its spokesman. Second, the British entered each conference with the idea that Indian unity must be preserved and that a plan was to be worked out that would help create national unity. These approaches neglected the fact that Jinnah and the League were determined that Muslims *must* have a nation of their own. The rioting and bloodshed grew worse, and all that the conferences produced was worse hostility among the Hindus and Muslims. Jinnah and the League were blamed by the Congress for this civil disorder. They preached hatred and division so thoroughly that violence was bound to erupt. The situation worsened every day, and even if no real hostilities had existed previously, it was obvious at this time that it would be impossible for Hindus and Muslims to live in an orderly society under one central government.

One more attempt at resolving Hindu–Muslim differences took place in 1946, when a Cabinet Mission was sent to India. As before, the mission's purpose was to urge the leaders to reach a common solution. They realized that the Congress would refuse to agree to the creation of Pakistan. The vehemence of their opposition to Pakistan was stated by Gandhi to the Cabinet Mission; "Pakistan which connotes division of India will be a sin and the two nation theory propounded by Mr. Jinnah is absurd."[7] However, Jinnah and the League were just as emphatic. "So far as Muslim India was concerned the conception of a United India was impossible. If any attempt is made to force a decision against the wishes of the Muslims, Muslim India will resist it by all means and at all costs."[8] Finally the British set up an interim government consisting of Hindus and Muslims. This was a temporary solution and did not solve the problem of to whom and to how many governments the British would transfer their power. No national constitution could be worked out, because the Muslims demanded the right to frame their own constitution exclusive of Hindu influence.

The League's policy of boycotting and sabotaging conferences paid off. The British, tired of waiting for an Indian resolution, announced by way of Prime Minister Atlee's address in the House of Lords that independence would be granted and power transferred to the Indians no later than June 1948. To whom and what form or forms of government it would be handed was left open. Atlee said:

> His Majesty's Government will have to consider to whom the power of the Central Government in British India should be handed over on the same date, whether as a whole to some form of Central Government for British India, or in some areas to the existing Provincial Governments, or in such other ways as may seem most reasonable and in the best interests of the Indian people.[9]

This announcement of British intentions encouraged the League to step up its activities of disruption, for the British had set a deadline on affecting unity. All that remained for the League to do was to incite turmoil, thus forcing the Congress to approve of partition as the only means to prevent chaos. Muslims began migrating from their strongholds to areas where neither Hindus nor Muslims held a distinct advantage. In these questionable areas civil disobedience movements and communal riots were started. Rioting ran rampant throughout every major city in which the Muslims had power. The horror and bloodshed were staggering.

The antagonists now were not the British; they tried to save the country from division, if it was possible at all. But the militant Muslim movement had gone beyond the point of no return. The idea of Pakistan satisfied the religious emotions as well as political instincts of the Muslims. The vision of a sovereign Muslim state was fascinating to them. It promised them the prospect of independence both from the British and from the Hindus. All this produced a vicious religious frenzy; the Indian government was not able to control the communal riots. The Congress took the only step open to them: they accepted, regretfully, the plan for partition of India, and the creation of the Islamic state of Pakistan.

Notes

1. Andrews, C. F. 1930. *Mahatma Gandhi's Ideas*. New York: Macmillan, 367.
2. Gandhi, M. K. 1971. *Autobiography*. Boston: Beacon Press, 441.
3. Bahadur, Lal. 1954. *The Muslim League: Its History, Activities, and Achievements*. Rawatpara: Agra, 259.
4. Ibid., 262.
5. Gandhi. *Autobiography*, 441.
6. Bahadur. *Muslim League*, 296.
7. Ibid., 315.
8. Ibid.
9. Ibid.

11
The Sikh Crisis in India: A Question of Identity

Arvind Sharma

AN ATTEMPT CAN BE MADE to arrive at an understanding of what is happening to the Sikhs in India in at least five different ways: (1) as a problem resulting from the normalization of an artificial polity created under British Raj (the "imperial model"); (2) as a consequence of the religious revival in India in the nineteenth and the twentieth centuries (the "revival model"); (3) as representing regional self-assertion against the hegemonizing tendencies of the central government (the "political model"); (4) as the result of forces unleashed by economic development (the "economic model"); and (5) as specially illustrative of the problems a minority may have to face in relation to a majority whose domination it fears (the "statistical model"). None of these "models," however, can be applied unless the basic question of the nature of Sikh self-identity is faced, for all of these models assume such an identity before they can even begin to explain the situation.

The question of Sikh identity is of contemporary, historical, and theoretical interest. Its contemporary relevance in conflict-torn India is too obvious to be stated. Its historical interest derives from the changing contours of Sikh identity over time since the sect was founded by Guru Nanak (1469–1539). Its theoretical interest lies in the light it sheds on the problem of identity in religion. As is well known, the Hindus are quite willing to regard the Sikhs as constituting a Hindu sect, but the Sikhs are unwilling to accept such an accommodation. Thus the question of Sikh identity comes to involve the following theoretical issue: how is the identity of a group to be understood when another tradition claims that the tradition in question is included within

190

that other? The Ahmadiyyas in Pakistan enable the issue to be posed in an opposite manner: how does a group identify itself when it regards itself as a sect of another tradition, which rejects it?

These remarks are intended to prepare the ground for the investigation of the question of Sikh identity that we now proceed to examine. It seems that Sikh identity could potentially be established along any of the following six lines:

(1) that Sikhism is a sect of Hinduism, influenced by Islam;
(2) that Sikhism is a sect of Islam, influenced by Hinduism;
(3) that Sikhism possesses neither a Hindu identity nor a Muslim identity but rather a composite Hindu–Muslim identity;
(4) that Sikhism possesses an independent identity all its own;
(5) that Sikhism really represents a regional as much as a religious identity, that is, to say, it possesses a Punjabi identity;
(6) that Sikhism really represents a case of linguistic identity on account of its association with the Punjabi language and the Gurumukhi script.

Let us now examine the case for and against each of these.

Sikhism and Hindu Identity

It could be argued for certain periods of Sikh history that the Sikhs were simply "Hindus who grew their hair long and did not cut their beards," as Khuswant Singh (1953, 89) points out, especially during the period when the Sikhs achieved temporal power. At the time of its origin as well, apart from the time of its political apogee, Sikhism could be regarded as a sect of Hinduism. Singh (1953, 182–83) writes, for instance, in a way reminiscent of the statement that Jesus was a Jew and Buddha was a Hindu:

> Guru Nanak, the founder of the Sikh religion, was a Hindu; so were the nine succeeding Gurus. Guru Nanak tried like his contemporary reformers to prune Hinduism of the many pernicious practices which were corroding Hindu society. His inspiration was essentially Hindu. The ideas were of necessity borrowed from Islam, the only other religion available for scrutiny. There is little evidence to support the belief that Guru Nanak planned the founding of a new community synthesizing Hinduism and Islam. He simply planned to reform Hinduism. He did so by reference to Islam. His emphasis on certain Islamic beliefs, e.g. the unity of God as opposed to Hindu pantheism, the equality of mankind as opposed to the Hindu caste system, the condemnation of asceticism, etc., aroused enthusiasm amongst Muslims. Many legends grew up about his being a Mussalman and going on pilgrimage to Mecca. All these are at the best wishful compliments from a community to which he owed so much.

However, this is only part of the story. Soon after Guru Nanak's death,

certain factors making towards a schism were introduced. A new script, Gur-
umukhi, was invented. A new religious literature was epitomized in the *Adi
Granth*. New centers of worship and social intercourse *(gurdwaras)* were erected.
New customs and conventions were introduced. Thus, for the Sikh the language
was Punjabi not Hindi; the script Gurmukhi not Devanagri; the scripture the
Granth Sahib and not the Vedas; the place of worship the *gurdwara* with the
Holy Book and not the temple with its stone idols. Hindu children shaved their
heads and celebrated Mundan. The Sikhs were baptized and swore an oath not
to clip their hair. . . . The Hindu was married round a sacrificial fire to the
chanting of the Vedas. The Sikh was married round the *Adi Granth* to the
singing of hymns. The dead Hindu had his skull smashed and his ashes cast to
the Ganges. The Sikh was cremated with different ceremonial and his ashes
simply scattered. (Singh 1953, 184)

Meanwhile historically, if Hindu–Sikh identity virtually fused during Sikh
rule over Punjab, the British annexation of the Punjab was followed by active
Hindu–Sikh schism.

Prominent among scholars who tend to identify the Sikhs as a Hindu sect
are E. Trumpp, Maurice Bloomfield, and Narang (Singh, 1966, 82). Khuswant Singh's position in this respect is interesting. He felt, at least in 1953,
that the tempo of Sikh merger into Hinduism was increasing and that

if the present pace of amalgamation continues, there is little doubt that before
the century has run its course Sikh religion will have become a branch of Hinduism and the Sikhs a part of the Hindu social system (Singh 1953, 185).

In this view, which sees Sikhism as emerging from and merging back into
Hinduism, its Hindu identity vis-à-vis any other is emphasized yet Sikhism,
for the duration of its existence, could still be considered virtually an independent religion.[1] The prediction of its merger into Hinduism, however, is
not accepted by all scholars. Thus W. Owen Cole (1980, 63–64) remarked:

It would be a rash person who would predict the nature and form that any
religion might take in the twenty-first century. Of Sikhism it can be said that
it has deep roots from which it can acquire new strength. Their worldwide
distribution is giving Sikhs a renewed sense of identity and this will carry them
forward. Twenty years ago some Sikhs were doubtful of their own future and
predicted their reabsorption into Hinduism. Today Sikhism may claim to be a
world religion.

Sikhism and Islamic Identity

The case for an Islamic identity of Sikhism is made less often than for the
Hindu one, but it has been made. F. Pincott makes this case forcefully in his
entry on Sikhism in *A Dictionary of Islam,* wherein he suggests that Sikhism

may "even be spoken of as the religion of a Muhammadan sect" (Bal 1969, 124). Four things incline one towards this view: the Sikh rejection of image-worship, the Sikh assertion on the unity of God, the Sikh emphasis on the role of God as creator, and the Sikh denunciation of caste. The obviously Hindu elements such as belief in karma in this view could be explained as simply arising "from the fact that he (Nanak) was born a Hindu" (Bal 1969, 138). W. L. McGregor states that "Nanak did not deny the mission of Mahomed, though he reprobated his oppressive cruelty and intolerance to the Hindoos" (Bal 1969, 64). He goes on to say that "Nanak considered himself a successor to Mahomed; and that he was destined to restore, by his example, precepts and writings, the whole of mankind to the worship of God."

That Sikhism is essentially Islamic is maintained most directly by Murza Ghulam Ahmad in his book *Sat Bachan,* in which

> after placing Nanak above all the Hindu Rishis, prophets and gods, he goes on to say that the knowledge contained in the hymns of Nanak is so subtle and divine that it is impossible to find the like of it in the Vedas or the other books of the Hindus. Having done so he maintains that Guru Granth is an exposition and a commentary of the Holy Quran and that Nanak was really a Mohammedan. Further on he analyses the teachings of Nanak in the same one-sided spirit and then quotes from Hughes' *Dictionary of Islam,* to support his contention of Nanak being a Muslim (Singh 1966, 89).

However, it is even more difficult to identify Sikhism as an Islamic sect than as a Hindu one. Apart from political rivalry between the two during Moghul rule, which may account for the last Guru forbidding Sikhs from having carnal knowledge of Muslim women, there are other divergences. The accounts of Nanak's life describe verbal contests with Faqirs and Shekhs, and Nanak, in some accounts is identified as a Hindu. Thus

> "a curious incident is next related to the effect that Makhdum Bahaad Din, the Pir of Multan, feeling his end approaching, said to his disciples, 'O friends, from this time the faith of no one will remain firm; all will become faithless.' His disciples asked for an explanation; and in reply he delivered himself of an oracular statement, 'O friends, when one Hindu shall come to Heaven there will be brilliancy in Heaven.' To this strange announcement his disciples replied, 'Learned people say that Heaven is not decreed for the Hindu; what is this that you have said?' The Pir told them that he was alluding to Nanak" (Bal 1969, 136).

McLeod (1968, 158) remarks that "Sikhism has commonly been regarded as a blend of Hindu beliefs and Islam, and if for Islam we substitute Sufism there appears, at first sight, to be much to support this view." On a closer examination, however, he concludes that the appearance is misleading so far as Sufism and therefore Islam is concerned:

> Affinities certainly exist, but we cannot assume that they are necessarily the result of Sūfī influence. Other factors suggest that Sūfism was at most a marginal influence, encouraging certain developments but in no case providing the actual source of a significant element.

McLeod (1968, 158–59) gives five reasons to support his conclusion: (1) that Sufis are condemned as vigorously as Quazis and Mullahs by Nanak; (2) that "there is a conspicuous lack of Sūfī terminology in the works of Gūrū Nānak;" (3) that purported Sufi affinities in Nanak's thought can be traced to "native Indian sources" with equal plausibility; (4) that some aspects of Nanak's teachings, like karma and transmigration, are in "direct conflict" with Sufi thoughts, and, most significant of all, (5) an examination of the more important point at which Muslim influence has been claimed can do little to support the claims made in this respect." Thus even Sikh monotheism could be Bhaktic rather than Islamic.

Sikhism: Composite Identity?

The previous review clearly indicates that Sikhism contains elements that could be identified as Hindu and Muslim. This has led to the view, apparently a fairly popular one, that Sikhism represents a synthesis of the two.

Thus the *Dabistan-i-Mazahib* of Mohsin Fani informs us that Nanak "professed the unity of God, which is called the law of Muhammad, and believed in metempsychosis," a popular Hindu doctrine, he "wore the rosary of the Muselmans in his hand, and the Zunar, or the religious thread of the Hindus, around his neck" (Bal 1969, 4). Later scholars add that

> after Nanak had visited all the cities of India, and explained to all ranks the great doctrines of the unity and omnipresence of God, he went to Mecca and Medina, where his actions, his miracles, and his long disputations with the most celebrated Muhammedan saints and doctors, are most circumstantially recorded by his biographers. He is stated, on this occasion to have maintained his own principles, without offending those of others, always professing himself the enemy of discord, and as having no object but to reconcile the two faiths of the Muhammedans and Hindus in one religion; which he endeavoured to do by recalling them to that great and original tenet, in which they both believed, the unity of God, and by reclaiming them from the numerous errors into which they had fallen (Bal 1969, 43).

The role of geography here may also be recognized, as Punjab was the major center of Hindu–Muslim encounter at this time, a fact that may explain the interpretation of Nanak's teaching that Nanak tried to "amalgamate the Hindu and Mohammadan religions" (Bal 1969, 95). The Sikh scripture contains the sayings of Hindu and Muslim saints and support the contention that Nanak's life

> was mostly spent in bringing Hindus and Muslims together. His personal success in this direction was remarkable. He was acclaimed by both communities. When he died, his body became a subject of dispute. The Muslims wanted to bury him, the Hindus to cremate him. Even to this day, he is regarded in the Punjab as a symbol of harmony between the two major communities. A popular couplet describes him: *Guru Nanak Shah Fakir. Hindu Ka Guru, Mussulman Ka Pir.* (Guru Nanak, the King of Fakirs. To the Hindu a Guru, to the Mussulman a Pir.)

The view that Sikh identity represents a composite Hindu–Muslim identity has not gone unchallenged. Thus Dr. Trumpp remarked that

> It is a mistake, if Nanak is represented as having endeavoured to unite the Hindu and Muhammadan idea about God. Nanak remained a thorough Hindu, according to all his views, and if he had communionship with Musalmans, and many of these even became his disciples, it was owing to the fact that Sufism, which all these Muhammadans were professing, was in reality nothing but a Pantheism derived directly from Hindu sources, and only outwardly adapted to the forms of Islam. Hindu and Muslim Pantheists could well unite together, as they entertained essentially the same ideas about the Supreme (Singh 1953, 123).

However, Sikh evidence itself seems to call the synthetic identity approach in question. The remark Nanak made after his three-day disappearance during which he is said to have communed with God is said to have been: "There is no Hindu, there is no musalman." Even F. Pincott who emphasizes the Islamic content of Nanak's life and teaching, as also his role as mitigating the opposition of Hinduism and Islam, remarks:

> This can mean nothing else than that it was Nanak's settled intention to do away with the differences between those two forms of belief, by instituting a third course which should supersede both of them (Singh 1953, 131).[2]

Sikhism: Independent Identity

Thus we are led to a fourth option in the matter of identity—inasmuch as the matter may be treated as a variable or a matter on some continuum—that Sikhism possesses neither a Hindu nor an Islamic nor even a composite identity; that in fact it possesses an *independent* identity. Early sentiment in support of this comes from the sayings of Guru Arjun.

I do not keep the Hindu fast, nor the Muslim Ramadan.
I serve Him alone who is my refuge.
I serve the one Master, who is also Allah.
I have broken with the Hindu and the Muslim,
I will not worship with the Hindu, nor like the Muslim
    go to Mecca.
I shall serve Him and no other.
I will not pray to idols nor say the Muslim prayer.
I shall put my heart at the feet of the one Supreme
    Being,
For we are neither Hindus nor Mussulmans
(Singh 1953, 27).

Modern Sikh scholars identify the Sikh tradition with this strand. Thus Sher Singh (1966, 146), after a comprehensive survey of the religious systems prevailing in the fifteenth century when Sikhism originated, concludes:

My purpose in this comparative survey of Sikhism was to show, that to say that it (Sikhism) is the branch of this or that religion is to shut out eyes to the multifarious trends of thought originating from all these sources and contributing to the general atmosphere in which the founders of Sikhism flourished. Just as the mere presence of the ideas of transmigration of souls and the law of Karma should not make us think that Sikhism is nothing but Hinduism; similarly its 'stern' monotheistic character should not persuade some writers to say that Nanak was a Mohammadan. If the Vedas and the Katebas, the Gita and the Gatha are the ancestors of Guru Granth; Zoroaster, Buddha, Christ, Mohammad, Sankara and Gorakh are in one way or the other, predecessors and precursors of Nanak. But this great geneaology and ancient inheritance should not make us believe that Nanak's ideas were all acquired by him. He did not start with a clean-slate-mind.[3]

An important point in the history of religions is involved here namely, the question: what makes a religion new or original?

Sikhism can claim to be an independent tradition beginning at its inception. Nanak's mystical experience, involving a disappearance for three days in a river, may be taken as its starting point. The incident has been alluded to earlier and is now described in more detail.

On the third day Nanak reappeared from the river, gave away his belongings, and joined a group of holy men. He remained silent under questioning, but when asked which path he was now following, for he seemed to be conforming to neither Hindu nor Muslim practice, he replied, "There is neither Hindu nor Mussulman so whose path shall I follow? I shall follow God's path. God is neither Hindu nor Mussulman and the path which I follow is God's" (Cole and Sambhi 1973, 8).

The traditional account of Nanak's death can also be seen as confirming that view.

> Tradition records that as news spread that he was about to die, Hindus and Muslims came to the famous man for a last audience. A dispute arose between them, the former claiming Nanak as a Hindu and saying that they would cremate the body, the latter saying they would bury it in accordance with Muslim custom. The Guru himself ended the dispute by instructing the Hindus to lay flowers on his right and the Muslims to place them at his left. Those whose flowers were fresh on the following day (and in September cut flowers do not last long in India) should dispose of his body according to their custom. The Guru covered himself with a sheet and went to sleep. The following morning both lots of flowers were found to be fresh but the body of Nanak had gone! 'There is no Hindu and no Mussulman.' To the end the affirmation remained the same. God's path was neither that of Hinduism nor of Islam, yet paradoxically (for both lots of flowers remained fresh) it included both (Cole and Sambhi 1973, 10).

Sikhism: Regional Identity

Sikhism is associated with one particular region of India—the Punjab—hence it seems logical to expect that Sikh identity could be seen as possessing not merely an ideological but also a geographical dimension. Political developments in post-independence India, in the form of a demand for a Punjabi Suba primarily by the Sikhs, tend to confirm this view. This view also gains some support from a perusal of Sikh history. Thus Khushwant Singh (1963, vii) writes in his preface to *A History of the Sikhs:* "The story of the Sikhs is the story of the rise, fulfilment, and collapse of Punjabi nationalism." He says later in the same preface that under Ranjit Singh (1780–1839):

> The Sikhs became the spearhead of the nationalist movement which had gathered the parent communities within its fold. The achievements were those of all Punjabis alike, Hindus, Muslims, and Sikhs. It was in the fitness of things that in the crowning successes of Punjabi arms, the men who represented the state were drawn from all communities. In the victory parade in Kabul in 1839 (a few months after Ranjit Singh's death) the man who bore the Sikh colours was Colonel Bassawan, a Punjabi Mussalman. And the man who carried the Sikh flag across the Himalayas a year later was General Zorawar Singh, a Dogra Hindu.

It is possible, however, to overstate this view. To assess the ethnic element in Sikh identity one must ask the question: Is Sikhism a missionary religion? Ethnic religions, as distinguished from missionary religions, tend to be associated with particular geographical regions. Thus the strong identification of Judaism with Israel, and of Hinduism with India comes to mind. There is some ambiguity on this point in modern works on Sikhism. Thus W. Owen Cole and Piara Singh Sambhi (1973, 45–46) remark:

> Nevertheless, ideally the Sikh is someone who is suspicious of ritual and sect. Although the first Sikhs were drawn from Hinduism and Islam, there have also been conversions to it from Christianity. In the main Sikhs are witnesses to the truth rather than missionaries, perhaps because to some extent the missionary must say that other faiths are untrue. The Sikh prefers to say that they are in danger of obscuring the truth, for rituals can become ends in themselves rather than ways by which God can be experienced and worship can be expressed. The critical Sikh recognizes that renewal or revival is constantly necessary in his own faith.

And W. Owen Cole (1980, 59) remarks elsewhere: "One may become a Sikh by conversion but Sikhism, holding the view that God may be found in any monotheistic religion, is not a missionary faith."

There is however evidence to indicate that conversion to Sikhism was not only possible but actually did take place. At one time Banda Bahadur (1672–1716), a Muslim, testified: "A large number of Mohammedans abandoned Islam and followed the misguided path" i.e., Sikhism (Singh 1963, 106). It is also well-known that during the time of Misls large numbers of Hindus accepted conversion to Sikhism, which they regarded as another branch of Hinduism.

Sikhism: Linguistic Identity

It is well-known that "The Granth Sahib is the central object of Sikh worship and ritual," that it "contains the writings of the first five Gurus, the ninth Guru, Tegh Bahadur, and a couplet by Guru Gobind Singh," and that the "language used by the Sikh Gurus was Punjabi of the fifteenth and sixteenth centuries" (Singh 1953, 39–40). This would seem to provide the basis for a strong linguistic identity with Punjabi on the part of the Sikhs, as it could be argued that Punjabi was the language of Sikh revelation. The following incident is one worth reviewing in this context:

> Guru Nanak was often accompanied by a friend, a musician named Mardana who provided the musical setting for the Guru's hymns. On one occasion Mardana was looking after a horse when the meditating Guru felt the word of God coming to him.
> "Mardana, touch the chords," he exclaimed.
> "The word is descending."
> "But Master, my hands are occupied in holding the reins of this horse," Mardana answered.
> "Let the horse go," was the Guru's unhesitating reply.
> "God's word does not wait upon man's convenience." (Cole 1980, 31)

These words were received in Punjabi and hence Punjabi could be regarded as the language of Sikhism. Sikhism also uses its own distinct script called Gurumukhi.

Yet even more than in the case of regional identity, the linguistic dimension of Sikh identity can be overstated. The Granth Sahib contains the words of not only the Sikh Gurus but also of Hindu and Muslim saints and Punjabi is not exclusively the language of the Sikhs. However, the fact that it is primarily associated with Sikhs and the fact that the agitation for a Punjabi-speaking state was led by the Sikhs does indicate the strength of this strand of Sikh identity.

Conclusion

Three points emerge from the foregoing discussion. First, one must distinguish between IDENTITY and IDENTIFICATION. The fact that for some periods of Sikh history Hindu and Sikh interests became identical and the two communities identified themselves with each other does not automatically mean that the separate identities were erased. It is possible for communities to merge and achieve a common identity but it should not be assumed to have happened just because the interests of the communities overlapped. Second, it is possible for a religious community to possess multiple identities. Thus the Sikhs could possess a linguistic as well as a regional identity in addition to possessing a religious identity. Third, identity is a variable. Religious communities may at one period in history define their self-identity in one way and in another period define it in another. One has only to contrast the initially pacific identity of the Sikhs with their subsequent martial identity to establish this point, which can also be substantiated from instances drawn from other religions of the world. To be sure, to a certain extent our identity possesses us, but it is equally true that to a certain extent we possess our identity.[4]

The present Sikh crisis in India contains elements that can be related to all five models. One of the Sikh grievances is their proportionate decline in the armed forces. This ties into the "imperial model." At one time the Sikhs constituted thirty percent of the British army in India while constituting barely three percent of the Indian population. The Sikh protest at being regarded as an "off-shoot of Hinduism" in the unmodified Indian constitution can be connected directly with the revival model just as the demand for greater autonomy can be connected with the political model. The Sikh demand for more industries in the Punjab (as distinguished from agriculture) reflects the operation of the economic model, while their willingness in the recent accord to yield Hindu areas to Haryana can be understood in terms of the statistical model.

However, the Sikh self-definition of its identity is crucial in this context.

The Sikhs have chosen to assert their independent identity above all else, with a strong dash of linguistic and regional identity. The assertion of an independent identity par excellence means in essence that the Sikhs can retain their linguistic and regional identities only on a narrower base just as Hindus have linguistically affiliated themselves with Hindi. The problem for Sikhs is that the geographical borders of Punjab have shrunk, first with the loss of West Punjab to the Muslims at the time of Partition and then of Haryana to the Hindus. An independent identity tied to geography clearly poses some risks.

The root of the Sikh crisis lies in the fact that Sikh identity cannot find full political expression even within the truncated Punjab: In order to gain power, the Sikhs have hitherto had to share power either with their own co-religionists belonging to different factions or with non-Sikhs or with both. But previously this seemed to be an acceptable if not an ideal situation. The current crisis arose when the Sikhs lost power qua Sikhs in the May 1980 elections, when the Akali Dal lost power. Earlier the Sikhs had shared the power. This phenomenon in itself is not new, for the Congress effectively controlled the Punjab prior to its division. But the division of the old Punjab in 1966 into a Hindu-majority Haryana and a Sikh-majority Punjab signalled the assertion of Sikh regional and linguistic identities and made the coexistence of an independent Sikh identity without a workable sharing of political power qua Sikhs difficult to endure in the Punjab.[5]

Finally, one aspect of Sikhism that has a special bearing on recent developments and has been a persistent factor in Sikh history needs to be identified. It is best characterized by the terms sectarianism and factionalism, where the former refers to the division of the Sikh community into sects and the latter to division within these distinct sects or, now, within political parties representing the Sikhs. Although a Sikh may be defined as "one who believes in the ten Gurus and the Granth Sahib," and the Sikhs represent a fairly homogeneous group basically consisting of (1) the orthodox *Kesadhari* (unshaven) Khalsa and (2) the clean-shaven *Sahajdharis*, Sikhism has also included sects that diverge in varying degrees from the main body. These include the Nirankaris and Namdharis, as well as schismatic sects before the Guruship was concluded by the tenth Guru (Singh 1944, 222).

Sikh sectarianism is recognized by Sikhs as a problem, and part of the activities of Bhindranwale were directed against these sects. Likewise, the Indian government had the damage that was done to the Golden Temple by Operation Blue Star repaired by making use of the internal divisions among the Sikhs and persuading a Sikh sect to undertake it. But overall, Sikh factionalism presents a more acute problem, apart from the issue of caste within the Sikh panth that also becomes a factor in these and other contexts.[6] At the present moment, the issue is one of factionalism in the Akali Dal, the party that represents the political aspirations of the Sikhs. It has witnessed the split between Master Tara Singh and Sant Fateh Singh in the past. More recently, it was torn between the radical position of Bhindranwale and the more moderate stand of Longowal. At the moment, factions have split over the issue of sending the police into the Golden Temple, after having assumed power in the state. What the future holds in store only time will tell.[7]

Notes

1. Sher Singh (1966, 88) says of Sikhism as an independent religion:

> The attempt to interpret Sikhism as Hinduism, apart from its cultural implications, or more precisely to interpret Sikhism as Brahmanism, has been as history shows, repudiated by the Hindus themselves. For instance in the days of Guru Amar Das the Brahmans took a deputation to Emperor Akbar and represented to him their complaint in the following words: Guru Amar Das of Goindwal hath abandoned the religious and social customs of the Hindus and abolished the distinction of the four castes. There is now no twilight prayer, no gyatri, no offering of water to ancestors, no pilgrimages, no obsequies, and no worship of idols or of the divine Salagram—no one now acteth according to the Vedas or the Simirtis—no gods or goddesses. Fani, so often quoted, did not fail to mark in the very days of the Gurus that Sikhism was developing as a separate religion. Thus he writes in the days of the Sixth Guru that the Sikh do not recite the Mantras of the Hindus, they do not venerate their temples, nor do they esteem their avataras. The Sanskrit language, which according to the Hindus is the language of the gods is not held in such great estimation by the Sikhs. Among them there is nothing of the religious rites of the Hindus; they know of no check of eating or drinking. When Partab Mal, a wise Hindu, saw that his son wished to adopt the faith of the Musalmans he asked him: "Why do thou wish to become a Musalman? If thou likest to eat every thing, become a Guru of the Sikhs (perhaps he meant a Sikh of the Gurus) and whatever thou desirest thou canst eat and drink."

2. Attention may be drawn here to W. H. McLeod's (1968, 161) statement on the point of Sikhism's synthetic identity:

> From this conclusion it follows that a common interpretation of the religion of Gurū Nānak must be rejected. It is not correct to interpret it as a conscious effort to reconcile Hindu belief and Islam by means of a synthesis of the two. The intention to reconcile was certainly there, but not by the path of syncretism. Conventional Hindu belief and Islam were not regarded as fundamentally right but as fundamentally wrong.
> Neither the *Veda* nor the *Kateb* know the mystery. The two were to be

rejected, not harmonized in a synthesis of their finer elements. True religion
lay beyond these two systems, accessible to all men of spiritual perception
whether Hindu or Muslim. It was the person who spurned all that was
external and who followed instead the interior discipline of *nām simaran*
who could be called a 'true' Hindu or a 'true' Muslim. Such a person had
in fact transcended both.

It is accordingly incorrect to interpret the religion of Gurū Nānak as a
synthesis of Hindu belief and Islam. It is indeed a synthesis, but one in
which Islamic elements are relatively unimportant. The pattern evolved by
Guru Nanak is a reworking of the Sant synthesis, one which does not depart
far from Sant sources as far as its fundamental components are concerned.
Gurū Nānak's concepts of the *Sabad*, the *Nām*, the *Gurū*, and the *Hukam*
carry us beyond anything that the works of earlier Sants offer in any explicit
form. It is Sant thought which we find in his works, but it is Sant thought
expanded and reinterpreted. The result is a new synthesis, a synthesis which
is cast within the pattern of Sant belief but which nevertheless possesses a
significant originality and, in contrast with its Sant background, a unique
clarity. It possesses, moreover, the quality of survival, for it remains today
the substance of a living faith.

One still wonders whether even such a synthetic approach will be accepted by the
Sikhs themselves.
3. Singh (1966, 90–91) elaborates:

> This brings us to the originality of the Guru or the newness of Sikhism.
> If we analyse the philosophy and religion of the Sikhs into bits and pieces
> then there is nothing what we can call original or new in it. But I do not
> think that in this sense anybody can assert absolute originality of any system,
> philosophy or religion of the world. This absolute newness is inconceiveable.
> What is new in Sikhism is not its bits and pieces of which it is made, but
> the form or the whole, in which those pieces are synthesized, such a synthesis
> in this form never existed before the times of the Guru in India, in Asia or
> even in the world.

4. For general discussion of identity and religion see Hans Mol, ed. *Identity and
    Religion: International, Cross-Cultural Approaches* (London: Sage Publications,
    1978).
5. One may add, as a point of general theoretical interest, that a seceding unit usually
    finds it easier to establish its self-identity (Sikhs not wanting to be considered
    Hindus) than an integrating unit (Ahmadiyyas wanting to be considered Muslims)
    which prompts the lapidary conclusion: it is easier to make enemies than friends!
6. The basic division here is between JAT and non-JAT Sikhs. See McLeod 1976,
    chap. 5.
7. In the Hindu-Sikh riots in Kanpur the Sikhs raised a slogan which translates:
    "Muslim and Sikh is brother, the Hindu is an other." The recent upsurge in hostility
    between the Hindus and the Sikhs has focused attention of the links between
    Sikhism and Islam. It should be recognized that Sikhism does not subscribe to

one key element of the Islamic creed: that Muhammad is the last prophet. If it were so it would be difficult to accept Nanak as the first Guru and the termination of the Guruship by Guru Gobind Singh would possess little meaning.

References

Bal, Sarjit Singh. 1969. *Guru Nanak in the Eyes of Non-Sikhs*. Chandigarh: Punjab University.

Cole, W. Owen. 1980. *Thinking About Sikhism*. London: Lutterworth Educational.

Cole, W. Owen and Piara Singh Sambhi. 1973. *Sikhism*. London: Wordluck Educational Company Ltd.

McLeod, W. H. 1976. *The Evolution of the Sikh Community*. Oxford: Clarendon Press.

McLeod, W. H. 1968. *Guru Nanak and the Sikh Religion*. Oxford: Clarendon Press.

Mol, Hans, ed. 1978. *Identity and Religion: International, Cross-Cultural Approaches*. London: SAGE.

Singh, Khuswant. 1963. *A History of the Sikhs*. Vol. I. Princeton, NJ: Princeton University Press.

Singh, Khuswant. 1959. *The Sikhs Today*. Bombay: Orient Longmans.

Singh, Khuswant. 1953. *The Sikhs*. George Allen and Unwin Ltd.

Singh, Sher. 1986. *Philosophy of Sikhism*. Delhi: Sterling Publishers.

Singh, Teja. 1944. *Essays in Sikhism*. Lahore, Punjab: Sikh University Press.

PART IV
PRECARIOUS
PLURALISM:
THE CASE OF ISRAEL

12

Self-Preservation and the Embattled Church: The Case of the Greek Orthodox Patriarchate of Jerusalem

Donald A. Luidens

THE PRINCIPAL PARADIGM that underlies the public pronouncements and behaviors of the Greek-born hierarchy of the Greek Orthodox Patriarchate of Jerusalem is this: The hierarchy perceives itself to be embattled and in the throes of a mortal struggle against overwhelming odds for its own self-preservation. It feels unjustly forced on the defensive, arbitrarily beset by political and ecclesiastical institutions from without the Church, and undermined by Arab parishioners from within.

Accordingly, the Patriarchal leadership has striven to establish and maintain a modicum of stability by resorting to two modes of response: on the one hand, all relations with individuals and groups external to the Patriarchate are conducted in the long-established formulae of international and ecclesiastical diplomacy, with all their attendant mechanisms of threat and cajolery, negotiation, and power play; on the other hand, the mode governing the hierarchy's relations within the Patriarchate, especially with the largely Arab membership, resolutely continues to be a "patriarchal" one. That is, the hierarchy envisions itself to be the patient father entrusted with the care and nurturing of his "children," who are frequently ungrateful and unruly.

On the basis of published material as well as interviews conducted with Arab lay and clergy Orthodox Christians, with Greek hierarchs, and with non-Orthodox participants in Jerusalem church circles,[1] I present an initial analysis of the life of the Jerusalem Patriarchate. Specifically, I consider the external factors, those involving relations with organizations and agencies outside the Church, which have historically had an impact on the social structures and actions of the Patriarchate. I also delineate the various ameliorative responses the Greek hierarchy has employed in order to ensure its ongoing stability and security in the face of pressures rising from the external factors.[2] These can be understood as falling into four broad categories: local and international political factors, and local and international ecumenical factors.

Historical Background

The Greek Orthodox Patriarchate of Jerusalem was one of the five original patriarchates of Christendom (the others were Rome, Constantinople, Antioch, and Alexandria). Jerusalem was granted autocephalous (autonomous) status by the Council of Chalcedon in 451 A.D. While its membership has never been large, it has held a special rank among the Orthodox faithful because of its claim to be the "Mother Church," a lineage it draws through the apostles' experience at Pentecost (Horner 1974, 41).

During successive governments—Christian, Moslem, and Jewish—the fortunes of the Patriarchate have fluctuated dramatically, reaching their nadir at the hands of the Roman Catholic Crusaders when the Greek Patriarch was expelled and the Church's properties were confiscated. Under the Ottoman Empire (1517–1917), the Greek Orthodox were pitted against other Christian communions, in particular the Franciscans, as each sought preeminence in the Holy Places (Cust 1930, 128). In 1852, in part as an outcome of the Crimean War (Fisher 1936, 942), the Ottoman Sultan decreed that the prevailing status quo in the Holy Places would henceforth be formalized and enforced (Germanos 1967, 24). This decree, and subsequent ecclesiastical/political compromises—known collectively as the Status Quo Agreements—have ensured that the Greek Orthodox would have the preferred position at such major pilgrim sites as the Church of the Holy Sepulchre (which houses the traditional Golgatha and Christ's Tomb), the Church of the Nativity (in Bethlehem), and The Tomb of the Virgin (originally a Franciscan sanctuary in the Gethsemane region) (Colbi 1976, 15–16). Subsequent British, Jordanian, and Israeli governments have reaffirmed this Status Quo arrangement with only minor alterations.

The Patriarchate continues to proclaim its Status Quo-based preeminence among the Churches of Jerusalem, as was evidenced in a recent interview with the current Patriarch, Diodoros I:

> The Patriarch of Jerusalem is the foremost, principal and decisive Christian spokesman in matters regarding Jerusalem and the Holy Places. This does not imply any prejudice to understandings previously established with Christian

confessions present in the Holy Places, not only about problems that may ensue, but also about matters concerning international rulings on the status of the Holy Places and of Jerusalem. (1981, 17)

The current Patriarchate consists of two distinct factions: the Greek-born hierarchy and the indigenous Arab membership. The former—deacons, monks, priests, bishops, and the patriarch—number around 140. They live primarily in Jerusalem, although several occupy monasteries throughout the Judean Hills. The monks, priests, and bishops are automatically members of the Brotherhood of the Holy Sepulchre, which is entrusted with the ownership and care of the Greek Orthodox Holy Places. The Brotherhood is guided on an executive basis by the Holy Synod, consisting of the Patriarch, the twelve bishops, and up to three archimandrites.

While membership statistics are somewhat suspect because they are based on family networks, unofficial church estimates, and incomplete reportings, there is general agreement that the Arab membership in "Palestine"[3] (including the West Bank, East Jerusalem, Gaza, and Israel) is around 40,000. An additional 45,000–55,000 reside in Jordan.[4] These members are participants in sixty-five parishes, largely in cities and towns; they are pastored by about sixty-one Arab clergy, all of whom are married and are therefore not eligible for membership in the Brotherhood (Benedictos 1972, 5).

Local Political Factors

According to Professor Ioannes Karmires of the University of Athens, the ideal form of church-state relations in the Orthodox world is one that promotes

harmony and mutuality ("symphonia" and "synallelia") which is based on the sufficiency and independence of the two co-existing and cooperating principles and powers without the subjugation either of the state to the Church or the Church to the state. (Harakas 1982, 5)

In the case of the Greek Orthodox Patriarchate of Jerusalem, this ideal has not been possible. Instead, the governments ruling "the Holy Land" have had determinative influence over the fortunes of the Church. For instance, under guidelines set up by the Ottomans in 1875, all nominees for the Patriarchal throne have had to have governmental approval (Colbi 1981, 63). Even during the last two elections, under Jordan in 1958 and under the joint supervision of Jordan and Israel in 1981, this governmental approval was still sought (Diodoros 1981, 2).

As a consequence of this imbalance of power, the Patriarchate has increasingly pursued compliance with the Status Quo as its main diplomatic and ecclesial objective. The Status Quo Agreements cover the minutest detail, as the following 1963 example illustrates:

We, the undersigned, the Greek Orthodox Patriarch of Jerusalem and the

Acting Custos of the Holy Land [the representative of the Franciscans] . . .
met on the thirtieth day of November 1963 . . . and agreed on the following
compromise, which will bind all members of both Communities:

(1) The ten northern windows of the Basilica of the Nativity at Bethlehem
will remain closed during the [annual, pre-Christmas] general cleaning, and
they will not be cleaned from outside by either parties [sic.]; while from inside
they will be cleaned by the Greek Orthodox from the beams of the ceiling by
means of poles covered with cloths.

(2) Throughout all the year the Greek Orthodox will light their candles, oil
lamps and electric bulbs in the Grotto during the Latin Feasts; and the Latins
will light their own during the Greek Orthodox Feasts. (Benedictos and Mancini
1963, 211–212)

Indeed, every step and pillar in the main pilgrim sites is parceled out. The
ongoing currency of these Agreements is witnessed at each Feast day as the
several communities carefully coordinate their respective, often simultaneous,
services.

In its effort to preserve its favored position under the Status Quo, the
Patriarchate has resorted to a variety of tactical approaches. The foremost of
these is its promotion of the Status Quo Agreements as immutable and absolute even in the midst of their evolution and clarification (as in the 1963
example above). For instance, since 1968 (that is, since the Six Day War)
the Israeli President has hosted an annual New Year's reception for the church
leaders of Jerusalem. As the doyen of this group, the Greek Patriarch expresses
words of appreciation on behalf of the Christians assembled. On the occasion
of the first such gathering, barely seven months after East Jerusalem had
come under Israeli jurisdiction, Benedictos I set the tone for subsequent
statements:

> We will direct all our endeavours . . . so that tranquility, security and peace,
> righteousness, mutual love and understanding may prevail in this Holy Land,
> wherein we have been living for centuries and are responsible for, and guardians
> of, the Holy Places, which constitute the focus of the world interest and whose
> *status quo*, therefore, has to be safeguarded, and where the privileges and rights
> of our institutions have to be respected and maintained, unaltered, forever.
> (1968a, 8)

From Benedictos' point of view, the Israelis took this proclamation and
warning to heart; four years later he praised the Israeli government which
"has, from the very start, shown absolute respect for the prevailing *status quo*
in the Holy Places" (Stern 1972a, 42). And four years later still, Benedictos
remarked:

> Let me once more assure Your Excellency that we of the Christian Churches
> wish to be in total harmony with all endeavors that aim to safeguard the *status*

quo in the Holy Places, respect for the rights and privileges of our religious institutions and communities and promotion of spiritual tolerance and intellectual understanding. (1976, 221)

While the Status Quo Agreements may be updated and adjusted to meet modern exigencies, the Patriarchate insists that they are a legally binding body of regulations and ecclesiastical compromises. As such, they are not to be abrogated by secular or religious authorities under any circumstances.

Orthodox supporters of the Patriarchate outside the country have joined this refrain. For instance, the Ecumenical Patriarch of Constantinople in 1974 called for the Greek and ecumenical churches to "offer aid and support to the Patriarchate of Jerusalem to protect the current status of the Holy Places." Similarly, in the same year, the clergy and laity of the Greek Orthodox Archdiocese of North and South America "adopted a resolution insisting that the rights and prerogatives of the Patriarchate of Jerusalem be respected and protected" (Bird 1975, 158).

Attendant with the Patriarchate's promotion of the immutability of the Status Quo has been a deliberate effort by the Greek leadership to limit the range of issues about which the Patriarchate will take an official stand. Even though the Status Quo is composed of a set of legal agreements that have inevitable political implications, the Patriarchate has insisted that preservation of the Status Quo is a religious issue, rather than a political one. As a consequence, the Patriarchate is within its rights to speak out on Status Quo related matters—even to heads of states and other governmental agencies. However, the leadership contends, it is not the Patriarchate's right to become entangled in non-religious—that is, "political"—issues outside the arena of the Status Quo Agreements. For instance, Metropolitan Vasilios, then the Chief Secretary of the Patriarchate and a leading contender in 1976 to succeed Benedictos as Patriarch, stressed this point in a statement calling for international guarantees of "les droits et les prérogatives de l'Eglise Orthodoxe en Terre Sainte" ("the rights and the prerogatives of the Orthodox Church on holy soil"). Vasilios carefully notes that the Patriarchate's relations with Israel "sont normaux" ("are normal"), and then states: "quant á l'internationalisation de la ville de Jérusalem, il a dit que c'est un probléme politique et non pas religieux" ("one could say that the internationalization of the city of Jerusalem is a political rather than a religious problem") (Diodoros 1976, 4). While the rights and privileges of the Orthodox Church should have international guarantees, the Church was not in a position to call for similar guarantees for the rest of Jerusalem.

Benedictos echoed this theme of noninvolvement in "political" matters in his 1974 New Year's greeting to President Katzir: "As heads of the Christian communities, *aloof from politics and dedicated wholly to our spiritual and sacred tasks*, tending to the Holy Shrines and the faithful committed to our care,"

they would pray for peace, justice, and goodwill [Emphasis added]. (Benedictos 1975, 96). Ironically, the very presence of Benedictos and his peers
as Christian leaders at the annual reception given by the President of Israel
is itself perceived by many Jerusalemites, from all political and religious perspectives, as a resounding political statement.

Another instance of the effort by the Greek leadership to act politically
while denying political intentions occurred in 1937 following the publication
of a British Mandate-sponsored study of prevailing conditions within the
Orthodox Church. The study, carried out by a Commission led by Sir Anton
Bertram, a noted British jurist, came in response to growing disquiet among
Arab members of the Orthodox Church. In July 1923 a conference of Arab
Orthodox parishioners "presented a 30-point proposal demanding reform"
of the Orthodox Patriarchate's structure (Kuttab 1984, 16). Bertram's com-
mission was appointed in 1925 and issued its findings, *Report of the Commission
on Controversies Between the Orthodox Patriarchate of Jerusalem and the Arab
Orthodox Community*, in 1928. The *Report* called for sweeping reforms to
increase Arab involvement in the control and operation of the Patriarchate.
In reply, the Greek hierarchs published a strongly worded *Refutation of the
Allegations Put Forward by Sir Anton Bertram Against the Patriarchate of Jerusalem* (1937). In a point-by-point rebuttal, the *Refutation* denounced the
findings of Sir Anton and his Commission.

However, after making their very political rebuttal (which documents official decrees from as early as the Constantinian Empire and on through the
Ottoman era), the *Refutation* concluded by reaffirming that it had no desire
to abrogate the political prerogatives of the Mandate power, and that the
Greeks' case was based solely on religious precedent and reasoning. The
wording of this final disclaimer is most revealing:

> In fact no one has in mind to deny the right of legislation over its subjects
> by the Successor Sovereignty [i.e. the British]. But when certain legal rules are
> also the rules of the Church and constitute its existence, and especially, when
> legislative innovations threaten to destroy rights not only for centuries enjoyed,
> but interwoven with the very existence of the Patriarchate of Jerusalem, we feel
> sure that the Authorities although having, as aforementioned, undoubted right
> to legislate will consider themselves bound by a status, which they have found
> and taken over. (Osterbye 1937, 55)

Thus, by carefully delineating its objective as the preservation of the immutability of the Status Quo Agreements, and by further arguing that its
concerns are with ecclesiastical ("religious") rather than political matters, the
Greek Orthodox Patriarchate has insulated itself against external efforts to
bring about change in its structure and behaviors. In addition, it has shielded
itself from the pressing needs of its Arab membership as they struggle to
survive in a politically tumultuous time.

However, the Patriarchate has not been totally immune to the winds of change. Frequently governmental pressures for change have occurred. In the face of these pressures the leadership of the Patriarchate has resisted as long as it was feasible and then yielded as little as possible. Perhaps this was most evident during the time of Jordan's sovereignty. In 1957, Patriarch Theodoros died. Under intense politicking from Jordanian and West Bank Arab lay Christians, King Hussein initiated legislation to grant Arabs additional powers in the conduct of the Patriarchate's affairs. According to Saul Colbi (1981, 63–64), Israel's leading authority on Christian relations in the Holy Land, the initial legislative proposals gave Arabs considerable responsibility, including roles in both the nominating and electing phases of the Patriarch-selection process. However, Arab "participation was considerably reduced in the final draft due to the Greek element inside the Jordanian government."

Among the official reforms that were successfully promulgated by the Government of Jordan, several are especially noteworthy. The Patriarchate agreed that all future candidates for the Patriarchal throne should be Jordanian citizens and should be able to read and write Arabic (Ibid., 64). The former requirement was rendered toothless, however, by a wholesale granting of Jordanian citizenship to all Greek monks who joined the Brotherhood of the Holy Sepulchre. The requirement that Arabic be spoken has also been a hollow one. Leading Arab lay members of the Jerusalem and Bethlehem congregations indicated in interviews with the current author that Arabic is poorly spoken by most members of the Greek hierarchy; as one put it, the Greeks speak "broken Arabic" and can barely read it. It is instructive to note that Benedictos I, the Patriarch elected shortly after King Hussein's regulations were enacted, was accompanied during a 1972 visit to Amman by "Mr. Stavros Papado-poulos, interpreter" (Rodoussakis 1973a, 179). However, competent Arabic is spoken by some individuals in the hierarchy, as the author found through his personal interviews. (One Greek cleric indicated that he had had four years of Arabic language training, which he received while studying in Russia. Despite living and studying in Jerusalem for almost ten years, it was to Russia that he went in order to learn Arabic.)

Thomas Idinopulos, an American professor of religion who has written widely on the churches in Jerusalem, provides further evidence of Patriarchal obfuscation in the face of government imposed reforms:

> King Hussein approved the election of Benedictos because the patriarch supported the new rules. But no sooner had the Greek been installed in office than Benedictos sought to turn Jordanian politicians against the rules, which died in committee. (1982, 19)

Elsewhere, Idinopulos (1981b, 374) records that the reforms that were passed by the Jordanian legislature were never fully implemented by Benedictos.

However, "to appease Arab interests he appointed the first Arab bishop of modern times, Simon Gharafeh, who happened to have a Greek mother."

Arab Orthodox lay interviewees were at least as scathing in their comments about this period. A Jerusalem lawyer was particularly incensed by the fates of the "Mixed" and "Local" Councils that were promised by the Patriarchate. The former—reportedly composed of eight Greek prelates, six Arabs (lay and clergy), and the Patriarch—was finally elected in the early 1960s. By agreement with the Jordanian government the Mixed Council was given control over one-third of the presumed receipts of the voluntary offerings given by pilgrims and other benefactors to the Patriarchate. However, no significant action was ever taken. With the departure from the West Bank of several prominent Arab members following the Six Day War in 1967, the Mixed Council was disbanded by the Patriarch for lack of a quorum. No successor Council has been elected.

"Local" Councils, which were promised a role in the affairs of individual parishes, were less fortunate still. By 1967, only the Jerusalem and Bethlehem Councils had been elected; no subsequent elections have been called by the Patriarch. Without Patriarchal approval, a Local Council "election" would have no credibility or legal status. In effect, the Patriarchate has inferred through its behavior that these Councils were imposed upon it by an unfriendly government, and since their existence contravened the hierarchy's understanding of the Status Quo precedents, which give the Greek hierarchs exclusive rights of governance, they need not be followed.

In order to assure that such crisis-point encounters with governments are not reached, the Patriarchate has diligently curried favor with the reigning authorities. As an Arab accountant put it, the principal organizational objective of the Patriarchate is "to attract the side of the governor, regardless of who it is." In an interview with Archimandrite Timotheus, the current Chief Secretary of the Patriarchate, I was told that the Patriarchate has had cordial relations with all of the most recent authorities—although the Secretary felt that the British had meddled unnecessarily in the internal affairs of the Church: "They turned our Arab flock against us with their propaganda." The findings and recommendations of Sir Anton in 1928 remain rancorous to the Greeks.

Relations between the Orthodox Patriarchate and the government of Israel have been particularly cordial. Besides the annual mutual expressions of goodwill exchanged at the New Year's receptions by the Patriarchs and the Presidents, a regular stream of receptions and visits takes place, particularly on the traditional visitation days (Modestos 1975a, 98). These informal ties have been reinforced by more concrete gestures.

Within days of the 1967 Six Day War, the Israeli Government unilaterally announced that it would recompense the Churches of East Jerusalem for war-related damages that they had incurred in the fighting after 1948, regardless of which military group had caused the damage. In all, about $1.5 million was paid to fifteen churches and religious orders by the Israeli government for these repairs (Modestos 1968, 495). In response to this governmental largesse, the Greek Patriarch and the Franciscan Custos (who oversees Roman Catholic Holy Sites):

> placed at the disposal of the State a 9,000 sq. metre belt of land outside and adjoining the Old City wall, between the Jaffa and Damascus Gates, so that it may be transformed into a green landscaped area for the embellishment of Jerusalem and the pleasure of citizens, pilgrims and other visitors. (Bird 1968, 5–6)

This "landscaped area" has, indeed, enhanced the environs of the Old City wall—and has served as an important security belt for possible Israeli military use in case of civil (i.e., Arab) disturbances.

In 1982, the Israeli "Administrator of Judea and Samaria" (the Israeli government's term for the West Bank) responded to a request from the Patriarch to facilitate resumption of the celebration of Epiphany on the shores of the Jordan River—the de facto border between Jordan and Israel. According to *Christian News from Israel,* the Israeli military went to considerable pains to assist the Patriarch:

> The Israeli Defense Forces prepared the site for the renewed rites. They cleaned the abandoned monastery and cleared a path to the river, removing both land mines and a thick overgrowth of wild shrubs, canes and thistles. A contingent of Israeli soldiers insured the safety of the participants in the ceremony, the river's edge being no more than eight metres from Jordan territory. (Diodoros I 1982, 203–204)

Significantly, "the participants" consisted of Patriarch Diodoros, thirty members of the Jerusalem clergy (all Greek) and a few lay parishioners, presumably Arabs.

In another significant gesture, Israeli Defense Minister Moshe Dayan responded quickly and generously in 1971 when a fire broke out in the Greek Orthodox Monastery of St. Catherine in the Sinai. He directed Israeli firefighting equipment to be dispatched to aid the monks. At the time, because of the Israeli military occupation of the Sinai, the Jerusalem Patriarch had assumed oversight responsibilities for the tiny, yet officially autocephalous, monastery (Bird 1968, 47; *Eastern Churches Review* 1972, 83). Subsequently, "His Beatitude [Patriarch Benedictos] flew down to the famed and ancient Monastery in Sinai in a helicopter readily put at his disposal by Mr. Moshe Dayan" (Rodoussakis 1972a, 155). Such gestures elicited public praise from the Patriarch, who gratefully acknowledged Israeli assistance—despite claims by Arabs, such as Patriarch Stephanos of the Coptic Catholic Church in Cairo, that the fire had been started by the Israelis (Idinopulos 1971, 11). These claims proved to be groundless but are symptomatic of a deep suspicion on the part of Arabs of the Greek hierarchy's intentions toward the Church's Arab Christians and toward the Israeli authorities.

Indeed, it has been in the face of growing Arab Palestinian nationalism that the Patriarchate has apparently courted, and received, the good will of the Israeli government. As Idinopulos has observed:

> What worries the Israelis is the politicization of the Arab laity of the Christian churches. This concern explains Israeli support of the Armenians and the Greek Orthodox hierarchy, both regarded as forces countering Arab radicalism. (1978, 501)

In these and other instances, the Greek hierarchy is seen by many Arab parishioners to be colluding with the Israeli government against the interests of Arab Christians.

Fully conscious of the volatility of the local political climate, however, the Patriarchate continues to work for the favor of Jordan as well. Patriarch Diodoros, who served for eighteen years prior to his enthronement as Archbishop of Jordan, has been especially supportive of projects in his old territory. According to Archimandrite Timotheous, since his elevation in 1981 Diodoros has undertaken construction of three new churches in Jordan, completed a large community center in Amman, and created a new titular bishopric in Idris, Jordan. In addition, while the Patriarchate is located in a part of Jerusalem that is currently governed by Israel, Diodoros delayed his coronation ceremony until "aprés la promulgation du décret royal jordanien, exigé par la loi" ("after the promulgation of the royal Jordanian decree, executed by law") (Diodoros I 1981, 2). These measures are tacit acknowledgments by the Patriarchate of the importance of continued Jordanian good will.

One Arab scholar sums up the efforts of the Patriarchate to seek support from all possible rulers: The Greek Orthodox hierarchs "are politicians, not spiritualists. They are more concerned with their political position than their spiritual one." This perspective may be unwittingly reflected in a statement by Archimandrite Timotheus: "We're like a small state, with a Foreign Minister, a Secretary of State, a Head of Finance, and so on." Benedictos makes a similar point when he compares the members of his Brotherhood with the monks who serve in the monasteries of Mt. Athos, in Greece:

> In the holy places of pilgrimage the duty [of the monk] does not have the characteristics of monastic confinement and of spiritual meditation as it is understood on Mount Athos; the Holy Sepulchre monk is a knight of the ancient order of the "Important." He must combine piety with bravery and faithfulness to tradition with an open attitude to life. (Diodoros I November 1, 1980, 6)[5]

Spiritual meditation may be the lot of the monks of Mt. Athos, but the monks of the Brotherhood of the Holy Sepulchre must struggle like "knights" with forces that would undermine the Status Quo, and thereby jeopardize the historic rights of pilgrims as well as the traditional preeminence, security, and stability of the Patriarchate.

International Political Factors

For the last century, the Greek Orthodox Patriarchate of Jerusalem has been engaged in a precarious balancing act between two sponsoring nations and their respective Orthodox churches. Greece, the primary source of personnel (only a few of the monks who join the Brotherhood come from Greek communities outside Greece, such as from Asia Minor and Cyprus) and a significant source of financial revenue, has inevitably played a major role in the life of the Patriarchate. However, this has not always been the case. When the Ottoman Empire, the "weak old man of Europe," began to show signs of decay during the nineteenth century, Russia stepped forward as the self-proclaimed advocate of the Orthodox faithful living in the Empire. In this proclamation they were following the precedent of the French, who had long shielded the Empire's Roman ("Latin") Catholics (Cust 1930, 127–128).

Prior to 1917, Saul Colbi (1976, 4) writes, "pilgrims, in their annual thousands, used to come from Tzarist Russia." However, after the Revolution, this source of pilgrims, and of the revenue they brought with them, virtually dried up. To compound the situation, the Patriarchate had been given vast land holdings in Russia and the Balkans; most of these were confiscated, thereby throwing the Patriarchate's finances into turmoil (Runciman 1971, 78). Thus, the October Revolution in St. Petersburg had the effect of pushing the Jerusalem Patriarchate into dependence upon Greece.

The Patriarchate continues to maintain active contact with the Russian Orthodox Church, even though the Soviets have discontinued governmental support. On his return from Moscow in 1981, Diodoros described the relations as "sont normaux ainsi que c'est le cas avec les autres Eglises auto-céphales" ("are normal as is the case with the other independent churches") (Tsimhoni 1981, 2). Regular exchanges of deputations, a steady flow of Jerusalem's monks to Moscow, and a common retention of the Julian calendar (in the face of strong pressure from most other Orthodox Churches, including the Ecumenical Patriarch), continue to undergird the relationship. In addition, the Jerusalem Patriarchate has been cautious to avoid being ensnared in the ongoing claims by "White Russians" to Russian Orthodox facilities that are under the present control of the Moscow-based church (Bird 1969, 47; Bird 1972, 167; Modestos 1973, 57–94; Zander 1971, 91; Luidens 1982, 186).

The warm association with the Russian Church has been at the sufferance of the Greek Church, headquartered in Athens. No visit by a delegation from Jerusalem to Russia or the Balkans takes place without a reciprocal stop or visit to Athens (see Bird 1968, 5–23; Diodoros I 1982, 188), and when deacons are sent to Russia for further training, others are sent at the same time to Athens (Modestos 1976, 222). Furthermore, in intra-Orthodox disputes, the Jerusalem Patriarchate generally supports Greece over Moscow. Such was the case when Patriarch Benedictos refused to recognize the autocephalous status of the Orthodox Church of America—previously known as the Russian Orthodox Greek Catholic Church of America—a status that was unilaterally declared by Moscow and rejected by Athens (Stern 1972b, 43).

For all intents and purposes, Greece is the international guarantor of the Greek ascendence in the Orthodox Patriarchate of Jerusalem. It is to Greece that the Patriarch turns in all matters of difficulty. The government of Greece has been instrumental in funding and carrying out reconstruction in a number of Holy Sites (in particular, the Church of the Holy Sepulchre—Rodoussakis 1972c, 108; Diodoros I 1982, 188). According to David Kuttab, a reporter for *Al Fajr*, an English-language Palestinian newspaper, the Greek government is also the source of salary payments for many of the Orthodox clergy (Kuttab 1984, 16).

Contributions of Greek pilgrims to the activities of the Patriarchate are also extremely important. Reconstruction of the Mar Elias Monastery and the Orthodox Church of Jericho relied on pilgrims' contributions (Kyprianos 1979, 27). Annual pilgrimages by thousands of Greek and Cypriot faithful (estimates of the number of Orthodox pilgrims at Christmas are over 3,000, and at Easter, over 5,000) is a major source of ecclesiastical revenue, for most pilgrims are housed in monasteries and Church- and parishioner-owned homes. If these were to be discontinued, as happened with the Russian pilgrims, the effects would be financially and politically devastating to the Greek hierarchy and to many Arab parishioners.

A final source of financial dependence is the large number of properties, movable and otherwise, that the Patriarchate has in Greece. Every monk, upon acceptance into the Brotherhood, deeds all of his earthly goods to the Brotherhood. Since almost all monks come from the mainland and islands of Greece, the Patriarchate has accrued untold wealth in Greece. According to Archimandrite Timotheus, this is the principal source of the Patriarchate's revenues. Indeed, the Patriarchate maintains a permanent liaison in Athens as its overseer of Greek relations and properties.

The perennial problem that confronts the Patriarchate is that of recruitment of youths who would become members of the celibate Brotherhood. Since these novices have been exclusively Greek and Greek-Cypriot, there have been frequent "appeals" to the Church in Athens to supply young recruits for Jerusalem (Benedictos 1972, 5–7; Osterbye 1978, 15–16; Diodoros 1984, 7). One of the more ingenious of such appeals involved setting up a rotation system under which non-married priests and monks from Greece could travel to Jerusalem and serve for short, predetermined periods to fill temporary vacancies that would arise in the Brotherhood. At the end of their brief stays, they would return to their prior assignments in Greece. In this way a Greek native would have experience in "the Holy Land"—and the Patriarchate would be assured of a supply of non-Arab, celibate clergy to fill its ranks (Tsimhoni 1980, 6). The latest in this series of recruitment appeals has resulted in the creation of a six-member commission, headed personally by Archbishop Seraphim, the primate of Greece (Idinopulos 1984, 12).

In recognition of these major dependencies it has on Greece, and in blatant contravention of its "nonpolitical" self-description, the Patriarchate celebrates most of the important Greek national holidays. An annual calendar reveals that—among others—the anniversary of the Greek revolution (begun in 1821 against the Ottomans), the anniversary of the "Ochi!" ("No!") movement commemorating the Greek resistance to the Nazis, the name day of former Greek King Constantine (before his deposition in 1974), and modern Greek Independence Day, are all acknowledged annually with celebratory masses in the Church of the Holy Sepulchre. In addition, most of these masses are followed by the gathering of the "Greek community" (diplomatic, business, and ecclesiastical) in the Greek Consulate-General. (For example, Rodoussakis 1972b, 33, 1973B, 257 and Modesto 1975b, 160 refer to Greek Independence Day observations, while Modesto 1975a, 97 recounts "Ochi" celebrations.) This pattern is in stark contrast to the virtual absence of recognition granted significant national days in the life of the Arab membership.

Local Ecumenical Factors

While political factors have had a significant impact on the life of the Patriarchate, their role has been emphasized chiefly in times of social and political crisis. On a day-to-day basis, the local ecclesiastical environment in which the Patriarchate functions presents it with some of its most challenging episodes. Once again, these challenges have eventuated in a series of defensive and preemptive actions on the part of the Orthodox Patriarchate.

Within the territory of the Patriarchate, there are currently twenty Christian denominations. They come from Chalcedonian and non-Chalcedonian traditions, Eastern and Western Rites, and Catholic, Protestant, and Orthodox national backgrounds. Estimates suggest that there are a total of 120,000 Christians in Palestine, with another 80,000 in Jordan (Betts 1975, 43; Diodoros I 1982, 187). According to Professor Gerries Khoury (1984), many of these denominations are represented by small contingents of expatriate clergy who are sent from other countries (such as Russia, Rumania, Syria, Ethopia, and Egypt) to tend their pilgrim sites and carry on rituals in their traditional sanctuaries. These denominations carry out their tasks, even in the absence of an indigenous congregation. In effect, the denominations have "presences" in the Holy Land.

Other denominations, such as the Greek Orthodox and Armenian Orthodox, have more sizable local congregations but have also seen the ministry
to them as secondary to the preservation of their ethnic hegemony while
executing their appointed rituals and ceremonies in the Holy Places. In the
last century, a number of Western churches—Roman Catholic, Anglican, Lutheran, and Baptist among others—have begun to aggressively promote their
unique brands of Christianity and to develop active, indigenous followings.
As a result of their proselytizing, they have frequently drawn members from
the older, Eastern Orthodox communions, much to the distress of these more
established groups.

Consequently, it is not surprising that intercommunion cooperation is not
seen by the Patriarchate to be an appropriate end in itself. However, on a
number of occasions the Patriarchate has found it advantageous to join forces
with other local denominations. In recent years, there have been two motivations for the Patriarchate to engage in such ecumenical activities. One mo-
tivation has been direct governmental pressure for the Churches to cooperate
in the face of common, usually facility-related, problems. The second moti-
vation for cooperative effort has been related to those occasions when government policy is widely perceived as a direct or indirect threat to the common,
ecclesial welfare.

On several occasions, the prevailing civil authorities have felt it necessary
to directly intervene in interchurch matters in order to gain cooperation. Key
among these have been joint efforts to effect much-needed repairs on co-
owned sanctuaries. The Status Quo agreements require that no structural
repairs or changes may take place in most Holy Places unless all resident
religious groups agree to them. This applies, even though the repairs may
be required in only one denomination's facilities, and even if that Church is
willing to undertake the necessary expenses.

According to an example recounted by a prominent member of the Church
of the Nativity in Bethlehem, in the mid-1970s significant repairs were needed
for sections of that basilica's lead roof. The damage was primarily in the
Greek Orthodox sections of the building, so that denomination agreed to
assume most of the costs of the repairs. However, the Armenian Orthodox
and the Franciscan Catholics repeatedly obstructed corrective measures—their
altars were dry. Finally, after two years of intense squabbling, the Israeli military authorities (who currently govern the West Bank) stepped in and decreed,
and partly paid for, a solution.

Even seemingly minor matters have, on occasion, required significant governmental tact and cajolery. The *Ecumenical Press Service* of the World Council
of Churches recounts a recent case in which Israel had to take steps in order
to respond to significant safety hazards in the Church of the Holy Sepulchre:

> . . . For the repair of the column [between the Armenian and Coptic Chapels
> which threatened to collapse] Israel agreed to foot the bill. The government

has also obtained permission from the five [Greek Orthodox, Franciscan, Armenian, Coptic, and Syrian Churches] to install lighting and rope-off a three-foot-deep pit near several ancient tombs. (Harakas 1985, 5)

The ecclesiastical authorities could not agree among themselves on such minimal safety precautions.

Nor is this need for governmental intervention just a recent phenomenon. The keys to the main entrance of the Church of the Holy Sepulchre have been maintained, since the Moslem conquest of Jerusalem in 638 A.D., by two local Moslem families. Each morning these doorkeepers, following an elaborate ritual prescribed in the Status Quo, open the sanctuary for use by the Christian denominations. The Moslems are recompensed for their efforts by the five Holy Sepulchre-related communions. Some accounts (Danilov 1981, 43) contend that this practice was the inevitable result of Moslem intervention between disputing Christian groups. However, Arab Orthodox informants argued that it is more likely an instance of Moslem assertion of sovereignty over the Christian Holy Places. In any case, the practice has been firmly enshrined in the Status Quo Agreements, and each party is loathe to change it.

While there are numerous examples of such governmental intervention to intentionally bring about inter-Church cooperation, the twentieth-century powers have been very reluctant to become tangled in the disputes, as illustrated by the Israeli government's delay of two years before they forced resolution of the quarrel in Bethlehem.

Interdenominational cooperation is more frequently motivated by governmental practices that are perceived by the churches to be threatening to their collective interests, especially as those interests are formulated in the Status Quo. Two crises in recent years have generated such interdenominational cooperation: the debates between Israeli governmental agencies and the Churches surrounding the "bribery for conversion" law and the "pilgrim guide" regulations.

One of the legacies of the Holocaust of World War II has been a deep suspicion in many Jewish circles of Christian proselytizing. In Israel, this suspicion generated an aggressive campaign by some Jewish organizations to discredit all Christian programs. Osterbye (1970) gives a full account of this campaign. So intense has been the pressure, that from time to time the Christian communities have come together in order to deny the accusations.

One of the first of these collective denials took place via a declaration published on July 14, 1963. Among its signatories was the Greek Orthodox Metropolitan of Nazareth, the Patriarchate's ranking prelate in Israel at the time. In addition to him, Catholic, Anglican, and Protestant representatives were cosponsors of the denial that they took advantage of poor or unemployed

Israelis or used their charitable organizations in education or medicine (i.e., hospitals) to pressure Jews to convert (Osterbye 1970, 130–31).

During the leadership tenure of Menachim Begin and the Likud Party, this campaign of suspicion about alleged Christian missionary activities reached fruition in the passage of a Private Member's Bill (that is, one which rose from the floor of the Knesset rather than through party initiative) known as "The Encitement to Change of Religion Act of 1977." The bill prohibits the giving or receiving of "money or any other material benefit in order to entice a person to change his religion" (Osterbye 1978, 122). The bill was passed in short order, largely in response to what was perceived by legislators as a growing movement to draw Israeli Jews into evangelical Christianity.

The official news organ of the Israeli Ministry of Religious Affairs, *Christian News from Israel,* records the concerted reaction that this bill elicited:

> The enactment has aroused concern in Christian and inter-faith circles in Israel and abroad. For example, on 10 March 1978, the Greek Orthodox, Latin and Armenian Patriarchs of Jerusalem and the (Franciscan) Custos of the Holy Land signed a letter to the President of the State, Professor Ephraim Katzir, in which they expressed their opposition to the enactment and its implications. (Ibid.)

Most significantly, the response to this issue was on the highest—the Patriarchal—level, a degree of cooperation that is extremely rare.

In this particular case, the united opposition resulted in some governmental backtracking; in subsequent pronouncements the Government assured the Christian communities that the legislation was not necessarily directed at them, (Sable 1979, 41–53) and that irrefutable evidence of wrongdoing would have to be produced before any official action would be taken (Osterbye 1978, 122). While the law remains on the books, its application has been virtually ignored.

A second crisis that drew considerable cooperative effort on the part of the several churches arose in the wake of Israeli governmental regulations that required that all tourist groups visiting Israel (East Jerusalem, in which the major Christian holy sites are located, is considered by the Israeli government to be part of Israel) had to be led by government-licensed guides. This seemed to imply that Christian pilgrim groups, even those led by religious officials, would have to have Jewish guides. The 1978 regulations were sporadically applied by the Likud government. In 1981 the issue reached an impasse, and in league with the Catholic hierarchy of Jerusalem, the Greek Orthodox Patriarchate protested. Haim Shapiro of the *Jerusalem Post* wrote that, once again, concerted effort resulted in a concession to the Churches. Those groups that were "pilgrim" in nature (rather than "tourist") would be permitted to have their own "qualified" religious leaders (Shapiro 1981, 35). Subsequent accounts, however, suggest that this matter may not be finally resolved (Idinopulos 1984, 31).

Such instances of cooperative ecumenical effort, whether government promoted or government induced, are rare and firmly resisted by the Greek Patriarchate. Mayor Teddy Kolleck, the Jewish mayor of "united" Jerusalem, has worked with the ecclesiastical leaders since 1967. In a recent interview he remarked on the difficulty of achieving concerted action:

> "The Greeks," he stated, "only see the Greek Jerusalem, the one which never goes beyond the outer walls of the Patriarchate." And then he added, "But this is true of all the church communities in the holy land. You cannot get them together on a common project, because the only city, the only land they know about or care about is the one they occupy." (Idinopulos 1981a, 159)

Indeed, more regularly than cooperation, competition among the groups is evident. Archbishop Germanos is a leading figure in the Greek-born Orthodox hierarchy (in 1981 he was one of the three contenders for the Patriarch's seat). In December 1967, shortly after the Six Day War, he made the following comments in an article introducing the Greek Orthodox Patriarchate to Israeli readers:

> The rights and privileges specified in the *ahtname* of [Caliph] Omar [ibn el-Hattab in 638 A.D.] were subsequently confirmed in rescripts issued by the later rulers of Palestine. It was on the basis of these rescripts that the Patriarchs could, in more recent times, undertake their untiring struggle for the preservation of Orthodox rights *against Latin and Armenian encroachments* [Emphasis added]. (Germanos 1967, 23)

Thus, from the very highest level of the Orthodox hierarchy, the hallmark of the Patriarchate's relationships with other denominations is seen as a struggle over competing rights and privileges.

The "struggle" is not just a rhetorical one, nor is it clouded in mythic history; its vitality is ongoing. In 1967, according to then-Vice-Mayor of Jerusalem, Meron Benvenisti, the Israeli government was seeking ways to obtain Vatican recognition of Israel. Benvenisti writes that newly won political control of the Old City led Israel to make this unusual offer in exchange for Vatican recognition:

> Israel would recognize the pope as coordinator of all Christian interests in Jerusalem and would treat the Catholics as "first among equals" with regard to other Christian communities in the Holy City. (Cited in Idinopulos 1978, 500)

In this way, the Greek Orthodox preeminence would be lost, once again, to the Catholics. In the end, nothing came of this particular proposition. Yet the rivalry continues.

Indeed, the very presence of a Latin Patriarch is seen by the Greeks as an unholy vestage of the Crusades, when the Greek Patriarch was ignominiously exiled to Cyprus and replaced by a Latin successor. Although the Latin Patriarch was subsequently expelled with the other Crusaders, he was reinstated by the Ottoman Emperor at France's instigation in the mid-nineteenth century (Fowden 1972, 431).

While the Status Quo legislation is minutely detailed—to the extent of allocating individual ceiling beams and stair steps to be cleaned (see the 1963 Agreement described above)—there continues to be a simmering debate about several unresolved aspects. One matter that generates contention is the privilege of cleaning as yet unallocated sections of the Holy Sites. On the principle that a section cleaned becomes a section possessed, fisticuffs erupted between the Armenian and Greek Orthodox Communities in December 1984 in Bethlehem's Church of the Nativity. In dispute were the implications of a Status Quo stipulation giving the Greek Orthodox the right to clean overhead beams from a ladder. The Greeks claimed that they could climb from the ladder and the crawl along the beams, thereby extending their "territory," while the Armenians said that they could only clean the area within reach of the top of the ladder. According to news accounts, several monks were rushed to the hospital for treatment following this fray (Kuttab 1985, 16).

According to a resident of Bethlehem, so frequent are the disputes among the various Christian groups sharing custody of the Church of the Nativity, that the local populace treats them as spectator events. He reports that the Church bells are rung at regular intervals every day; if the bells ring at other times, Bethlehemites assume that a holy fracas has begun, and many gather in the courtyard to observe. Since the combatants are generally Greeks, Syrians, or Armenians, the Arab population, both Christian and non-Christian, feels particularly perturbed.

The second major issue that has elicited varying levels of cooperation and competition among the Churches is focused on changing Church membership patterns. According to demographer Daphne Tsimhoni:

> The proportion of Christians in the West Bank, as in Palestine at large, has steadily decreased since World War I as the result of constant Christian emigration and a higher Muslim birthrate. . . . The Christians' concentration in towns, and their having been educated in schools run by European Christians, facilitated their migration and settlement abroad. (1983, 55–56)

This dwindling of numbers would seem to be a common threat to all the Christian communities, and many Christians have expressed alarm about the situation (Kuttab 1984, 16). Among the most outspoken has been Patriarch

Hakim, the Melchite (Greek Catholic) primate of Antioch whose diocese includes Jerusalem:

> If present population trends continue, the Melkite Patriarch Maximos V Hakim has predicted, "in ten or fifteen years there will be no Christians in the land of Christ, the Palestine of early Christian history." (Modestos 1969, 327)

While this dire prediction has not been fulfilled, it is a theme that was repeated frequently in interviews with the Arab Orthodox faithful; they fear that their number is doomed.

The Greek Orthodox Patriarchate of Jerusalem has also appeared to have some recent disquiet about the trend. In 1982, together with the Greek Orthodox Patriarchs of Antioch and Alexandria and the Archbishop of Cyprus (of these, only the Antiochan Patriarch was an Arab), Diodoros "issued a joint appeal . . . to reaffirm the necessity of the Christian Orthodox presence in this region" (Luidens 1982, 64). However, even in this expression of concern, no direct mention is made about the loss of Arab membership; concern is just registered about the future of an "Orthodox presence." This letter is reminiscent of an earlier (1972), more pointed epistle from Patriarch Benedictos to the bishops of the Church in Greece:

> . . . The times in which we are living . . . have brought about changes in our Holy Brotherhood, and now, from day to day, it is dangerously declining, so that our monasteries are closing down and we cannot attract new monks to them. (Benedictos 1972, 6)

Indeed, over the years the Patriarchate has spent considerably greater effort on recruiting and retaining its Greek hierarchy than on securing its Arab flock; presumably the diminishing Greek "presence" is the one to which the joint 1982 statement also refers (Ware 1981, 102).

While the Greek Orthodox Patriarchate has been virtually silent on the political and human rights of Palestinians, Patriarch Hakim and the Melchites (Greek Catholics) have been outspoken public proponents of those rights. It would appear that this difference of political perspective has served to fuel a growing rivalry between the Melchite and Greek Orthodox Churches. The latter accuses the Melchites of enticing away its Palestinian members, especially through their extensive school system. This concern was articulated by each Orthodox interviewee, whether Greek or Arab, with whom I spoke.

Table 12.1 hows the extant data on sectarian membership trends in Palestine over the last half-century. It suggests that the Greek Orthodox have good cause to worry about the shifting affiliation patterns. While these data must be read with some caution, two "trends" are very apparent: proportionally, the Greek Orthodox have been losing members; at the same time, the Mel-

TABLE 12.1:
SECTARIAN CHANGES AMONG CHRISTIANS IN PALESTINE, 1931–1984
(INCLUDING ISRAEL, THE WEST BANK, AND JERUSALEM)

	1931[1]		1969[2]		1984[3]	
	Number	Percent	Number	Percent	Number	Percent
Greek Orthodox	38,100	47%	37,450	38%	40,000	34%
Latin Catholics	18,000	22%	23,900	24%	25,000	21%
Melchites	12,500	15%	24,800	25%	41,300	35%
Protestants*	5,500	7%	4,800	5%	3,400	3%
Others**	7,500	9%	8,550	9%	9,000	8%
TOTALS	81,600	100%	99,500	101%	118,700	101%

* "Protestants" includes Anglicans.
**"Others" includes both Chalcedonians and Non-Chalcedonians.
[1]Betts 1975, 66. Betts bases his 1931 data on the 1931 British Mandate census figures.
[2]Colbi 1969b, 191. Colby's data is taken from an Israeli government census, that was conducted after the Six-Day War.
[3]Khoury 1984, 33ff. Khoury drew his data from the records of the various churches as well as from official government statistics.

chites have been gaining members. From these data, it is not possible to demonstrate that there is large-scale switching, but such an interpretation would accord with the assessment of most observers with whom I spoke. The Melchite church, a uniate branch of the Roman Catholic communion, is an Eastern Rite Church (that is, it follows the Orthodox liturgy) and retains much of the structure and practice it brought with it from the Greek Orthodox Church when it splintered in 1724. As a result, it is a "natural" switch for disaffected Arab Orthodox to make. In addition, the Melchite Church has long been run by an Arab clerical hierarchy.

That this trend is not just a recent phenomenon is suggested in a comment by historian Robert B. Betts (1975, 66):

> During the late 18th century . . . the Roman Catholic Church began seriously to encourage local Orthodox Christians to identify with the newly created Greek Catholic Rite, and by the establishment of the British Mandate in 1920 had successfully recruited about 25% of Palestinian Orthodoxy, while another third had been lured away by the Latin Catholic and Protestant missions with their fine schools and dedicated clergy.

Movement from Greek Orthodox membership to that of other affiliations, especially Melchite, has been of long standing.

The differences between Melchite and Greek Orthodox membership trends become even more significant in light of the fact that the two primary enhancers of Palestinian Arab emigration—personal contacts in Europe and the Americas and higher levels of education attained via church-sponsored schools—are less significant factors in the Greek Orthodox community. As a consequence, Greek Orthodox out-migration is probably at a much lower level than that for the Melchites. Thus, while the Orthodox have barely replaced their departed members, the Melchites have grown even in the face of out-migration.

It would appear, at least until recently, that there has been minimal programmatic response within the Greek Orthodox hierarchy to the loss of Arab members. As late as 1982, Professor Idinopulos made the following observation:

> The Greek hierarchy looked with displeasure on all these [nineteenth century] missionary activities, but was not alarmed. The real threat to their power and privilege, they believed, lay with the Franciscans and Armenians, and they took a position in the Patriarchate of Jerusalem that continues to this day. Its primary responsibility is the safeguarding of Christian shrines in the Holy Land, and only secondarily the tending of the needs of the Orthodox Arab community. (1982, 17)

The Greeks' concentration on maintenance of the Holy Sites and promotion of their primacy as established in the Status Quo Agreements has resulted in an offhand, or even hostile, treatment of the Arab Orthodox parishioners.

However, according to Archimandrite Timotheus, a new effort has been launched under current Patriarch Diodoros to respond to the trends. In particular Timotheus cited the construction projects in Jordan and the recent (1982) opening of a secondary school in Jerusalem as evidence of this new resolve.

Indeed, other evidence suggests that the current hierarchy is more distressed than has previously been the case. At a recent Middle East Council of Churches meeting held in Cyprus, the Greek Orthodox delegates made it plain that they were upset with the encroaching on their membership by other denominations, even hinting that the Patriarchate might withdraw from this ecumenical agency if the trend persisted. They pledged a more vigorous school building program in order to counteract this perceived encroachment.

Perhaps the level of distress that prevails in the Patriarchate is best expressed in a recent interview given by Diodoros to the Orthodox Press Service:

> The Patriarch also says his earlier complaint about what he considers efforts by Roman Catholics to entice people away from the Orthodoxy has not changed the situation, and that before Christmas, Roman Catholics "systematically visited Orthodox households" to encourage them to take part in Roman Catholic liturgical celebrations. (1985, 52)

Within Jerusalem the Greek Orthodox Patriarchate has established a rather mixed record in building Christian renewal through local ecumenical activities.

The growing movement, stimulated in large part by Anglicans and Protestants, to present a united Christian front through cooperative worship, has placed a strong pressure on the Orthodox. Among the first such modern undertakings have been the joint worship services held annually during the "Week of Prayer for Christian Unity." After a rather halting start in the mid-1960s, this movement "came above ground" in 1967. A year later "an Anglican friend" shared the following account with the editors of the *Eastern Churches Review:*

> Last year there was a step forward, with Lutherans, Roman Catholics, and Anglicans holding some joint services—not well announced.
> This year we moved forward drastically—although the Orthodox (the Greeks) and the Syrian Orthodox (the Jacobites) would not participate. This was partly, but not wholly, because they were approached on behalf of Rome by a bearded Russian Uniate; but I think that they will have to do something to get in next year. (Anonymous 1968, 81)

However, this was not to happen so quickly. Indeed, following an announcement in 1969 by the Melchite archbishop of Akko that he was going to celebrate Easter according to the ancient, Gregorian calendar—a gesture intended, at least in part, to show that the Melchites were cognizant of their Roman Catholic affiliation—Patriarch Benedictos saw fit to issue a warning to his priests and lay members forbidding them from joining the Catholic services (Bird 1970, 32).

From this inauspicious beginning—and after the organizers learned more about the art of ecclesiastical diplomacy (no more "bearded Russian Uniates" as emissaries)—the Greek Orthodox were finally included in the Week of Prayer for Christian Unity in 1973. However, as late as the Spring of 1985, the Greek Orthodox presence in these services was largely confined to those celebrations at which they officiated. Unlike the Syrian Orthodox and Melchite clergy, the Greek Orthodox hierarchs are still not a major factor in these sessions.

On another level, that of collective Christian response to the ongoing occupation of the West Bank by Israel, the Greek Orthodox have apparently been ambivalent and even obstructionist. Unless there is a direct challenge to its position vis-à-vis the Status Quo Agreements, the Patriarchate has been reluctant to participate in actions that confront the government of Israel. One former Greek Orthodox Arab layman noted in an interview that some other denominational leaders recently tried to form an informal council to share concerns and provide the framework for corporate responses to perceived governmental injustices. However, when the invitations for the informal council's first meeting were distributed, the Greek Orthodox hierarchy was gravely vexed. It contended that, as the premier Church in Jerusalem, such an invitation was its prerogative. The other churches reportedly gave way and encouraged the Greeks to issue such an invitation. However, months later, no such invitation was forthcoming.

In summary, the Greek Orthodox Patriarchate has vacillated in its relations with other local denominations. While it has sought cooperation when preservation of the Status Quo demanded it, the Patriarchate generally sees cooperation as contravening its prerogatives as the preeminent Christian communion in the Holy Land. In the face of collective demographic changes and of growing local ecumenicity, the Patriarchate has engaged in ecumenical efforts on a minimal level, but its involvement has generally been reluctant or even obstructionist. In all such matters, the overarching concern of the Greeks has been their stability and security as the entrenched leadership of the Patriarchate.

International Ecumenical Factors

Relations between the Patriarchate of Jerusalem and the other autocephalous Orthodox Churches have been reflective of the Patriarchate's dependence on Greece. In general, it has followed the lead of the Greek Church in intra-Orthodox matters, as has been mentioned above in relation to the Russian Orthodox Church.

In recent years, the leading ecumenical figure in the Orthodox world has been the late Ecumenical Patriarch, Athenagoras of Constantinople, who was the nominal superior of the Church of Greece but with whom Athens grew restive. Athenagoras was an active proponent of such ecumenical endeavors as Orthodox membership in the World Council of Churches and closer cooperation between Orthodox and Catholic communions.

In 1964, amid considerable pomp and publicity, Patriarch Athenagoras met in Jerusalem with Pope Paul VI, thereby breaking a 900-year policy of mutual recrimination and excommunication between these two Christian communities. However, in the Jerusalem Patriarchate these ecumenical efforts were met with grim formality and growing displeasure. As the site of both Latin and Orthodox Patriarchates and as the initial center of Christianity, Jerusalem had been chosen to be the meeting place for Patriarch Athenagoras and Pope Paul.

However, it would appear from the record that the Jerusalem Patriarchate's participation was very much that of supporting cast. Although Patriarch Benedictos was the official host for Athenagoras, Benedictos' meeting with Pope Paul was brief and diplomatic (Osterbye 1964, 3–11). In his welcoming comments Benedictos addressed Pope Paul as "Very Holy Pope, who presides over the Roman Catholic Church . . . Zion, the venerable Mother of the Churches, joyfully salutes your happy arrival" (Zander 1971, 93). The tone of this greeting was warm and effusive. However, coming as it did from one who saw the Roman Catholic Church as a primary threat to his own institution's stability and existence, Benedictos' greetings made it clear that the Pope had no claim to headship over the other ancient patriarchates. Pope in Rome he may be, but in Mother Jerusalem, Paul was, at best, a welcome pilgrim. In the end, Benedictos acceded to Pope Paul's presence because it was the will of Athenagoras, the Patriarch over Greece and the Orthodox world's leading ecumenist.

Archimandrite Kallistos (Timothy) Ware, a leading American student of contemporary Orthodoxy, suggests the depth of resistance to ecumenism that was felt by Patriarch Benedictos:

> A kindly and courteous man, traditionalist in his theology, Patriarch Be-
> nedictos was critical of the "ecumenist" policies of Patriarch Athenagoras of
> Constantinople, and in his later years was more reserved over questions of
> Christian unity than any other Orthodox church leader. (1981, 102)

Further evidence of Jerusalem's dependence upon Greece to set the tone for its ecumenical efforts can be found in the delegations that the Patriarchate sent to Pan-Orthodox and other ecumenical conferences. These delegations of the Jerusalem Patriarchate regularly included theological faculty members from Greece (usually the University of Athens) among their number. The limited human resources of the Patriarchate, combined with its concern that theological orthodoxy as current in Greek circles be the paramount issue in every ecumenical encounter, served to limit the Patriarchate's ongoing involvement in meaningful, structure-altering, relationships (Bird 1968, 5; Modestos 1976, 221–222; Ware 1982, 179).

The depth of actual impact on the structure and activity of the Jerusalem Church is indicated by the report about the delegation that represented the Patriarchate at the World Council of Churches General Assembly in Nairobi in 1975. The two archimandrites (neither of whom sat on the all-powerful "Holy Synod") who formed the delegation came back to Jerusalem and "reported on the proceedings to the Synod" (Modestos 1976, 222). No action or official response devolved from their participation; two "back benchers" had made an appearance at this significant ecumenical gathering and then had merely recounted the Assembly's proceedings to their superiors.

The attitude of the Patriarchate toward the World Council of Churches, of which it has long been a full member, was summed up recently in an interview granted by Patriarch Diodoros:

> The primate of the Jerusalem church then expresses clearly his disapproval
> of the participation "of our Orthodox Church as one among the four hundred
> confessions united in the W.C.C." For him "the participation of the Jerusalem
> church in the W.C.C. is simply formal." (1984, 7)

While an active member of the WCC in terms of sending delegations to various conclaves of the Council, the Patriarchate sees this involvement as merely a "formal" one that is not intended to signify commitment to the policies, pronouncements, or programs of the WCC.

Among the key issues with which the WCC is currently wrestling is the matter of intercommunion across denominational boundaries. In addition to the historic members of the WCC, this particular dialogue has also involved Protestant denominations that are not members of the WCC as well as representatives from various Catholic constituencies, who are also non-members. At its 1983 General Assembly in Vancouver, British Columbia, the WCC endorsed a lengthy document dealing with the issue of intercommunion along with other matters (*Baptism, Eucharist, and Ministry* 1982). The document calls on participating communions to consider carefully the historical reasons for division among the churches and to consider the possibility of transcending these differences in the future. It was perhaps this document that sparked Diodoros' (1984, 7) comments about "formal" participation in the WCC. In any event, he continued the interview with an implicit rejection of the WCC document and an explicit criticism of the Catholics and the Copts:

> Finally, about intercommunion, His Beatitude clearly condemns the practice of giving the holy communion to the faithful from heterodox churches, for example to the Roman Catholic faithful and to the Copt.

Despite this ambivalent relationship with the WCC, the Patriarchate has been involved in a number of bilateral discussions with members of other communions, including the Lutherans (Ware 1982, 179) and the Anglicans (Rodoussakis 1973c, 55; Modestos 1978, 146). In 1974, Archbishop Vasilios represented the Jerusalem Patriarch in an audience with Patriarch Dimitrios of Constantinople. During their session, Vasilios expressed his expectation that a "niveau panorthodoxe" (pan-orthodox standard) would be applied to all such "dialogues bipartites" (bilateral dialogues). In effect, the policy that the Patriarchate employs in such dialogues is to discuss matters of mutual accord, but to refrain from concessions that might be considered "unorthodox" or that would change the Status Quo (Diodoros 1974, 4).

However, what constitutes a "niveau panorthodoxe" in ecumenical matters is still very unclear. Indeed, it is an issue that is very much under discussion among the Orthodox churches and will be one of the ten topics under consideration at some future Pan-Orthodox Council (Stern 1976, 3). This Council would be the first Orthodox conclave of its scale since the Second Council of Nicea, held in 787 AD; however, its date and site are undetermined (one Lutheran ecumenist commented to the author: "There will sooner be a Vatican III than a Pan-Orthodox Council").

Thus, while participating on a formal level in a number of international ecumenical arenas, the Jerusalem Patriarchate has no immediate intention of engaging in greater cooperation, much less "visible union." Preoccupied as it is with its own self-preservation, the Patriarchate perceives the ecumenical movement in general as one that blurs the boundaries that the Orthodox have worked so hard to establish. As claimant to the preeminent position among the Churches in Jerusalem, and as the self-styled "Mother Church" and historical preserver of the true "Orthodox" faith, the Patriarchate's instincts and actions are to shore up its sagging defenses and further isolate itself. This is accomplished in the face of considerable external ecclesiastical pressure to be more forthcoming.

Conclusions

Beset with a variety of pressures from without, the Jerusalem Patriarchate has established a firm shell of self-defense. Basing its overriding concern for self-preservation on the favored position it has been guaranteed under the Status Quo Agreements, it strives to absolutize those Agreements and promote them as immutable.

While it seeks the favor of Israel, the reigning government, the Patriarchate recognizes the vissicitudes of Middle East politics and retains friends in the Jordanian government as well. This reliance on informal contacts with political leaders is coupled with a persistent, formal disclaimer about its involvement in political matters. In this way it is able to remain aloof from the highly volatile confrontation between Palestinians and Israelis. While this "hands off" approach is not appreciated by the Arabs, it is warmly welcomed by the Israelis—who respond with conciliatory gestures.

The Greek hierarchy has long been reliant on international support for its financial and institutional stability. During the early stages of the formalization of the Status Quo agreements, the Russian government acted as the Patriarchate's proponent in the Empire's courts. Subsequent to the Russian Revolution in 1917, the government and Church of Greece assumed the roles of protector and advocate for the Jerusalem Patriarchate.

Greece's involvement continues to grow to the point that the Patriarchate's financial solvency and personnel recruitment are absolutely dependent upon Greece. In the immediate future, this involvement can be expected to remain crucial for the Orthodox Church of Greece will increasingly be able to effect change within the Jerusalem Patriarchate. As Greek national interests shift, especially in relations with the oil-rich Arab countries, the implications for the life of the Jerusalem Patriarchate's Greek hierarchs are also profound. In sum, the Patriarchate's international tightrope walk will continue for the foreseeable future.

In recent years, under Patriarch Diodoros, there has been a growing awareness in the hierarchy about the disquiet among the Arabs and about their consequent departure from the Church. While a clear policy has not been enacted, it is likely that this awareness will lead to new programs on behalf of the Arabs. However, if the Patriarchate becomes a public advocate of the political causes of the Palestinians, it will inevitably jeopardize its favored position with the Israelis. Since governmental support—from whomever is in power—is a keystone of the Patriarchate's policy of self-preservation, a sudden or dramatic shift towards the Arabs is highly unlikely. Instead, the Patriarchate will undoubtedly continue its hazardous balancing act in this arena as well.

While the ecumenical movement has waxed and waned worldwide, the participation of the Jerusalem Patriarchate has been formal and noncommittal. As a virtual ward of the Church of Greece, it has had to rely for its international ecumenical cues on Athens' lead. The latter's ecclesiastical struggles with Moscow and Constantinople have made the Jerusalem Patriarchate cautious and have thereby limited its involvement. Furthermore, Jerusalem's reliance on a conservative policy of distinction between "orthodox" and "heterodox" communions continues to be a retarding factor in its ecumenical endeavors.

In the end, the Greek Orthodox Patriarchate has succeeded in preserving its own stability according to the Status Quo regulations. However, this stability has been accomplished at the cost of virtual isolation from other local communions and from the wider ecclesial and political trends of the day. By withdrawing into its own community and traditions, the hierarchy has effectively removed itself from meaningful external engagements.

In a recent interview, Archimandrite Timotheus said that when monks join the Patriarchate they agree that "their only mother is the Brotherhood, their only father is the Patriarch, and their only country—regardless of where they come from, Greece or Australia or America—is the Holy Places." Measured against this rather limited yardstick, the Patriarchate has been masterfully successful.

Notes

1. While there are a number of English-language accounts of the history of the Greek Orthodox Patriarchate of Jerusalem, they tend to be subsumed in larger works on the Christian communities of "the Holy Land." As a result, the distinctive experiences of the Jerusalem Patriarchate are nowhere systematically nor sociologically assessed on their own terms.

Nevertheless, several publications have recorded the comings and goings of the members of the Patriarchate, thereby providing some evidence of the inner workings of the hierarchy. Chief among these sources has been the official publication of the Israeli Ministry of Religion, *Christian News from Israel (CNFI)*, which has been published irregularly since the late 1950s. Beginning in 1970, *CNFI* has included a section that recounts the most recent "events" in the life of the Patriarchate. This short piece (generally known as "Event and Comment: Chronology of the Greek Orthodox Patriarchate") has usually been written by a member of the Holy Brotherhood and effectively reflects the "official" slant of that exclusively Greek body, as modified to appear in an Israeli government document.

In addition, *CNFI* has regularly included "News Items" that recount Patriarchate-related matters that are considered of potential interest to its Israeli readership. In these articles, the government's perspective is only thinly disguised. However, in presenting a record of activities (such as those that occurred during the visits to Jerusalem of Pope Paul in 1964 and of Patriarch Pimen from Moscow in 1972), accuracy can be assumed.

Other periodic accounts of the pronouncements and actions of the Greek members of the Orthodox hierarchy are included in *Episkepsis* (the biweekly publication of the Orthodox Center of the Ecumenical Patriarch in Chambesy, Switzerland), *Eastern Churches Review* (in a biannual article entitled "News and Comment" that presents the activities of the Orthodox churches throughout the world), and *Diakonia* (in the annual "Survey of Orthodoxy," initiated by Thomas Bird in the late 1960s). Additional information, although more ecumenical in its focus, is available from the *Ecumenical Press Service* of the World Council of Churches, of which the Patriarchate is a member.

In all of these sources, the vantage point is that of the Greek hierarchy of the Patriarchate; the Arab membership's perspective is virtually absent. While some published material reflecting the Arabs' attitudes and actions has appeared in *Al Fajr* (*The Dawn*, an English-language, Palestinian weekly that is available—after Israeli government censorship—in Jerusalem) and the *Jerusalem Post*, this perspective is not generally available in printed form.

As a consequence of this paucity of information, interviews were conducted with Arab members and former members of the Patriarchate who must remain anonymous. While the interviewees did not constitute a "representative" sample of opinion (almost all were professionals—from education, journalism, medicine, and the law; all were males; and all were from Jerusalem, Bethlehem, or their immediate environs), they represented a very articulate segment of the Arab faithful. Their perceptions were remarkably candid and uniform. In order to better assess the validity of their arguments, additional interviews were undertaken with Arab and Western academics who were not members of the Patriarchate but who had observed the Patriarchate close hand. Again, the unity of supportive assessment was strong.

The principal resource for the myriad rules and regulations that constitute the Status Quo Agreements is Bernardin Collin's helpful *Recueil de Documents Concernant Jérusalem et les Lieux Saints (Collection of Documents Concerning Jerusalem and the Sacred Places)*, an exhaustive compendium of the Agreements from Ottoman days to the 1970s.

Archimandrite Timotheus, the Chief Secretary of the Patriarchate, was a ready and cordial informant. He graciously provided the hierarchy's perspective on the local scene—one that was reflective of the official image that is presented in the aforementioned published sources. Other interviews were held with a Greek monk from the Holy Brotherhood and with two Arab priests in the Patriarchate.

In sum, there is little available sociological analysis of the contemporary Greek Orthodox Patriarchate of Jerusalem. Those sources that exist are selective, periodic, and are generally focused on the Greek-born hierarchy of the Church. This initial examination of the social and political structures of the Patriarchate relies on extant sources as well as on open-ended interviews with a variety of members of the local community. As such, it represents a limited vantage point, but it is an important first step in the process of analyzing this ancient and isolated communion in the Christian tradition.

2. Elsewhere (Luidens, 1986), the factors relating to the internal dynamics of the Patriarchate, especially the relations between Greeks and Arabs, are examined.
3. In the political atmosphere of Middle East rhetoric, place names are highly charged. In this paper, the term "Palestine" refers to a geographic entity, that included in the British Mandate, rather than a contemporary political one.
4. For Palestine data, see Betts 1975, 76; Colbi 1969b, 189–190; Khoury 1984, 33. Tsimhoni 1983, 60 refers to only the West Bank and East Jerusalem. Betts (1975, 76) presents realistic estimates for the total Jordanian and Palestinian region.
5. The author wishes to express appreciation to Dr. Catherine Schutter for translating assistance.

References

Anonymous. 1982. *Baptism, Eucharist, and Ministry: Faith and Order Paper No. 111.* Geneva: World Council of Churches.

Anonymous. 1972. "Around the World." *Eastern Churches Review* 4: 83–84.

Anonymous. 1968. "An Anglican Friend." *Eastern Churches Review* 2: 81.

Benedictos I, Patriarch. 1976. "The Reply of His Beatitude Patriarch Benedictos to the Greetings of the President." *Christian News from Israel* 25: 4, 221.

Benedictos I, Patriarch. 1975. "President Katzir's New Year's Greetings to the Heads of the Christian Communities; The Reply of Patriarch Benedictos." *Christian News from Israel* 25:2, 95–96.

Benedictos I, Patriarch. 1972. "Appel du Patriarche de Jerusalem en faveur de la Fraternite du Saint-Sepulchre qui 'decroit dangereusement.' " *Episkepsis* 52 (April 18), 5–7.

Benedictos I, Patriarch. 1968a. "Chronicle of Events." *Christian News from Israel* 19:1–2 (May), 8.

Benedictos I, Patriarch. 1968b. "Letter to Israel Minister of Justice Yaacov Shapiro." *Christian News from Israel* 19:1–2 (May), 17–18.

Benedictos I, Patriarch and Father Iganzio Mancini. 1963. "Agreement for the Basiclic of the Nativity." Reprinted in *Recueil de Documents Concernant Jerusalem at les Lieux Saints,* Bernardin Collin, ed. Jerusalem: Franciscan Printing Press (1982), 211–212.

Bertram, Sir Anton and J. W. A. Young. 1928. *Report of the Commission on Controversies*

Between the Orthodox Patriarchate of Jerusalem and the Arab Orthodox Community. London: Oxford University Press.

Betts, Robert Brenton. 1975. *Christians in the Middle East*. Athens: Lycabettus Press.

Bird, Thomas E. 1975. "A Survey of Orthodoxy: 1974." *Diakonia* 10: 131–167.

Bird, Thomas E. 1974. "A Survey of Orthodoxy: 1973." *Diakonia* 9: 157–187.

Bird, Thomas E. 1972. "A Survey of Orthodoxy: 1971." *Diakonia* 7: 150–181.

Bird, Thomas E. 1970. "A Survey of Orthodoxy: 1969." *Diakonia* 5: 16–41.

Bird, Thomas E. 1969. "A Survey of Orthodoxy: 1968." *Diakonia* 4: 47–77.

Bird, Thomas E. 1968. "A Survey of Orthodoxy: 1967." *Diakonia* 3: 40–73.

Bird, Thomas E. 1968. "Chronicle of Events." *Christian News from Israel*. 19:3–4 (December), 5–23.

Colbi, Saul P. 1981. "The Patriarchs of Jerusalem: How They Are Elected." *The Holy Land* 1:2 (Summer), 62–64.

Colbi, Saul P. 1976. "The Christian Churches in the State of Israel: A Survey." *The Israel Economist* (August).

Colbi, Saul P. 1969a. "Christian Churches in Israel: Recent Developments in the Relations Between the State of Israel and the Christian Churches." *The Israel Economist* (February).

Colbi, Saul P. 1969b. *Christianity in the Holy Land*. Tel Aviv: Am Hassefer.

Cust, L. G. A. 1930. "The Status Quo in the Holy Places." Reprinted in *Recueil de Documents Concernant Jerusalem et les Lieux Saints*, Bernardin Collin, ed. Jerusalem: Franciscan Printing Press.

Danilov, Stavro. 1981. "Dilemmas of Jerusalem's Christians." *Middle East Review* 13 (Spring-Summer), 41–47.

Diodoros I, Patriarch. 1984. "Declaration du Patriarche Diodore de Jerusalem sur le C.O.E. et l'Intercommunion." *Episkepsis* 307 (January 15), 7.

Diodoros I, Patriarch. 1982. "Epiphany Again Celebrated on the River Jordan Near Jericho." *Christian News from Israel* 27: 203–204.

Diodoros I, Patriarch. 1982. "Event and Comment." *Christian News from Israel* 27: 187–189.

Diodoros I, Patriarch. 1981. "The Significance of Jerusalem for Eastern Christians." *Episkepsis* (July 1); reprinted in *MECC Perspectives* 3 (October/November), 17.

Diodoros I, Patriarch. 1981. "Election du nouveau patriarche de Jerusalem." *Episkepsis* 246 (February 15), 2.

Diodoros I, Patriarch. 1980. *Episkepsis* 240 (November 1), 5–6.

Diodoros I, Patriarch. 1976. "Les droits du Patriarche Diodore de Jerusalem en Terre Sainte." *Episkepsis* 307 (January 15), 7.

Diodoros I, Patriarch. 1974. "Un envoye special du patriarche de Jerusalem aupres du Patrirche Oecumique Dimitrios." *Episkepsis* 97 (March 19), 4–5.

Fisher, H. A. L. 1936. *A History of Europe*. London: Edward Arnold & Co.

Fowden, Garth. 1972. "Christian Communities in Jerusalem." *Sobornost* 6 (Winter), 430–434.

Germanos, Archbishop. 1967. "The Greek Orthodox Patriarchate in Jerusalem." *Christian News from Israel* 8 (December): 22–26.

Harakas, Stanley. 1985. "Holy Sepulchre Church Maintains Status Quo." *Ecumenical Press* 52:16 (May 1–10), release #5.

Harakas, Stanley S. 1982. "Church and State in Orthodox Thought." *The Greek Orthodox Theological Review* 27:1 (Spring), 2–21.

Horner, Norman A. 1974. *Rediscovering Christianity Where It Began: A Survey of Contemporary Churches in the Middle East and Ethiopia.* Beirut: Heidelberg Press.

Idinopulos, Thomas A. 1985. "Jerusalem Patriarch Pessimistic on Dialogue." *Ecumenical Press Service* 52.

Idinopulos, Thomas A. 1984. "Israeli Guides Forced on Christian Pilgrims." *Al Fajr* (March 21); reprinted in *MECC Perspectives* 3: 31.

Idinopulos, Thomas A. 1984. "Une initiative en Grece pour venir en aide au Patriarcat de Jerusalem." *Episkepsis* 326: 12.

Idinopulos, Thomas A. 1982. "Religious Colonialism and Ethnic Awakening: In Jerusalem the Orthodox Hierarchy Remains at the Center of Sanctity and Strife." *Worldview* 24, 17–19.

Idinopulos, Thomas A. 1981a. "Christians and Jerusalem." *Encounter* 42: 155–161.

Idinopulos, Thomas A. 1981b. "A New Patriarch for the Holy City." *Christian Century* 48, 373–375.

Idinopulos, Thomas A. 1978. "Jerusalem the Blessed: Religion and Politics in the Holy City." *Christian Century* 48: 373–375.

Idinopulos, Thomas A. 1971. "Un incendie au monastere orthodoxe du Sinai." *Episkepsis* 44: 11.

Khoury, Gerries. 1984. *Guide to the Church in the Holy Land.* Nazareth: Al-Hakem Printing Press.

Kuttab, Daoud. 1985. "The Right to Clean." *Al Fajr* (February 1), 16.

Kuttab, Daoud. 1984. "The Greek Orthodox Church: Gaps between clergy and laity." *Al Fajr* (January 8), 16.

Kyprianos, Archimandrite. 1979. "Church Chronicles." *Christian News from Israel* 27: 27–28.

Luidens, Donald A. 1986. "Divisive and Mitigative Factors in a Bi-ethnic Church: The Case of the Arabs and Greeks of the Jerusalem Orthodox Patriarchate." Unpublished manuscript: Hope College, Holland, Michigan.

Luidens, Donald A. 1982a. "Mid-East Primates in appeal." *Ecumenical Press Service* 49:17 (May 23–31), release #64.

Luidens, Donald A. 1982b. "Miscellaneous news." *Christian News from Israel* 27: 186.

Modestos, Archimandrite. 1978. "Church Chronicles." *Christian News from Israel* 26:4, 146–148.

Modestos, Archimandrite. 1976. "Event and Comment." *Christian News from Israel* 25:4, 221–223.

Modestos, Archimandrite. 1975a. "Event and Comment." *Christian News from Israel* 25:2, 97–98.

Modestos, Archimandrite. 1975b. "Event and Comment." *Christian News from Israel* 25:3, 160–161.

Modestos, Archimandrite. 1973. "News and Comment." *Eastern Churches Review* 5:1, 57–94.

Modestos, Archimandrite. 1969. "News in Review." *Eastern Churches Review* 2:3, 321–328.

Modestos, Archimandrite. 1968. "Notes on Church-State Affairs." *Journal of Church and State* 10:3, 490–503.

Osterbye, Per. 1978. "Patriarchat de Jerusalem: problemes et perspectives." *Episkepsis* 201 (December 15), 15–16.

Osterbye, Per. 1978. "Outlawing the Use of Bribery for Religious Conversion." *Christian News from Israel* 26:3–4, 122–123.

Osterbye, Per. 1970. *The Church in Israel*. Denmark: Vinderup Bogtrykkeri.

Osterbye, Per. 1964. "The Pilgrimage of Pope Paul VI to the Holy Places in Israel." *Christian News from Israel* 15:1, 3–11.

Osterbye, Per. 1937. *Refutations of the Allegations Put Forward by Sir Anton Bertram Against the Patriarchate of Jerusalem*. Jerusalem: Greek Convent Printing Press.

Rodoussakis, Archimandrite Cornelius. 1973a. "Event and Comment." *Christian News from Israel* 23:3 (11), 178–179.

Rodoussakis, Archimandrite Cornelius. 1973b. "Event and Comment." *Christian News from Israel* 23:4 (12), 256–257.

Rodoussakis, Archimandrite Cornelius. 1973c. "Event and Comment." *Christian News from Israel* 24:1 (13), 55.

Rodoussakis, Archimandrite Cornelius. 1972a. "Event and Comment." *Christian News from Israel* 22:3–4 (7–8), 154–156.

Rodoussakis, Archimandrite Cornelius. 1973b. "Event and Comment." *Christian News from Israel* 23:1(9), 32–33.

Rodoussakis, Archimandrite Cornelius. 1972c. "Event and Comment." *Christian News from Israel* 23:2 (10), 108–109.

Runciman, Steve. 1971. *The Orthodox Churches and the Secular State*. Trentham, New Zealand: Auckland University Press.

Sable, Thomas F. 1979. "A survey of Eastern Christianity: 1978." *Diakonia* 14: 41–53.

Shapiro, Haim. 1981. "Priests granted permission to guide pilgrim groups." *Jerusalem Post* (July 6); reprinted in *The Holy Land* 1:2 (Summer), 35.

Stern, Gabriel. 1976. "Ten themes adapted for Pan-Orthodox Council." *Ecumenical Press Service* 43:35 (December 2), release #3.

Stern, Gabriel. 1972a. "Patriarch Pimen in Israel." *Christian News from Israel* 23:1 (9), 40–42.

Stern, Gabriel. 1972b. "News item." *Christian News from Israel* 23:1 (9), 43.

Tsimhoni, Daphne. 1983. "Demographic trends of the Christian population in Jerusalem and the West Bank: 1948–1978." *Middle East Journal* 37:1, 54–64.

Tsimhoni, Daphne. 1981. "Visite officielle de S. B. Patriarche Diodore de Jérusalem au Patriarcat de Moscou." *Episkepsis* 260 (October 15), 2.

Tsimhoni, Daphne. 1980. "Visite de S. B. le patriarche de Jérusalem á Athens. *Episkepsis* 238 (October 1), 6.

Ware, Archimandrite Kallistos (Timothy). 1981. "Obituaries: Patriarch Benedict of Jerusalem." *Sobornost* 3:1, 102.

Ware, Archimandrite Kallistos (Timothy). 1982. "The Year in Review." *Christian News from Israel* 27:4, 178–179.

Zander, Walter. 1971. *Israel and the Holy Places of Christendom*. New York: Oxford University Press.

13
Christian Zionism and Jewish Zionism: Points of Contact

Roland Robertson

THE EMPIRICAL STARTING POINT for the present discussion arose from the increasing conspicuousness in the early 1980s of a link between some American fundamentalists, on the one hand, and some Israeli leaders and other avid proponents of Israeli foreign policy, on the other. This is most clearly exemplified by then Prime Minister of Israel, Menachem Begin, handing a Jabotinsky Award, for service to the cause of Israel, to Jerry Falwell in the fall of 1980. Even though that was by no means the beginning of the relationship, very few students of religion took much interest in it. Indeed, when inquiries were made in 1980 of other scholars, much doubt was expressed about its existence. There was a widespread assumption that resurgent American fundamentalism drew much of its support from the bastions of anti-semitism in the South, while the explicit political activism of a major wing of fundamentalism was only surfacing at that time. Moreover, even though the situation was in great flux, the idea of militant support for Israel being a distinctively right-wing cause was still relatively new.

Thus began, in spite of academic skepticism, an attempt to comprehend not only the roots and nature of Christian fundamentalist support for Israel but also the origins and *raison d'être* of Israeli interest in Christian fundamentalism in the United States. That set of inquiries rather quickly revealed that the histories of American fundamentalism and the formation of the modern state of Israel, beginning with the crystallization of the Zionist movement in Europe and the U.S. at the end of the nineteenth century, have been intriguingly related. As fundamentalism developed during the 1890s, beliefs about the fulfillment of Biblical prophecy with respect to the return of the Jews to the Holy Land and the eschatological significance of that prospect were important, if not the most central, matters of concern. The rise of modern

239

Zionism within Jewish communities and the extensive pogroms against Jews in Eastern Europe that precipitated a massive Jewish migration, much of it to the U.S., occurred at precisely the same time as those developments. Indeed they influenced the thinking of some of the fundamentalist thinkers.

While the formation of fundamentalism—in the very definite sense of the explicit advocacy of a return to allegedly Fundamental Christian principles—had no explicit impact upon the nascent Zionist movement, the increasing visibility of the latter did have some impact upon the former. Indeed, a few figures in the growing fundamentalist movement openly and adamantly advocated the establishment of a modern homeland for the Jews, although that does not mean that they backed the Zionist movement *per se*. Moreover, the large waves of Jewish immigration in the later years of the nineteenth century and the early years of the twentieth century constituted a significant part of the ethnic pluralization of American society. This in turn had an important impact upon certain segments of the existing American populace, stimulating a "nativistic" and theologically fundamentalistic response. In other words, the dynamic of fundamentalism itself was partly set in motion in response to the dislocation of values concerning American identity and the future status and role of long-established groups, whose ancestors had mainly migrated to America from the British Isles (Marsden 1980).

This is not to say that the return of the Jews to the Holy Land was clearly advocated as a way of cleansing America of alien groups and values—although there was certainly some of that—but rather that the fates of two very different sets of people from very different parts of the world came into a very complex conjunction. Certainly the Jewish migration to America, and numerous other events and circumstances involving Jews in many different societies, was a factor in the rise of American fundamentalism. While the latter did not so definitely affect the early growth of the Jewish Zionist movement (not least because that movement started on European soil), there can be little doubt that even at that embryonic stage there was a realization in Jewish Zionist circles that non-Jewish American groups were going to affect the future of the Jewish Zionist movement.

In other words, early Jewish Zionists realized that the fate of their movement was to be bound up with the political activities of various segments of organizations and movements within a number of societies on the global scene. While there is little or no indication that those early Zionists considered nascent American fundamentalism to constitute such a segment or collectivity, the fact that there was a reservoir of theological and religious support for the idea of a new Jewish Zion could not have entirely escaped their attention. Early in the twentieth century it was becoming clear that "the Jewish issue" was an ingredient of American political life, mainly in terms of the political significance of the growing Jewish population in some of the major Northeastern urban areas. There was, in any case, evidence of a long-existent Christian, theologically based support for the idea of a new Jewish homeland. The extent to which early Zionists recognized the strong strain of "peculiar ambivalence" concerning the Jews that had existed in America since colonial times—i.e. "pro-Jewishness" (whether in the form of ancient Israel as a model for America or the fate of the Jews as a test of America's fidelity to God's writ) combined with a reluctance "to accept contemporary Jews because of their stubborn refusal to accept the true faith" (Feingold 1974, 27)—is probably not possible to ascertain. Nevertheless, by the early years of World War I in the Zionist movement, and among activist Jews generally, it had become clear that the complexity of non-Jewish attitudes toward Jews had to be understood if something was to be done about the plight of the Jews, particularly as far as the controversial idea of the establishment of a "new" home for the latter was concerned.

Two analytical problems in the modern sociology of religion arise in conjunction with these preliminary indications of the contours of one of the most fateful sets of problems of our time. The first problem concerns the relationship between ideal and material interests (as Weber described them), as well as with related distinctions between the sacred and the secular, the religious and the non-religious. The second problem centers upon the global aspect of the rise and fate of social movements.

I am more concerned in the present discussion with the American-Christian fundamentalist (or Christian Zionist) orientation towards "the Jews" and the state of Israel than I am with the foundation and history of the latter. However, it should be said that both the history of modern Zionism and of the varying attitudes towards Zionism and Israel itself display such a complex mixture of interests and motives as to confound any attempts to make simple and neat categorizations of the type with which sociologists have become familiar. While it is not difficult to treat American fundamentalism as a "primarily religious" phenomenon, its recent political activities and televangelistic misadventures (e.g., the Jim Bakker–PTL scandal) notwithstanding, it would be inappropriate to analyze either Zionism or the history of support or opposition to it (as well as to the state of Israel) along those lines. Thus the present discussion should not be regarded in any straightforward sense as an exercise in the sociology of religion.

Moreover, as I have implied, there is a very important sense in which both American fundamentalism and Zionism have been phenomena of global significance and have been rooted in global circumstances. Both were—although fundamentalism less so in comparison with Zionism—initially responses to European events and circumstances of the later years of the last century and the early years of the present one. Both were also bound up with the international thematization of the quest for national independence and societal identity that flowered in that same period (Gluck 1985; Gong 1984).

The Early History of Fundamentalist Zionism

Since academic interest in millenarianism and revitalization was first crystallized by historians and anthropologists in the 1950s intellectuals have increasingly learned of the significance of that phenomenon not merely in primitive and pre-industrial but also in the modern history of a number of Western societies including Britain and the U.S. (Robertson 1985a). While modern fundamentalist "non-Jewish" Zionism can in one sense only be dated as far back as the 1880s, when dispensational premillenarianism crystallized as a significant component of American evangelicalism, the concurrence of millenarianism (particularly premillenarianism) and beliefs about the congregation of the Jews in their "homeland" has constituted a definite thread of Protestant Christianity since the seventeenth century. Indeed, it can be traced back much further in the history of predominantly Christian societies (Tuchman 1956).

The religio-political attempts on the part of radical Protestants in mid-seventeenth century England to "turn the world upside down" (to use Hill's evocative phrase) involved in some quarters prophetic beliefs concerning special treatment of the Jews, as part of the generalized sense of millennial expectation of that period (Hill 1975). In the American colonies the Puritans, enraptured as they were with the Old Testament and "thinking of themselves as the real Hebrews, sought to draw the professing Jews among them back into the fold from which they had supposedly strayed" (Feingold 1981, 27). By the later part of the seventeenth century the basic contours of the denominational matrix from which would spring virtually all of the main features of modern Protestant Christianity in Britain and America had been established. The theme of Israel and the significance of the Jews seems to have abated (other than in the form of America as the new Israel), although ideas concerning the return of the Jews to the Holy Land remained prominent in some American Puritan circles. In the American context both that period and the eighteenth century saw a considerable degree of (post)millenarianism, at the base of which was the notion of "The City on a Hill." In the Great Awakening of the mid-eighteenth century the millennial emphasis was considerably intensified, notably manifested in Jonathan Edwards' conviction that the Kingdom of God was imminent.

The mixture of postmillennial expectation and popular anticipation of the Second Coming, both centered on the belief that God had determined a special role for England and/or America as the New Jerusalem, greatly increased in the last third of the eighteenth century. The combined effect of the revolutions in France and America accentuated millenarian tendencies in Britain and the newly founded U.S. Yet it was not in the American but rather in the British context in the late eighteenth and early nineteenth century that a premillenarian kind of orientation crystallized, involving a flowering of interest in biblical prophecy with particular reference to the Jews. Early nineteenth century American interest in "the Jews" appears not to have had such a distinctive flavor. Such interest as there was in the Jewish people (who numbered only about 1,500 in a population of nearly four million) was confined to attempts to convert Jews to Christianity and/or the expression of hope, in terms of Christian doctrine, for the recongregation of the Jews in the Holy Land (Grose 1983, 6–8).

In 1795 Richard Brothers proclaimed that London would soon be struck by an earthquake, which would be followed by the restoration of the Jews to the Holy Land. "England was specially called to make that great event possible; and he, the Revealed Prince of the Hebrews, would soon lead all Jews, including those 'hidden' within the population of England, to Palestine in order to await the coming of Jesus Christ" (Garrett 1975, 14–15).

England was thus regarded as the New Israel, with Brothers cast in the role of the king of the Jews. More specifically, as with many previous English millenarians, Brothers said that before the Jews could return to Israel the Lost Tribes had to be found. He believed that they were, indeed, to be found among the English. That esoteric idea subsequently developed during the nineteenth century in the form of the British Israelite Movement, which persists to this day (Wilson 1967). Brothers himself appears to have lost interest in his mission concerning the Jews and the number subscribing to his doctrines was certainly not large. The prophetess Joanna Southcott obtained the idea for the mission that consummated her own prophetic career, when in 1814 she announced that she was miraculously pregnant (Garrett 1975, 214). Southcott claimed that she would give birth to Shiloh, the second Messiah. (Brothers had labeled himself "God's Anointed King, and Shiloh of the Hebrews.") Shiloh would lead the Jews back to Palestine.

That particular form of early nineteenth century renewal of English interest in the condition of the Jews constituted one of the three main aspects of the millenarian revival that was eventually to play an important role in the American fundamentalist-evangelical movement on behalf of Israel. The two other aspects were great concern with the prophetic scriptures and with the doctrine of the premillennial advent (Sandeen 1970). Only the latter appears to have been significant in America in the early years of the century, eventuating in the ill-starred prophecy concerning the end of the world issued by William Miller in the early 1840s. (Miller did not subscribe to ideas concerning the restoration of the Jews to Israel. In fact he thought that "the Jew had had his day.") While premillenarian ideas were certainly not insignificant in America during the first half of the century, they were overshadowed by an almost orthodox postmillennialism—of oscillating intensity—concerning the special religious significance of America, with little mention of Jews.

In contrast, in Britain people such as Brothers, Southcott, and Lewis Way set the scene for a burst of premillenarianism. Way was responsible for reviving the fortunes of the London Society for Promoting Christianity among the Jews six years after its formation in 1809. The return of the Jews to the Promised Land, an idea stemming directly from interpretation of prophecy, became in the columns of the LSPCJ's organ (*The Jewish Expositor*) "firmly established as a plank in the millenarian creed" (Sandeen 1970, 11). The scriptural passages that, it was claimed, predicted the circumstances of the French Revolution predicted also Christ's Second Coming and the restoration of the Jews. More specifically, the scene was set for the tendency to identify one or more nations in negative roles (such as the anti-Christ and the Beast of the North) and others in the role either of the New Israel and/or as destined to play a crucial role in the fulfillment of prophecy in relation to the Jews being restored to Palestine.

This revival of British millenarianism did not, however, involve political activism. It was widely believed that man's capacity to effect significant change through politics or through the church was negligible. Christ's imminent return was foretold by the upheavals of the period; and the Second Coming would lead to salvation for only a few. For the most part, the only "activism" encouraged was the kind advocated with little successful result by the LSPCJ, namely the conversion of Jews in Palestine and worldwide to Christianity. However, an influential section of the British upper-class, notably Lord Shaftesbury, was deeply involved in promoting Christian Zionism on an eschatological basis. (American Protestant Missions in that and the subsequent period focused largely on conversion of Muslims.)

During the period 1820–1850 adherents to British premillenarianism continued to maintain beliefs about the return of the Jews as a central ingredient of their doctrine. Among the major figures of that period were, in addition to Way, Edward Irving and Henry Drummond. In 1829 Drummond summarized the main result of recent conferences on prophecy by emphasizing the cataclysmic end to the present dispensation, an end involving judgment and the restoration of the Jews to Palestine (Sandeen 1970, 21–22).

Meanwhile, in America the Millerites had encountered widespread and intense scorn through the failure of their prediction concerning the end of the world in 1843 (and then 1844). Some have argued that the Millerite disaster discredited explicit millennialism in the U.S. for some decades. Others argue that it was only premillennialism that was damaged. Denominations with premillennial emphases prior to the Miller debacle were forced into a postmillennial stance, which then became part of a widespread postmillennial orientation in America in the period before and after the Civil War (Smith 1980). The history of premillennialism in America after the Millerite debacle was marked by a dispensationalist emphasis that it had not possessed before. It also emphasized a deepening concern with the fate of the Jews (which, as we have noted, was greatly at odds with Millerite doctrine) as well as what eventually made it distinctively American (in purely doctrinal terms)—namely, biblical literalism.

Opinion differs as to how much the emphasis upon dispensationalism derived from the teachings of John Nelson Darby, leader of a schismatic group within the British sect known as the Plymouth Brethren (Kantzer 1977). Dispensationalism had not been an issue in the schism among the Brethren. Indeed dispensationalism is sometimes not even mentioned in scholarly discussion of Darby's teaching. Darby seems to have been relatively uninfluential during and after his visits to the U.S. and Canada in the 1860s and 1870s. The ideas that were most salient to him, particularly the notion of the ruin of the churches and his low estimate of human ability to improve individuals or the world—his dispensational ideas—attracted strong attention in some American evangelical quarters.

The core doctrinal feature of the dispensational premillennarianism that developed rapidly towards the end of the nineteenth century was that the prophecy in Daniel 9 should be interpreted as meaning that "seventy weeks" actually involve 490 years (70 sevens). The first 69 "weeks" refer to the period lasting from the rebuilding of Jerusalem to Christ's death, while the period of the church intervenes between the end of the 69th "week" and the beginning of the last "week," that consists of the final days prior to the return of Christ and the instigation of the millennium. In the final days there will, *inter alia*, appear the anti-Christ and "the Beast" (who will form a new version of the Roman Empire in the mode of Babylon). The Jews will return as unbelievers to the Holy Land, with some of them being converted, and will be subject to great persecution during the second half of the last "week." The actual return of Christ is to involve the overthrow of the Gentile world powers, the Beast and the anti-Christ.

Finally, of the more important dispensational motifs mention should be made of the belief that the "true saints" of the church living at the onset of and/or during the final days will be plucked out of the world in a "rapture" (Marsden 1980, 52–55). Darby had placed great emphasis upon the idea of the "secret rapture." In so doing he had prescribed separation from the church and the world, in contrast to the political activism within the world (if not necessarily the church) that has periodically characterized some sections of the dispensational premillenarian community since the late nineteenth century, most notably in the late 1970s and 1980s.

The Founding of American Premillennarian Zionism

Partly in response to the impact of the "higher biblical criticism" (much of it of "alien" German origin) and the Darwinian theory of evolution, those subscribing to the inerrancy of scripture in combination with dispensationalist views began to form a relatively coherent movement in the U.S. during the last quarter of the nineteenth century, especially through the Niagara and International Prophetic Conferences that were periodically held from 1868 onwards. By the time of the 1895 conference dispensationalists had become increasingly inspired by the expanding Jewish movement into Palestine (Rausch 1979, 79–146).

Prior to that, however, a prominent dispensationalist, William Blackstone, had issued a striking message. In his *Jesus is Coming,* published in 1879, Blackstone rendered Darbyist dispensational conceptions in popular form, paying explicit attention to the return of the Jews to the Holy Land. *Jesus is Coming* sold as many as one million copies and was translated into a number of languages, including Hebrew. At one time it was the practice to present every graduate of Princeton Theological Seminary, the early anchor of the commitment to Biblical inerrancy, with a copy of the book (Ehle 1977, 306). With several associates Blackstone founded the Hebrew Mission in Behalf of Israel in Chicago in 1887, an organization that engaged in humanitarian activities as well as attempts to convert Jews to Christianity—it survives today in Chicago as the American Messianic Fellowship. Blackstone eagerly evangelized among Jews believing that Israel's acceptance of Jesus would restore all the things spoken of by the ancient Jewish prophets (Ibid.).

Blackstone's concern with the provision of a refuge for Jews resulted partly from his visit to Palestine in 1888. Greatly impressed by the Holy Land, he became convinced that it could be developed agriculturally and commercially if it were populated by people with talent, energy and drive—qualities he ascribed to the Jewish people. Shortly after his return, news of the brutal Russian pogroms against the Jews came to Blackstone's attention. Believing that there could be no better solution for the predicament of Russian Jewry than for them to emigrate to Palestine, he organized an ecumenical conference in Chicago on "The Past, Present, and Future of Israel." Several well-known clergymen and rabbis participated, endorsing Blackstone's plea for sending the beleaguered Russian Jews to Palestine and unanimously passing a resolution of sympathy with the oppressed Jews of Russia, a copy of which was sent to the Tsar.

Christian premillenarians at the Chicago conference apparently expressed much interest in the settlement of Jews in Palestine. Jewish speakers, while voicing compassion for their Russian brothers, did not, on the other hand, favor a regathering of Jews in Palestine on Biblical (or other) grounds. For example, a prominent rabbi summarized the view then widely held in the American Jewish community: "We, the modern Jews do not wish to be restored to Palestine. We have given up hope in the coming of a political, personal Messiah. We say 'the country wherein we live is our Palestine, and the city wherein we dwell is our Jerusalem' " (Fink 1954, 56). Nevertheless the Chicago conference encouraged Blackstone to press ahead with his proposal for Jewish emigration from Russia to Palestine. He thus drew up a Memorial to send the President, securing 413 signatures from influential political and business leaders including the Chief Justice of the U.S. Supreme Court, a state governor, the Speaker of the House of Representatives, Ohio

Congressman (later President) William McKinley, mayors of three large cities, John D. Rockefeller, J. Pierpont Morgan, Cyrus McCormick, and Charles Scribner.

The Blackstone Memorial, sent to President Harrison and his Secretary of State in 1891, opened with the question: "What shall be done for the Russian Jews?" and went on to maintain that with autonomous government "the Jews of the world would rally to transport and establish their suffering brethren in their time-honored habitation." They had waited patiently for over seventeen centuries for "such a privileged opportunity. . . Let us now restore them to the land of which they were so cruelly despoiled by our Roman ancestors" (Grose 1983, 36). The Memorial called for an international conference to consider the circumstances of the Jews and their claims to Palestine as their ancient home, as well as to lessen suffering.

In a cover letter, Blackstone added some further points, such as the fact that the European powers would probably be pleased with the plan because they did not want to take the persecuted Jews themselves, but his strongest overt appeal was expressed religiously. Men and women had a privileged opportunity to further the purposes of God with respect to his originally chosen people. The Blackstone Memorial attracted considerable interest and discussion. According to Feldstein (1965, 65) no other "nineteenth century document dealing with the Jewish question and Palestine, including Herzl's Jewish state, evoked so much editorial comment in this country as the Blackstone Memorial." In his Annual Message to Congress in 1891, the president responded to the latter. He called attention to the plight of the Jews in Russia, stating that the government had made clear to the Tsarist government its great concern about the harsh treatment of the Jews. The Memorial was subsequently presented to President Wilson in 1916 and has been credited with playing a role in Wilson's favorable response to the Balfour Declaration (Malachy, 1978, 130).

In 1892, five years before the unrelated first Jewish Zionist congress, Blackstone wrote an article entitled "Jews," which was printed as a religious tract and distributed by the millions over a period of twenty-one years in North America, Europe, and the Middle East. The tract deplored the persecution of the Jews at the hands of Christians through the centuries and contended that, when Jews are given a chance, they beat all competitors and rise to leadership in every society (Ehle 1977). The relationship of Jews to Biblical prophecy was one of the tract's major themes:

> They have literally fulfilled prophecy and are living evidence of truth of God's word. . . Surely all these things ought to quicken our interest in this peculiar, wonderful people, for whose conversion Paul said he could wish himself separated from Christ. . . May we not conclude the Lord is even now setting his hand again the second time for the restoration of his people? (Mouly and Robertson 1983, 100).

The reaction of the Jewish community to Blackstone's activities was very mixed. The Reform Jews were opposed to the settlement of Jews in Palestine, while Jews of various persuasions found Blackstone's theology either ludicrous or a threat to the integrity of their own faith (or a bit of both). But these objectives were generally muted, while Blackstone's efforts on behalf of the hapless Russian Jews were emphasized. His support of the idea of a return to Palestine before large audiences all over the country, as well as his publications, did much to stimulate public interest in the Zionist cause. Blackstone was critical of the secular Zionism of Theodor Herzl on the grounds that it showed no recognition of God's purpose in the advocacy of a Jewish state (Grose 1983, 37). Some Jews who did embrace Zionism expressed gratitude to Blackstone. A letter to Blackstone, written in 1916, expressed not only the appreciation of a Jewish friend but also that of Justice Brandeis, for the positive role that this premillennarian Christian had played in popularizing Zionism in the U.S.:

> Mr. Brandeis is perfectly infatuated with the work you have done along the lines of Zionism. It would have done your heart good to have heard him assert what a valuable contribution to the cause your document [the Memorial] is. In fact, he agrees with me that you are the father of Zionism, as your work antedates Herzl. (Rausch 1979, 8–9)

Some of the nuances of the fundamentalist-evangelical, dispensationalist position in relation to the Jews in the early years of the present century can be seen in a speech that Blackstone gave in 1918. There were, said Blackstone, only three choices available to the Jew. He or she could become a "true" Christian, embracing Christ as Lord and Savior. Few Jews were likely to accept that path, he observed.

The second option was to "hold fast to the ancient hopes of the fathers and the assured deliverance of Israel . . . through the coming of their Messiah, and complete national restoration and permanent settlement in the land which God has given them." That was the "true" Zionist choice.

The remaining option was to become an assimilant (what has been called by other fundamentalists an apostate Jew). The assimilants, said Blackstone, were the Jews who will not be either a Christian or a Zionist; "they wish to remain in various nations enjoying their social, political, and commercial advantages" (Rausch 1979, 284–315).

It is, of course, the second option that groups of fundamentalists advocated then and that constitutes a central feature of the beliefs and political activities of many fundamentalists now. Aside from the issue of the degree to which emphasis was, and is now, put upon the conversion of the Jews during "the end days," the sharp distinction made by Blackstone between the Zionist and assimilationist options (leaving no room for genuine, non-Zionist Jewishness) provides clues on how fundamentalists have been accused of being anti-semitic and the type of response to that accusation that the fundamentalist Zionists have made over the years. Their argument has been that their concern is with the Jewish collectivity and that many mainline Protestants are anti-semitic through their opposition to the collective-national welfare of the Jews.

Whatever may be the most persuasive case within the modern controversy about the development of the fundamentalist-evangelical movement during the first quarter of the century, there can be little doubt that attitudes toward dispensational interpretation of the Bible and orientations towards the Jews played a significant part. The foundational series of twelve books, *The Fundamentals,* dealt intermittently with matters pertaining to the theological-historical importance of the Jews, which is not necessarily out of line with a prophecy-based stance in favor of Jewish nationalism. Jewish issues were mentioned quite frequently. The second editor of the series, published in the years 1910–1915, was a "Hebrew Christian" named Louis Meyer. Though not as much in favor of Zionism as Blackstone, Meyer welcomed it as a fulfillment of prophecy. The single article devoted specifically to prophecy was by Arno C. Gaebelein who—although a gentile Christian—acquired enough Yiddish to engage in missionary work among the Jews in New York in that tongue (Rausch 1979, 212–83).

Gaebelein, who was the editor of the radical dispensationalist journal *Our Hope,* argued that the apparently accurate Biblical prophecies concerning the Jews constituted proof of the inerrant, supernatural status of the Bible. Thus, for radical dispensationalists, events and circumstances pertaining to the condition of the Jews became a part of the battle with the modernists. Independent Jewish settlement in Palestine and, in particular, the founding of modern Zionism by Herzl gave succor to the dispensationalist standpoint. Regardless of the agnostic, secular basis of Herzl's ideas concerning a modern Jewish homeland—announced in 1896 in his short book, *The Jewish State*—the pages of *Our Hope* recorded and interpreted his ideas and the activities of the Zionist Congress, notably in its section entitled "Notes on Prophecy and the Jews." One contribution to the latter was provided by C.I. Scofield, whose *Scofield Reference Bible* (1909) was probably the single most influential publication on crystallization and diffusion of the dispensationalist orientation.

Generally, the period of World War I greatly heightened interest in the interpretation of prophecy. The Balfour Declaration (1917) concerning the need for a modern homeland for the Jews and then the seizure of Jerusalem by British troops provided the premillennialists' prophetic conferences of that time with added significance. Some premillennialists were taken with the fabricated, anti-semitic *Protocols of the Elders of Zion,* while Gaebelein wrote a book that spoke in clearly anti-Jewish terms (Marsden 1980, 210), indicating a split within American premillenarianism regarding the Jews that persists to this day. By the end of World War I the joining of extreme American patriotism (not in evidence for much of the 1914–18 period) to a commitment to the developing Zionist cause had been established.

My main concern thus far has been simply to outline the growth of dispensationalist concern with the global circumstances of the Jews and the idea of Jewish recongregation in Israel. By the end of World War I these themes constituted a salient, although not dominant, feature of American fundamentalism. They had also played some part in stimulating the rapid growth of interest among political leaders in the U.S. in the idea of a homeland for Jewish people. However, it was in Britain that the Zionist movement achieved its first truly tangible success with the Balfour Declaration of the British war cabinet in 1917 (Sanders 1984).

Following Herzl's founding of the Jewish Zionist movement along secular lines during the last few years of the nineteenth century and the centering of Zionist diplomatic activities in London in 1902 (Laqueur 1972, 119), much of the Zionist effort was directed at seeking political support from the British and American governments, support which—when it was forthcoming—involved a wide range and complex mixture of motives and rationales (O'Brien 1984). Among the more significant motives and rationales on both sides of the Atlantic (but in different proportions) were: (1) the concern about the rapid influx of Jews, particularly those escaping pogroms in Tsarist Russia; (2) the desire to influence Russia (via the Zionist sympathies of Russian Jews) to stay in the war against Germany; (3) the concern that Germany might weaken commitment in the allied societies, notably America and Russia, were it to become the first to declare in favor of a Jewish homeland; (4) imperial ambition, mostly in Britain, in relation to the Middle East, and the goal of keeping French influence there to a minimum (the French actually issuing their own "Balfour" in 1916); and (5) what O'Brien (1984, 34) has called "transcendental (or sentimental) considerations," which in the U.S. had largely flowered in the wake of the Blackstone Memorial and which in Britain included the Biblical commitments of the British Prime Minister, Lloyd George, and the "personal and philosophical commitments of the then foreign secretary, Arthur Balfour" (Ibid.).

Thus, in the overall development of a favorable attitude toward the establishment of some kind of Jewish homeland (not necessarily in Palestine), the American fundamentalist movement played only a very small role. The fact that the movement's own identity was partly forged in terms of dispensationalist interpretations of the significance of matters affecting Jews was to have very important consequences well after the state of Israel was established in 1948.

My main concern here is not to address the topic of the influence of the nascent fundamentalist movement in the years preceding the event that nearly destroyed it—namely, the Scopes trial in Tennessee in 1924—but rather to underline the fact that the origins and fates of both Jewish and Christian

Zionism have intersected and been affected, in different ways, by overlapping circumstances. In the early years of the century perhaps the most important of these circumstances was the large-scale migration of displaced and fleeing Jews from Eastern Europe to the U.S. At least indirectly that wave of immigration constituted an important part of the "de-Americanization" of the U.S. to which many of the early fundamentalists responded negatively and in reaction to which it forged the "nativistic" components of its identity (Marsden 1980). A "*pro*-Jewish" orientation, in the form of advocacy on the basis of Scripture of a Jewish return to the Holy Land, fitted neatly with that undercurrent of resentment concerning what was, according to Marsden's (1980) persuasive argument, an internal and culturally enforced "migration" of potential adherents to the fundamentalist cause (in the sense that the latter suffered culture shock as a consequence of the waves of "alien" European immigration).

Fundamentalists, Evangelicals, Jews, and Israel: The Recent Years

I cannot in the present context explore the extent to which dispensationalist commitment to Jewish Zionism continued between the early 1920s and the 1970s. Much research has yet to be done on the fundamentalist movement after the symbolic defeat of the latter at the Scopes trial. If we know less than we ought to about that period of American fundamentalism, we know even less about the pro-Jewish dispensationalist segment within it. The view has been expressed that the dispensationalists came to dominate fundamentalism, as the latter was reconstituted as "the defeated party [which] understood the corporate roots of belief and . . . retired to build a powerful subculture which has now re-emerged" (Martin 1981). That does not mean that we can definitely speak of the recently re-emergent fundamentalist-evangelicalism—the movement remaining after the split with evangelicalism in 1947—as being dominated by a consensus on the doctrine of the Second Coming and associated matters. In fact there is evidence of considerable disarray in the contemporary fundamentalist movement on precisely that theme—there being differences among premillennialists, amillennialists, postmillennialists, pretribulationists, posttribulationists, and other groups.

The period of fundamentalism's decline in conspicuousness—the mid-1920s through the early or mid-1970s—was tumultuously conspicuous for the Jewish Zionist movement and Jews generally. The Zionist movement grew in strength in the 1920s and 1930s as the British Mandate in Palestine became increasingly problematic in respect to both Arabs and Jews, many of the latter being Zionistic immigrants. By the early 1930s the Nazi persecution of the Jews was rapidly gaining momentum in Germany—to culminate in the Holocaust. The dreadful events of the Nazi period constituted the immediate backdrop to and the final precipitant of the events and circumstances leading to the partitioning of Palestine and the establishment of Israel as a nation-state. In the process, concern with Israel became institutionalized within the fabric of American political life (Spiegel 1985), both as a topic of political controversy and foreign-policy formation, and as a focal point of Jewish mobilization of manifest or latent positive orientations toward the position of the Jews in the Middle East.

Thus during the late 1940s the scene was fully set for the operation of a complex array of military-strategic, political, economic, idealistic, and religious motives that has paralleled the situation in the early years of the century, but which has been inflated in order to relate to Islam and Islamic fundamentalism, especially since the oil crisis of the early 1970s.

The academic skepticism about a militant pro-Israeli stance among fundamentalists during the early 1980s largely rose from general ignorance of the "sleeping giant" of American fundamentalism, stereotyping of those believed to be fundamentalists, and failure to realize the inadequacy of research conducted on anti-semitism and differential religion-based attitudes toward Jews. Research on "Christian anti-semitism" has typically failed to isolate fundamentalists, and even more so, dispensational fundamentalists, primarily because they are spread across denominations. The discussion of anti-semitism generally has not been subtle enough to deal with the theological nuances provided by fundamentalist ideas.

Another aspect of the explanation concerning the initial strangeness of not merely the pro-Israeli views of some fundamentalists but also the concrete encouragement of those views by some Israelis and Jewish-Americans involves even more complexity. The reformation of the fundamentalist movement that has gained so much recent attention in fact occurred at the same time as the founding of the state of Israel, the late 1940s. In the early years of the state of Israel there was not a great deal of enthusiasm about it among fundamentalists, in large part because Israel was perceived to be secular, materialistic, and socialist. Enthusiastic support for Israel was thus more typical of a minority of mainline, liberal Protestant groups and the more premillennial groups within the evangelical community (the latter having split from the hardline fundamentalists in the late 1940s).

It would appear that the accentuation of dispensational interest in Israel developed through the confluence of a number of trends in the mid-1970s. First, there was a diminution of the vacillating support for Israel in the mainline Protestant denominations. Second, dissensus grew among American Jews concerning Israeli foreign policy, especially after the 1973 war, thus attenuating the perception of the Jewish-American as a liberal. Third, Israel, particularly after the coming to power of Begin, appeared in a much more religious, indeed, millennial, light. Fourth, there developed in the American, "non-left" evangelical context—a context much broader than that of fundamentalism—a sharpened interest in Israel in the light of scriptural prophecy, relating to the perception of the late 1970s as "a time of trouble," especially in the Middle East. And fifth, the late 1970s and early 1980s witnessed a heightening of interest in the Holocaust that had devastated European Jewry.

In the early 1970s, an Israeli scholar, Yona Malachi, explored the orientation of the fundamentalist churches to Zionism and the state of Israel, concentrating upon premillennarians, mainly considering the works of seminarians and theoreticians. Except for the *Moody Monthly*, Malachy paid little or no attention to the popular evangelists and the publications directed at the ordinary churchgoer. He concluded:

> There is no doubt that both Zionism as it has developed and the nature of the Jewish state have strengthened the view of many conservative Christians that modern Jewish nationalism is indeed worldly, materialistic and even secularist, and that there is, therefore, no theological justification for actively supporting the state.
>
> Whatever the reasons, it is clear that for some decades now Dispensationalism has refrained from all cooperation with Zionism, in spite of its positive attitude toward Zionism in the early years... Its Zionist belief now has a strictly eschatological significance, and its sole mission is intensive evangelization among the Jewish people.

Regardless of the possibility of Malachy having failed to examine the appropriate sources and looking, from his point of view, fruitlessly at such groups as the Jehovah's Witnesses and the Seventh Day Adventists (successors of the Millerites), it seems that well before the actual publication of his book (in 1978) there had been an expansion of concern with Israel among dispensationalists and some other premillennialists. Notwithstanding Malachy's conclusion, pessimistic from an Israeli point of view, a shift occurred in some Israeli and Jewish-American quarters toward a more optimistic view of the possibility of enlisting support for Israel among fundamentalists. This shift culminated in Begin's claims in 1980 that the major pressure-group resource for Israel within the U.S. was the evangelical community, of which the dispensationalists were seen to constitute the most significant section. There were deeply held reservations within Israel and the American Jewish communities about, as well as denial of, links between Christian premillenarians and Jewish Zionists. Nevertheless, the links were strengthened rapidly during the mid-1970s to mid-1980s period. If we consider the fact that Zionism has been articulated continuously and forcefully by premillenarians in America since the beginnings of modern Zionism and that, traditionally, Jewish agencies in this country have been active in courting Protestant groups that show promise of providing political support for the idea of, and subsequently the concrete state of, Israel, then the recently developed links should not surprise us.

254ROLAND ROBERTSON

The increasing interest among fundamentalists in the phenomenon of Israel and the significance of "the Jews" in the 1970s has to be seen in three, overlapping frames of American reference. First, in spite of certain kinds of fundamentalist reservations about his theology and ideology, Billy Graham, widely regarded as the father of contemporary Protestant publicists, exerted considerable influence in terms of his fervently expressed admiration for the existence of modern Israel. (Graham was a predecessor of Falwell in receiving the Jabotinsky Award from the Israeli government.) Second, the increasing awareness of the strategic importance of Israel following the Six Days War in the Middle East, enhanced by the strong showing of Arab nations opposed to Israel in the war of 1973 and the associated oil crisis, provided an ideological opening to the more fundamentalist of the evangelical forces that had been held back by the radicalism and liberalism of the 1960s. Third, the 1970s witnessed a remarkable expansion of TV evangelism in the U.S., with a number of the more prominent and successful TV preachers promoting a premillennial perspective on events of global significance, with particular reference to the attack on Israel by "the Anti-Christ" and the eschatological significance of the Middle Eastern situation (Hadden and Swann 1981, 95–96). From that standpoint Israel and the "end time" significance of the Middle Eastern situation received special attention within the context of the perceived American defeat by North Vietnam and its allies. Support for Israel was declared to be a desideratum of the blessedness of the United States.

Thus during the 1970s and the early 1980s there were issued from within fundamentalist and neo-fundamentalist camps a number of widely disseminated proclamations about the Biblical significance of events in the Middle East and the need for political engagement "in order to" be on God's (and America's) side in that respect (Mouly and Robertson 1983, 104–108). These developments were understandably encouraged by influential or would-be influential leaders in Israel and within the American Jewish community. By the early 1980s support for Israel and the policy of American action in favor of Israel had become something of a litmus test in some American conservative circles.

Conclusion

I have been emphasizing both the historical and contemporary significance of theologically legitimated—but surely not only theologically motivated—militant Zionism in important sections of the Christian premillenarian community in the U.S. I have also indicated that the activities of some premillenarian and some of the more hardline Jewish Zionists have become intermingled. What is of particular interest about the latter is that it shows how the fortunes of a religious movement can be affected by political and international factors, leading possibly in the long run to the reshaping of theological emphases on both sides of the "alliance." I cannot pursue here the phenomenology of the *modus vivendi* that, however fragile, seems to have been reached by the end of the Begin period in Israel. I can only offer some speculations concerning the overall theme of the public emergence and increase in attractiveness of dispensational millenarianism in America in the 1970s and early 1980s and its focus on international relations with specific reference to the relationship between America and Israel.

Aside from the claim that there is something millenarian about American society itself, there is growing support for the general proposition that American society periodically undergoes phases of revitalization or awakening, when cultural forces are regenerated, bonds between individual and society are reformulated and the national identity is refocused (McLoughlin 1978; Huntington 1981). Moreover, we have good reason to believe that not only in America have times of rapid juxtaposition of social, political, economic, and cultural factors often involved an upsurge of millennial, or at least, regenerational, expectation. Within the Christian cultural context, particularly its Protestant segment, it would appear that interest in the restoration of the Jews as an element of eschatological expectation has accompanied such concern frequently.

Narrowing the analytical focus, we can see that American evangelicalism as a whole has gone through phases of withdrawal, only to emerge later in activist form (Gordon-McCrutchan 1981). The recent re-emergence of evangelicalism is part of a discernible rhythmic pattern. Indirectly the concern with the Jews was part of the resistance to modernism and opposition to the Social Gospel among the fundamentalists. The rapid growth of Zionism and increasing signs of the return of the Jews to the Holy Land in the period 1890 through the early 1920s enhanced dispensational premillennialism by, *inter alia,* demonstrating the inerrancy of the Bible (because prophecy was proving accurate) and showing that modernity was a manifestation of the corruption and disorder that would attend the end-days.

If indeed dispensationalism, in its various forms, did become the central motif of the fundamentalist retreat after the Scopes trial, then it is not surprising that it was a core feature of fundamentalism when it re-emerged in activist form in the 1970s. The fires of the rapid changes of the 1960s and early 1970s and the increasingly difficult global position of Israel since 1973 caused many premillenarian leaders to effect theological and ideological links between the alleged corruption and lack of global power of America, an outcome that has been diminished by the "televangelical scandal" of 1987. America is cursed, so it is said, as long as it does not exert itself unambiguously for Israel. In that regard the very identity of America, as well as the "salvational identity" of individual Americans, centers upon Israel. Activity in "the world" has been demanded, in contrast to some previous periods of premillenarian withdrawal, precisely because the final battle is imminent. But new complexities may push that battle into the more-or-less distant future.

These considerations have been formulated in mid-1987, when a number of circumstances pertaining to my primary theme are sharply in the public view. I think, particularly, of the discrediting of, at least, certain aspects of televangelical dispensationalism via "the Bakker affair," the confusion about U.S.-Israel relations affairs created by "the Pollard spy problem," and the Iran-contra hearings. It may well be that American dispensational millenarianism is on the brink of its "Second Scopes," its second major defeat since its birth. American "neoconservatism" may well go down with it. Just as Jewish migration to the U.S. was stemmed in the same year as the Scopes trial (1924), so may 1987 become a year of significance in Israel's relationship with the U.S. Such are the global-sociological fates.

Note

1. Ruth Mouly first brought my attention to the significance of this event and was generous in sharing with me much of what she had already discovered about resurgent Protestant fundamentalism in the U.S. and attitudes towards Israel. Subsequently we researched that topic together in 1981 and 1982 (with particular reference to the impact of Christian Zionist ideas and organizational activities on the formation of American policy in the Middle East) with the help of a grant from the Society for the Scientific Study of Religion and wrote "Zionism in American Premillenarian Fundamentalism." (1983) Certain of the more empirical parts of the present essay draw closely upon the latter, while I also invoke a section on the origins of modern American millenarianism, which I wrote for our jointly published paper but which was omitted by the editor of the relevant issue of the *American Journal of Theology and Philosophy* (4, 3, 1983) because of space constraints. It should be emphasized that although I am indebted to Ruth Mouly she bears no responsibility for the interpretations that I offer in the present paper.

References

Cohen, Steven M. 1983. *American Modernity and Jewish Identity*. New York: Tavistock Publications.
Dobson, Ed and Ed Hindson. 1981. *The Fundamentalist Phenomenon*. New York: Doubleday-Galilee.
Ehle, Carl F., Jr. 1977. *Prolegomena to Christian Zionism*. Ph.D. dissertation, New York University.
Feingold, Henry L. 1981. *Zion in America: The Jewish Experience from Colonial Times to the Present*. New York: Hippocrene Books, Inc.
Feldstein, Marning. 1965. *American Zionism 1884–1904*. New York: Herzl Press.
Fink, Reuben. 1954. *America and Palestine*. New York: Herald Square Press.

Fishman, Hertzel. 1973. *American Protestantism and a Jewish State*. Detroit: Wayne State University Press.

Garrett, Clarke. 1975. *Respectable Folly*. Baltimore: Johns Hopkins University Press.

Glock, Charles Y. and Rodney Stark. 1966. *Christian Beliefs and Anti-Semitism*. New York: Harper & Row.

Gluck, Carol. 1985. *Japan's Modern Myths: Ideology in the Late Meiji Period*. Princeton, NJ: Princeton University Press.

Gong, Gerritt W. 1984. *The Standard of 'Civilization' in International Society*. Oxford: Clarendon Press.

Gordon-McCutchan, R.C. 1981. "The Irony of Evangelical History." *Journal for the Scientific Study of Religion* 20 (4): 309–26.

Grose, Peter. 1983. *Israel in the Mind of America*. New York: Alfred A. Knopf.

Hadden, Jeffrey and Charles E. Swann. 1981. *Prime Time Preachers: The Rising Power of Televangelism*. New York: Addison-Wesley Publishing Company, Inc.

Hill, Christopher. 1975. *The World Turned Upside Down*. Harmondsworth: Penguin.

Huntington, Samuel P. 1981. *American Politics: The Promise of Disharmony*. Cambridge: Belknap Press.

Kantzer, Kenneth S. 1977. "Unity and Diversity in Evangelical Faith." In *The Evangelicals*, David F. Wells and John D. Woodbridge, eds. Grand Rapids, MI: Baker Book House, 58–87.

Laqueur, Walter. 1972. *A History of Zionism*. New York: Schocken Books.

Liebman, Charles S. and Eliezer Don-Yehiya. 1984. *Religion and Politics in Israel*. Bloomington: Indiana University Press.

Liebman, Charles S. 1985. *The Religious Component in Israeli Ultra-Nationalism*. Cincinnati: Judaic Studies Program, University of Cincinnati.

Lindsey, Hal. 1970. *The Late Great Planet Earth*. Grand Rapids, MI: Zonderan Press.

McLoughlin, William G. 1978. *Revivals, Awakenings, and Reform*. Chicago: University of Chicago Press.

Malachy, Yona. 1978. *American Fundamentalism and Israel*. Jerusalem: Hebrew University.

Marsden, George S. 1977. "From Fundamentalism to Evangelicalism: A Historical Analysis." In *The Evangelicals*, David F. Wells and John D. Woodbridge, eds. Grand Rapids, MI: Baker Book House, 146–62.

Marsden, George M. 1980. *Fundamentalism and American Culture: The Shaping of Twentieth-Century Evangelicalism 1870–1925*. New York: Oxford University Press.

Martin, David. 1981. "Back to the Beginning," *Times Literary Supplement*, Dec. 18: 1461–62.

Mouly, Ruth and Roland Robertson. 1983. "Zionism in American Premillenarian Fundamentalism." *American Journal of Theology and Philosophy* 4 (3): 97–109.

Neusner, Jacob. 1985. *Israel in America: A Too-Comfortable Exile?* Boston: Beacon Press.

O'Brien, Conor Cruise. 1984. "Israel in Embryo." *New York Review of Books*, March 15: 34–38.

O'Brien, Conor Cruise. 1986. *The Seige: The Saga of Israel and Zionism*. New York: Simon and Schuster.

Rausch, David A. 1979. *Zionism Within Early America Fundamentalism: 1878–1919*. New York: Edwin Mellen Press.

Roberts, Oral. 1963. *The Drama of the End-Time*. Tulsa: Oral Roberts Press.

Robertson, Roland. 1985a. "The Development and Modern Implications of the Classical Sociological Perspective on Religion and Revolution." In *Religion, Rebellion, Revolution*. New York: St. Martin's Press, 236–65.

Robertson, Roland. 1985b. "The Relativation of Societies: Modern Religion and Globalization." In *Cults, Culture and the Law*, Thomas Robbins et al., eds. Decatur, GA: Scholars Press, 31–42.

Robertson, Roland. 1981. "Consideration on Church-State Tension from within the American Context." *Sociological Analysis* 42(4): 193–208.

Robertson, Roland and JoAnn Chirico. 1985b. "Humanity, Globalization and Worldwide Religious Resurgence: A Theoretical Exploration." *Sociological Analysis* 46 (3): 219–42.

Sandeen, Ernest R. 1970. *The Roots of Fundamentalism*. Chicago: Chicago University Press.

Sanders, Ronald. 1984. *The High Walls of Jerusalem: A History of the Balfour Declaration and the Birth of the British Mandate for Palestine*. New York: Holt, Rinehart and Winston.

Smith, Timothy L. 1980. *Revivalism and Social Reform*. Baltimore: Johns Hopkins University Press.

Spiegel, Steven L. 1985. *The Other Arab-Israeli Conflict: Making America's Middle East Policy, From Truman to Reagan*. Chicago: University of Chicago Press.

Toon, Peter. 1970. *Puritans, the Millenium and the Future of Israel*. Cambridge: James Clark.

Tuchman, Barbara W. 1956. *The Bible and the Sword*. New York: New York University Press.

Wald, Kenneth D. 1987. *Religion and Politics in the United States*. New York: St. Martin's Press.

Wilson, Dwight. 1977. *Armageddon Now*. Grand Rapids, MI: Baker Book House.

Wilson, John. 1967. "British Imperialism: The Idological Restraints on Sect Organization." In *Patterns of Sectarianism*, Bryan Wilson, ed. London: Heinemann, 345–76.

14

A Christian Love for Israel

Grace Halsell

I FEEL THAT I have been born-again—twice. I experienced one conversion in Texas and another in Jerusalem. Let me begin with Texas.

I grew up in a small, windblown town on the high, dry plains of West Texas. It was said that out there one could see further—and see nothing—more so than almost anywhere.

One summer when I was nine, I visited my maternal grandmother in Arlington, Texas, located between Dallas and Fort Worth, and in that era a dusty, quiet village of so few people that everyone knew everyone else.

A "great revivalist"—as grandmother identified a visiting preacher, otherwise known as Brother Turner—came to town, put up his tent and preached for a week.

Grandmother and I attended every night. Brother Turner preached fire-and-brimstone sermons, telling us that the world is divided into the wicked and the good, and the wicked will go to hell and only those who are born-again will escape an everlasting fire. Repent or perish! he warned.

All of us listening to him were spellbound. We had no radio, television, or public cultural events, and we depended to a great extent on the "great revivalists" such as Brother Turner to bring us knowledge and understanding.

Each night I experienced a sense of excited, growing anticipation. Then came the final night of the revival. Brother Turner held a large Bible in his left hand, quoted directly from God, and in conclusion asked those who had not witnessed for Christ to come forward. Mrs. Triplett, who played the piano, then struck the notes for the well-known hymn, "Just as I am."

We stood to sing. Grandmother and I held a hymnal, but we knew the words by heart:

> Just as I am/ and waiting not
> To rid my soul/ of one dark blot. . .

No one came forward. Brother Turner asked us to be seated. Then he

259

asked Mrs. Triplett to continue playing while we all bowed our heads. He
asked those who knew they were saved to raise their hands, and those who
had not raised their hands to come forward and be saved.

Everyone seemed to be thinking of me in those moments. Everyone was
softly singing. I rose from the wooden bench and moved forward, alone, to
where the evangelist was standing. He welcomed me, put his arms around
me, and soon my grandmother and neighbors and friends were there to embrace me.

I felt myself shaking, uncontrollably. Tears were streaming down my face.
I felt certain that God himself had orchestrated the holy happening.

When I was growing up, being saved was a prime topic of conversation.
It was not, in our small town, considered unusual for a man like my father
to encounter a stranger and without preliminary words of salutation ask,
"Are you a Christian? Are you saved?"

What does a fundamentalist, born-again Christian believe? He or she generally believes the Bible is "true," that it is the word of God, that every "i"
has been dotted and every "t" has been crossed, and that's that. If the Bible
says it, we were told, do not use your mind. Accept it as God's word and
God's will.

We had only a few books in our home, but among them we had a set of
some dozen volumes called *The Book of Knowledge*. In one of these books I
first saw a sketch of a dinosaur and read that scientists said the huge creatures
had roamed the earth 65 million years ago. But I had been told that God
created the earth 6,000 years ago, and that He did it all in only six days.
Therefore I accepted the idea that He created dinosaurs and Adam and Eve
all in the same week.

The ministers I heard all scoffed at the idea of evolution. What Darwin
wrote, they insisted, was plain heresy. Once I heard the well-known Texas
evangelist J. Frank Norris ridicule the evolutionists by bringing apes and
monkeys to his pulpit and shouting: "According to Darwin, let me introduce
you to your kinfolk."

We went to church twice on Sundays. We also went to Wednesday night
prayer meetings.

Generally, the Christians of my town accepted every word they found in
the Bible as spoken by God himself. We believed in these cardinal "truths":

Mary, the mother of Jesus, was a virgin.

The Jews were God's Chosen People.

And God gave the Holy Land to His Chosen People, the Jews.

And because the Jews were his Chosen People, God would bless those
who blessed the Jews and curse those who cursed the Jews.

All of this was very much a part of my early indoctrination. It was, I might
say, part of the air that I breathed.

Now I want to move on to my second conversion, in Jerusalem—or at least near there. The year is 1979, and I had gone to the Holy Land without knowing anyone. I began to meet women and men of the three faiths, Christians, Muslims, and Jews. As part of my research for a book, I lived in the homes of families of these faiths.

I went to the portion of Palestine that is called the West Bank. I talked with Palestinians who had been forced—at gunpoint—to leave the land that they said their fathers' fathers' father, back as long as memory served, had farmed.

I stayed in the home of a third generation American couple, Linda and Bobby Brown, who talked about life back in the Bronx and Brooklyn. As Jews they had immigrated to Israel, where they were issued rifles and Uzi machine guns. Along with other recent immigrants, they confiscated land from the Palestinians to build a colony called Tekoa.

One evening, as we sat under the stars looking at the flickering lights of Arab villages, Bobby Brown said:

"All the Arabs must leave this land. God gave this land to us, the Jews."

Suddenly all that I had been taught as a child flashed back to me. God had Chosen People—and God gave the Holy Land to his Chosen People.

Now I was in the Holy Land. It was not Brother Turner speaking the words, back in the days when there was no modern political entity called Israel on our maps. Rather, it was a man from Brooklyn speaking. And the land on which we sat was not a mystical, other-worldly biblical Zion but the land, and the livelihood, of Palestinians who had lived there for the past 2,000 years.

The reality of the situation struck me with what others who have gained a new understanding of an issue have termed a "shock of recognition." I had in a moment come face-to-face with a very important issue that had been with me since childhood. All of a sudden it came together, and I had a new awareness.

Bobby Brown's words, that God gave the Holy Land to the Jews, made me realize that people like me were part of the problem—the problem of the Arab-Israeli conflict. I had been accepting the Israel of the Bible as the Israel of today—and now I was there. I was in that place, which I had only been seeing through the Bible.

The allegorical Zion was not the same as the Zionist state. That was my shock of recognition. Christ had taught that the New Jerusalem was not a piece of real estate, but a journey within—that no one should make a cult of land. But I knew that literally millions of Americans had not been able to disengage themselves from this cult of land, a cult of Israel.

As in any cult worship, I felt it could spread and represent a danger for all of us because the cult links America to a modern, political entity, Israel, and does so in an emotional, unnatural, and politically explosive way.

I wanted to know why we say we have a moral commitment to Israel and why we as taxpayers each year give every Israeli man, woman, and child the equivalent of $1,700; why Americans annually give about five billion dollars to a modern, sovereign state, based on their worship of a God of Israel.

As part of my research, I made two trips to the Holy Land with Jerry Falwell—in 1983 and again in 1986. On the first trip, Brad, 35, from Georgia, unmarried, neatly dressed, a financial adviser (he told me he made good money) gave me the reason why Americans support a modern Israel. I was seated beside Brad on the tour bus when he said almost word for word what the dual American–Israeli citizen Bobby Brown had said:

"The Arabs have to leave this land because it belongs only to the Jews. God gave all of this land to the Jews."

And did God give the land of Palestine to the Jews, I asked, because the Jews were his Chosen People?

"Yes, definitely," he said. "The Bible tells us that. You recall the promises God made to the Jews, regarding this land." And then naming chapter and verse he quoted from memory a text from the Old Testament's Book of Genesis about God telling Abraham to cast his eye before him and around him and all that he could see would belong to him and his seed.

Because of such verses, Brad and others of the New Christian Right found it easy—and for them, perhaps, necessary—to block from their view the Palestinians who were all around us.

My roommate on the first trip was named Mona. She was about 55, a native of Indiana now living in Florida. She always carried a Bible with her, often referring to it as a guide for everyday living.

One day after visiting the Sea of Galilee, we boarded our bus for a drive to Jerusalem. It was five o'clock and after we were seated, our Israeli guide told us:

"We've about a two-and-a-half-hour drive. You won't see anything, so why don't you put your heads back, close your eyes, and take a siesta." Like robots, the pilgrims reclined their heads and closed their eyes. We were entering into the West Bank land of the Palestinians, but our guide did not mention the word Palestinian.

"Mona," I whispered to my roommate who sat beside me, "we are passing through the land of the Palestinians. There are Palestinian homes and Palestinians all around us. They have always lived here."

I pointed to a small stream, the Jordan river, so famous in our Christian hymns, that flowed on our left. "Mona," I continued, "this land is called the West Bank of the Jordan—but our guide does not mention it by name. He calls this land inhabited by Palestinians by the old biblical names of Judea and Samaria, but for four million Palestinians this is Palestine."

Dusk was bringing mysterious colors to the land. We saw distant and flickering lights of villages. As I whispered my comments about Palestinians being all around us, I could see Mona's body undergo a physical transformation. I saw her shoulders move forward in a protective, hunkering down, defensive stance, as if I were literally assaulting her with a weapon. She was attempting not to hear what she had assumed she should not know. Eventually she asked:

"Palestinians? Who are Palestinians? Isn't everyone living here Jewish?"

That, of course, was the way she had read it in her Bible. Mona had grown up, as I had, in a Christian home, reading the Bible, listening to the Bible. We had not learned about the Middle East in our schools. All we knew was what we had read in Scripture penned by the Hebrews. We studied the Old Testament stories of the sojourn of Hebrew people in Palestine, the wars of the Kings of Israel, and the special dealings of God with the Chosen People. Every hero was a Hebrew and the others hardly mattered.

Mona read her Bible every day. But she knew little or nothing about current Middle East history or the 2,000 years that had intervened since the Hebrews, for a brief period, controlled Jerusalem. That one brief period, out of the dozens of conquests by various tribes, was the only history engraved on Mona's mind.

After a moment, as if pleading for a reassurance that non-Jews did not exist in this land, she asked:

"Are the Palestinians also Jews?"

Palestinians, I reminded her, were Christians and Muslims.

But she could not seem to get the concept of another people, equally real, into her mind. She, having accepted the concept of a Chosen People, also had a concept of an unChosen People. She placed the Chosen and the unChosen into her system of belief that calls for the Jews to be in Palestine—and the Palestinians to be outside. Or, if actually there, then invisible.

Mona's belief system is a very prevalent one. It is held by most major TV evangelists including Falwell, Jimmy Swaggart, Jim Bakker, James Robinson, Pat Robertson, Oral Roberts, and many others. This belief system holds that Christ cannot return for his second visit until seven time periods, called dispensations, occur. The first of these is the ingathering of the Jews into Palestine.

Falwell and others hold that the next step in the countdown on history must be the rebuilding of a Jewish temple. This belief has great political ramifications. For Jewish fanatics and Christian dispensationalists both say the temple must be built atop Haram al-Sharif, holy grounds to 800 million Muslims around the world.

On the 1983 Falwell tour, our group went to the Old City of Jerusalem and we approached the large Muslim grounds where the Dome of the Rock and Al-Aqsa Mosque are located. Here, too, is the Wailing Wall, where Jews gather to pray, believing the wall to be a relic from Solomon's Temple, destroyed about 2,000 years ago.

"There," said our Israeli guide, pointing to the Dome of the Rock and Al-Aqsa Mosque, "we will build our third Temple."

As we left the site, I remarked to Clyde, about 70, a retired Minneapolis business executive, that the guide had said a temple would be built there. But, I asked, "What about the Muslim shrines?"

"They will be destroyed," said Clyde. "One way or another, they must be removed. You know it's in the Bible that the temple must be rebuilt. And there's no other place for it except in that one area. You find that in the law of Moses."

Did it not seem possible, I asked Clyde, that the Scripture about building a temple would relate to the time in which it was written, rather than to events in the 20th century?

"No, it is related to the End Time," Clyde said. "The Bible tells us that in the End Times the Jews have renewed their animal sacrifice."

So Clyde was convinced, I asked, that Jews, aided by Christians, should destroy the mosque, build a temple and reinstate the killing of animals in the temple—all in order to please God?

That, said Clyde, was the way it had to be. It was in the Bible.

Now many Christians who feel the same as Clyde have formed a Temple Mount Foundation to help Jewish terrorists destroy the Muslim shrines. An oil-and-gas man, Terry Reisenhoover of Oklahoma, heads the foundation. I have talked with several leaders of this Temple Mount Foundation, several of whom are very wealthy. They are not ashamed of their plans to destroy the Dome of the Rock and Al-Aqsa Mosque.

The Reverend James DeLoach of Houston's Second Baptist Church visited me in my Washington, D. C. apartment. He told me that he and others in the Temple Mount Foundation had raised and spent tens of thousands of dollars to defend Jewish terrorists charged with criminal assaults on the mosques.

What, I asked, if the Jewish terrorists they support are successful and destroy the mosques? What if this triggers World War III and a nuclear holocaust? Would he and Reisenhoover not be responsible?

No, he said, because what they were doing was God's will.

We hear in this country a great deal about Shiite fanatics who go on suicidal missions because they believe they are doing the will of God. We hear much less about Christians who are millionaires, dress in fine suits, and look like our brothers or our uncles. They do not look like the stereotypical fanatic or terrorist. Yet they believe that if they start a nuclear war, they are doing God's will.

It might be easy to dismiss Brad, Mona, Falwell, DeLoach, and the New Christian Right as representing only an insignificant fringe element. However, they are far more than that. The New Christian Right is the rising star of the Republican Party. And they increasingly gain power through their sym-biotic relationship with Israel.

Christians form the single most important bloc of support for Israel. There are about six million American Jews who give unconditional support for Israel. But there are also about 40 million Christians who do the same thing.

Moreover, the fundamentalists-dispensationalists who make a cult of Israel are the fastest-growing segment of Christianity. They are aggressively seeking and winning political power. They dominate the Moral Majority. *The Moral Majority Report* goes to more than two million readers, including 82,000 clergy, and every Senator, Congressperson, governor, and all major media in this country. The New Christian Right owns 1,400 radio stations, three Christian television networks and thirty TV stations. Through their television programming, they send their messages every week into the hearts and minds of about 15 million Americans.

Moreover, an increasing number of Americans are reading, and perhaps starting to believe, the dispensationalists' basic textbooks. Eighteen million Americans bought copies of Hal Lindsey's *The Late Great Planet Earth*. This is based entirely on a cult of Israel, that is, a theology centered entirely on developments that must take place in Israel.

Many televangelists openly collaborate with the Israeli government. They use their pulpits, direct mail campaigns, and their TV and radio stations to advocate total support for Israel. They favor giving Israel whatever billions of dollars Israel requests. They "rejoiced" (to use the word of one TV evangelist) over the invasion of Lebanon. They favor Israeli occupation of Arab lands: the West Bank, Gaza, the Golan Heights, southern Lebanon, and Arab East Jerusalem.

The alliance between the New Christian Right and the state of Israel seems strange until one studies how both gain from it. Israel originally sought this alliance back in 1967. In 1980 Menachem Begin, then prime minister, gave Jerry Falwell Israel's highest honor, the Jabotinsky award. And in 1983 in Jerusalem I personally heard Falwell thank Moshe Arens for the gift of an Israeli Windstream jet.

The New Christian Right purportedly spends more than $500,000 each day to organize support for its political goals, and its investment is paying off. Pollster George Gallup once gave Falwell credit for swinging the 1980 election for Reagan. Not only are TV Evangelists seeking to become political power brokers, but they are also attempting to take over the presidency itself. Friends and acquaintances of Pat Robertson are encouraging his run for president; he's well-funded, well-known and has a following pre-made by his years on TV. In 1985 the idea of Pat Robertson for President seemed far-fetched; by the fall of 1986 no one was laughing; and in the winter of 1988, he came in second in the Iowa caucuses.

Besides their growing influence in politics, the New Christian Right poses another danger: they push us towards more wars. As his stellar attraction in 1983, Falwell produced Defense Minister Moshe Arens. Arens talked to our group of pilgrims about the Israeli 1982 invasion of Lebanon, saying, "We went into Lebanon to kill all the terrorists. We wanted to wipe them out!" The Christians around me seemed transformed. They were energized, the adrenalin was flowing, as if a lion were loose in our midst. As Arens called for renewed dedication to military strength and a new and bigger war, the Christians jumped to their feet in sustained applause. They interrupted him eighteen times with standing ovations. They stamped their feet, and shouted "Amen!" and "Hallelujah!"

On Falwell's 1985 tour, he produced as his star attraction another military man, General Ariel Sharon, mastermind of the 1982 Israeli invasion, which killed 20,000 Palestinians and Lebanese, most of them civilians. Introducing Sharon, Falwell said, "In all the history of the world there comes along only a few great men." Then he named George Washington, Abraham Lincoln— and Ariel Sharon!

Now I want you to imagine for a moment that you have signed on a journey sponsored by Falwell. You and your group land in Tel Aviv, rest overnight and the next morning are on a bus, headed for Megiddo.

To get there, we travel north for fifty-five miles. We arrive at a site that lies south of Haifa, about fifteen miles inland from the Mediterranean Sea. On leaving the bus, my steps fall in with Clyde, the Minneapolis retired businessman. We walk a short distance to a tell or mound (i.e., remains of ancient communities).

I suggest to Clyde that this site, once a city of great importance and a strategic crossing of important military and caravan routes, had been a battlefield through the centuries.

"Yes," Clyde agreed. "Some historians believe that more battles have been fought here than at any other place in the world." We all continue walking to a vantage point, and then we stop, to absorb a commanding view of the Jezreel valley below. My companion seems overcome with emotion.

"At last!" Clyde remarks. "I am viewing the site of Armageddon!"

Had Clyde, I asked, read much about Armageddon?

"You know we find the word Armageddon only once in the Bible. That of course is in the Book of Revelation, that's chapter 16, verse 16." And then Clyde quotes the short verse:

"And he gathered them together into a place called in the Hebrew tongue Armageddon."

Clyde tells me that in that final battle, a 200-million man Oriental army will move westward and destroy the most populated area of the world and arrive at the River Euphrates.

"And in this final battle," Clyde said, "the forces of the Anti-Christ and the huge Oriental army will have tremendous nuclear power."

"But," he continued, "the Anti-Christ will be fighting against King Jesus who will utterly devastate millions. It will be history's bloodiest battle!"

And did Clyde, I asked, visualize Christ rather like a five-star general, a Supreme Commander, who will use nuclear weapons to destroy forces allied against him?

"Yes," he said. "In fact, we can expect that Christ will make the first strike. He will release new, very powerful nuclear weapons, not yet developed."

Clyde's demeanor and words made it appear inevitable: the world going up in a big bang. He seemed certain of his details regarding the final conflagration.

Yet this battle, Clyde said, was to be waged in a field before us, a valley so small it would fit in a Nebraska farm, and be lost if placed in a big Texas ranch. Gesturing toward the minuscule, quiet valley of terraced fields, I remarked to Clyde:

"It looks very small for the last, great decisive battle."

"No," he said, quite serious, "you can get a lot of tanks in there."

"Tanks!" I repeated. "And all the armies of the earth! And atomic bombs falling from airplanes?"

"All of this," said Clyde. "And several million will die right here."

"But why," I asked, "would a God who is all sovereign want this?"

"Because of Israel," Clyde said. "Don't forget the armies of the East will march against Israel. God will enter into this battle to protect Israel. And His people, the Jews."

"And how," I asked, "will he protect Israel? What will happen to the Jews living in Israel?"

"Two-thirds of all the Jews living here will be killed," Clyde said. "And the others will convert to Christ."

Clyde seems typical of millions of American Christians who see Armageddon bringing terror, destruction, and rivers of blood, as well as the eradication of most Jewish people and the great religion of Judaism. But they nevertheless contend that God has ordained it in order to usher in the Second Coming of Christ.

Armageddon theology was not only on Clyde's mind but also on the minds of many American voters in 1984 when the question was raised: Does Ronald Reagan believe God has foreordained the destruction of the earth? On at least seven occasions, Reagan raised the subject of Armageddon. Many associates suggest that Reagan is a dispensationalist. He has not denied it. His remarks tend to confirm that he is. On one occasion, he said, "We may be the generation that sees Armageddon." Asked to explain the statement, he said no one knows when Armageddon might occur. He did not deny that he believes it will—and must.

Reagan shuns all mainline church leaders, all nuclear freeze and peace advocates. And he associates and honors those who preach an Armageddon theology. He singled out two dispensationalists, evangelists James Robinson and Jerry Falwell, to give the opening and closing prayers at the 1984 Republican National Convention.

Many alarmed citizens now feel that Robinson and Falwell and other dispensationalists—the leaders in the New Christian Right—represent the greatest danger of our time, because they openly push for a nuclear Armageddon.

There is a vast difference between the fundamentalism of my childhood and the fundamentalism of today. In my childhood, preachers often denounced movies, dancing, whisky, and evolution. All of this was fairly unsophisticated, consisting of down-home vices. Brother Turner and even J. Frank Norris had only limited funds, they did not have television and there was no state of Israel—that is, no actual site for an Armageddon theology. And there was no atomic bomb.

Now Falwell, Pat Robertson, and other dispensationalists have all of these. They actively use all of them to preach, promote, and actually to sell Americans on the idea we must build more bombs and then use them to destroy the earth in a nuclear Armageddon.

Falwell and other TV evangelists claim this is going to happen in our lifetime. But they do not worry. They will not be here when the nuclear bombs start falling. They will be raptured, lifted up into the clouds—and then Christ will build them a new heaven and a new Earth.

For Falwell, Hal Lindsey, and others, the Apocalypse becomes almost a wish fulfillment, a thing they welcome and look forward to seeing. It is as if huge flames threaten to engulf all of us, while they stand by pouring on kerosene. Meanwhile, most of us face the hideous possibility that we humans will utterly destroy not only ourselves but our species, all future generations, thus bringing the entire human project to an abrupt and final halt. We ourselves would be exclusively responsible for this.

Today American Christians are largely in two groups: The first group has perhaps 40 million persons who, based on their interpretation of Scripture, make a cult of Israel. As part of this cult of Israel, they believe we must fight a nuclear Armageddon.

In the second group are all the other Christians who do not dare criticize this cult of Israel for fear someone will say, "You are anti-Semitic."

The unprecedented novelty of our historical situation, which had its roots in Christian communities such as mine, seems to have escaped most of us.

A religion based on the cult of Isreal created the problem. And the crisis remains primarily a religious one.

Yet we as lay persons along with our religious leaders have done and are doing virtually nothing to provide knowledge and resources to solve the crisis. In short, we are doing little to stop the Armageddon theology in its tracks.

Yet, I think we do have the knowledge and resources to overcome this doomsday ideology.

Most of us know about the nuclear winter that will result if one country strikes another with nuclear bombs. The clouds of dust will envelope us all. No one can win. We will all lose. We will destroy the possibility of all life on our planet Earth.

Thus we must return to the most religious of convictions: We are one people. We are bound together.

This conviction will, I hope, bring us to a new understanding. And with this understanding, we may somehow learn to live in peace. Teilhard de Chardin put it this way:

> Someday, after we have mastered the winds,
>   the waves, the tides and gravity,
> We shall harness for God
>   the energies of love.
> Then, for the second time in the history
>   of the world,
> Man will have discovered fire.

Contributors

Eileen Barker, Dean of Undergraduate Studies, London School of Economics, London, England

M. Gerald Bradford, Administrative Director, Hutchins Center, University of California, Santa Barbara, California

Thomas C. Bruneau, Professor of Political Science, McGill University, Montreal, Canada

Michael Dodson, Professor of Political Science, Texas Christian University; Fort Worth, Texas

William R. Garrett, Chairman and Professor of Sociology, St. Michael's College Winnoski, Vermont

Bonganjalo Goba, Faculty of Theology, University of South Africa, Pretoria, South Africa

Jeffrey K. Hadden, Professor of Sociology, University of Virginia, Charlottesville, Virginia

Grace Halsell, Author and Lecturer, Washington, D.C.

John Heinerman, Director, Anthropological Research Center, Salt Lake City, Utah

Theodore E. Long, Chairman and Associate Professor of Sociology, Washington and Jefferson College, Washington, Pennsylvania

Donald A. Luidens, Professor of Religious Studies, Hope College Holland, Michigan

Armand L. Mauss, Professor of Sociology, Washington State University Pullman, Washington

Jerry G. Pankhurst, Associate Professor of Sociology, Wittenberg University Springfield, Ohio

K. L. Seshagiri Rao, Professor of Religious Studies, University of Virginia Charlottesville, Virginia

Roland Robertson, Professor of Sociology, University of Pittsburgh, Pittsburgh, Pennsylvania

Arvind Sharma, Professor of Religious Studies, University of Sydney, Sydney Australia

Anson Shupe, Professor of Sociology and Chair, Department of Sociology and Anthropology, Indiana University-Purdue University at Fort Wayne, Indiana

Index